Climate Change

A Guide to Carbon Law and Practice

Consulting Editor **Paul Q Watchman**

Consulting editor
Paul Q Watchman

Publisher
Sian O'Neill

Marketing manager
Alan Mowat

Production
John Meikle, Russell Anderson

Publishing directors
Guy Davis, Tony Harriss, Mark Lamb

Climate Change: A Guide to Carbon Law and Practice
is published by
Globe Law and Business
Globe Business Publishing Ltd
New Hibernia House
Winchester Walk
London Bridge
London SE1 9AG
United Kingdom
Tel +44 20 7234 0606
Fax +44 20 7234 0808
Web www.gbplawbooks.com

Printed by CPI Antony Rowe, Chippenham, Wiltshire

ISBN 978-1-905783-12-0

Climate Change: A Guide to Carbon Law and Practice
© 2008 Globe Business Publishing Ltd

DISCLAIMER
This publication is intended as a general guide only. The information and opinions which it contains are not intended to be a comprehensive study, nor to provide legal advice, and should not be treated as a substitute for legal advice concerning particular situations. Legal advice should always be sought before taking any action based on the information provided. The publishers bear no responsibility for any errors or omissions contained herein.

Table of contents

Carbon dioxide levels now stand above their highest levels for the last 650,000 years. In early 2008 we learnt that the North Polar ice cap is melting so fast that some scientists are predicting that in seven years time it will completely disappear in Summer. This is thoroughly alarming news which should galvanize us into urgent action. Each and every one of us has a responsibility to respond – the whole world is in this together and together we must act.

This is why I am delighted to introduce this book, by practitioners drawn from different continents, on climate change and the law. Global warming is an issue for every part of society and it must change the way in which business is conducted. That is why it is essential that the right legal frameworks are in place and embedded into every-day business behaviour as quickly as possible.

Starting from a look at how climate change law has evolved from public international law in the 1970s and moving into practical issues associated with the current law around carbon projects, particularly those under the Kyoto Protocol, I hope this book provides one of the inputs needed to underpin a future expansion of climate change solutions by enhancing the understanding of the legal aspects of a future global carbon market. It also covers a range of legal practices, and not just those directly involved in creating new markets, such as accountancy, taxation, corporate social responsibility, corporate transactions, competition, litigation and real estate.

Over the last twenty-three years I have been heavily committed to encouraging responsible business through Business in the Community, of which I am President, through my Business and the Environment Programme and also my International Business Leaders Forum. This is why I launched my Accounting for Sustainability initiative in 2006 to help companies understand how to incorporate this type of global challenge into their practices. It is enormously heartening to find a genuine determination amongst many companies to show real leadership on climate change, not least the legal sector.

I can only congratulate the authors for producing this most important reference book, the value of which is most likely to grow. For the sake of our children and grandchildren, I hope and pray that it will accelerate the pace at which we achieve a genuinely low carbon global economy.

Introduction

Paul Q Watchman
Dewey & LeBoeuf

"We can't cure the planet, we haven't the power, but we just might be able to make it go into reverse phase and cure itself."[1]
Lovelock and Rapley

Until the 1990s the most common twentieth century fictional depictions of the end of the world, Armageddon, were the invasion of Earth by aliens from outer space, some cute and others scary, or the destruction of the planet by Earth colliding with a meteor or other very large object from outer space. In more recent years, as the Wellesian and other science fiction threats of invasion or planetary destruction from outer space have receded in the popular imagination, these harbingers of the doom of mankind have been replaced, at least in popular culture, by much more anodyne or prosaic events. There is now recognition of the very real threat that the Earth is being destroyed within the Earth itself by man's careless stewardship.

It is not the threat of the silent rising tide of greenhouse gases (GHGs), which being both invisible and odourless would fail any test of dramatic arts, from the traditional values of an Olivier to the method acting contortions of a Stanislavski, but rather the impacts and consequences of climate change and global warming, which provide the drama. The more frequent severe weather conditions which result from climate change or global warming in the form of perfect storms, tornadoes, typhoons, tsunamis, floods, rising sea levels, reversal of the flow of the Gulf Stream, the destruction of native habitats, species of flora and fauna and the way of life of communities, indigenous people and vulnerable tribes and groups, the melting of the polar ice caps and a return to severe winters as portrayed by films such as *An Inconvenient Truth* and *The Day After Tomorrow* are all very dramatic.

Far more than dramatic, they are tragic in the proper use of that term – that is, predestined and unavoidable. Climate change brings apocalypse now and it would appear that at present it is beyond our control to influence it, at least in the short and medium terms. The lead-in times for weather patterns to change are very lengthy and what can be done today may take decades to have any meaningful effect on the weather. There is therefore no immediate answer, no silver bullet.

---

1   Letter from James E Lovelock and Chris G Rapley, "Ocean Pipes Could Help the Earth to Cure Itself", *Nature*, 449 (September 27 2007), p 403.

Waking up after sleeping for 100 years

So great is the perceived threat of global warming that it has been variously described by leading scientists, economists, businessmen and politicians as a "unique challenge",[2] "a more serious threat than global terrorism",[3] and "the greatest threat that society faces today".[4]

The most recent Assessment Report by the Intergovernmental Panel on Climate Change (IPCC)[5] of 2007 concluded that the scientific uncertainties of global warming are essentially resolved. The Fourth Assessment Report "Climate Change 2007"[6] states that warming of the climate system is unequivocal, adding that there is clear evidence for a 0.74C rise in global temperatures and an average rate of 1.8 mm/yr rise in sea level during the twentieth century. The IPCC synthesis predicts that global temperatures could rise by between 1.8C and 4C and sea level could rise by between 0.18 and 0.59 mm/yr by the year 2100. The IPPC also envisages that weather patterns will become less predictable, and that the occurrence of extreme climate events, such as storms, floods and droughts, will increase.

The *Stern Review on the Economics of Climate Change*,[7] released in October 30 2006, is another watershed in the climate change debate as it represents one of the most important reviews of the economics of climate change. The report examined the latest evidence on the economic impacts of climate change itself, and explored the economics of stabilising GHGs in the atmosphere. It also analyses the policy challenges involved in managing the transition to a low-carbon economy.

It states that "climate change presents a unique challenge for economics: it is the greatest and widest-ranging market failure ever seen".[8] Also, it claims that "the evidence shows that ignoring climate change will eventually damage economic growth. Our actions over the coming few decades could create risks of major disruption to economic and social activity, later this century and in the next, on a similar scale to those associated with the great wars and the economic depression of the first half of the 20th century".[9]

Stern goes on to conclude that, given the gravity of the risk and the very narrow window for taking action, radical measures must be taken immediately to address the problem of climate change. Accordingly, 1% of the world economic activity should be invested to reduce the impact of global warming and failure to do so could risk

---

2   *Stern Review on the Economics of Climate Change* (October 30 2006), Part I, p 1.

3   Sir David King, "Climate Change Science: Adapt, Mitigate, or Ignore?", *Science*, 303 (January 9 2004), pp 176 to 177.

4   Speech by the Rt Hon David Miliband MP at the launch of Natural England, London (October 11 2006).

5   In 1988, the United Nations Environmental Programme and the World Meteorological Organization established the IPCC. It was created due to increasing concerns regarding the possibility of global warming. The most important aim of the IPCC is the continued assessment of the state of knowledge on the various aspects of climate change, its multiple impacts and response strategies.

6   IPCC, *Climate Change 2007: Synthesis Report* (IPCC 2007).

7   *Stern Review on the Economics of Climate Change* (October 30 2006).

8   *Stern Review on the Economics of Climate Change* (October 30 2006), part I, p 1.

9   *Ibid.* Executive Summary, p 2.

10   In April 2008, Lord Stern admitted that the current situation is far worse than the assumptions that formed the basis of the Stern Review. GHG emissions are growing faster than previously thought because of several factors that were not fully appreciated before, including the release of methane from thawing permafrost, the acidification of oceans, and the decay of carbon sinks. See Danny Fortson, "Stern Warns that Climate Change is Far Worse than 2006 Estimate", *The Independent* (April 17 2008).

future economic damage equivalent to a reduction of up to 20% in global gross domestic product. These figures are substantially higher than earlier estimates of the costs of global warming.[10]

Among many others, two noted economists have tried to understand the reason behind such high estimates. William D Nordhaus[11] has focused on the "social rate of time discount", the rate used to compare the wellbeing of future generations to the wellbeing of those alive today, and by using a different percentage has arrived at very different numbers. Sir Partha Dasgupta[12] has also focused his critique on intergenerational equity, as well as on a savings rate. Different ideas on how costs and benefits should be imposed on different generations have been put forward and choices may ultimately depend on ethical judgements. However, these have not diminished the importance of addressing climate change.

An equally stark warning on the need for society and industry to meet the challenges of climate change was given by Dr John Llewellyn, Senior Economic Policy Advisor of Lehman Brothers, according to whom "the pace of a firm's adaptation to climate change is likely to prove to be another of the forces that will influence whether, over the next several years, any given firm survives and prospers; or withers and, quite possibly, dies".[13] This warning to the finance industry is matched by leaders in insurance and reinsurance. For example, Rolf Tolle, Lloyd's Director for Franchise Performance, has stated that "climate change is today's problem, not tomorrow's. If we don't take action now to understand the changing nature of our planet and its impact, our industry will face extinction."[14] In February 2008, Citi together with JPMorgan Chase and Morgan Stanley announced the formation of the "Carbon Principles", which are climate change guidelines for advisors and lenders to power companies in the United States.

As for politicians, a long time passed after world leaders seriously discussed climate change in 1992 and in the years that led to the adoption of the Kyoto Protocol. In the Summer of 2007, in the G8 Summit held in Heiligendamm, climate change made the news again, and a commitment to the United Nations Framework Convention on Climate Change (UNFCCC) was reaffirmed.[15] At the end of 2007, the United Nations Climate Change Conference, held in Bali, culminated in the adoption of the Bali Road Map, which, though modest in scope, consists of a number of forward-looking decisions with the main goal of reaching a secure climate future. At the end of the Bangkok Climate Change Talks, held between March 31 and April 4 2008, it was announced that a timetable had been agreed for the negotiating process leading to a long-term international climate change agreement to be

---

11   William D Nordhaus, "A Review of the Stern Review on the Economics of Global Warming", *Journal of Economic Literature* (May 2 2007) and "Critical Assumptions in the Stern Review on Climate Change" Science, 317 (5835) (July 13 2007), pp 201 to 202.
12   Sir Partha Dasgupta, Comments on the Stern Review's Economics of Climate Change (December 12 2006).
13   John Llewellyn, Lehman Brothers Report, *The Business of Climate Change: Challenges and Opportunities* (February 2007), p 4.
14   Lloyd's, "Lloyd's urges insurers to take climate change seriously or risk being swept away" (June 5 2006).
15   Joint Statement by the German G8 Presidency and the Heads of State and/or Government of Brazil, China, India, Mexico and South Africa on the occasion of the G8 Summit in Heiligendamm, Germany, June 8 2007 and Summit Declaration: Growth and Responsibility in the World Economy.

concluded in Copenhagen two years later. "The train to Copenhagen has left the station", Yvo de Boer, Executive Secretary of the UNFCCC, said. In Europe, the European Parliament Temporary Committee on Climate Change considered the "scientific basis of climate change as settled".[16]

What are GHGs and how did we get into this mess?

GHGs are gases which control energy flows in the Earth's atmosphere by absorbing infrared radiation and which reduce the loss of heat into space. They are essential to maintaining the temperature of the Earth. GHGs have both natural and anthropogenic sources.

Global GHG emissions due to human activities have grown since pre-industrial times, with an increase of 70% between 1970 and 2004. CO_2 is the most important anthropogenic GHG.[17] Its annual emissions have grown between 1970 and 2004 by about 80%, from 21 to 38 gigatonnes, and represented 77% of total anthropogenic GHG emissions in 2004. The rate of growth of CO_2 was much higher between 1995 and 2004 than during the period of 1970 to 1994.[18]

The largest growth in GHGs between 1970 and 2004 has come from energy supply, transport and industry, while residential and commercial buildings, forestry (including deforestation) and agriculture have been growing at a lower rate.[19]

On a geographic basis, there are important differences between regions. North America, Asia and the Middle East have driven the rise in emissions since 1972. Developed countries (UNFCCC Annex I countries) represent 20% of the world's population, but account for 46.4% of global GHG emissions. In contrast, the 80% of the world population living in developing countries (non-Annex I countries) account for 53.6% of GHG emissions.[20] However, China, with approximately 8% higher emissions than those of the United States, now tops the list of CO_2 emitting countries.[21]

Given the dire pronouncements on the gravity of the threat posed by global warming or climate change – the terms sometimes seem to be used popularly if not logically or scientifically as having equivalent meaning – it is reasonable to ask how the problem arose and why it took so long for the need for intervention to be appreciated fully.

The first thing to note is that the effect of GHGs on global warming has been long accepted. It is now over 100 years since global warming was officially discovered by Svante Arrhenius, who is credited with recognising the effects of GHGs on the atmosphere in 1896.[22] To put this in historical context, in that year Queen Victoria became the longest reigning British monarch, William McKinley became President of

---

16   European Parliament, Draft Interim Report on the scientific facts of climate change: findings and recommendations for decision-making. 22.1.2008 2008/2001 (INI).

17   Other GHGs include methane (CH_4), nitrous oxide (N_2O), perfluorocarbons (PFCs), hydrofluorocarbons (HFCs), sulphur hexafluoride (SF_6) and ozone depleting substances (ODSs: chlorofluorocarbons (CFCs), hydrochlorofluorocarbons (HCFCs) and halons).

18   IPCC, *Climate Change 2007: Synthesis Report* (2007), p 36ff.

19   *Ibid.*

20   *Ibid.*

21   www.mnp.nl/en/dossiers/Climatechange/moreinfo/Chinanowno1inCO2emissionsUSAinsecondposition.html.

22   Svante Arrhenius, "On the Influence of Carbonic Acid in the Air upon the Temperature of the Ground", *Philosophical Magazine and Journal of Science*, 41 (1896), pp 237 to 276.

the United States and the shortest war in world history, the Anglo-Zanzibar war, was concluded in 38 minutes. This was also a year of unusually severe weather conditions. In May and August, respectively, the costliest tornado in the history of the United States levelled St Louis in Missouri, killing more than 250 people[23] and a tsunami and earthquake devastated Japan killing 22,000 people.[24]

Both Arrhenius and Thomas Chamberlin (who subsequently confirmed that human activity could warm the Earth by adding CO_2 to the atmosphere) abandoned their research. At the time, scientists felt that human influences were minimal in comparison to the more powerful forces of astronomy and geology. These ideas were reinforced by studies during the 1940s. However, subsequent research put together by Gilbert Plass in 1955 concluded that adding more CO_2 to the atmosphere would intercept more infrared radiation, preventing it being lost to space and thus warming the planet. Also in the 1950s, the conviction of the dissolution of CO_2 in the sea was contested, and Roger Ravelle's calculations showed that the complexities of the surface ocean chemistry are such that it returns much of the CO_2 it absorbs. In the late 1950s and the early 1960s, Charles Keeling used the most modern technology available at the time to measure the concentration of atmospheric CO_2 in Antarctica and Mauna Loa. The resulting Keeling CO_2 curves, which ultimately demonstrate global warming, have become famous.

The twentieth century, punctured by two world wars and global recessions, was a period of rapid economic expansion and population growth. However, such expansion and growth in many Western countries was brought at the cost of water pollution and declining air quality. As Blake's Satanic mills gave way to Boz's grim towns, where serpents of smoke spiralled to the heavens, those urban sources of disease and effluvia in turn gave way to an age of coal, steam, mass electric light, gas and electric heating and the automobile, all fuelled by what seemed to be inexhaustible and cheap sources of energy supply.

With advances in technology came an age dominated by the careless and prodigious use of fossil fuels. Year after year, as air quality declined respiratory disease and death increased. In London, killer smog led to clean air legislation in the 1950s; smog from automobiles and factory plants choked Los Angeles' inhabitants in the 1990s; and smog put those living and working in industrial areas in India and China in the first decade of the twenty-first century under threat of serious risk of disease or death.

The 10 warmest years on record have all occurred since 1990 in the balmy decade of the 1990s, which Robert Watson, former IPCC chairman, stated was "the hottest in the last century".[25] Not so much a case of fiddling as Rome burns, but not heeding warnings while sweating at home, in the train and in the office.

The 1980s saw an expansion in the environmental movement following Rachel Carson's *Silent Spring* (1962), the image of the Earth seen from the Moon in 1968 and

---

23   See www.usgennet.org/usa/mo/county/stlouis/cyclone.htm.
24   See www.agu.org/sci_soc/sanriku.html.
25   RT Watson, *et al* (eds), IPCC: Climate Change 2001: Synthesis Report. A Contribution of Working Groups I, II, and III to the Third Assessment Report of the Integovernmental Panel on Climate Change (IPPC 2001).

the Earth Day the following year, the Club of Rome's Limits to Growth and the Stockholm Conference in 1972, the Three Mile Island nuclear reactor accident in 1979, Chernobyl in 1986, and the *Exxon Valdez* oil spillage in 1989.

After the discovery of the depletion of the ozone layer – with the societal and political interest in the topic, which culminated in the signing in 1985 of the Vienna Convention for the Protection of the Ozone Layer and the 1987 Montreal Protocol on Substances that Deplete the Ozone Layer – it was the time for climate change.

In 1988 the IPCC was established, with its first report being released in 1990. In 1992, the UNFCCC was signed at the Rio Earth Summit. It represented the creation of the first international-law climate change instrument.

The second international-law mechanism, the Kyoto Protocol, was adopted under the Framework Convention in 1997 and came into force in 2005 when it was ratified by Russia (albeit that the United States has refused to ratify it). The Kyoto Protocol sets out binding targets for developed countries for the reduction in GHGs in a first commitment period, the period between 2008 and 2012, when it expires. The Kyoto Protocol introduces three flexible mechanisms: the Clean Development Mechanism (CDM), Joint Implementation (JI) and International Emissions Trading.

The anatomy of GHG emissions schemes

Simultaneously with the entry into force of the Kyoto Protocol,[26] the EU Emissions Allowance Trading Scheme (EU ETS) – the world's largest, comprising approximately 11,500 industrial emitters – became effective on January 1 2005.[27] The scheme introduces tradable quotas as an environmental instrument. The idea of a scheme based on quotas is to limit a total emission (a "cap") within a determined area (a "bubble") by allowing a certain amount of emissions (a "quota") to a polluter, which is to receive allowances equal to its quota. The possibility of trading allowances generates efficient allocation by the market. This scheme has created an important new tradable commodity.

The EU ETS was created and is regulated at the EU level by Directive 2003/87/EC of the European Parliament and of the Council of October 13 2003 establishing a scheme for GHG emission allowance trading within the Community and amending Council Directive 96/61/EC (the Emission Trading Directive (the Directive), as amended.[28]

Although other GHGs[29] are covered by the Emission Trading Directive, carbon

---

26   Under the Kyoto Protocol, the European Union agreed to reduce GHG emissions by 8% below 1990 levels during the commitment period of 2008 to 2012, a target which was shared among the 15 member states prior to enlargement. Under Council Decision 2002/358/EC of April 25 2002 (OJ L130, 15.5.2002, p 1), a burden-sharing agreement was also established setting differing targets for each of the member states. The new member states, except for Cyprus and Malta, which do not have any commitments, have individual targets under the Kyoto Protocol.

27   The EU ETS is divided into two phases: a pilot phase to operate until 2007, and Phase II which coincides with the EU's Kyoto commitment period of 2008 to 2012.

28   OJ L 275, 25.10.2003, p 32. The Directive was amended by Directive 2004/101/EC of the European Parliament and of the Council of October 27 2004, amending Directive 2003/87/EC establishing a scheme for GHG emission allowance trading within the Community, in respect of the Kyoto Protocol's project mechanisms (OJ L 338, 13.11.2004, p 18).

29   Methane (CH_4), nitrous oxide (N_2O), hydrofluorocarbons (HFCs), perfluorocarbons (PFCs) and sulphur hexafluoride (SF_6).

dioxide (CO_2) is its primary target and it is currently the only tradable emission. At present, the Directive is also limited to certain industries: energy activities,[30] production and processing of ferrous metals,[31] minerals industries (cement, glass and ceramics)[32] and pulp and paper industrial plants. Proposals are well advanced to include the aviation sector in the EU ETS and discussions have been held to include shipping.[33]

The first phase of the EU ETS ran from 2005 to 2007 and the second phase will run until 2012, to coincide with the first Kyoto commitment period.

On January 23 2008, the European Commission published its draft proposals for the review of the scheme, required under Article 30 of the EU Directive on the EU ETS. The role of the review is to develop the EU ETS in a positive way post-2012 and learn from experience to date.

However, the EU ETS is not a unique scheme. There are other examples in Japan, Australia and New Zealand, and several different emissions trading schemes exist in the United States (eg RGGI and California's Carbon Regulation). These are discussed in the chapter by Steven Ferrey and Courtney Queen.

The impact of climate change and carbon in the law

For lawyers, climate change and carbon have offered legal challenges and opportunities almost unequalled since the steam age. Just as the Industrial Revolution caused traditional legal doctrines to be re-examined in light of the needs of the sponsors of railways and shipping and the investors in the stock exchanges which fuelled their enterprises and of the property owners and communities which opposed their progress, climate change has changed everything.

In essence, the legal issues relating to climate change can be divided into three main areas. First, the mechanics of trading carbon units; second, potential liabilities arising not only in respect of trading carbon units, but also for damage caused to property and people; and, third, the impact of climate change and the carbon market on existing areas of legal practice. This book addresses these three areas: on the mechanics of trading carbon units (see parts II and III), projects, credits and trading are all discussed; on liabilities, there are key chapters in part IV on litigation, accountancy and taxation, corporate social responsibility and corporate transactions; on the impact of climate change and the carbon market on existing areas of legal practice, the later chapters of Part IV discuss the implications of climate change and competition, real estate, and carbon capture and storage.

Following further introductory analysis by Professor Peter Cameron, which reviews the principal steps in the climate change debate that have laid the foundations of a distinct body of law on climate change, projects are discussed.

Christopher Carr and Flavia Rosembuj analyse, among other topics, the structuring and financing options for Clean Development Mechanism (CDM) and

---

30 Combustion installations with a rated thermal input exceeding 20MW, mineral oil refineries and coke ovens.
31 Metal ore roasting or sintering installations and those for the production of pig iron or steel with a capacity exceeding 2.5 tonnes per hour.
32 Of a certain capacity.
33 Road transportation, agriculture, residential and office use, which are also important emitters, have so far not been considered.

Joint Implementation (JI) projects, how the purchase of "verified" (instead of "certified") emission reductions provide for an innovative financing technique, and how risks in CDM and JI projects can be managed. According to the World Bank, the market for carbon credits had grown to over US$5 billion in 2006. It is therefore important in this emerging and rapidly growing market that lawyers get it right for their clients and that potential elephant traps are avoided, insofar as they can be.

The work of these experienced carbon trading lawyers is augmented by the practical experience of John McMorris on running a carbon project. McMorris offers a project developer's view on how to develop CDM and JI projects by identifying different steps to be achieved, and possible strengths and limitations of a project.

At the start of Part III, Christopher Norton explores how the trading of emissions reductions has developed and focuses on key contractual provisions that deserve particular attention when negotiating Emission Reduction Purchase Agreements (ERPAs); and Seb Walhain discusses the development of carbon trading and how the carbon market is likely to evolve.

In a very important chapter, Martijn Wilder sheds light on the nature of carbon credits. These are defined as any instrument that represents a tradable right in GHG emissions reductions, which is not determined by the Kyoto Protocol or most domestic laws. It is important to determine the nature of a carbon credit in the event of a dispute between different entities involved in a project generating the credit, or the insolvency of the holder, in order to establish how credits are to be executed and secured.

Anju Sanehi discusses emissions trading in terms of who is trading, what is being traded, trading documentation and its architecture and provisions specific to emissions trading. In particular, this chapter discusses the main standard emissions trading agreements: those produced by ISDA (the International Swaps and Derivatives Association, Inc), EFET (the European Federation of Emissions Trading) and IETA (the International Emissions Trading Association).

Anthony Hobley closes Part III with a fundamental chapter. This provides for an overview of the carbon market by explaining the UNFCCC, the Kyoto Protocol, the Marrakech Accords and the Kyoto flexibility mechanisms. The chapter further discusses the genesis of emissions trading, the leadership of the European Union and what is happening in the world, including the United States.

In Part IV, the chapter on litigation provides important commentary on the liabilities that may be associated with climate change.

Greater scientific and social awareness leaves unresponsive governments or corporations prone to litigious action which, once commenced, raises a multitude of legal challenges and opportunities of which both plaintiffs and defendants must be aware. These challenges and opportunities are discussed by Jose Cofre, Nicholas Rock and Paul Watchman. They include the scope and breadth of potential causes of action, the issue of legal standing in courts and tribunals, justiciability and judicial competence, expert evidence, the challenge of the science of causation and the question of appropriate remedies.

It may well be in the case of climate change litigation that the outcome for plaintiffs and defendants – if not their lawyers – is no more satisfactory than tobacco or asbestos litigation, or litigation by third-world plaintiffs against first-world defendants.[34] Climate change litigation is likely to clarify some minor and some important constitutional, public and administrative law issues whilst leaving unsettled the crunch issues relating to human rights and tort as it applies to climate change and its victims. Now that plaintiffs are better aware of judicial attitudes prevailing in their respective jurisdictions, they are formulating new types of legal claims. One of the most recent of these is a claim commenced by the Native Village of Kivalina and the City of Kivalina against 24 global energy companies under not only public and private nuisance, but also civil conspiracy and concert of action, alleging that certain defendants have entered into agreements to participate in the contribution to global warming and to mislead the public with respect to the science of global warming.

Non-climate-change-related case law is also importantly relevant to the way emerging climate change litigation claims are presented, and interpreted by the judiciary. For example, as recently as May 2008 the English Court of Appeal[35] clarified the current law on public nuisance in England (a much relied-upon cause of action in climate change suits). The Court of Appeal held that damages may be awarded in public nuisance where a person's life, safety or health has been adversely affected by an unlawful act which need not necessarily involve interference with the enjoyment of land.

Whatever the final outcome of nascent climate change litigation, it is clear that with the range of potential litigants, the scope of laws which may apply and the political weight of the issue of climate changes we are in the foothills of climate change litigation.

Other topics which may concern liability are addressed in the chapters on accountancy and taxation, corporate social responsibility (CSR) and corporate transactions.

Iain Calton, Helen Devenney and Sarah Nolleth discuss the challenges of GHG accounting and taxation, and market participants continue to wait for clear guidance on both. The chapter, which is divided into two main portions, begins with the evolution and current developments in emissions' accounting, particularly in respect of allowances held and of forward contracts to acquire allowances. There are important consequences arising from different accounting treatments for emissions and these relate to profit and loss and financial performance more generally. The taxation implications of emissions rights are considered in the second major portion of the chapter, in particular from the UK perspective. Globally, emission allowances are taxed differently in different jurisdictions and, while some specific rules have been established in certain countries, others have relied on principles in established tax law.

Angela Delfino, Mike Wallace and Paul Watchman ask how climate change is affecting CSR. Their conclusions are bold yet important: firstly, there is more

---

34   Goldman Sachs has stated that carbon emissions could create corporate liability comparable to that caused by asbestos impacts. See Evan Mills and Eugene Lecomte, *From Risk to Opportunity: How Insurers can Proactively and Profitably Manage Climate Change* (Ceres, 2006), p 7.

35   *Corby Group Litigation v. Corby Borough Council* [2008] EWCA Civ. 463 (Lord Justice Ward, Lord Justice Dyson and Lady Justice Smith).

reporting; secondly, in relation to CSR reporting there are better perceived business opportunities; thirdly, the nature of CSR is changing as disclosed information is being quantified progressively.

This fact reflects the sea change at political, legal and market levels whereby greater transparency and accountability are sought by means of disclosure. This may be achieved through company returns as in the United States,[36] or directors and pension fund trustees' duties in the United Kingdom,[37] or voluntary schemes such as the Carbon Disclosure Project and the revised Equator Principles.[38] There is, however, some deserved scepticism regarding the methodology for measuring carbon emissions, reporting, auditing and the value of some carbon offsetting mechanisms and programmes.

Some legal jurisdictions make special provision for companies to disclose actual, potential or future environmental liabilities as part of their annual financial reporting obligations, or in respect of listing or general company reporting, or for directors and pension fund trustees to report the impact of their businesses on the environment and communities. Existing legislation has also been helpful in forcing businesses to re-examine their practices, so as to reduce their environmental impacts. Even companies that have not been in the vanguard of those that have accepted the scientific validity of climate change and the need for GHG emissions reduction do at least recognise that they can save – and have saved – substantial expenditure by good environmental husbandry and financial housekeeping, including carbon management strategies.

Equally relevant to corporate and mergers-and-acquisitions (M&A) lawyers is the impact of the carbon market and carbon trading on corporate transactions. In some cases, the free allocation of large excess amounts of carbon units under Phase I of the EU ETS to energy and other manufacturing companies resulted in large windfall profits. Ownership of, or security relating to, these units may be very valuable. Indeed, in the case of one European steel company which was put up for sale it was said, no doubt apocryphally, that the value of the allocation of carbon units to the installations owned and operated by the company was greater than all the other assets owned by it.

In the due diligence process and the sale and purchase agreement, it is necessary to establish rights of ownership of and security over carbon units, and in relation to their registration and transfer, and to ensure that each party is clear whether the vendor or the purchaser will retain or have title to the carbon units transferred to it. Likewise, it is important to understand the carbon allocation laws in relevant jurisdictions, as it is possible in some countries that carbon units may be lost if a plant is mothballed or closed, and for swingeing cuts to be focused on one industry or a group of industries rather than being reduced on an equitable or equal basis. For

---

36   For example, the Attorney-General of New York recently started an investigation under state securities legislation into five energy companies to determine whether financial risk had been adequately disclosed in respect of their association with coal-fired power plants. Also see the CERES Petition Before the United States Securities and Exchange Commission; Petition for Interpretive Guidance on Climate Risk (September 18 2007); Petition Number: 4-547.

37   Namely, the Occupational Pension Schemes (Investment) Regulations 2005 SI 2005/3378.

38   www.cdp.org and www.equatorprinciples.com.

example, those energy companies which took early action after the re-unification of Germany were unhappy when, during the process of allocating carbon units, the German government did not, in their view, give them sufficient recognition for early action in terms of the carbon units allocated to energy plants.

Finally on this point, although the EU ETS is a carbon emissions reduction scheme, it is not true that all countries will be forced, under national or regional state implementation of the Kyoto Protocol or post-Kyoto, to reduce their levels of carbon emissions. Indeed, in recognition of the fact that certain member states are more developed than others, it is essential that the nuances of each of the carbon allocation schemes under each Phase of the EU ETS for each member state are known. For example, new entrants' allowances may be more freely available in the United Kingdom than in the rest of Europe. Similarly, industries thought to be of high importance to the development of local or regional economies, such as the ceramics industry in Portugal or Spain, may be granted more allocations, whereas other local or regional industries may not be given preferential treatment in allocating carbon credits – for example, the cement industry in Germany, which is one of the principal consumers of energy and emitters of carbon dioxide, may with some justification feel aggrieved at the allocation given by the German carbon allocation scheme to the production of cement.[39]

These and other corporate due diligence issues are examined in detail by John Bowman and Simon Read in their chapter on corporate transactions. This chapter, therefore, focuses on the impacts of carbon issues on corporate transactions and how a failure to consider fully the potential carbon liabilities of a company could result in the acquisition of a completely different business. The chapter also considers how climate change issues may impact on each stage of a transaction, from the due diligence stage through to the drafting of contractual documentation.

Climate change and the carbon market may have implications for other areas of legal practice.

Peter Crowther and Lucie Fish look at EC competition rules which apply to carbon trading and to the allocation of emission allowances. Specifically, their chapter looks at agreements, decisions and concerted practices harmful to competition, and the unilateral conduct of dominant firms which use their power in an anti-competitive manner, both prohibited under EC law. The chapter also looks at state aid rules which apply where aid is granted by a member state or through state resources; confers an advantage on its recipients; favours certain undertakings or the production of certain goods; distorts or threatens to distort competition; and affects trade between member states.

Tim Baines and John Bowman discuss green buildings and green cities. Their chapter begins by introducing the concept of energy efficiency in buildings in international, national and local initiatives. It also discusses legislative measures. Emissions trading, the concept of "green" in commercial agreements and the

---

39   Wolf Spieth and Martin Hamer, "The Implementation of the EU ETS Directive in the EU Member States in the Light of the German National Allocation Plan", *Journal for European Environmental and Planning Law*, vol 2 (2005).

implications of climate change for property leases are then addressed. The chapter ends with a wider policy discussion as to what legal mechanisms should be used in mitigating the possible climatic impacts of buildings.

Juliette Addison, John Bowman and Paul Watchman discuss carbon capture and storage and carbon sequestration. This technology has assumed greater importance in recent years and is seen by some as a panacea in the mitigation of climate change impacts. However, scientific, economic, social, and environmental challenges as well as legal constraints make carbon sequestration and carbon capture and storage an important case study.

Climate change relates to many other areas of the law, which cannot all be addressed in a publication of this nature. A particularly important area is human rights.

Climate change has many interfaces with human rights. To refer to just a few examples, climate change relates to the right to life, the right to health, the right to property and the rights of indigenous peoples, because global warming can trigger poverty, famine, mass migration and the spread of infectious diseases, such as malaria and dengue fever.

Recent studies and communications[40] point to the link between climate change and the propensity for violent conflict, which in turn will leave communities poorer, less resilient and less able to adapt to climate change. The terms "climate refugee" and "environmental migrant" are now beginning to be used.

A study by Dan Smith and Janani Vivekananda,[41] for example, highlights four key elements of risk – political instability, economic weakness, food insecurity and large-scale migration. The study identifies a group of 46 countries in which the effects of climate change interacting with economic, social and political problems will create a high risk of violent conflict. Second, a group of 56 countries was identified, in which the interaction of climate change and other factors creates a high risk of political instability, with a potential for violent conflict in the longer term.

The conflict in Sudan has been called the "first climate change war" and on top of all the economic and ecological implications of global warming, the prospect of climate change resulting in more conflicts like Darfur could be a distinct possibility.

Mitigation and adaptation to climate change

Policy and legislation are essential for dealing with unavoidable impacts of climate change.

As defined by the IPPC, "mitigation is an anthropogenic intervention to reduce

---

40   See for example, "Climate Change and International Security", Paper from the High Representative and the European Commission to the European Council (S113/08), of March 14 2008; German Advisory Council on Climate Change, *Climate Change as a Security Risk* (London: Earthscan 2008); Christian Aid, *Human Tide: the real migration crisis* (London: Christian Aid 2007); DD Zhang *et al* "Climate Change and War Frequency in Eastern China over the Last Millennium", *Human Ecology* (2007) (this study links climate change to 1,000 years of conflict in China); Julian Borger, "Climate Change Could Lead to Global Conflict, says Beckett", *The Guardian* May 11 2007. In April 2008, the United Nations Security Council held its first debate on the impact of climate change on peace and security. See Security Council SC/9000.

41   Dan Smith and Janani Vivekananda, *A Climate of Conflict: The links between climate change, peace and war* (London: International Alert 2007)

the anthropogenic forcing of the climate system; it includes strategies to reduce GHG sources and emissions and enhancing GHG sinks".[42] Adaptation, on the other hand, is defined as the "adjustment in natural or human systems in response to actual or expected climatic stimuli or their effects which moderates harm or exploits beneficial opportunities".[43] Various types of adaptation can be distinguished, including anticipatory, autonomous or spontaneous and planned adaptation. Adaptation is the response available for the impacts that will occur before mitigation measures have an effect. The challenge to adaptation will be particularly acute in developing countries, where greater vulnerability and poverty will impose limits on the ability to act.

The reduction of GHGs will require significant changes in human behaviour and technology. However, changes may also be implemented using existing technology. For Pacala and Socolow[44] the fundamental scientific, technical and industrial knowledge to solve and abate global warming in the next 50 years already exists Although there is no single technology that could meet the world's energy needs and limit atmospheric CO_2 to a trajectory that avoids a doubling of the pre-industrial concentration, a portfolio of technologies does exist. Pacala and Socolow outline their 50-year solution using "stabilization wedges", which represent parts of a global energy pie (one billion tonnes of carbon per year). These can collectively be executed to reduce current emissions with existing technologies. In this model, seven wedges of savings must be deployed to reduce global emissions, in order to avert catastrophic global warming.

In the model, three economic options exist to reduce atmospheric carbon: energy efficiency and conservation (with four options: improved fuel economy, reduced reliance on cars, more efficient buildings, and improved power plant efficiency); removal of carbon from electricity and fuel production (with nine options: substitution of coal with gas, storage of carbon captured in power plants, storage of carbon captured in hydrogen plants, storage of carbon captured in synfuels plants, nuclear fission, wind electricity, photovoltaic electricity, renewable hydrogen, biofuels); and biological storage of carbon in natural sinks (with two options: forest management and agricultural soils management).

Whilst relying on existing technology, investment and creativity is still required. These represent risks and opportunities for businesses (eg renewables or carbon capture and storage). Moreover, climate change, mitigation and adaptation bring other opportunities and risks.

Climate change opportunities

In the 1970s British sitcom, *Dad's Army*, the redoubtable Scottish actor, John Laurie, cast as Private Fraser, would see destruction of mankind in every difficulty, no matter how petty or minor. Hence his catchphrase, "We are all doomed, doomed!". This sentiment has recently been adopted by the tabloid press in describing James

---

42   IPPC, *Climate Change 2007: Synthesis Report, Glossary of Terms* (IPCC 2007).
43   *Ibid.*
44   S Pacala and R Socolow, "Stabilization Wedges: Solving the Climate Problem for the Next 50 Years with Current Technologies", *Science* vol 305 (August 13 2004).

Lovelock's vision of famine, flood, droughts, displacement, civil war and more parochially the rising level of the River Thames, engulfing the Houses of Parliament and much of the Thames Embankment north of the river and the London Eye on the South Bank.[45]

Europe, China, India and the United States form the key to success in tacking global warming. In China, India and the United States, greenhouse gas emissions are largely unregulated or poorly regulated; and India and China are now using fossil fuels to power their economic growth. Both India and China, however, along with other developing countries, can with some justification point to the fact that the developed countries have had the advantage of unregulated GHG emissions for centuries. That the developed countries now expect developing countries to limit, pause or halt their development for a problem created by the developed counties smacks of irony at best and hypocrisy at worst.

Students of the literature of climate change, particularly as it relates to rising sea and river levels, tsunamis, hurricanes, typhoons and other radical weather changes, may come to see life in much the same way as prophets of doom such as Private Fraser. However, climate change is not just about risks and liabilities; it also creates opportunities. Business and financial institutions may choose to change, and to consider where opportunities lie – for example, by using the CDM and JI flexible mechanisms or by creating gothic edifices of derivatives and securitisation.

On November 2 2006, *The Times*, by way of contrast to the doom-laden predictions of those caught in the eye of the maelstrom of climate change, noted that climate change is not all gloom and doom: "Climate change is a different kind of enemy. But for some, the battle will be very profitable."[46]

The press[47] has also reported on the rebirth and reinvention of Silicon Valley due to clean environment or green technology. In Silicon Valley, the investment in alternative energy products, nanotechnology and other innovative techniques went from US$34 million in the first quarter of 2006 to US$290 million in the third quarter. Vinod Khosla, who helped to co-found Sun Mycrosystems and who arguably made the most money of any venture capital during the internet boom in the late 1990s, is now investing in clean technology such as batteries, ethanol and coal gasification.

This is not all. Our green utopia, a step away from our brown dystopia, comprises more than just new sources of energy or hybrid cars. Green buildings proliferate, as well as environmental hotels such as "1" Hotels and Residences. Green opportunities exist in sustainable farming and organic and environmental food and drink, such as the Charles Krug Winery, the Niman Ranch, Green & Black's Organic Chocolate, Organic Valley, Amy's Kitchen and Duchy Originals. Eco-fashion is in a boom, with fully dedicated brands such as "Edun", or as part of certain designer brands such as Stella McCartney. The same is happening with natural care products such as the Body Shop range or Burt's Bees. Seventh Generation and Method are helping us clean our houses – this time, in a sustainable way.

---

45   Sarah Sands, "We're all Doomed! 40 years from global catastrophe", *Daily Mail* (March 22 2008).
46   Camilla Cavendish, "Who will Clean up Carbon?", *The Times* (November 2 2006).
47   Laurie J Flynn, "Silicon Valley Rebounds, Led by Green Technology", *New York Times* (January 29 2007).

Climate change risks

Climate change risks are of three types: first, those directly related to climate change, such as extreme events like flooding, heat waves, hurricanes and tornadoes; second, those associated with investing in mitigation and adaptation technologies, such as renewables and carbon capture and storage; and, third, those related to sustainable practices, which may not be sustainable at all.

All of these represent well-known risks to different sectors of activity: power generators, the transport sector, the insurance and reinsurance industries, and banking and financial institutions.

The UK government, however, is also concerned that the green market and climate change industry is being populated by rogues and people without necessary professional competence and that this is bringing the market and the industry into disrepute.

Conclusions

In *Americans and Climate Change*,[48] Abbasi describes global warming as the "perfect problem": it is complex and of inaccessible scientific content; it involves a substantial and uncertain time lag between cause and effect; and there is inertia in all the key drivers of the problem, from demographic growth to long-lived energy infrastructure to ingrained daily habits at the household level. Moreover, it is beset by the following forces: psychological barriers that complicate comprehension and processing of the issue, due in part to its perceived remoteness in time and place; the partisan, cultural, and other filters that cause social discounting or obfuscation of the threat; motivational obstacles, especially the futility associated with what is perhaps the quintessential "collective action problem" of our time; and the mismatches between the global, cross-sectoral scope of the climate change issue and the jurisdiction, focus, and capacity of existing institutions.

This book is our contribution to the debate and, hopefully, to action. Our aim is to examine some of the more interesting aspects of the law and practice relating to climate change and the management of carbon assets and liabilities which have emerged in recent years, and to provide a practical guide to those who toil in the various vineyards that have been planted as part of the carbon market in recent years.

We have been very fortunate in persuading unrivalled energy and carbon market leaders and leading carbon law practitioners to join us at Dewey & LeBoeuf in this venture. I would like to thank each of them and my friends and colleagues in the climate change practice group at the firm for the work they have done. I hope that, in the production of the book, I have not damaged or abused too many friendships along the way.

The last word on climate change in this Introduction is given to Jeff Immelt, CEO of General Electric, who put his company's money where his mouth is in supporting the GE "ecomagination" initiative personally in order to encourage GE to develop

---

48   Daniel R Abbasi, *Americans and Climate Change: Closing the Gap Between Science and Action* (New Haven: Yale School of Forestry and Environmental Studies 2006).

clean technologies and green businesses. Updating in 2005 for the boz 'n' hood generation the parable of the ostrich with its head in the sand, Immelt said: "I see the way trends change, and [the climate] is changing. You can either sit with a hood over your head and pretend things won't change or you can get ready for it."

Paul Q Watchman is co-chair of Dewey & LeBoeuf's global environmental, health and safety practice group and the leader of its climate change group.

Having practised law for more than 30 years, Paul's climate change practice now includes advising on the development of carbon projects under the Kyoto Protocol, carbon capture and storage projects, renewable energy projects and green buildings, as well as emissions trading. He has advised major energy and oil and gas clients, insurance companies and financial institutions on climate change litigation.

In addition, Paul has a wide-ranging practice in environmental, planning and regulatory issues. Paul has represented a large number of industrial conglomerates buying and selling businesses around the globe. This has involved multijurisdictional due diligence and the negotiation of complex forms of environmental protection for clients.

Paul also has a particularly keen interest in corporate social responsibility, human rights and business practices. He has been involved in ground-breaking work for the United Nations on the fiduciary duties of pensions funds, unit trusts and insurance companies. In 2006, Paul was named as one of the six key international figures in the development of sustainable finance.

History of climate change law and policy

Peter D Cameron
University of Dundee

The key driver behind the introduction of law on climate change mitigation has been the growing body of scientific evidence to support the proposition that a change of climate is taking place, resulting directly or indirectly from human activity and which is altering the composition of the global atmosphere in addition to natural climate variability. As the scientific evidence has mounted, the pressures for law-making have come from two principal directions: the development of global cooperative solutions, perhaps by way of regional actions as a first step (most notably the EU Emissions Trading Scheme, but also the various US schemes); and the introduction of national schemes, expressing leadership by example and a belief by some states that an incremental approach may yield some benefits. At both national and international levels, there has been a continuing tension between proposals for preventive action and resistance based on perceived negative impacts on competitiveness or economic development. For many sectors of industry, the uneven development of climate change law presents a significant risk of regulatory uncertainty.

The sections below review the principal steps in the climate change debate that have laid the foundations of a distinct body of law on climate change at international and regional levels. To some extent they represent a "history", but this should not mislead; the international legal framework in this area is very much a "work in progress". It will be adapted and elaborated as more states become involved in cooperative actions and as further evidence of the socio-economic impacts of climate change adds urgency to the need for such cooperation.

1. The beginnings: Stockholm

The earliest evidence of the need for collective action on climate change emerged from the Stockholm Conference on the Human Environment in 1972. It acted as a catalyst to developments in the United Nations (UN) for the next decade and beyond. In particular, it established the principle that the use of the Earth's resources has to be regulated in line with the aim of maintaining developmental opportunities. The way in which this was to be achieved was not made clear at that stage, but the principle was established. The conference adopted a non-binding Declaration of Principles for the Preservation and Enhancement of the Human Environment, which was designed to "inspire and guide the peoples of the world in the preservation and enhancement of the human environment".[1]

---

[1] Report of the UN Conference on the Human Environment, UN Doc.A/CONF.48/14 at 2-65, and Corr.1 (1972); 11 ILM 1416 (1972).

Institutionally, it led to the creation of the UN Environment Programme (UNEP) which was to administer an Action Plan for the development of environmental policy. This Action Plan consisted of 109 recommendations for environmental action at the international level.

The most important of the 26 principles in the Stockholm Declaration were Principles 21 and 22. Principle 21 drew on existing treaty and customary law to proclaim:

"States have, in accordance with the Charter of the United Nations and the principles of international law, the sovereign right to exploit their own resources pursuant to their own environmental policies, and the responsibility to ensure that activities within their jurisdiction or control do not cause damage to the environment of other States or of areas beyond the limits of national jurisdiction."

Essentially, the normative force of the provision is that trans-boundary environmental harm has to be controlled. Principle 22 requires states to cooperate in the development of international law with respect to liability and compensation for the victims of pollution and other environmental damage, insofar as this is caused by activities within the jurisdiction or control of these states into areas beyond their jurisdiction. Most of the other Principles were policy-oriented, rather than normative in character. Responsibility for future generations was set out in Principle 1, and Principle 2 states that the "natural resources of the earth, including the air, water, land, flora and fauna must be safeguarded for the benefit of present and future generations through careful planning or management, as appropriate". Some of the tensions that have figured in subsequent discussions on climate change were apparent, however. Principles 8 to 11 recognise that economic and social development is essential and that environmental policies should "enhance and not adversely affect the present or future development potential of developing countries". The approach to environmental and resource management in Principles 12 to 17 is very similar to that adopted 20 years later in the Rio Declaration (see below).

The Stockholm Declaration introduced some key ideas on how environmental and developmental issues would in future be handled in international relations: it treated environmental protection and economic development as linked subjects; it envisaged the need for cooperation between states and for coordination of activities addressing the issues identified, within and outside the UN system; and it promoted the idea of inter-generational equity. However, for more than a decade very little progress was made in applying these ideas. Indeed, with respect to climate change issues, little progress was made in developing a common response for an even longer period.

2.   The formation of IPCC

Although there were a number of intergovernmental conferences on climate change issues from 1979 onwards,[2] it was not until 1988 that UNEP and the World

---

2   The principal initiatives were the WMO's World Climate Conference in 1979 and the UNEP/WMO/ICSU Conference in Villach, Austria: "Assessment of the Role of Carbon Dioxide and of Other Greenhouse Gases in Climate Variations and Associated Impacts".

Meteorological Organisation (WMO) established the Intergovernmental Panel on Climate Change (IPCC). The IPCC was given the task of assessing current scientific, technical and socio-economic information relevant to understanding the scientific basis of risk of human-induced climate change, as well as the potential impacts and options for adaptation and mitigation. It was not charged to conduct research, nor to monitor data or other relevant parameters, basing itself instead on the available literature. In this sense, it is policy relevant but not policy prescriptive. It has three working groups and a task force on national greenhouse gas inventories. Its secretariat is hosted by WMO in Geneva and supported by UNEP and WMO. A principal activity of the IPCC is to provide an assessment of the existing knowledge on climate change at regular intervals. The fourth of these assessment reports was published at the end of 2007. The first report was published in 1990 and was used by the Intergovernmental Negotiating Committee as the scientific basis for the United Nations Framework Convention on Climate Change (UNFCCC). Subsequently, the second report in 1995 included socio-economic aspects of climate change and was influential in the negotiations on the Kyoto Protocol. The fourth and most recent report built on previous work and declared with greater confidence that "the warming of the climate system is unequivocal".[3] From time to time, special reports and technical papers have been produced by the IPCC on specific issues such as emissions scenarios.

Although there was no universal agreement among scientists on the nature of the problem, the direction of thinking became very much clearer throughout the 1990s. The general thrust of the scientific argument is contained in the second assessment report of the IPCC, which states that "the balance of evidence suggests a discernible human influence on global climate".[4] The IPCC indicated that the projected growth of greenhouse gases (GHGs) was likely to lead to an increase in global temperatures ranging between 1C and 3.5C by the end of the next century. These GHGs (carbon dioxide (CO_2), methane (CH_4) and nitrous oxide (N_2O) were shown to "have grown significantly" by about 30%, 145% and 15% respectively between 1750 and 1992, owing mostly to industrialisation. The evidence in terms of temperature records throughout the 1990s also indicated increases. Insurance companies noted the growing costs of weather-related losses, especially after the effects of the El Niño hurricane. Estimates put the damages at US$33 billion for El Niño related weather disasters alone.[5] A little later, such events provoked negotiators in the Kyoto Protocol Conference of the Parties (COP) to act. When Hurricane Mitch caused disasters in Central America, some blamed this on global warming and a resolution was passed to urge all parties to take steps to achieve the early entry into force of the Kyoto Protocol.[6]

In practice, GHGs are not without positive effects upon the Earth's climate. Without these gases, especially water vapour and carbon dioxide, the Earth's surface

---

3   IPCC, *Fourth Assessment Report, Climate Change 2007: Synthesis Report; Summary for Policy-Makers*, November 2007, p 2.
4   Second Assessment Report, 1995.
5   Reuters (Germany), December 29 1998.
6   Resolution 1/CP.4, November 14 1998.

would be so cold that it would be impossible for human life to exist. Their function is to trap the infrared radiation reflected by the Earth's surface, thus warming the surface and the atmosphere. Conversely, an excess of these gases in the Earth's atmosphere would lead to a greater absorption of the infrared radiation, which in turn would increase global warming. The critical issue is maintaining the right balance. The metaphor of the greenhouse was first used as long ago as 1863 to describe this phenomenon.

The general view was that, on available evidence of trends of increase in the atmospheric concentrations of gases, there was a strong likelihood that global average temperatures would rise, causing severe changes in the global atmospheric system. Among these were a shift in climatic zones and in mean and extreme weather conditions, a melting of glaciers at the North and South Poles (already in progress by that time), and an expansion of water leading to a rise in sea levels and a submerging of most coastal regions. The overall impact on economic, social and ecological systems could be unprecedented.

The importance and controversial role of the various IPCC reports throughout the 1990s should not be underestimated. At that time, the scientific community was not unanimously behind the conclusions in their assessment reports. Some of the counter-arguments were that its results were based on the following:

- insufficient data with respect to water vapour and the negative feedback effect of CO_2 and aerosols, as well as the complicated role of the oceans as sinks for CO_2;
- ignoring the impact of CO_2 emissions on increasing the growth rate of plants;
- exaggerating the impact of anthropogenic (ie man-made) emissions on the global climate system;
- unrealistic models and minimising the uncertainty in data; and
- arguments made by vested interests that create political, not scientific, assessments.

Nevertheless, a consensus began to emerge among policymakers that a problem did indeed exist. They seemed to have been won over partly by the increasingly apocalyptic predictions of the IPCC (eg the idea that global warming may not be a gradual process, but may instead involve a sudden switch to a new climate system), and partly by the growing evidence of temperature reduction in the atmosphere. This trend has been accelerated by the later work of the IPCC.[7] Indeed, the precautionary approach, as an instrument of environmental policy, would certainly lend support to the adoption of timely measures to prevent possible serious or irreversible damage to the environment or health in the face of scientific uncertainty of the exact cause of such risk.

---

7   For example, Climate Change 2001: Impacts, Adaptation and Vulnerability, approved by IPCC Working Group II in Geneva, February 13 to 16 2001.

3.   The Rio Conference

Some 20 years after the Stockholm Conference, the UN convened a new conference intended to build upon the principles it adopted. The UN Conference on Environment and Development (UNCED) included two novel features. First, non-governmental organisations (NGOs) were permitted to play a significant role in preparatory committees. Secondly, it was sponsored not only by states, but also by major companies and foundations. Eventually, at the Earth Summit in Rio de Janeiro in Brazil on June 14 1992 a Declaration on Environment and Development and the UNFCCC were agreed by delegates from the 176 participating states.[8]

The Rio Declaration contained 27 Principles which set out the basis on which states and people were to cooperate and further develop "international law in the field of sustainable development". Although it is non-binding, it has more significance than its Stockholm predecessor. Its core lies in Principles 3 and 4, which declare that the right to development needs to take into account the role of environmental protection in the development process. Principle 10 sets out a number of important procedural requirements, such as public participation in environmental decision-making; adequate public access to information, and access to any relevant judicial proceedings. In these respects, the provisions of the Rio Declaration are much more specific than those in the 1972 Declaration. Both the key Principles of the latter – Principles 21 and 22 – are transposed into the Rio Declaration in its second and thirteenth Principles. Principle 12 also supports an open trading system by requiring that trade restrictions for environmental purposes are not to constitute "a means of arbitrary or unjustifiable discrimination or a disguised restriction on international trade".

The different contributions of states to regional and global environmental degradation were recognised in Principle 7 with the notion of "common but differentiated responsibility". Standards applied by some states "may be inappropriate and of unwarranted economic and social cost to other countries, in particular developing countries".

The UNFCCC was another important achievement of the Rio Conference. It has been the centrepiece of the international community's efforts to combat climate change since its adoption.[9] The UN General Assembly approved the start of negotiations in December 1990 through resolution 45/212, and a Convention was finalised on May 9 1992 – all in the short period of 15 months. The aim was to secure universal participation and achieve a consensus among the many diverse positions, not least over responsibility for the problem. The many serious differences between states – including developed and developing nations and within the developed nations between the European bloc and the United States – had important consequences for the final text. The FCCC that emerged was a framework for a

---

8   There was also agreement on a Convention on Biological Diversity and an ambitious Agenda 21, but these are less relevant to our purposes in this chapter. For more on this see Chapter 2 of Philippe Sands, *Principles of International Environmental Law* (2nd edn), Cambridge University Press, 2003.

9   (1992) 31 I.L.M. 849. The Convention was adopted on May 9 1992 and opened for signature in June 1992. It entered into force on March 21 1994, after deposit of the fiftieth instrument of ratification. See generally, D. Bodansky, "The United Nations Framework Convention on Climate Change: A Commentary" (1993) 18 *Yale J.Int.L.* 451 to 558.

process of negotiating further agreements and taking specific measures to address climate change. It was signed by 154 countries in Rio the following month and has the objective of "stabilisation of greenhouse gas concentrations in the atmosphere at a level that would prevent dangerous anthropogenic interference with the climate system".[10] The countries listed in Annex I of the FCCC (the industrialised countries) agreed to work to return greenhouse gas emissions to 1990 levels and to demonstrate a reversal in the trend toward growing emissions before the year 2000. The FCCC established several institutions, including the Conference of Parties (COP) which meets annually as the governing body of the FCCC and deals with the issues related to it. It is the main supervisory institution of both the FCCC and the Kyoto Protocol (discussed below). Table 1 sets out the various meetings up to end 2007 and the main developments in each case.

The FCCC also stated that the industrialised countries "may implement policies and measures jointly with other Parties". This short reference in an otherwise long document sowed the seeds for the so-called "flexible mechanisms" of Joint Implementation (JI), the Clean Development Mechanism (CDM) and emissions trading. However, the FCCC is a framework agreement that depends upon supplementary protocols and agreements for implementation. The Kyoto Protocol is an example of this process at work.

It was in the second half of the 1990s that the international response to climate change started to gather real momentum. In Berlin in 1995 (at the first Conference of the Parties, known as COP-1), it was agreed that the emissions reductions targets provided for in Articles 4(2)(a) and (b) of the FCCC were insufficient, that new commitments would be needed for the post-2000 period and that these commitments should be laid down in "a protocol or another legal instrument" at the COP-3 in Kyoto, Japan, in December 1997. However, it was also agreed that no new commitments would be applied to developing states.

In December 1995, the IPCC's Second Assessment Report stated that "the balance of evidence suggests that there is a discernible human influence on global climate". In July 1996 at COP-2, negotiators agreed that the IPCC report justifies "action by Annex I countries to limit and reduce emissions of greenhouse gases". During the 16 months that followed, there was intense negotiation to meet the schedule for completion of a new instrument at COP-3 in 1997.

4.   The Kyoto Conference

The Protocol to the United Nations Framework Convention on Climate Change, agreed to in December 1997 at Kyoto in Japan, envisages legally binding steps to achieving reductions in emissions of GHGs. Many of these heat-trapping gases are produced by carbon-intensive industries, so implementation of the Protocol will impact upon the energy industry. Some of the impacts will be positive, creating opportunities for new products and services to assist companies that need to reduce their greenhouse gas emissions (through trading schemes and investment funds). Other impacts are likely to be negative, such as those affecting electricity generating

---

10   FCCC, Article 2.

Table 1: Chronology of events

Event	Date	Development
UN Conference on Human Environment	June 16 1972	Declaration of Principles adopted, linking environmental protection to economic development
UNFCCC, Rio de Janeiro	May 9 1992	Convention signed by 160 states, entering into force on March 21 1994
COP-1, Berlin	March 28 to April 7, 1995	Berlin Mandate agreed, calling for negotiation of stronger commitments for Annex I countries than goals set at Rio; treaty instrument thought necessary to include measures to reduce emissions and quantified emissions objectives as a way of measuring progress
COP-2, Geneva	July 8 to 19 1996	Geneva Declaration made, in which a number of Annex I countries announced their intention to adopt legally binding mitigation commitments; idea mooted of tradability of commitments
COP-3, Kyoto	December 1 to 10 1997	Kyoto Protocol adopted, with differentiated goals for parties
COP-4, Buenos Aires	November 2 to 13 1998	Action Plan adopted, setting out timetables for the completion of necessary technical work and decisions to fill in the details of the Protocol
COP-5, Bonn	October 22 to November 5 1999	Decisions taken to prioritise technical work to define more precisely provisions on technology transfer and capacity building (for developing country parties) as well as draft decisions for COP-6 to define the flexible mechanisms
COP-6, The Hague	November 13 to 24 2000	Talks break up after deadlock in negotiations, so technical work not completed by deadline set in Buenos Aires
EU ETS	January 1 2005	EU's domestic emissions trading scheme launched

Event	Date	Development
Entry into force of Protocol	February 16 2005	Russian ratification leads to entry into force; triggers discussions on new ideas, and progress at COP-11 in Montreal in December
Stern Report	October 2006	Conclusions of expert report by Sir Nicholas Stern attracts considerable publicity; claims that problem more acute than previously thought and that the longer action is postponed, the more dramatic and costly the changes required
UK Climate Change Bill published	March 2007	British government stakes its claim to leadership in climate change mitigation by introducing a draft bill and consultation process; bill aims to put a strong legal framework in place, aiming at a 60% reduction in CO_2 emissions by 2050, with real progress by 2020.
Australia announces emissions trading scheme	June 2007	Hitherto a strong opponent of the Kyoto process, Australia announced a carbon trading scheme, only for this to be superseded by more radical plans of a new government, which ratified the Protocol in December 2007
IPCC Fourth Report published	November 2007	Report in four parts concludes that warming of climate is "unequivocal" and that most of the increase in global warming is man-made; synthesis report timed to be published before COP-13 at Bali, Indonesia
COP-13 agrees on a roadmap for designing a post-Kyoto framework	December 2007	The roadmap charts the course for a new negotiating process to be concluded by 2009 and ultimately lead to a post-2012 international agreement on climate change

companies that rely upon coal and oil for much of their power generation, or heavy industry and manufacturing industries that use coal or oil in their heating systems, as well as those industries that are energy intensive.

The heart of the Kyoto Protocol is its legally binding character, its core idea being that without this element of multilateral legal constraint the sovereign states of the globe are unlikely to make any significant progress in addressing the problem of climate change. Amid the considerable body of scientific data, the shifting sands of negotiating positions and the complex economic arguments over methods of implementation, the simplicity of this feature cannot be overstated. Legal constraint on the exercise of sovereign power is an essential element in the solution of the climate change problem, and Kyoto is a first – and far from perfect – step in the development of a legal response on a multilateral basis.

The Third Conference of the Parties (COP-3) at Kyoto marked a significant step forward in the UNFCCC process. With the conclusion of a Protocol[11] to the FCCC in December 1997, the UNFCCC process moved in a distinctly practical direction. The Kyoto Protocol imposes legally binding commitments, and offers radical new mechanisms, to combat climate change.

The main features of the Kyoto Protocol may be summarised as follows:

- Signatories to the Protocol have undertaken to make a legally binding commitment to achieve its objectives.
- The developed countries listed in Annex I to the Convention (Annex I Parties) have each signed up to a binding individual emission limitations target to be achieved by the years 2008 to 2012 (the EU, which ratified the agreement as a bloc in May 1998, is a special case). Collectively, the Protocol provides for differentiated Annex I targets which amount to an average reduction of 5.2%. This affects six GHGs.[12] The base year is 1990 for cuts in the three most important gases: carbon dioxide, methane and nitrous oxide.
- Most important of all is probably the inclusion of so-called flexible mechanisms of JI, CDM and emissions trading. These are market-based mechanisms which can be used by industrialised countries to lower their compliance costs. The CDM was a real surprise and emerged from the negotiations very much at the last minute. Included for similar reasons was a limited category of carbon sequestration activities or "sinks".
- No quantitative commitments are included for developing countries, reflecting the guiding principle of common but differentiated responsibility, under which the industrialised countries are required to take the lead.

There were three main issues in the negotiations leading to the conclusion of the Protocol. The first of these was the level of GHG reductions for the developed countries. The second concerned the role of the developing countries and the countries in transition (ie the post-Communist countries of Central and Eastern Europe) in limiting GHGs. The third issue was the mechanisms to implement GHG reductions, such as the flexible mechanisms under the third bullet above. The other two issues concerned the inclusion of man-made GHGs and the use of forests as sinks

---

11   Kyoto Protocol to the United Nations Framework Convention on Climate Change, UN Doc.FCCC/CP/1997/L.7/Add.1. Unless otherwise specified, all references to Articles below are to Articles in the Kyoto Protocol. A good account of the origins and negotiations on the Protocol provisions is contained in *The Kyoto Protocol: A Guide and Assessment*, by Michael Grubb with Christian Vrolijk and Duncan Brack, Royal Institute of International Affairs/Earthscan, 1999.

12   Carbon dioxide, methane, nitrous oxide, hydrofluorocarbons, perfluorocarbons and sulphur hexafluoride.

to offset emissions from fossil fuels. These were issues of a much lesser order than the first three. Of all of them, the one that turned out to be the most contentious was the role of developing countries in limiting GHGs. The issue highlighted a paradox: the major polluters were the developed countries who were signing up to legal obligations, but by the year 2010 the developing countries are expected to become the major producers of GHGs in the world and yet under the Kyoto regime their legal obligations will be either distinctly weaker or non-existent. For some Annex I Parties this represents a serious shortcoming in the final text signed at Kyoto.

Kyoto left open this crucial question of participation by the developing countries. Developing countries (or at least some of them, such as China, India and Brazil) are expected to be the major contributors of GHGs by 2010, so that efforts by the industrialised countries alone will be inadequate to deal with the problem. In such cases, there may also be problems of implementation even where the legal obligations have been accepted by governments, due to weak legal and institutional frameworks, as well as in some cases a high degree of centralisation and little input from industry into decision-making. This is a highly unsatisfactory context for the implementation of long-term projects such as emissions trading schemes or indeed a CDM project. In addition, the application of controls on Annex 1 countries may result in industries relocating to developing countries to avoid the restrictions. However, for some developing countries or countries in transition, the prospect of joining in an emissions trading scheme is an attractive one. By exporting quotas they could generate hard currency income. Examples of this financial aspect proving an incentive include Argentina and Kazakhstan.[13] For other developing countries, there is some resentment that a problem which has been created over the past 200 years largely through industrialisation by the developed world is one that they are now being expected to pay for.

Many of the participating countries at Kyoto accepted that the rules for implementing the Protocol needed to be worked on. For example, the Article on emissions trading (Article 17) could be interpreted with a wide discretion by states even though the basic ideas were ones that most participants were agreed upon. However, the parties agreed on the basic principles and postponed the details to a later COP. The Kyoto Protocol remains a landmark environmental agreement which, once ratified and complied with, offered the potential for a transformation in the way energy is produced and used, and in the way transport systems are utilised. The socio-economic impact could be considerable – and it would be global. In addition, the legal implications would be very wide ranging.

4.1   After Kyoto: the short-term effects

Three meetings of the parties to the UNFCCC were convened between 1998 and 2000. The first, COP-4, was convened on November 2 1998 at Buenos Aires, Argentina. It concluded with the adoption of a "Buenos Aires Action Plan" establishing deadlines for finalising work on the Kyoto Mechanisms, compliance issues and policy measures. These issues to be addressed include the following:

---

13   Christian Vrolijk, "The Buenos Aires Climate Conference: Outcome and Implications", RIIA Briefing Paper New Series No 2, April 1999.

- financial mechanisms for assisting developing countries to respond to the challenges related to climate change;
- further work on policies and measures introduced by the European Union later at the conference;
- development and transfer of technologies;
- rules governing the Kyoto flexible mechanisms with priority on the clean development mechanism; and
- an undertaking to discuss supplementarity, ceilings, long-term convergence and equity issues.

The parties broke a four-year deadlock on the issue of technology transfer. The conference decision outlines a process on how to overcome the barriers to the transfer of environmentally sound technology. On compliance, the parties reached a common understanding that a strong and comprehensive regime is needed to ensure an effective implementation of the Kyoto Protocol. On financial arrangements, countries that were particularly vulnerable to the impacts of climate change will receive further support from the Global Environment Facility (GEF) to plan concrete measures for adaptation.

Meanwhile, further urgency to the issues under discussion was provided by the Third IPCC Assessment Report in 2001, which highlighted new findings of research into climate change. They included an increasing body of observations that support a picture of a warming world and other changes in the climate system, stronger evidence that recent warming is attributable to human activities and a finding that those with the least resources have the least capacity to adapt and are therefore the most vulnerable. The emphasis in that report on a comprehensive assessment was the last of its kind, however. The IPCC decided to emphasise new findings in its fourth report, published in 2007, and to organise data around certain cross-cutting themes such as sustainable development, water and technology, integration of mitigation and adaptation and regional integration.

5.   The current position

Interpretations of the growing body of scientific evidence on climate change continue to act as a driver to policy and legal initiatives. In this context, the Stern Report and the IPCC's fourth assessment report have played important roles in influencing policy makers. At the same time, the impatience of some nations and states within federal regimes to turn the Kyoto mechanisms into workable schemes within their territories is evident from the growth of regional emission trading schemes.

5.1   The Stern Report

In October 2006, the UK Government published a comprehensive report on the economics of climate change – probably the most sweeping carried out so far.[14] It had an international perspective on the impacts of climate change and the stabilisation of GHGs in the atmosphere. Describing climate change as "the greatest market

---

14   Nicholas Stern, *The Stern Review: the Economics of Climate Change*, Cambridge University Press, 2006.

failure the world has seen",[15] it argued that ignoring climate change would eventually damage economic growth and that the benefits of early action would greatly outweigh the costs. The impacts will be unevenly distributed, imposing heavier burdens on the poorer countries. Increased international cooperation was required in areas such as creating price signals and markets for carbon, sponsoring technology research, development and deployment and promoting adaptation, particularly for the developing countries.

Although the report took full account of the latest scientific evidence of global warming, its innovation lay rather in the economic analysis and its recommendations for action. In particular, it argued that establishing a carbon price, by means of tax, trading or regulation, is an essential requirement for climate change policy. At the heart of the report was the idea that policy needs to promote sound market signals, overcome market failure and give a central role to equity and risk mitigation. Its conclusions were optimistic in their emphasis on the opportunities for growth, and in their belief that the regional schemes emerging on the foundations laid down by the UNFCCC and Kyoto could be linked up into a global scheme for carbon emissions trading. The EU's Emissions Trading Scheme (ETS; see also section 5.2 below) third phase commencing after 2012 offered considerable potential in this respect.

The considerable publicity surrounding the report's conclusions assured it of some influence, not least on the emerging EU integrated policy on energy and climate change. A few months later, the European Commission published its Energy Policy for Europe, which favourably commented on the Stern Report's analysis.[16] Soon after, the United Kingdom introduced a Climate Change Bill that explicitly referred to the Stern Report in its justification for proposals to establish carbon budgets for 15 years ahead and for the creation of an expert Committee on Climate Change to advise the government on the best way forward in this area.[17] However, the report's emphasis on the potential for linkage of regional schemes to the EU ETS highlighted the present lack of connection between that scheme and other important areas of the globe which are major sources of GHG emissions (on a scale that the EU is not and never will be): principally, the United States and China. The challenge of bringing these major polluting nations within the global and sub-global framework established by the UNFCCC remains considerable, but the vigour with which the Stern Report analysed the problem as well as the opportunities it identified may have positive effects on policy development.

5.2   Growth of regional trading schemes

An important development at the regional level has been the growth of regional schemes for emissions trading. The best known of these is the EU's Emission Trading Scheme, which is the largest in the world and is expressly linked to the Kyoto Protocol. It is the only mandatory emissions trading scheme in the world. The first phase of the ETS commenced in January 2005 and ended in December 2007. It

---

15   HM Treasury Press Release, "Publication of the Stern Review on the Economics of Climate Change".
16   Commission of the European Communities, "Limiting Global Climate Change to 2 Degrees Celsius; the Way Ahead for 2020 and Beyond", COM (2007) 2 final, 10.1.2007, at 3 to 4.
17   Foreword by Secretary of State to Climate Change Bill, March 2007, p 5.

imposes a cap on the amount of carbon that may be emitted by large installations, and allows participants in the ETS to trade among themselves. The scheme is linked to the developing world through the CDM, so that trading may take place in validated credits. Allowances were allocated rather generously in the first phase, but this is unlikely to be repeated. Criticism was also levelled at the use of grandfathering rather than auctioning as a distribution mechanism. However, the first phase did lead to the creation of a market in carbon for the first time across the European Union. During phase 2, the ETS will be linked to other countries that are participating in the Kyoto trading regime.

Other schemes are at an early stage of development by comparison. In the United States there are two notable regional schemes, involving respectively groups of eastern and western states. The Regional Greenhouse Gas Initiative (RGGI) was initiated by the State of New York and commits 10 states from the north-east United States to a cap-and-trade CO_2 programme for power generators. It aims to reduce the carbon "budget" of each state by 2018 by as much as 10% below respective 2009 allowances; it is scheduled to commence on January 1 2009. In the West, California is among a group of five states and one Canadian province that have set up the Western Climate Initiative, with the aim of creating a regional GHG control and trading system. Separately, California has passed legislation in 2007 which is designed to curb CO_2 emissions, using flexible mechanisms in the form of project-based offsets.

In Australia, the new government has promised to introduce a cap-and-trade system by 2010. However, below the federal level there have already been efforts to explore this area; for example, in New South Wales and Tasmania. Under the New South Wales Greenhouse Gas Abatement Scheme the state government aims to reduce emissions from the electricity sector by requiring generators and large users to buy certificates to offset a proportion of their GHG emissions.

5.3   The IPCC Fourth Assessment Report and Bali

The latest report from the IPCC was directed largely at influencing opinion at COP-13, which met at Bali, Indonesia, in December 2007. This was a crucial meeting in setting the agenda for the work to be done for a new international instrument to enter into operation once the Kyoto Protocol expired in 2012. The report did not pull any punches. It argued that warming of the climate system is now "unequivocal" and that most of the increase in the past 50 years is very likely to be man-made. However, many (but not all) impacts can be reduced, delayed or avoided by mitigation. Governments have a wide variety of policies and instruments available to them to create the incentives for mitigation action. Delayed reductions in emissions will significantly constrain the opportunities of achieving lower levels of stabilisation and "increase the risk of more severe climate change impacts".[18]

The Bali meeting was attended by representatives from more than 180 countries with observers from NGOs. It delivered important evidence of progress. The roadmap called for four negotiating sessions in 2008, which would set out the basic elements

---

18   IPCC Synthesis Report, *ibid*, p 20.

of a new legal instrument. It reaffirmed the principles of binding and quantitative commitments for developed countries, and "common but differentiated responsibilities" for all countries. None of this constituted an earth-shaking step forward, but did ensure that a formal procedure was in place to start work on the next stage in international climate change law, which will probably include a deepening of the commitments entered into in the Kyoto Protocol a decade before the Bali Conference.

6.   Conclusions

The problems associated with tackling climate change are essentially global in both their causes and effects, respecting no national boundaries. As such, they require a significant element of global cooperation if they are to be tackled properly. Few would disagree with this unremarkable statement, but the difficulties in achieving this international cooperation in the context of nation-states driven by self-interest has been evident in all of the negotiations on Kyoto implementation since 1997. However, to some extent this is now a matter of history. By the end of 2007, attention had definitively shifted to the development of a successor instrument to the Kyoto Protocol for the period after 2012.

The problems in climate change regime design do not lie only in the instruments of international law that have been developed to address them. The shortcomings of national and regional measures have been equally and perhaps even more evident. While this subject matter goes beyond the scope of this chapter, the discrepancy between rhetoric and reality in the implementation of the EU ETS in its first and second phases may be noted. Progress at the international level may nevertheless eventually achieve agreement on how the post-Kyoto principles can be designed so that the more intensified national and regional efforts are harmonised and become much more effective in achieving climate change mitigation.

The past decade shows beyond a shadow of doubt that a consensus now exists behind the central role of market mechanisms and legal frameworks (international and regional) for tackling climate change. Currently, this consensus is strongest in the European Union, but it is also evident in varying degrees in other parts of the world. In the next few years the potential for linking these regional approaches will become apparent. In that sense, the pre-history of climate change law and policy may be coming to an end and the real history only just be commencing.

Annex

The flexible mechanisms

The Protocol proposed three principal mechanisms to implement GHG reductions. These are briefly considered below. It may also be noted that since that time the relatively new concept of carbon capture and storage (using, for example, a depleted oil or gas field for the storage of CO_2) has been accepted as a flexible mechanism.

(a)   Joint implementation[19]

Annex I Parties may trade among themselves Emission Reduction Units (ERUs) resulting from projects aimed at reducing anthropogenic emissions by sources or enhancing anthropogenic removals by sinks of GHGs in any sector of the economy. This is subject to a number of conditions, however. Such projects have to provide a reduction in emissions or an enhancement of removals by sinks additional to any that would otherwise occur. Newly planted forests, for example, act as "sinks" by absorbing CO_2 from the atmosphere. These projects also require the approval of the parties involved in the project. The ERUs may not be acquired if such action is not in compliance with obligations under Articles 5 and 7. Finally, the ERUs are to be supplemental to domestic actions for the purposes of meeting commitments under Article 3.

Joint implementation raises a host of difficult issues that have to be resolved if further guidelines for implementation are to be developed.

(b)   *The Clean Development Mechanism (CDM)*

A new mechanism was set out in Article 12 to assist parties not included in Annex I to achieve sustainable development and attain the ultimate objective of the Convention. Under the CDM the developed countries receive GHG credits or Certified Emissions Reductions (CERs) by sponsoring actual GHG offset projects or other actual technology transfer in a developing country. The credits acquired in this way effectively raise the number of tonnes the acquiring country may emit above its Article 3 "assigned amount". Parties not included in Annex I therefore benefit from project activities which result in certified emission reductions. However, it was also designed to assist those parties to Annex I in achieving compliance with their quantified emission limitation and reduction commitments under Article 3 of the Protocol.

Other provisions of the Protocol relevant in this respect are the following:

- non-Annex I parties will benefit from project activities even if a project does not yield CERs because the project must be initiated first;
- Annex I parties can use the CERs to contribute to their compliance with a part of their targets;
- CERs must be certified by operational entities to be designated;
- modalities and procedures are to be elaborated;
- participation in the CDM is voluntary and may involve public and private entities; and
- CERs obtained during the period from the year 2000 up to 2008 can be used towards compliance in the first commitment period (2008 to 2012).

It may be noted that CERs will be additional to the overall assigned amount for Annex I. For the energy sector, this mechanism has potential for limiting the impact of the Protocol on its profitability. There are currently more than 860 registered CDM projects in 47 developing countries, and about 2,000 projects in the project registration pipeline.[20] The UNFCCC Secretariat administers a CDM Registry and an International Transaction Log (ITL) and transfers issued CERs from the CDM Registry

---

19   Article 6 of the Kyoto Protocol.
20   UNFCCC Secretariat, Press Release: "Kyoto Protocol's Clean Development Mechanism passes 100 millionth certified emission reduction milestone", 18 December 2007.

to the national emissions registries. The registries of Japan, New Zealand and Switzerland are linked to the ITL, and CERs have been transferred to the registries of Japan and Switzerland.[21]

(c) *Emissions trading*[22]

Parties are allowed to participate in emissions trading for the purpose of fulfilling their commitments. Essentially, the developed countries may purchase GHG credits or allowances from other developed countries that have emissions below their targets set by the Protocol ("target-based credits"). The COP is required to define the relevant principles, modalities, rules and guidelines in particular for verification, reporting and accountability for emissions trading. Given the high volume of GHG emissions it generates, the energy sector is the one most affected by the emissions trading schemes.

---

21   *Ibid.*
22   Article 17 of the Kyoto Protocol.

Structuring and financing projects[1]

Christopher Carr
Vinson & Elkins LLP
Flavia Rosembuj
World Bank

1   Introduction

The Kyoto Protocol, through its Clean Development Mechanism (CDM) and Joint Implementation (JI) provisions, has provided innovative mechanisms for encouraging projects that reduce greenhouse gases. However, the Kyoto Protocol rules do not establish how an individual CDM or JI project is to be structured. This chapter provides an overview of certain structuring options.

In simple terms, a CDM or JI project involves a physical activity that reduces greenhouse gas emissions. These projects can range from capping a landfill, improving efficiency at an industrial facility or planting trees, to a variety of other projects that reduce greenhouse gas emissions. The emission reductions from the physical activity form the basis for a revenue stream based on carbon credits.[2] Issues then arise as to how to finance the physical activity, and how the benefits of the revenue stream will be allocated.

Financing techniques have evolved rapidly to meet the opportunities and challenges that the CDM and the JI mechanisms present. The market for carbon credits from these projects has rapidly grown, to more than US$5 billion in 2006 and even more in 2007.[3] Multiple approaches to structuring or financing CDM and JI have arisen, as underlying project dynamics vary widely. The appropriate structure for a CDM or JI project depends on issues such as the extent to which the project requires external finance and expertise, or is to be financed and managed by the project developer itself based on the anticipated revenue stream from the emission reductions.

The World Bank has been an early pioneer in the CDM and JI markets, forming some of the first carbon funds designed to purchase emission reductions. It has continued to be a significant purchaser of emission reductions on behalf of client countries and non-sovereign entities, although other entities – including numerous private-sector participants – have entered the market and developed a variety of

---

1   The first two sections of this chapter are based on Carr and Rosembuj, "World Bank Experiences in Contracting for Emission Reductions", 2 *Environmental Liability*, 2007.
2   All projects seeking to create carbon credits under the Kyoto Protocol must take place in countries that have ratified the Protocol. CDM projects take place in developing countries and generate "certified emission reductions" (CERs). JI projects take place in countries that have committed to binding emission limits (ie developed countries or countries with economies in transition) and generate "emission reduction units" (ERUs). "Carbon credits" as used in this chapter refers to both CERs and ERUs.
3   See World Bank, "State and Trends of the Carbon Market 2007" (World Bank, 2007) (hereafter "State and Trends of the Carbon Market").

approaches to financing CDM and JI projects.

This chapter cannot cover the whole range of structuring or financing options for a CDM or JI project, but it seeks to provide the reader with an overview of certain structuring options, focusing on those utilised by the World Bank while also surveying some of the other available options.

Section 2 of this chapter explores the establishment of World Bank carbon funds and their approach to structuring CDM and JI projects. Section 3 articulates how the purchase of "verified" versus "certified" emissions serves as an innovative financing technique. Section 4 discusses the management of risks in CDM and JI projects. Section 5 explores a sample of other approaches to structuring projects undertaken beyond the World Bank.

2. Establishment of World Bank funds and their approach to purchasing emission reductions

The basic concept of a World Bank carbon fund is quite simple: a fund collects contributions from participating entities and uses those funds to facilitate projects that reduce greenhouse gas emissions. The emission reductions generated from those projects are then distributed to the entities that contributed to the fund pro rata based on the amount of their respective contributions.

In 1999, the World Bank established a Prototype Carbon Fund (the PCF) to promote purchasing greenhouse gas emission reductions in the developing world. The PCF has, in many respects, pioneered the global carbon market, undertaking transactions several years before the Kyoto Protocol to the United Nations Framework Convention on Climate Change (the UNFCCC) entered into force. Moreover, the PCF has acted as a role model for other similar funds that have been launched by the World Bank (the "Carbon Funds"), other international financial institutions, and the private sector. The basic concept of the PCF was endorsed by the 17 private entities and six governments that contributed US$180 million to it. Subsequently, the PCF has purchased emission reductions from projects ranging from biomass, to hydroelectric, to energy efficiency and conservation projects, in more than 15 countries.

Over the past seven years, the World Bank's carbon finance programme has grown from the PCF to include ten carbon funds and facilities, with a total capitalisation in excess of US$2 billion.

The carbon funds largely focus on purchasing emission reductions that fund participants can use to meet compliance obligations in the first commitment period established by the Kyoto Protocol. This first commitment period runs from 2008 to 2012. However, in addition to focusing on compliance obligations, the World Bank has created the Community Development Carbon Fund that delivers verifiable additional sustainable development benefits in addition to emission reductions. Similarly, the World Bank established the BioCarbon Fund to pioneer opportunities in carbon sequestration. Additionally, the World Bank has expanded the market beyond generating emission reductions under the current limits of the Kyoto Protocol, including by purchasing emission reductions that are generated after 2012.

The carbon funds are just one type of trust fund administered by the World Bank.

World Bank trust funds mobilise resources to support poverty reduction across a wide range of types of projects and regions. Trust funds support development activities or programmes with administration by the World Bank and contributions from one or more donors. Trust funds have grown in number and scope in response to the international community's desire for the World Bank to help manage broad global initiatives through multilateral partnerships, such as the Global Environment Facility, the Heavily Indebted Poor Countries (HIPC) initiative, and the Global Fund to Combat AIDS, Tuberculosis and Malaria.[4]

The PCF represented a new business type for the World Bank, one in which public and private participants wanted to be actively involved in a fund's management, and in which a fund had a goal of generating measurable returns for the trust fund's contributors.[5] Returns were in the form of emission reductions. To accomplish this, the World Bank devised a governance structure for the PCF that actively involved fund participants in governance matters. The PCF governance structure was a new framework for the World Bank. Although the World Bank had experience acting as a trustee (it now serves as trustee to 1,000+ trust funds, holding more than US$16 billion in trust[6]), it typically had substantial discretion to administer the funds placed with it under trust agreements, which usually contained broad objectives. The PCF represented some reduction in the trustee's broad discretion, including actively soliciting the input of fund participants on matters such as in which projects to invest.

Governance structures similar to the PCF have been included in other World Bank carbon funds, with the exception of the Umbrella Carbon Facility. The World Bank, as trustee of the Umbrella Carbon Facility, pre-identifies the project or projects specific to a given tranche, and then reports annually to participants on how funds have been used to purchase emission reductions. Therefore, as opposed to other carbon funds, Umbrella Carbon Facility participants do not need to choose the projects in which the facility would invest; the World Bank, as trustee of the Umbrella Carbon Facility, is solely responsible for the Umbrella Carbon Facility's governance. The Umbrella Carbon Facility does not involve donor participation, other than by their contributing to the relevant tranche in which they participate.

The World Bank's role in purchasing emission reductions for parties that wish to use them for compliance purposes has diminished relative to the overall size of the market in some sectors where the private sector has been increasingly active. However, the World Bank continues to assist market participants in realising the benefits of carbon finance through innovative funds and projects. Two examples of this innovation include the Umbrella Carbon Facility and the Carbon Fund for Europe.

The Umbrella Carbon Facility has aggregated multiple sources of funding to purchase carbon emissions from large, pre-identified projects. These funding sources have included the World Bank's existing carbon funds and other buyers who were not fund participants. The first tranche of the Umbrella Carbon Facility involves the purchase of carbon credits from two Chinese chemical companies for two large HFC-

---

4   See 2006 Trust Funds Annual Report from the World Bank available at http://www-wds.worldbank.org.
5   See S Smyth, "The Prototype Carbon Fund: a New Departure in International Trusts and Securities Law", *Sustainable Development Law & Policy*, 2005, V(2) at 28.
6   See Note 4 above.

23[7] destruction transactions. These two transactions combined were the largest carbon purchase at the time.[8] They showed the possibility of purchasing emission reductions on an unprecedented scale. These two HFC-23 emissions reduction projects will finance the purchase of approximately 19 million tonnes of carbon dioxide equivalent per year of emission reduction credits.

However, under the terms of the HFC-23 European Reduction Purchase Agreements (ERPAs), the two companies will not receive all the revenues earned from the sale of the emission reductions. As part of its participation in the purchase, the World Bank supported the Chinese Government with a major policy initiative to create a revenue-sharing feature. This feature channelled 65% of the proceeds to a special Sustainable Development Facility to fund sustainable development activities in China. This revenue sharing also applies to all other Chinese Kyoto Protocol transactions. However, different degrees of revenue sharing apply to different sectors. For instance, the revenue sharing is lower for renewable energy projects than HFC projects, based on the different expected financial returns by companies involved in such transactions. Through China's Sustainable Development Facility, projects will further the Kyoto Protocol's objectives by channelling carbon revenues into activities that support sustainable development.

The Umbrella Carbon Facility represented a shift from the World Bank's previous approach to structuring carbon funds. In the past, the World Bank had pursued portfolios of projects on behalf of emission reduction purchasers. The Umbrella Carbon Facility represented a first and an important step towards helping sellers access the market by structuring strategic transactions.

As increasing numbers of public and private purchasers, developers and financiers enter the market, it is possible that multiple entities will increasingly be involved in a given transaction, either through formal or informal partnerships. As an example of possibilities for collaboration, the World Bank has commenced co-managing the Carbon Fund for Europe with the European Investment Bank. This fund seeks actively to encourage the participation of private entities in implementing transactions in which the fund invests.

3. An innovative financing technique: purchasing "verified" versus "certified" emission reductions

As the World Bank pioneered the development of carbon funds, it has also been innovative in the field of contractual provisions in ERPAs. World Bank ERPAs have undergone various changes from early PCF purchases. Early PCF ERPAs incorporated contractual structures from project finance agreements and World Bank loans and credits, providing varying amounts of up-front financing in order to obtain rights to the future delivery of emission reductions.

However, the World Bank subsequently developed a "payment on delivery" ERPA approach, whereby it made payment upon the actual delivery of future emission

---

7   HFC-23 is one of the most potent of the six greenhouse gases recognised under the Kyoto Protocol. It
     has a global warming potential 11,700 times that of carbon dioxide.
8   See www.cdmpipeline.org.

reductions.[9] Even under this "payment on delivery" approach, the World Bank can offer some up-front financing, which can be offset against future payments for delivered emission reductions, in order to facilitate developing the project that reduces greenhouse gas (GHG) emissions. This approach is designed in part to facilitate private-sector opportunities to provide financing (see section 5).

3.1 Purchasing carbon credits amidst regulatory uncertainty

As already mentioned, the PCF began purchasing emission reductions roughly five years before the Kyoto Protocol took effect. However, even these initial PCF ERPAs were designed to catalyse generating emission reductions that could ultimately be converted into certified emission reductions (CERs) under the Clean Development Mechanism.[10]

In order to purchase an emission reduction "asset" the value of which largely arises from a still-developing regulatory programme, the PCF began purchasing "Verified Emission Reductions" (VERs). These VER contracts generally define "emission reductions" as all existing and future legal and beneficial rights arising from one GHG reduction, including the right to any CERs arising from that GHG reduction.[11] By using this definition, purchasers seek to obtain the future regulatory rights that arise from the seller's physical act of reducing emissions. Under these contracts, the World Bank pays for emission reductions when they are "verified" against a contractually agreed-upon monitoring protocol. Once a project becomes registered by the CDM Executive Board, any necessary adjustments to the monitoring protocol are made, to maximise the delivery of CERs from the project.[12]

Purchasing VERs can catalyse environmental markets in uncertain regulatory environments. Although the Kyoto Protocol typically drives the value in an international carbon transaction, a VER contract allows the parties to create, transfer and pay for emission reductions amidst regulatory uncertainty. This same approach can be used by market participants (other than the World Bank currently), to contract for emission reductions in the United States, where various federal and sub-national greenhouse gas regulations are being considered or are under development.

In the international marketplace, with the entry into force of the Kyoto Protocol, many market players focused on purchasing CERs – that is, signed contracts that only paid for a "compliance grade" asset. Under CER contracts, purchasers only make payment for the delivery of CERs that have been issued by the CDM Executive Board. Under these CER contracts, the seller bears the risk of the project not producing CERs, including the risk of a project never being approved by the CDM Executive Board.

Even after the Kyoto protocol took effect, the World Bank continued to use VER

---

9   See, for example, the World Bank, "General Conditions Applicable to Verified Emission Reductions Purchase Agreement" (hereafter "VER General Conditions") and the "General Conditions Applicable to Certified Emission Reductions Purchase Agreement" (hereafter the "CER General Conditions"), both of which are dated February 1 2006 as at the time of writing and available at www.carbonfinance.org.
10   Because the CDM market has been more active than the JI market in terms of the number of transactions and overall volume of emission reductions generated, this section refers to the CDM market. However, many of the contracting principles are comparable for JI ERPAs.
11   See, for example, the definition of Emission Reductions at Section 2.01 of the VER General Conditions.
12   The CDM Executive Board supervises the CDM, under the authority and guidance of the Conference of the Parties serving as the meeting of the Parties to the Kyoto Protocol (COP/MOP). For additional information, see http://cdm.unfccc.int/EB/background.html.

contracts, as well as CER contracts, to allow maximum flexibility to sellers interested in contracting with the Bank and to support sellers in the development of difficult projects and new methodologies.

VERs have also become significant as the World Bank contracts for purchasing emission reductions that are expected to be delivered after the Kyoto Protocol's first commitment ends in 2012. World Bank funds buying emission reductions for post-2012 delivery can contribute to market stability, helping to provide continuity between the Kyoto and any post-2012 regimes in the evolution of the global carbon market. This can be particularly true where projects need revenue for more than the approximately five years remaining in the first commitment period. To purchase post-2012 emission reductions, the Bank has usually taken a hybrid approach and purchased CERs for emission reductions delivered up to and including 2012, and purchased VERs thereafter.

Thus, VER contracting has come full circle. Whereas VER contracts allowed for the purchase of emission reductions before the Kyoto rules were fully developed, they also provide a contractual mechanism for purchasing emission reductions after the first commitment period ends in 2012. For post-2012 emission reductions, payment can be made against emissions that are verified according to a pre-determined monitoring plan as agreed between the contracting parties. As with other VER purchases, the buyer could obtain whatever compliance value might arise from those GHG reductions.

3.2   VERs, CERs, risk and pricing

A comparison of VER and CER contracts reveals an important feature of the market for carbon credits: the allocation of risk impacts pricing. This risk allocation can be seen in applicable remedies for events of default, as well as in the contractual allocation of certain key risks such as "project risk" and "Kyoto risk". For example, in the year 2006, according to one study, CER prices averaged above US$10, but a significant range in CER prices existed from around US$6 to up to US$24. This range was indicative of varying risk between projects, including by way of example the choice of remedies, the existence of a delivery guarantee, or other aspects of risk allocation. Further reflective of the importance of risk in emission reductions pricing, this study found that average CER prices in 2006 were demonstrably higher than VER prices.

An important issue in ERPA contracting relates to the remedies that are available if a seller breaches its obligations to deliver emission reductions under an ERPA. Both the World Bank VER and CER General Conditions provide for the following two remedies in the event of a seller's unintentional failure to deliver the contracted-for emission reductions: allow delivery in subsequent years; or if, and only if, the delivery failure persists for three consecutive years or in any of the last three years of the contract, terminate the ERPA and recover the World Bank's costs.[13] Notably, the World Bank forgoes the right to terminate for just one or two years' delivery failure,

---

13   See Section 13.03(a)(i) of the CER General Conditions and Section 13.03(a)(i) of the VER General Conditions. Additionally, under these General Conditions, in cases where the ERPA provides for call options, the World Bank, upon the sellers's unintentional failure to deliver, is also entitled to convert the amount of emission reductions subject to a delivery failure to a call option.

as long as the breach is not an intentional breach.[14] Rather, there must be a continuing delivery failure in order for the World Bank to have the right to terminate. The approach enhances the income flow stability to the seller, to facilitate the seller's obtaining financing for the project.

By comparison, some CER contracts by other buyers in the market require the seller to guarantee delivery of the carbon credits. Under such guarantees, if the seller fails to deliver emission reductions from a project, it may be required to deliver CERs from a different source to the buyer. Guarantee provisions can convert an ERPA from an asset to a liability for the seller. This would occur if a project fails to deliver emission reductions and the seller incurs higher costs for obtaining those emission reductions from a different source. However, sellers that offer guaranteed delivery can obtain significantly higher prices for carbon credits for which delivery is guaranteed.

While not risks per se, ERPAs should also allocate certain responsibilities in creating the carbon asset between buyer and seller. For instance, ERPAs should allocate the responsibility between buyer and seller for paying for the "share of proceeds" required to fund certain CDM administrative expenses and adaptation measures.[15] Under the VER General Conditions the buyer pays the share of proceeds, while under the CER General Conditions the seller pays the share of proceeds.[16] This allocation mirrors which party is expected to bear the regulatory risks involved in developing a Kyoto-compliant project.

One common feature in ERPAs is that the seller typically bears the "project risk". Project risk means the risk that the agreed-upon physical activity will take place, whether capping a landfill, installing renewable energy generation, or some other activity that reduces or sequesters greenhouse gas emissions.

Reasons for a project failing to perform can include construction delays or technology failing to function as anticipated. Additionally, raw materials necessary for the project (which may be as varied as biomass from crops, water for hydroelectric facilities, methane from a landfill, or traditional fuels such as oil or gas) may increase in price or be unavailable. Counterparty risk may also exist, arising from whether parties to various project contracts (such as contracts to purchase power from a facility) are reliable. Projects might fail to perform for a number of reasons, but generally speaking the seller bears the "project risk". This allocation of project risk is based on the seller being best-positioned to assess and bear project risk.

On the other hand, World Bank VER and CER contracts have significant differences in the allocation of "Kyoto risk". Contracting for CDM and JI credits involves contracting for an "asset" the value of which arises from a regulatory programme – the Kyoto Protocol. Risks that these credits will not be created or transferred under the Kyoto regulatory regime can be understood as "Kyoto risk". A key "Kyoto risk" is that

---

14   Both the CER and VER General Conditions provide for more stringent remedies in the event of an intentional breach.

15   The adaptation share of proceeds involves a 2% deduction from CERs issued for projects (except those located in least developed countries). The fee for the share of proceeds for administrative costs is calculated as US$0.10 per CER issued for the first 15,000 tonnes of CO_2 equivalent for which issuance is requested in a given calendar year and US$0.20 per CER issued for any amount in excess of 15,000 tonnes of CO_2 equivalent for which issuance is requested in a given calendar year.

16   See Section 5.05 of the CER General Conditions and Section 5.05 of the VER General Conditions.

the CDM project may never be registered by the CDM Executive Board (or may be rejected as a JI project). The World Bank VER and CER contracts show how this risk can be allocated in different ways. Under the VER General Conditions, the buyer bears the risk that the project may not be registered, and will make payment based on the agreed-upon monitoring protocol if the registration does not occur within a specified time period. By comparison, under the CER General Conditions, the seller bears the risk that the project will not be registered.

Another important risk occurs if the methodology is not approved by the CDM Executive Board, or a less favourable methodology is applied to the project. Under the World Bank's VER General Conditions, the Bank bears this risk. By comparison, in a CER contract, the seller would bear these risks.

A distinction can be made between risks involved in creating the carbon asset, versus transferring that asset. A market exists for trading Kyoto credits that have already been issued – for example, CDM credits that have already been issued by the CDM Executive Board. For transactions involving credits that have already been issued, "project risk" is eliminated, and those "Kyoto risks" involved in creating the carbon credits are eliminated. However, regulatory risks still remain regarding the transfer of credits. Transfer risks include risks, by way of example, that either the buyer or seller country (or the countries that authorise private buyers or sellers to participate in a transaction) will not be eligible to engage in international emissions trading under the requirements of Article 17 to the Kyoto Protocol.

Other regulatory risks exist, but the above discussion illustrates that the allocation of these risks is an important part of structuring the sale and purchase of Kyoto credits. Under World Bank VER contracts, the buyer typically bears most regulatory risk, although this increased incurring of risk is reflected in lower pricing for carbon credits. Pricing aside, as mentioned above, VER contracts can provide a valuable mechanism for contracting amidst regulatory uncertainty.

4. Managing risks

By their nature, CDM and JI projects typically involve a higher degree of risk than other infrastructure or industrial projects as they involve a new and developing area of law and a cross-jurisdictional transfer of rights. The allocation of two key types of risk has already been discussed above: "project risk" and "Kyoto risk". Other types of risk arise, including risks such as: "political risk", when a project is located in a developing country or economy in transition with political and regulatory uncertainties; "market risk", whereby the market for the credits may move in such a direction as to create an incentive for one of the parties to breach an ERPA; and reputational risks.

4.1 Political/country risk

Significant diversity exists among developing countries and economies in transition. Generally, the less developed a country's political and legal infrastructure, the greater the perception that it may present political risk for investors.

Many facets of political risk can impact on a CDM or JI project. For instance, a change in law in the host country could impact the project. This could occur, for example, by creating a special tax on CER or ERU revenues, by nationalising the carbon asset or the underlying project, or by introducing new legislation applicable to CDM or JI projects. Other risks include that due to a lack of clarity in government regulation, whereby the parties may not be able to establish legal title to the CERs; or where a change in the government challenges the previous government's acts. Strong currency fluctuations could also disrupt a project. Alternatively, a host country could establish an administrative procedure so lengthy, complicated or unclear that it may render impossible the approval of a CDM or JI project.

Political/country risk can be allocated through the *force majeure* provisions in an ERPA, allowing a right of termination or other contractual relief. Some insurance products may also be available to mitigate political risk.

4.2   Market risk

"Market risk" includes the risk that the market for the credits may move in such a direction as to create an incentive for one of the parties to breach the ERPA. This risk is increased for long-term purchase agreements, as the time is increased over which prices may fluctuate.

Several options are available to mitigate market risks. One option is to have shorter-term contracts, although this is not always feasible given the timing of delivery of the emission reductions and the need for a longer-term revenue stream to justify investment in a project.

Another option to mitigate market risks is through pricing. Many ERPAs involve a fixed price over the term of the agreement. In the event of a dramatic change in market price, the parties may have an incentive to breach the agreement. For instance, in the event of a dramatic price rise, the seller may want to sell the emission reductions to a different buyer that will offer a higher price. In the event of a collapse in price, a buyer may desire to escape its obligation to purchase the emission reductions at what now seems a high fixed price. One technique for reducing these incentives to breach is to index the emission reduction price to the prevailing market price. Other options include having both a floor and a ceiling to the indexed price, or a combination of both a fixed and indexed price for certain tranches of emission reductions from a project.

Other options to handle market risk include providing adequate contractual remedies so that if one party breaches, the other party is made whole. Either a buyer or seller could also be required to post a letter of credit, or obtain a third-party guarantee, to secure performance of certain obligations.

Finally, acting as the focal point responsible for communicating with the CDM Executive Board (or the various authorities responsible for a JI project) can increase a party's control over a project and mitigate its risk. For instance, if a buyer serves as a focal point with the CDM Executive Board, a seller may be unable to redirect the CERs to a different buyer in breach of the contract.

4.3   Reputational risk

In addition to the CDM project risks described above, parties may face reputational risk, whereby participation in a project may invoke criticism from third parties, such as non-governmental organisations (NGOs), that damages the goodwill and reputation of a company or institution. To mitigate reputational risk, World Bank carbon finance projects must comply with World Bank safeguards policies.[17] Including these policies in World Bank ERPAs imposes further obligations on emission reduction sellers that are not standard in other ERPAs, but which are deemed necessary for the World Bank to be engaged in carbon finance.

Of course, non-World Bank actors may also face reputational risk. Some private-sector participants may seek to avoid certain projects, due to their own assessment of reputational issues. For instance, a company operating in a country where NGOs strongly oppose a given landfill facility may want to avoid such a project.

However, the rigour of the CDM process was designed to help to mitigate reputational risk, for example by establishing the checks and balances of the independent UNFCCC process, which should help to legitimise projects. Market participants can further mitigate reputational risks through due diligence and attention to potential opposition of communities where projects are located.

While discussing every type of risk that may present itself in a carbon finance transaction is beyond the scope of this chapter, suffice it to say that individual transactions should be carefully evaluated for the specific risks that are material to that transaction, and how those risks are best mitigated.

5. Additional project structures

The World Bank Carbon Finance Unit's approach to carbon finance projects is relatively straightforward: the carbon finance unit purchases the carbon "off-take" or carbon CER or VER stream, paying on delivery (with a limited possibility for up-front payments). However, many other possible mechanisms for project involvement are possible.

As mentioned above, carbon finance projects involve a physical activity and a revenue stream arising from the reduced emissions. The question then becomes how that physical activity will be financed and how the benefits of that revenue stream will be allocated. In addition to requiring financing for the physical activity that reduces emissions, carbon finance projects often require both new technology (equipment) as well as expertise in navigating the Kyoto regulatory process in order to derive the value from the emission reductions. The simplest project structure would involve a project entity that was able to self-finance the project, had available in-house expertise, and could arrange for the necessary equipment for the project through conventional financing. However, this simple structure is not the rule in carbon finance.

This section provides a brief sample of other approaches, beyond that of the World Bank, that have been taken to finance CDM and JI projects.

5.1 Equity, JV and BOOT arrangements

Figure 1 shows a typical project structure in which there is an ERPA for emission

---

17   The World Bank's Safeguards' Policies address both environmental issues (natural habitats, forestry, pest management, safety of dams, international waterways and disputed areas) and social issues (involuntary resettlement, indigenous people, cultural property, forced labour and harmful child labour). These operational policies were created to provide internal guidance to Bank staff in dealing with environmental and social issues in order to foster a harmonised approach within the Bank.

reductions between the buyer and seller. However, the entity undertaking the project often requires an infusion of either financing or expertise to give effect to a transaction. The question that then arises is, if this financing or expertise comes from a third party, how is that third party compensated?

Figure 1: Typical project structure

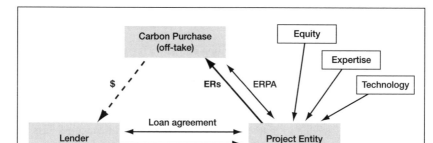

Financing may be provided by a loan agreement with a lender. Alternatively, a party providing financing, equipment or expertise may take equity in the entity undertaking the project, form a joint venture, enter into a build-own-operate-transfer agreement, or enter into some other mechanism by which expertise or financing is provided and compensation returned.[18]

Note that carbon finance projects may, in many cases, also have an additional revenue stream associated with the project activity in addition to the carbon credit stream. For instance, both revenues from generating carbon credits and selling electricity may arise from installing renewable energy or capping a landfill (if the captured methane is used to generate electricity). Similarly, forestry projects may both sequester carbon as well as generate valuable forest products. These additional revenue streams can assist in funding the project activity, as well as help to secure a loan or other external financing.

5.2 Assigning payments to lenders and ERPA bankability

Another approach to facilitate the financing of payments is to assign ERPA payments directly to a lender to pay for the loan. Indeed, the World Bank CER and VER general

---

18   For an overview of approaches to financing projects, see Sami Kamel, *Guidebook to Financing CDM Projects* (UNEP Risoe Center, 2007).

conditions readily allow for this.[19] Alternatively, a lender may take the ERPA as a form of collateral, obtaining rights to the contractual revenue stream in the event of a default in a loan payment.

A significant question then arises as to the "bankability" of the ERPA (the ability to borrow against the emission reduction revenue stream), as viewed by a lender. Generally speaking, if the revenue stream arising from the emission reductions is more reliable, the ERPA is more bankable.

As indicated above, a World Bank VER contract can significantly increase the bankability of an ERPA. This is done by means of:

- the Bank (the buyer) assuming a significant measure of the Kyoto risk;
- remedies that restrict the Bank from terminating an agreement due to a short-term, unintentional failure in delivery; and
- the Bank not requiring a delivery guarantee.

One challenge to financing is the fact that carbon finance projects involve at least some up-front costs, both in order to fund the physical activity that reduces emissions, as well as the costs for processing the project under the Kyoto mechanism. For renewable energy projects, these up-front costs can be a significant share of overall project costs, as these projects have intensive initial capital costs (such as installing wind turbines or solar panels).

One implication of these up-front costs is that significant financing may be required in advance of the carbon revenue stream. Lenders have taken a variety of approaches to loans for carbon finance projects. In one CDM project in Brazil, the lender was willing to mirror debt service payments so that they were due at the time of, and in amounts equalling, projected revenues from the emission reductions.[20]

Even when loan payments do not precisely mirror expected emission reduction revenue, they can provide a significant revenue stream that makes obtaining a loan possible. For instance, the Inter-American Investment Corporation (the "IIC", a member of the Inter-American Development Bank Group) financed a hydroelectric CDM project in Ecuador relying in part on the carbon revenue for the project to meet its investment criteria. These investment criteria required more than 50% of the facility's sales to be under contract and assigned to the lender in order to secure the loan's debt service.[21] In that project, the emission reduction revenue was projected to account for between 19% and 57% of annual debt service.

5.3 Seniority in purchasing emission reductions

CDM and JI projects can also involve multiple purchasers of the emission reductions from a project. A simple arrangement could involve one purchaser buying the emission reductions over one discreet time period, followed by another purchaser. For instance, one purchaser could buy emission reductions generated by a project

---

19 See, for example, VER General Conditions, Section 15.06(a).
20 See Ken Newcombe, "The Global Carbon Market and Carbon Economics" (hereafter "Carbon Economics"), Workshop on the Carbon Market and Brazilian Carbon Transactions, October 26 2005 (presentation), available at http://www.bioclimatico.com.br/pdf/biblioteca/evento_Ken_1.pps.
21 World Bank, *Carbon Finance Annual Report* (2005), p 20.

from 2008 to 2012 (the first Kyoto commitment period), followed by a second purchaser who buys the emission reductions generated after 2012.

However, if multiple purchasers are interested in buying emission reductions in the same time period, an important issue arises as to which purchaser has "senior" rights. If a CDM project underperforms, the parties will need to look to the contractual arrangements to determine who receives what credits. One option is for a lead buyer to have seniority over all other purchasers, so that the lead buyer would receive its credits before any other purchaser. Another arrangement would be for multiple buyers to participate on a *pari passu* basis, so that credits would be distributed pro rata among the buyers in proportion to their respective rights in the event of a delivery shortfall.

By way of simple example, consider a project that is expected to generate a million tonnes of emission reductions each year, with two purchasers each buying 500,000 tonnes each year from 2008 to 2012. If the project only generates 500,000 tonnes each year in total, if one buyer were to have full seniority, then that buyer would receive its full allotment of credits in the year of the shortfall, and the other buyer would receive no credits. If the buyers participated on an equal, *pari passu* basis, then in the year of shortfall each buyer would receive 250,000 credits. From these two simple examples spring multitudes of options for structuring transactions, including multiple buyers contracting for various tranches of emission reductions. For instance, one buyer could take the first 200,000 tonnes generated in a given year, followed by a second buyer taking the next 200,000 tonnes, followed by a third buyer taking whatever generation might remain.

5.4   Other approaches to structuring and financing

As mentioned above, discussing the entire range of structuring or financing options for a CDM or JI project is beyond the scope of this chapter. Other entities taking innovative approaches to structuring transactions include the International Finance Corporation, a member of the World Bank group, which among other things has developed a mechanism to guarantee delivery of carbon credits from projects. Both specialist financiers and main-line international investment banks have committed expertise, ingenuity, and substantial resources to financing CDM and JI transactions. Approaches to structuring CDM and JI transactions are likely to be varied given the significant variety in types of projects, parties to those transactions, and countries in which the transactions take place. However, as indicated in this chapter, the assessment and allocation of risks will be a common feature for financing a project.

6.   Conclusion

The structuring of CDM or JI project is evolving dynamically, and financing terms are being driven by a combination of powerful forces from both within multilateral institutions and from the financial world. The experience of the carbon market so far shows that, in the right policy environment, the carbon market could generate $100 billion or more annually in the future.[22]

---

22   According to Yvo de Boers, UNFCCC Executive Secretary, see unfccc.int/files/press/news_room/press_releases_and_advisories/application/pdf/20060919_riyadh_press_release_vs5.pdf.

Running a carbon project

John McMorris
Forest Systems LLC

1.   Introduction

A few years ago I was asked to help train an experienced auditor (from outside the climate change arena) who was to perform internal reviews of company-run projects. After a few weeks of training he made a telling observation: "At first glance I thought this was an incredibly simple industry. The overall goals can be described in just a few words: You select a qualified site, implement a greenhouse gas mitigation solution, monitor the project to determine the amount by which emissions have been reduced, and file appropriate regulatory paperwork to document the process. *Yet, if I touch my finger to any part of the process, it explodes in complexity and nuance!"*

As simple as this process is to describe, the devil is truly in the detail. This is true whether a project is implemented under the Kyoto Protocol or the European Union's Emissions Trading Scheme (EU ETS), any of the several regulatory regimes emerging in the United States or Australia, or in non-regulated (voluntary) markets.

First, a perspective issue: this chapter is written from a project developer's viewpoint and contains certain biases as a result. While I alternate between general observations/cautions and specific guidance for running a successful project, my end goal is simple – to alert prospective project proponents or financiers to issues deserving of thought. Second, the chapter touches upon several subjects (including financing, Emissions Reduction Purchase Agreements and taxation) that are treated in greater depth in other chapters – but only to highlight decision consequences or to give project-based context. After reading this chapter you may have new thoughts/insights and should refer back to these reference chapters. My hope is that reading this chapter will enable you to identify a project's potential strengths and limitations while avoiding various painful lessons many of us have learned along the way.

2.   What makes for a successful project?

This chapter examines essential project and organisational characteristics for projects which proudly withstand public scrutiny. Before this, however, consider what carbon projects are supposed to do. Irrespective of any other political and environmental goals, they reduce greenhouse gas (GHG) emissions, which can then be traded as carbon offsets. Who should care about this?

The International Emissions Trading Association (IETA) notes, "Offsets play an important role as they are currently the only mechanism through which developed and developing countries cooperate in combating climate change. They raise awareness in developing countries of climate change and the value of reductions and also bring into the effort sectors that are not covered by ETS as well as jurisdictions that do not have regulatory regimes". Indeed, offsets raise awareness in *all* countries – even those lacking formal climate change programmes. In addition to creating public sensitivity to the consequences of climate change, offsets make a valuable near-term contribution to atmospheric carbon levels while giving industry time to develop truly "needle moving" technologies that can forever change our future. Projects may have other social, cultural, environmental or local political benefits in addition to offset production. It is easy to see that almost everyone can and will be affected by carbon offset development.

What does it take to succeed? Irrespective of regulatory regime or location, the "public" metrics for project success are largely the same: good organisation, credible and reliable technical solutions, conservativeness, transparency, data quality and audit process integrity. Other metrics are "inward looking" and for the moment I will simply assume they are present: project implementation integrity (including construction quality, if applicable), availability/use of competent project staff, participant and stakeholder training, project safety, reliability, adequate cash flow (important for maintaining good contractor relations!), and adequate commercial margin for operations that sell their offsets to finance the project. Project proponents should develop a "to do" matrix to help identify organisational and data shortfalls – and to define internal "decision thresholds" that move the process along.

The need for complete, accurate data – gathered and recorded pursuant to a publicly vetted monitoring plan – cannot be overemphasised. Commercial project success ultimately requires the project proponents to convert unverified emission reductions to some form of certified offsets (used to satisfy regulatory compliance requirements or to create a project revenue stream). This requires a third-party audit of data completeness, accuracy, timeliness and presentation. Project data must be retained (typically for several years), as noted in the project design document (PDD) and monitoring plan.

Even in unregulated markets, data quality and verification are key value drivers. I recently saw an eBay auction for "carbon offsets" from a tree named Herb, located in the seller's back yard. Needless to say, these offsets commanded low value! On the other hand, well-defined projects – using legitimate science, conservative methodologies and receiving competent third-party verification – create high-quality verified emission reductions (VERs). These offsets are increasingly in high demand among both consumers and large emitters seeking either to position themselves in the public's eye, or to gain experience with project management and internal emissions accounting. As such they have a correspondingly higher value.

Another success factor, often difficult to characterise, is the "expertise" of prospective project proponents. One of my greatest frustrations when talking to people who are considering establishing a GHG mitigation project (no matter the location) is how many of them "don't know what they don't know". This comes back to the "simple" vs "complex" issue – and a prevailing natural belief that intelligent people can quickly sort out challenges and intuitively find ways to "maximise" project offsets. Unfortunately, this is not always true. Not surprisingly, some proponents attempt to establish projects after little research and preparation – and find the going quite tough. Others invest significant time and become self-made experts; yet others engage consultants or project developers to enable the process. However, *nothing* can substitute for experience and perspective. You should give serious thought to the most efficient way to add such expertise to your project and the pros/cons of each approach. Also give some thought to the intent behind the project and the audience (and possible optics) you are playing to. Of course, if you are seeking to develop an internal corporate "projects" department with self-contained expertise, you may want initially to combine consultants with full-time staff. On the other hand, if you are seeking efficiently to develop one or more projects – be it for public acclaim, environmental positioning, or enhanced operations – and do not want the overhead of an internal group, an experienced project developer is more likely the answer.

Given what I have said above, does a project's success require engaging a project development company? No – but such companies have dedicated their existence to building relevant infrastructure and expertise and quite often establish functioning projects more efficiently than someone (or a group) for whom project management is but one responsibility. Project development companies actively follow the fast-paced regulatory environment and have a good knowledge of the factors (including methodological changes, current or pending) that may impact on a given project and of ways to minimise their negative impact. This combination of experience, exposure and infrastructure can be compelling.

In reality, projects can be developed in *many* ways: they can be undertaken directly by the site owner/operator or run by external project development staff. They can be self-funded or rely upon external funds. They can "forward sell" their offsets (more on this later), or wait until offsets are certified, selling into the "spot" market. Different elements of the process – such as methodology development, PDD development, technical solution design and/or implementation, ongoing maintenance and monitoring and eventual disposition (including sale) of the certified offsets – can be let out (either singly or severally) to consultants, or they can be handled via dedicated internal staff. Coordination and consistency tie these elements together.

Be careful not to sell short the role of networking: successful projects are built upon myriad relationships. Having the capacity to call upon a host country DNA (designated national authority) or DFP (designated focal point) (or to be called by them), a host country ministry, a designated operational entity (DOE), financiers or a technology provider can help identify non-obvious problems and their speedy resolution. Indeed, without these relationships a licence or necessary approval may appear to grind to a halt when a simple, well-placed phone call may be enough to speed it on its way. When building your network, remember to include both "worker level" contacts (who can be *outstanding* sources of information) and more senior decision makers. Lastly, membership in one or more (local or international) industry associations enables networking and an increased awareness of the dynamic regulatory environment and its potential project impacts.

3. **So, you are starting a project: what should you do first?**

Before starting a project, your organisation should answer a range of questions. Regard these as "setting the stage" for your project(s) in a given region:

- Does undertaking this project require you to have "new" dedicated staff?
- If so, and the project is in a different location from that of your core business, does it require you to establish a separate organisation or legal entity – or can you work from afar? and
- Will the project(s) and staff be located in a foreign country?

This simple line of questioning already suggests trade-offs which should be carefully considered. You might not establish a foreign project development operation for only a single project, as the friction costs could surpass related benefits. If you plan to build on many sites, however, the advantages of a local company may well outweigh the "costs". In-country businesses often enjoy significant advantages in banking, contracting, communications, employment issues and taxation – especially VAT. That said, many countries do not allow "single shareholder" foreign-owned subsidiaries (although there are often work-around solutions).

While there are few "wrong" answers, your organisation's decision on whether to establish an in-country entity will affect overall project cost and schedules. I will leave aside related governance and liability considerations, as these are complex and vary from country to country. You are recommended to consult qualified legal counsel before choosing an optimal business structure for project execution. Further issues are as follows:

- For CDM projects: will the project be bilateral or unilateral? CDM was conceived as a bilateral model between developed (financier/buyer) and developing (producer) nations, to benefit developing countries via new financial resources, better technology and the achievement of their sustainable development criteria; the corresponding Annex I (developed) nations' benefit is access to less-expensive emission reduction (ER) opportunities than would be domestically available. Since this model was first conceived, many developing nations have chosen to catalyse project development under the "unilateral" projects provision (projects without formal Annex I approval), which was later allowed by the United Nations Framework Convention on Climate Change (UNFCCC). Under this approach, developed-nation involvement typically occurs after project registration. When first contemplating a project, check with the host DNA to ascertain whether certain rules apply for converting unilateral projects to bilateral projects – or whether the conversion is allowed at all (unilateral projects are not allowed in some countries).
- For CDM projects: does the host country have special taxation provisions (or dispensation) for CERs? Some countries levy specific CER taxes, while other countries instead offer special incentives. In addition, other taxes such as import duties may be waived or reduced for CDM projects that have made proper in-country filings. In yet other cases, projects may qualify for special tax provisions/treatment if they create alternative energy or use it to power project-related equipment. It is worth exploring such discounts before finalising the project design. Further, does the host or participating DNA charge a fee for the review and issuance of the letter of approval (LoA)? I have observed a significant fee basis in some Annex I countries.

- JI projects between Annex I parties follow an overall process analogous to CDM (and other regulated environments), but they are approved and administered by the involved parties (rather than by an executive board) and may include less oversight than CDM. A host country can be designated "Track I" or "Track II", which are terms relating to the host's compliance with UN participation requirements. Both tracks share common characteristics: they must establish a DFP office, essentially the equivalent of a CDM country's DNA, and develop national guidelines and procedures for LoAs, assigned amounts (the various accepted units of emission reductions and allowances), and a national registry. Also, "determination" (validation) of a PDD and monitoring reports are made by an applicant independent entity (AIE) – the equivalent of a CDM designated operational entity.

  The most immediate difference is that Track II country projects are subjected to a rigorous review process under Article 6 of the Supervisory Committee – baseline and monitoring work is reviewed by the Joint Implementation Steering Committee (JISC), inspired by the work of the CDM Executive Board (EB) – whereas Track I countries can stipulate their own approval procedures for projects, PDDs and monitoring reports. In addition, Track I allows the conversion of surplus Assigned Amount Units (AAUs) into Emission Reduction Units (ERUs) via what has become known as a "greening" process. Because Track I nations are allowed self-determination, ERUs from Track I projects have a potentially lower delivery risk, as there is no risk the project will fail to pass JISC procedures. On the other hand, such projects have enhanced exposure to host country risk (target compliance), as Track I nations are directly liable for offset overestimation.

  After establishing whether your host is Track I or II, next determine whether the host identifies your prospective project as an environmental priority (important to receiving local support and approval) and whether a memorandum of understanding (MoU) exists between the two relevant Annex I countries. Also, determine if there are special qualifications or requirements for projects or project developers; some countries will not allocate resources in the absence of specific accreditation. Additionally, some Annex I countries are uninterested in establishing certain project types via an Annex I partner, but may be interested in establishing these projects under a domestic trading scheme (DTS). In these cases, project performance may result in the issuance of domestic offsets that can only be used by in-country emitters. In all cases the "benefit" and approval mechanisms should be confirmed.
- Project finance: This is a complex topic and I will cover it only briefly. Let us divide this into two parts: how much; and through whom? Note that there are many more variations than are covered here, and creativity and persistence are the hallmarks of success.
  - *How much:* this may take you several iterations. In simple terms, what funding will you need to establish a given project or projects including the staff, infrastructure and tools needed for success? Recognise that certain parameters are unknowable (eg will the CDM EB change the rules mid-

stream?). Also, organise your estimates to withstand a rigorous review by all interested players.

A project budget needs to include the obvious – such as capital expenditures (CAPEX) and operating funds (OPEX) – but may also include project-allocated OPEX for an ongoing (or remote) staff/organisation, local filing/permit fees and a medley of regulatory and audit-related costs. The project's technical "solution cost" is, itself, a function of technology choice, technology maturity, your team's (or sub-contractor's) familiarity with the technical solution and its optimisation, methodology choice, monitoring needs, site remediation issues, time line and many other factors. Do your best to tally the estimates, recognise they are interdependent with other decisions such as whether to form a separate entity, legal costs, etc and then (experience suggests you should) increase the overall budget by at least 50% to account for schedule uncertainty, regulatory changes (affecting monitoring, project yield and documentation), etc. Less obvious costs include "cost of money" charges and your organisation's overhead or governance and administration charges. Your financiers will most likely require you to perform model variations and/or sensitivity analyses before issuing funds.

– *Who pays for it?* The simplest case is a site owner/operator who undertakes a project directly and self-finances or arranges financing based on an existing credit facility. From here, there are near-infinite variations with myriad rights/obligations. Common variations include:

  – third party financing secured by a "forward sale" of offsets at pre-agreed pricing (which may or may not include partial prepayment funding provisions);
  – leveraging other project value streams (electricity that can be sold under a power purchase agreement, "green" electricity, other environmental credits, project enabled/derived products, dramatically reduced operating costs, etc) of demonstrable value; and
  – working with a project developer that is willing to advance project-related expenses for an ownership position in the resulting offsets.

Each approach has different merits and finance terms vary as a function of who bears the risk.

Many forward-sale instruments now recognise ER value post-2012 (the end of Kyoto's first period), although offers based on net present value recognise little value for outward years. Make sure you have built conservative assumptions into your project yields as IPCC emission coefficients conservatively estimate country-level emissions – meaning they tend to estimate to the high side – but may not be "spot on" for project-based emission reductions. Remember: if your financing terms appear workable with deep ER yield or pricing discounts, your paybacks will be even safer with stronger yields. Also, consider that project cycles can be quite long and it may be years before your project yields certified offsets. If offsets are the principal motive for establishing a project, ensure that your cash flow will carry you to receipt of them.

- Land use: if the project proponent does not own the target site/operation or additional land is needed, is it necessary to negotiate local land use or access rights? What licences or permits are needed? Who needs to apply for them and what are normal cycle times? What workarounds may exist if the normal licence cycle time far exceeds what your project can tolerate? A provincial minister once told me that one licence often took years because of departmental staff shortages. We ultimately provided short-term staff to help clear his department's backlog. To what extent are politics involved and what can be done to mitigate their impact? If you seek to develop a project on behalf of a separately held operation, you should execute an agreement defining commercial relationships/terms – especially if you retain project equipment ownership and require land use/access.
- If the land is owned by a private entity other than the operation owner/operator, you may need additional agreements. The agreements should define who retains title to the offsets, who is responsible for interfacing with regulatory and audit authorities regarding project issues (to prevent future confusion) and relevant commercial terms. Some countries require the use of an emissions reduction purchase agreement (ERPA) that defines (among other things) offset sales price. Rights and taxation consequences vary by country.
- Land ownership: if the project (site) land is not owned by a private entity (perhaps it is owned by the state), are there land grant papers or licences conferring land use privileges to the site operator for at least the duration of the proposed project? If not, the project term may be in jeopardy. What legal limits (if any) are associated with this land grant paperwork? If the land is owned by the state, check with the DNA and issuing ministry to determine whether special filings or licence amendments must be made before establishing the project. Use agreements to define (and limit) the obligations or liability associated with the design and/or installation of project-related equipment.
- Who (associated with the project) will ultimately own the ERs (whether VERs, CERs, ERUs, VCUs, etc)? The site owner? A separate developer? A municipality or state government? Multiple parties? Local title, ownership and conveyance issues should be understood. In the case of CDM, actual CER "creation" occurs when the UNFCCC "accepts" a "request for issuance" with associated monitoring, verification, and certification reports. (Some voluntary offset systems, such as VCS, recognise ER creation when project documentation is accepted by an accredited registry, which then issues the appropriate instrument (such as VCUs).) Once issued, the CERs are deposited to pending accounts in the CDM Registry until forwarding instructions are issued by the project participants. Failing to follow issued forwarding procedures precisely may have taxation consequences. ERUs are recognised by the parties (sovereign governments) responsible for project recognition. VERs generally lack government recognition/backing, but are still an asset with tangible value.
- As noted above, an emissions reduction purchase agreement may be an

effective instrument for defining offset ownership issues and sales terms – including "who gets what", price guarantees and/or limits, payment terms, delivery failure consequences and so forth. Forward sales terms contemplate risk profiles, delivery terms and a net present value determination based upon a forecast of risk, offset demand and pricing. Countries requiring bilateral projects sometimes require an ERPA firmly to establish Annex I partner identity and relevant terms. ERPAs can be crafted to suit a project's unique needs or can be built upon an industry standard template (eg World Bank or IETA). If other contracts are used between the participants, it may be possible to incorporate ERPA terms directly into one of the other documents.

- What documents are needed adequately to describe or "qualify" a project? The regulatory environment, the methodology, auditor requirements and local statutory requirements will define the documents needed for validation, registration, verification and offset issuance. In general, you will need documents that substantiate claims and descriptions in the PDD – things like production records, energy usage, copies of licences and permits (especially those showing that the pre-project operation complies with statutory requirements), proof of baseline, a project barriers analysis, proof of project "intent" (this can be established via contract, public announcements, other corporate papers and much more) and engineering documents about your proposed solution(s). Whenever possible, get copies of actual records rather than simply extracting key figures for your records. Determine whether local law requires specific document certification or notarisation to be valid – particularly if copies have to be provided to the DNA.

  In unregulated environments, the existence or lack of formal documentation (especially audit documents) is one of the biggest determinants for offset pricing – not to mention public scrutiny – particularly audit documents that establish the "realness" of the VERs or prove these credits have not been double sold. This process and associated documents are already implicitly assumed in CER/ERU pricing.

- Essential relationships: several "local" service relationships will be critical to your success. The most important include your project auditor, local counsel and an accountant. If possible, choose an auditor with sectorial experience and/or one located in your region. In the case of CDM/JI projects, also confirm UNFCCC accreditation status. While you can work with an auditor to overcome any of these deficiencies, it will add several months to your schedule and additional challenge to the overall validation process, covered below. If your project is located in another country, you will want local counsel to harmonise your agreements with local laws and to inform you of contractual and social limitations. Employment law, in particular, varies from country to country and should be considered when tendering employment offers. Assuming you hire local staff, an accountancy firm will keep you on top of local taxes and filings – which can be profoundly complicated. They will also give guidance for dealing with local banking and/or the central bank.

4.   Project-specific terms

There are several specialised terms and concepts relating to project qualification and documentation. We will discuss some of these before reviewing specific project steps.

4.1   Project design document (PDD)

In many regards, PDDs are the "business proposal" of the climate change space. They follow a prescribed template and include many elements: a general description of the pre-project operation and proposed project, methodology choice and application, project activity crediting period (typically seven or 10 years; forestry projects have other guidelines), monitoring methodology and plan, specific analyses/discussion regarding "baseline emissions", "project emissions", leakage (ie additional energy use and resulting emissions caused directly by project activities), (calculated) emission reductions, a review of implementation barriers, a delineation of related environmental impacts, a study of project "additionality" and consideration of "sustainable development", a summary of the global stakeholders' process, project participant contact information, information regarding public funding, and more. PDDs rarely include funding details, but must confirm that certain types of (assistance) funding are not used. CDM and JI PDD templates can be downloaded from the UNFCCC website and must be strictly followed.

While all PDDs are structured similarly, well crafted ones carefully explore methodology options to avail themselves of specific site operating characteristics. Review existing registered PDDs for relevant clues, giving careful thought to how a modest change in process or equipment may yield additional offsets. Strive to use simple and unambiguous language in the PDD; it will be read by a varied audience.

Take good care to use the most current version of your chosen methodology, which can be downloaded from the UNFCCC website. Be sensitive to revision changes as these may occur with little warning after EB meetings. Projects using older methodology versions will have to be updated prior to validation.

Your document will be judged on the quality (versus quantity) of its data and descriptions, themselves a function of our understanding of both the pre-project operation and the methodology/process used to modify it. Also, remember to answer the "question" asked in each template heading. All too often project proponents enter data which is not appropriate for a particular section; for example, if the heading is related to technology, avoid a discussion on additionality.

4.2   Baseline/project activity

One of the concepts important to a PDD is defining an "emissions baseline". The baseline is the scenario that reasonably represents the anthropogenic emissions by sources of greenhouse gases that would have occurred in the absence of the proposed project activity. Different scenarios may be considered, as different options may have existed prior to the proposed project activity. Of course, continuation of the current activity could be one of them; implementing the proposed project activity absent registration as a CDM project may be another; and many others may be possible. In simple terms, the baseline determination may be (but generally is not) different from the "business as usual" approach at the project site. To the extent that there is a difference, this difference has to be accounted for when calculating project-related emission reductions.

A baseline scenario must take into account relevant national and/or sectorial policies and circumstances, such as sector reform initiatives, local fuel/technology availability, sector (and infrastructure) expansion plans, and the economic situation in the project sector. If local regulations have recently required an upgrade or switch away from the project site's "business as usual approach", it may not be possible to take credit for the proposed project change (or at the least, the offsets associated with the change will likely be reduced).

Paragraph 45(b) of the Modalities and Procedures also require a baseline to be established in a "transparent and conservative manner". This means all baseline assumptions must be detailed and all choices substantiated. If there is uncertainty regarding values of variables and parameters, the baseline is considered "conservative" if the resulting projection does not lead to an overestimation of ERs attributable to the project activity. The PDD should clearly define the assumptions and factors with their associated uncertainty and how the uncertainty will be addressed.

In simple terms, five steps are identified for the definition of a project's baseline:

- set the project boundary;
- define applicable project conditions;
- discuss project barriers;
- select the most appropriate baseline methodology; and
- calculate baseline emissions.

Developers of a new baseline methodology must review paragraph 48 of the CDM Modalities and Procedures and select the approach most consistent with the context of applicable project type(s) and with the underlying algorithms and data sources used in the proposed baseline methodology. While there may be overlap between the three options offered under paragraph 48, only one approach should be used for calculating baseline emissions or baseline emissions rates.

4.3   Additionality

Article 12.5 of the Kyoto Protocol requires UNFCCC projects to demonstrate "additionality" – that is, they must provide that "reductions in emissions are additional to any that would occur in the absence of the certified project activity". In lay terms, would the ERs have occurred in the course of normal/profitable business upgrades (also known as "business as usual")? If so, these reductions will not qualify for project credit. Conversely, if economically attractive alternatives exist (to the "unattractive" project), or other barriers (eg technological, labour, or social) stand in the way of project implementation, it will probably meet the tests for additionality.

This concept is one of the most difficult to define unambiguously and many early projects applied less stringent guidelines than are in use today. Even as I write this chapter, there is a CDM EB call for input regarding this subject. In simple terms, a proposed project has to suggest an operation/site change that would not be made without the CDM/JI project (and the value incentive of the associated ERs).

Recent EB meetings have provided both guidance and tools for determining additionality. They include a "barriers analysis" and qualitative and quantitative assessments of different potential options with an indication of why the non-project option is more likely. What is the common element to each of these approaches? They provide a systematic step-by-step procedure for determining whether a proposed project activity is, or is part of, the baseline scenario, thereby helping to determine whether the project activity is additional.

Additionality should *not* be assumed – it must be demonstrated. Project proponents should highlight the key logical assumptions and quantitative factors that help establish project activity additionality. Kyoto project guidelines suggest this should be done in as much detail as needed, but avoiding repetition that is not needed for reasons of clarity.

Guidelines and procedures on how to document additionality are available from the UNFCCC website.

4.4 Leakage

Leakage is technically defined as the net change of anthropogenic emissions by sources of greenhouse gas emissions occurring outside the project boundary that is measurable and attributable to the implementation of the project activity. The use of project electrical equipment – such as pumps, monitoring equipment, chillers, etc – is one example of potential leakage. The PDD should identify sources of leakage, and which of them can be neglected (see the guidelines in EB20, Annex 2). Even if the calculation of leakage is to be performed *ex post*, the PDD should include the determination of an *ex ante* estimate.

4.5 Sustainable development

While projects should conform to the host nation's goals for sustainable development, this consideration is most relevant for projects located in developing nations. The World Commission on Environmental Development (1987) defined sustainable development as "development that meets the needs of the present without compromising the ability of future generations to meet their own needs". While it is the responsibility of the host nation DNA to determine whether a proposed project contributes to its country's goals by assessing the project's impact, most nations perform this task by evaluating three main dimensions: environmental, social and economic sustainability.

5. Project (and process) steps

Once you have set the stage by answering (most of) the "what makes for a successful project?" questions it is time to dig into the project process. Project steps can be resolved into two phases: "project preparation and development" and "project implementation". Key project preparation and development steps are set out in sections 5.1 to 5.4 below.

5.1 Project design and formulation

This may require a Project Idea Note (PIN) followed by a Project Design Document (PDD) – or only a PDD. Depending on the project type (and prospective ER yield) the

PDD may utilise either a small-scale or large-scale methodology. Small-scale projects have somewhat simpler administrative standards and can use a single DOE for validation and verification. If a suitable methodology does not yet exist, the project proponent may submit a proposed new methodology along with a proposed PDD and both will be considered by appropriate panels of experts. An individual PDD may group multiple (similar) project sites within an overall project, or may group multiple methodologies relevant to a single site. The recently released guidance on Programmatic CDM should be considered when multiple sites are involved. Either a PIN or PDD may have associated local filing fees. All will later become part of the overall project validation process.

These "steps" are those associated with CDM projects – but the principles are similar for JI projects and will likely be similar in *most* regulated environments. In fact, there has been growing convergence between "systems" in recent months. The JI system, US-based Regional Greenhouse Gas Initiative (RGGI) and Voluntary Carbon Standard (VCS), for instance, all allow the use of CDM methodologies in their projects. RGGI even accepts CERs in satisfaction of its (proposed) compliance targets.

5.2 Host and participating nation approval

CDM and JI projects require a host nation letter of approval (LoA), received from the designated national authority (DNA) or designated focal point (DFP) respectively. Typically, a PDD and application are required to petition host-nation DNA/DFP consideration; sometimes an application fee is required. Host-nation LoA issuance typically follows a multi-step review of an acceptable global stakeholders' process, statutory conditions, licensing, the proposed project and pre-project operations, and a determination of whether the project is harmonised with national statutory and sustainable development goals. In some cases, project validation is a prerequisite to receiving the host nation LoA; an emission reduction purchase agreement may also be required. Host nation LoAs can be a bit challenging to secure – and are a function of the individual nation's review process, attitudes and staffing levels. Figure out how to help your host nation to look good and the DNA/DFP will become your friend!

Counterparty (Annex I) LoAs are often easier to receive, as they generally consist only of an administrative review of the project and its participants.

5.3 Project validation/determination

This process is known as "validation" under CDM and "determination" under JI. This critical step utilises an UNFCCC accredited (third party) auditor – the designated operational entity (DOE) for CDM or accredited independent entity (AIE) for JI – to assess and recommend a project registration. Validation or determination generally takes place prior to project implementation (more on this later) and is the qualifying examination for the estimated generation of emission reductions (either CERs or ERUs, respectively). Under CDM, this is also the point at which a project is posted on the UNFCCC website to invite public critique.

In effect, the DOE/AIE is empowered as the "eyes and ears" of the COP to ensure a project meets all necessary professional and regulatory standards. Project validation is the first of four key functions a DOE/AIE performs in the overall project process.

The others are: to verify a registered project's emission reductions; to certify these emission reductions; and to request (of the appropriate board) issuance of certified offsets.

For each project, the validating DOE/AIE performs both a desk review of the project design document (and related documents) and a site audit. The PDD is essentially a carefully scripted "business plan" for climate change activities, including descriptions of the pre-project activities, the proposed project-related changes, emission reduction calculations, and much more. The audit ensures the project proponents have (i) made proper use of a relevant methodology, (ii) used diligence in gathering relevant and consistent data, (iii) publicly disclosed the project through a global stakeholders' process including a Q/A process, and (iv) addressed constituency needs, whether a next-door neighbour or a government ministry. During this review, the DOE/AIE issues clarification requests, corrective action requests (CARs) and forward action requests (FARs) to seek additional clarity or to help correct process or calculation errors. Upon receipt of clear answers and appropriately amended documents the DOE/AIE issues a Validation Report. While some proprietary underlying data can be kept confidential (or redacted), the validation process is intended to be an open, transparent process. All key findings (including corrective action responses) are made public.

Why such a formal process? It needs to be remembered that ER offsets are both invisible and intangible; their existence needs to be established and verified. In effect, validation confirms that a proposed project conforms to both host nation and Kyoto Protocol requirements, applies the science and technology correctly, and has properly set the stage for project implementation.

So, what is the best way to survive the validation/determination process? First, work with your DOE/EIA to determine what documents and process will be used to qualify the project. Often, a DOE/EIA will supply a "protocol" specifying the key points. In advance of submitting your PDD for desk audit, gather the cited documentation and forward copies along with the PDD and payment.

Consistency and clarity are critical. If underlying operating documents (such as production records, licences, local audit results, etc) contain data inconsistencies or have been transcribed inaccurately into your own data records system and the PDD, you will slow the audit process and various documents may have to be amended. It is essential to develop internal quality control (QC) checklists and review your documentation package before transmittal. While you may choose to forward imperfect documents, you will at least know which documents need to be "upgraded" and you can start the effort. Be aware that reviewers often speak multiple languages, and the language used by the PDD or associated documents may not be the reviewer's native tongue.

When the DOE/AIE performs a site audit, personnel familiar with both the pre-project site and the proposed project should accompany the auditors and facilitate the review process when asked. The team members who are familiar with the project should have good perspective on the whole project, or you risk creating as many questions as you hope to solve! Make careful notes and follow up quickly with promised (additional) documents or answers. *The DOE/AIE is liable for the quality of this audit. They have purview to ask any question necessary (of site personnel, local officials, project staff, etc) to satisfy themselves regarding project quality and process.*

Once the project proponents have satisfactorily answered all CARs and amended the PDD (and associated documents) to suit, the DOE/AIE will release a final Validation Report. This report is a prerequisite of registration and may also be required by the host DNA prior to LoA issuance.

5.4   Registration

A project that has been validated and has received its LoA(s) is ready to be submitted for registration as a CDM or JI project. In effect, this step is included to recognise the receipt of documents and process verification steps confirming a project's baseline definitions, additionality and contribution to sustainable development and to allow the public to review *all* project-related documentation. Application for registration must be accompanied by a Request for Registration application and a fee (this fee has a "staircase" structure and charges projects according to predicted offset yield). Registration is the first formal recognition of a project and is prerequisite to entering the monitoring phase and crediting period.

CDM project registration applications are reviewed by the Registration and Issuance Team (RIT), a 20-expert panel established by the CDM Executive Board to streamline the registration and issuance process. The RIT is chaired by a member of the EB on a rotating basis. The RIT is empowered to impose additional clarification requests (beyond those which may have been asked by the DOE) and will not pass a project to the EB for registration until these requests are satisfactorily answered. In this way the RIT ensures that project validations (which are performed by different DOEs) are performed to a common standard.

Project implementation is the next project phase and consists of "execution", monitoring, and verification and certification of ER offsets.

5.5   Execution (or "practice change" or "construction")

Most project development guidelines define attendant process steps from a regulatory or documentation perspective – often skipping the actual "execution" of the project changes. This said, after deciding how to build a team, choosing an overall project approach, qualifying a project site, executing agreements, hosting a stakeholders' meeting, designing a technical solution, writing a PDD, validating and registration – it is necessary to make the actual project changes before commissioning and entry to the monitoring phase.

While project proponents may choose to execute project-oriented changes prior to registration, they do so at their own risk – since the CDM EB (or JI nations) may choose not to approve the project or, worse, may deny certification or acknowledgement of emission reductions at a later stage in the process. Having no approval, of course, means the project will never qualify to receive certified offsets. What is more, if execution/construction occurs prior to public disclosure (as a CDM or JI project), it may seriously jeopardise project additionality during the validation process. Moreover, the host country DNA/DFP may impose LoA delays for process non-compliance.

Execution may, depending on the project and methodology, be a relatively simple "process" change or may include significant infrastructure changes – what I have called "construction". Once this step is completed and the project site is running smoothly under the new configuration, the site can be commissioned.

5.6   Monitoring

Monitoring begins after PDD-described project changes are made and the site is commissioned – that is, "new" operations start. The monitoring plan requires the collection and recording of specified parameters at a given (or shorter) time interval. While this would seem to be the "easiest" part of a project, this phase often suffers from inadequate staff training and may result in incomplete data. Depending on monitoring plan requirements, monitoring staff may be site resident or may visit at regular intervals. During the verification and certification phase, incomplete data or process irregularities will reduce the quantity of certified offsets available to the project developer. Nonconforming projects may require a Request for Deviation prior to certified offset issuance.

Methodologies (and projects) employing sampling to derive parameters used to estimate ERs must quantify these parameters at the 95% confidence level. Check your instrument manuals to determine how many readings must be made to reach this confidence level. Also remember to choose upper/lower bounds used in estimating ERs in such a way to foster conservative results.

Some projects employ sensors with local memory/recording or data transmission that enable remote monitoring. Such tools can increase the reliability of monitoring, provided they meet all Monitoring Plan requirements. What is important, however, is the completeness and consistency of the data, the confidence the DOE/EIA can have in the data and measuring devices (including their calibration), and the process by which data is recorded and stored.

While this overall process sounds simple, experience suggests that smoothly run projects require well-defined processes, trained staff and outstanding record keeping. Your QC staff should work closely with project personnel to ensure success.

5.7   Verification and certification

The project developer is responsible for creating regular monitoring reports to document project performance and problems. These reports document actual project emissions (distinguished from the predictions made in the PDD) and form the basis for third-party "verification" of the emission reductions. Report intervals should be consistent with methodological guidance and a project's natural cycles. An agricultural project, for instance, may require roughly annual monitoring whereas an industrial project may be relatively insensitive to report intervals. Some methodologies require a "lesser than" approach – where actual results are compared with the baseline or other parameters and the most conservative result taken. Once the DOE/EIA verifies the monitoring report and its data, the DOE/EIA submits the report to the EB (or Annex I nations for JI) for approval and certified offset issuance.

The first time a DOE/EIA verifies project performance, it will also go through a project implementation validation whereby it confirms that the project was implemented as described in the PDD and other project documentation. It will confirm that permits were applied for and approved, that "as built" or "marked up" drawings document minor variations from the original plans or prints and that sensors conform to minimum monitoring requirements. It will determine whether specific construction shortcomings – including material, workmanship, lack of QA/QC processes, etc – represent a "risk" to achieving claimed results. Because the DOE/EIA is liable for this verification, it takes a conservative view towards risk issues and may require the monitoring report to take additional discounts.

5.8 Issuance

Upon receipt of necessary DOE and project participant paperwork, including a Request for Issuance, the Registration and Issuance team will review all applicable paperwork for consistency, conservativeness and transparency. If the project exhibits post-PDD changes (or the project is nonconforming), they will require a Request for Deviation and may seek other clarifications or requirements prior to certified offset issuance. Once satisfied that a project has met the necessary tests, a recommendation for issuance is passed to the EB.

5.9 Sale

Project offsets may have been forward sold to finance the project or may be contracted under ERPA terms. Some offsets may be available for "spot sale" into the market.

Projects often take some 18+ months before the first monitoring report and DOE review of project performance, with regular reporting thereafter. Projects may be verified over either a seven-year period that may qualify for additional period renewals (for a total of 14 or even 21 years) or for a fixed period of ten years. The project PDD and validation determine whether a project period is ten years or seven, seven possibly qualifying the project for an additional (or two additional) seven-year period(s).

6. Working with the CDM Executive Board/JI Supervisory Committee

We shall begin with definitional issues:

- The *CDM Executive Board (EB)* supervises the Clean Development Mechanism (CDM) under the authority and guidance of the Conference of the Parties serving as the Meeting of the Parties to the Kyoto Protocol (COP/MOP), and is fully accountable to the COP/MOP. CDM's overarching principles are defined in the Modalities and Procedures of the CDM.
- The *Joint Implementation Supervisory Committee* (JISC) also works under the authority and guidance of the COP/MOP, *inter alia*, and supervises the verification procedures defined in paragraphs 30 to 45 of the document entitled "Guidelines for the implementation of Article 6 of the Kyoto Protocol".
- The *Secretariat* (also known as the Climate Change Secretariat) services the Convention and its bodies, including the parties, as outlined in Article 8 of the Convention. It now employs some 200 staff from around the world.

While project participants and industry are permitted informal access to individual members of the EB and JISC, no direct formal mechanism exists for dialogue with these groups. Historically, the DOE/EIAs have represented project constituency needs to these groups and IETA is given occasional time to brief members at specific meetings. EB and JISC members take care to ensure that all formal exchanges are transparent in nature.

The Secretariat has limited – typically project-specific – dealings with the project development community, particularly during reviews by the RIT. Recently, recognising that further industry evolution requires embracing new thoughts, the Secretariat has been making an effort to extend itself on behalf of the UNFCCC. Early in 2007, for instance, the Secretariat extended an invitation to IETA's Project Developers' Working Group (PDWG) to review systemic inefficiencies and to explore alternative approaches. This day-long meeting was quite successful and additional meetings are being planned.

It is admittedly unusual for an industry to keep the regulators and regulated completely apart; most industries foster structured communications with predefined agendas, meeting minutes and resolutions. As the parties gather to negotiate Kyoto's next (post-2012) phase, the project development community is hopeful the COP/MOP will make provisions allowing the EB and JISC to meet their constituencies on an occasional, if not regular, basis.

Postscript

November 2007 saw the launch of the Voluntary Carbon Standard (VCS), developed over a two-year period through discussions with a wide range of carbon market stakeholders and in consultation with the International Organization for Standardization (ISO). While other VER systems exist, the VCS is a global standard that can be used in all jurisdictions and geographies (and with nearly all project types, including the avoided deforestation projects highlighted at the Bali COP/MOP) for certification of credible voluntary offsets. Because the VCS has established such high standards for rigour and transparency, many believe it will emerge as the leading standard against which all voluntary offset projects will be judged.

While individual project-administrative steps may vary (when contrasted with CDM/JI), the overall architecture – including project documentation and project implementation steps – will seem quite familiar to those who have read this chapter. VCS provides means to ensure that voluntary project offsets are from a credible source, and are not double traded or double counted.

Selling carbon credits

Christopher Norton
Lovells LLP

1. Introduction

Investment in carbon emission reduction projects through CDM and JI will generally involve parties entering into forward contracts associated with the promise of a future delivery of greenhouse gas (GHG) emission reductions. As with any technology-based investment project, an appropriate allocation of non-delivery risks between sellers and buyers will have value and will need to be properly reflected in the contractual arrangements.

As with other projects and transactions, an emission reduction project can be structured, and the emission credits arising from that project sold, in a variety of ways. There is not yet a universal approach to the way in which the creation and sale of such credits is documented. However, even before the Kyoto Protocol entered into force, attempts were made to develop standard emission trading contracts, including by the International Emissions Trading Association (IETA). (The latest version of IETA's standard approach to the CDM market is discussed in section 6 below.) In addition, early carbon funds adopted fairly standard contractual approaches that were simply modified to take account of project-specific issues.

Now that the Kyoto Protocol is in operation and the predicted secondary market in emissions trading is rapidly developing, the use of more standardised contracts is becoming increasingly common. That is not to say that the story is complete. The emissions market is, by and large, still in its infancy and will continue to develop as the international legal regime in which it sits evolves. In addition, key differences between the various types of emissions credits ensure that agreements relating to their sale and purchase necessarily involve a range of drafting and negotiating approaches. This chapter explores how the trading of emission reductions has developed and focuses on key contractual provisions that warrant particular attention when negotiating Emission Reduction Purchase Agreements (ERPAs).

2. ERPAS – contracting approaches

2.1 ERPAs in context

The sale of emission reductions is, of course, similar to the sale of any commodity from a project (such as electricity under a power purchase agreement). However, emission reduction projects present particular risks due to the developing nature of the international framework upon which they are based. These risks need to be carefully identified and managed in the ERPA.

The focus in this chapter is on emission credits arising from primary projects, whether they are Certified Emission Reductions (CERs) arising from the Clean Development Mechanism (CDM), Emission Reduction Units (ERUs) arising from Joint Implementation (JI), or Verified Emission Reductions (VERs) in the voluntary market. In this context, and except where otherwise stated, reference to emission reductions (ERs) is made as a generic term.

This chapter also puts to one side the possibility of the sale or transfer of ERs that are incorporated in another project agreement. For example, ERs may be used as part payment on an equity investment or as part repayment of a financial loan to an emission reduction project. In other cases, a project developer and his private entity joint venture partner may share emission credits in accordance with agreed pro-rata distributions. However, experience to date has indicated that, in the majority of emission reduction projects, the sale of ERs is a separate venture from the development of the project infrastructure.

2.2   **Contracting approaches: (i) finding buyers and sellers**
From the early years of the emissions market, there have been varying approaches to match buyers with sellers. These include:

- sellers implementing a competitive tender or auction process for potential buyers;
- buyers issuing a request for ERs from the market;
- sellers approaching potential buyers with a term sheet or project description to propose investment in an emission reduction project; and
- sellers arranging with independent brokers to transact their ERs on the open market.

Before the Kyoto Protocol entered into force, many CDM project developers tendered to the World Bank and other carbon funds (discussed in 3 below). As the ER market has grown, so some of the other approaches mentioned have become more popular. The development of the international legal regime has also played its part. For example, the endorsement of programmatic CDM projects (ie where the CDM Executive Board authorises a series of emission reduction projects, rather than requiring an individual registration for each) may increase the popularity of bullets one, three and four above, as project developers have an increased number of ERs at their disposal.

2.3   **Contracting approaches: (ii) types of ERPA**
Approaches to contracting for ERs have also varied greatly. This has largely been influenced by levels of knowledge of the CDM, JI and voluntary projects, an increasing number of sellers and buyers in the market and the gradual consolidation of the international rules on CDM, JI and voluntary standards (although it should be noted that the development of the latter is still some way behind the Kyoto-based mechanisms). Contracts for the sale and purchase of Kyoto units and VERs bear a number of similarities, but what ultimately distinguishes them are the provisions relating to transfer and delivery – a VER is effectively a contractual right in the underlying greenhouse gas emission reduction whereas Kyoto units are credits held

in an electronic registry account. Over time approaches will continue to shift, as will the dynamics of contracts and the stringency of commercial clauses.

There are a number of ways in which ERs can be sold into the market, including:

- a direct and immediate sale of ERs which have already been generated by a project over a certain period (ie a spot transaction);
- a direct sale of ERs to be generated from the future activities of an emission reduction project (ie a forward sale); and
- an option or pre-emption to purchase agreed volumes of ERs at a later date.

It is not unusual for ERPAs to include a combination of the above structures and buyers are increasingly looking to contract forward to the post-2012 period, usually through options and pre-emption rights.

3. Early experience

3.1 Introduction

The most extensive experience of early emission reduction projects came from first movers under the auspices of the CDM. The World Bank's Prototype Carbon Fund (PCF) and the Dutch Government's Certified Emission Reduction Unit Procurement Tender (CERUPT) were the primary buyers of ERs in the early carbon-trading market. Due to the fact that these early transactions occurred in an embryonic legal framework, both the World Bank and the Dutch government attempted to manage the uncertainties in the market through contractual arrangements with their fund participants and project developers. An overview of the early World Bank projects can be found in the introductory chapters to this book.

Notwithstanding the fact that the early ERPAs of the PCF and CERUPT were completed before the entry into force of the Kyoto Protocol, certain key areas emerged that are still important for those considering entering the market today. An overview of these issues is presented here and each is explored in more detail in subsequent sections.

3.2 Consistency with international rules

Both the PCF and CERUPT attempted to ensure that the projects from which they purchased ERs were consistent with the CDM procedure under Kyoto Protocol rules, in the expectation that these projects would ultimately be eligible to create CERs. CERs are now a reality, but compliance with international rules is still a significant issue and one that should be addressed during the process of due diligence.

3.3 Management of risk

The PCF comprised a number of participant countries and companies. Investment in the fund was made on the basis that the World Bank would be trustee of the PCF, and that it would be used to purchase ERs in a "learning by doing" approach. This inevitably involved risk in the nascent CDM market. This risk finds parallels in the emerging voluntary emissions market in which legitimacy is largely dependent on high-quality VERs underwritten by robust monitoring and verification standards.

Since the PCF, the World Bank has developed (and continues to develop) other funds, including the Community Development Carbon Fund (CDCF). The remit of the CDCF includes purchasing CERs from projects in least developed countries that otherwise would not receive finance from traditional investors due to high levels of risk. This country risk is, notwithstanding the entry into force of the Kyoto Protocol, as relevant today as when the CDCF took its first steps in the CDM market.

3.4   Delivery risk

In recognition of the fact that developing country project participants may face a range of obstacles in operating a CDM project, the early World Bank ERPAs generally provided for a degree of flexibility in the event of delivery failure. The World Bank's Carbon Finance Business (CFB) would work with the seller to remedy the shortfall and establish alternative delivery arrangements, with rights of termination and damages only for persistent failure, fraud, gross negligence or wilful misconduct.

In contrast, the ERPAs that CERUPT negotiated were more commercial in nature. CERUPT tender documents, for example, incorporated stringent penalties for non-delivery. One of the penalties was established at 2.5% of the total contract value each month that a delivery remained outstanding, regardless of the amount of shortfall (although it should be noted that this was subsequently amended and was in any event subject to "reasonableness" under Dutch law, which was the governing law of CERUPT ERPAs).

Today, the risk of delivery failure remains a fundamental concern both for compliance buyers and institutional buyers as we examine in section 5 of this chapter.

4.   Pre-contractual arrangements and due diligence

4.1   Introduction

As competition in the marketplace increases, it is likely that there will be a greater number of buyers seeking to secure ERs from reliable emission-reduction projects. As the lead time to develop a project may be lengthy, buyers are likely to seek at an early stage to obtain exclusive rights to secure ERs from projects that meet international standards and that have a lower commercial risk. For those beginning the negotiation process, there are two key questions:

- How do you ensure exclusivity during the negotiation of the ERPA?
- What level of project and legal due diligence should be undertaken?

These will be discussed in turn.

4.2   Pre-contractual negotiations

Once a potential emission-reduction project is identified, generally both the project developer and the buyer of ERs are eager to enter into binding legal arrangements for the sale and purchase of the ERs at a certain price. For their part, project developers may rely on the projected revenue from ER sales to make the project economically viable, whilst potential buyers of ERs realise that the market price for ERs can be volatile and may quickly increase beyond their means.

These factors are, of course, to a certain extent competing. Project developers would like an increase in projected revenue whereas potential buyers want to benefit from the ERs at the lowest cost. Accordingly, where sellers and buyers agree in principle over a project, there is a balance between the two parties at the start of negotiations. However, as noted above, ERPAs are generally negotiated in accordance with the particular circumstances of the project and such negotiations can take a significant period of time to finalise. This passage of time increases the risk of imbalance.

Therefore, the parties may seek to enter into an agreement to deal exclusively between themselves for a defined period, and which fixes the ERs at a certain price, particularly where projects are at an early stage of development. The early agreement could be in the form of an exclusivity agreement under which the parties agree to negotiate solely with each other for a fixed period, a binding letter of intent setting out the basic agreement between buyer and seller for the transaction of ERs, or a term sheet providing a summary of the major terms that will ultimately be contained in the ERPA.

The parties can and do seek to make these "pre-agreements" legally binding, but since the final form of the ERPA will almost certainly remain to be negotiated at this stage, it is difficult to say whether in practice such an agreement that purports to be legally binding can be enforced in a timely fashion.

4.3   Due diligence

The effort and time devoted to due diligence will depend to large degree on the type of ERs being purchased and the type of project from which they originate. The due diligence involved in a spot purchase of ERs that have already been generated may be limited to ensuring that the seller has good title to the ERs and is selling what he purports to sell. By contrast, the due diligence involved in a forward sale of ERs from a project that has yet to be validated or registered with the appropriate body and/or built will be correspondingly more laborious.

As mentioned above, emission reduction projects involve similar considerations to those which apply in more "traditional" projects (such as power purchase agreements). These include identifying project partners, technology suppliers, lenders, construction contractors and key regulatory approvals (etc). However, emission reduction projects add a layer of complexity to "standard" project due diligence, including (assuming that the project is not yet registered):

- Does the project have host country approval (as required)?
- Is the project likely to meet the registration threshold of international rules (such as approved baseline and monitoring methodology and verification requirements)?
- Are there any other investors and, if so, what are their entitlements?
- Are there any other local law issues that could impact on the ability of the project to generate and deliver ERs?
- As a buyer or other investor, am I at risk under local law for project-related liabilities?
- Is the host country (or investor country) likely to impose taxes on the ERs generated by the project? and
- Are there adequate legal mechanisms for the enforcement of parties' rights?

Very often, developers of emission reduction projects are small or medium-sized enterprises that are unused and sometimes resistant to responding to lengthy due diligence questionnaires. Therefore, for the buyer one issue will be what level of due diligence should be undertaken having regard to such potential seller sensitivities.

4.4   Insurable risks?

Employing an insurance-based Carbon Emission Credit Delivery Guarantee (CECDG) may allow parties involved to mitigate aspects of the project-based risks which could otherwise affect the level and timing of the predicted emission reductions. The types of risks which can be covered by a CECDG policy include design and operational risks, financial and credit risks, performance risks, political risks and Kyoto Protocol specific risks such as those associated with project approval and emission verification. A number of insurance and reinsurance companies offer so-called "wrap products" aimed at providing coverage for all or some of these project-related risks. This type of insurance available will generally be designed specifically to provide financial compensation where a covered risk affects the delivery of the promised GHG emission credit.

5.   Key legal issues in ERPAs

5.1   Introduction

For any emission-reduction project, the major issues to be addressed in the ERPA will include:

- at what point the contractual obligations of the parties will take effect (the use of conditions precedent);
- defining what type of ER is to be sold under the ERPA;
- determining who has the legal entitlement to the ERs and ensuring that this is properly transferred to the party which is purchasing them;
- determining how ERs are to be sold and transferred;
- determining the quantity of delivery and terms of payment;
- responsibility for payment of various project development and regulatory costs;
- responsibility for taxes;
- appropriate seller warranties and covenants;
- managing a shortfall in the delivery of ERs;
- assignment and novation provisions;
- appropriate termination provisions; and
- resolving disputes and choice of law.

These are considered below in turn.

5.2   Conditions precedent

In view of the uncertain nature of many CDM and JI projects in terms of obtaining regulatory (etc) approvals, it is not unusual for many ERPAs to be conditional upon matters such as registration or determination and commissioning of the project. In this way, the buyer (in particular) can limit his exposure to a long-term contractual commitment on a non-viable project.

5.3   **Defining what type of ER is to be sold under the ERPA**

Before the Kyoto Protocol came into force, the scope for entering into ERPAs was limited to VERs in the hope or expectation that these VERs would ultimately become tradable Kyoto units. Today, however, a buyer is faced with a myriad of purchase options: CERS (of various types), ERUs, AAUs, VERs from the voluntary sector etc.

However, the buyer may wish to specify, where it is buying Kyoto units, that any CERs or ERUs delivered to it must be acceptable for compliance purposes under the EU Emissions Trading Scheme (the EU ETS). Currently, the EU ETS does not recognise credits from forestry projects, and this looks set to remain the position until after the end of Phase II of the Scheme. Similarly, if the buyer is purchasing credits from a large hydroelectric project (in excess of 20MW installed capacity), it may wish to make it a condition that the project complies with the criteria set forth in the World Commission on Dams report. The buyer should also check whether the designated national authority (DNA) through which it intends to seek approval to participate in such a project has particular requirements for confirming such compliance.

The choice of "commodity" to be sold under the ERPA may well have a significant bearing on the structure of the rest of the agreement. The basic difference between ERs arising from a compliance market (CERs, ERUs and AAUs) and those arising from voluntary projects (VERs) may be obvious. Procedures for developing and registering projects, verifying emission reductions and issuing credits vary considerably between project mechanisms in both the compliance and voluntary markets. These differences will need to be reflected in the contract, meaning that an ERPA for ERUs may look very different from an ERPA for CERs.

5.4   **Determining who has the legal entitlement to the ERs and ensuring that this is properly transferred to the buyer**

One of the major risk-management issues in contracting to purchase ERs is to identify the underlying legal ownership and to ensure that such ownership is securely transferred through contractual arrangements. For example, in the case of ERs generated from a landfill methane capture or reduction project, which entity has ownership of the methane gas – the owner of the landfill or the operator?

This is of particular concern in the case of VERs, which, as mentioned above, are contractual rights in the underlying emission reductions. With Kyoto units, the electronic registries in which such credits are held act as a quasi title guarantee. For this reason and in an attempt to provide credibility to the VER market a number of VER registries are being developed. In any event, as a minimum the ERPA should require the seller to provide general warranties as to the ownership of the underlying ERs and to guarantee clear and unencumbered legal title.

As for the risk of revocation of ERs, in the case of CERs the risk is mitigated by the fact that the CERs are created and issued direct to a project participant buyer by a UN body, the CDM Executive Board, and also by the fact that international emissions trading under Kyoto operates on a "sellers liability" model. Therefore, once issued, CERs cannot be revoked and, if too many CERs have been issued because of the negligence of the designated operational entity (DOE), it is the DOE that is obliged to reimburse the excess volume to the CDM Executive Board and not the project developer or buyer.

5.5   Determining how ERs are to be sold and transferred

The ERPA should clearly provide the mechanism for transferring the ERs to the buyer and the point at which title passes. We take each of these in turn.

(a)   *Effecting the transfer*

On the face of things it should be a simple enough matter to effect a transfer of Kyoto units from one electronic registry (the CDM Registry or, in the case of JI, the host country registry) to the buyer's account in a national registry. However, in the case of CERs from CDM projects this transfer process must take account of the fact that, as a general rule, the buyer under a primary ERPA must also be a project participant approved by an Annex I Party to the Kyoto Protocol. This enables the issuance of the CERs from the CDM Executive Board's pending account direct to the buyer's national registry account (ie the CERs do not flow through the project developer or seller). The ERPA should contain clear and precise provisions governing this process. In particular, under the CDM Modalities and Procedures, the project participants must nominate a focal point (one or more of the project participants) on whose instructions the CDM Executive Board will act when issuing CERs. The project participants are obliged, therefore, to determine at an early stage who will bear the responsibility of liaising with the appropriate international body.

Naturally, the buyer will feel that if it has control over the issuance process this will largely mitigate the risk of non-delivery, whereas for its part the seller will not wish to relinquish total control of this process, particularly when payment is on delivery.

Moreover, the seller will generally only be prepared to accept obligations to perform tasks that are actually within its control. It will not want to be in a position where it will be in breach of the ERPA if, for example, the CDM Executive Board refuses to issue CERs or the buyer's national registry cannot receive CERs.

At the time of going to print, an additional problem for the issuance of CERs to national registry accounts is that the International Transaction Log (ITL) is not yet operational. For this reason some buyers have agreed to accept delivery of CERs into their temporary accounts in the CDM registry and thereby take the risk of delayed ITL operations.

In the case of ERUs from JI projects, the buyer will want the seller to take all reasonable steps to ensure that the host country issues the contract ERUs direct to the buyer's national registry account.

Delivery of VERs is somewhat different because VERs are contractual rights in ERs rather than credits held in an electronic registry. The VER sale agreement will therefore need to provide for the creation and transfer of these exclusive contractual rights and this is often achieved through the provision of a title transfer form combined with delivery to the buyer of the verification report corresponding to the ERs that are being purchased.

(b) Transferring title

The ERPA should provide that the legal and beneficial title to ERs is to be transferred to the buyer and clearly provide the exact point at which such title transfers. For example, should beneficial title transfer upon the issuance of ERs by the CDM Executive Board under the CDM or the submission of a verification report under JI, with legal title to transfer on delivery to the buyer's registry account, or is transfer of title contingent upon receipt of payment from the buyer?

The seller will want to ensure that the buyer is obliged to pay for the ERs at the same time as it receives title to them. This way, if the buyer fails to pay for the ERs the seller will be able to sell them to another market buyer, although in practice difficulties will arise if the ERs have been transferred into the buyer's account prior to payment. For this reason, the use of paying agents and/or collateral agreements (such as letters of credit or security for any payment due from the buyer) have become increasingly common.

The buyer will generally prefer to receive legal title to ERs as early as possible after the emissions credits are created, but in accordance with general commercial practice it is likely to accept that transfer of legal title will only occur upon delivery plus payment.

5.6 Determining quantity of delivery and terms of payment

The ERPA should clearly specify the quantity of ERs being acquired and the timeframe in which they are to be acquired. It should also clearly specify the ER unit price and whether that price is tax inclusive.

(a) Quantity of delivery

The seller will want to be certain of its delivery obligations under the ERPA in order to plan the operation of the project, and it should also be comfortable that its minimum delivery obligations are well within the expected project capacity.

The buyer will also want to be certain of the total amount it is obliged to pay under the ERPA for the ERs and the number of ERs that it should expect from the seller. It may also wish to have an option to purchase further ERs from the project on either the same terms as the contract ERs, or at the contemporary market price.

Given the desire for certainty for both parties, the ERPA should specify a delivery schedule for the ERs which accords with the expected performance of the project. This may be by reference to the estimated volume specified in the Project Design Document once validated. However, it may be wise to leave a "buffer" of expected GHG reductions from the project, so that any minor delay in the project will not lead to the seller being in breach of the ERPA. This is often done by including absolute minimum delivery requirements some way below the expected performance of the project so that only delivery failure beyond these shortfalls will be a breach of the ERPA. Similarly, where a buyer is purchasing credits from a "project pool" he may require the seller to "ring fence" a quantity of credits in excess of the contract volume and grant the buyer exclusivity over that ring-fenced volume.

(b)   ***Price***
As emission reduction projects are generally long-term projects – five years or more – many ERPAs are in the form of forward contracts under which buyers seek to purchase future streams of ERs over the lifetime of a project. The agreed price for each ER will vary depending on whether the ERPA provides for guaranteed or qualified delivery obligations, up-front finance (generally higher risk for the buyer, so lower price for the ERs), or payment on delivery (less risk for the buyer). Options in the ERPA on price setting could include:

- providing for a fixed unit price for each ER delivered;
- providing a floor price, plus an uplift based on the market price for ERs at the time of delivery – in the absence of a credible Kyoto unit market price this is sometimes by reference to the EU Allowance (EUA) market price in the EU ETS;
- providing an agreed fixed price, with an adjustment factor should the ER later be on-sold for a significantly increased price; or
- including prepayment clauses, discounting to present value and drafting appropriate triggers for reconciliation and/or security arrangements.

5.7   Payment of project development and regulatory costs
The costs involved in developing a CDM or JI project can be significant, including preparation and validation of the PDD, registration and verification fees. The general approach in commercial sale contracts is that the seller would be responsible for covering all costs involved in creating the ERs and that it should factor these costs into the price it receives for ERs under the ERPA. There are, however, buyers who are willing to take a share in "project risk" and pay for or contribute to the costs of validation, registration and verification etc; and, where this is the case, consideration should be given as to when such payments are to be made and the circumstances in which the buyer may be entitled to be reimbursed (eg on non-delivery or termination).

5.8   Responsibility for taxes
Consideration of taxation issues goes beyond traditional project concerns. This is a result of the developing legal status of ERs. (Here, it should be noted, the focus is primarily on ERs generated in the compliance market.) For example, host countries are at liberty to impose a levy on emissions credits generated by projects in their jurisdictions, such as those levied in China, and parties entering into an agreement to purchase those credits will want to ensure that responsibility for payment of such taxes and levies rests with the seller. In addition, other project mechanism specific taxes may apply. The CDM for instance imposes a Share of Proceeds levy, consisting of a deduction of a 2% of CERs generated by the project ("Adaptation Share of Proceeds") and fees which are paid to the CDM Executive Board on registration and issuance ("Administrative Share of Proceeds"). As a general rule, the parties to an ERPA will agree that the seller bears all taxes up to the date of delivery (therefore, including the Share of Proceeds) and the buyer bears all taxes levied on or after deliver of the ERs.

In addition, the purchase price would usually be net of VAT.

5.9 Seller warranties and covenants

In addition to standard warranties as to incorporation, capacity and compliance with law etc, the buyer may also seek a number of Kyoto and/or project-specific warranties and covenants from the seller, including in relation to:

- the selection of the DOE and the provision of information (including warranting the accuracy of the information submitted) to the DOE;
- the timely preparation of the PDD and faithful compliance with validation, registration, monitoring and baseline requirements (as applicable) under international rules;
- doing everything necessary to ensure that the creation and transfer of the buyer's rights, interests and entitlements are effected under the ERPA;
- confirming that the seller has unencumbered legal and beneficial title to the ERs at various stages of the project, that the seller will not encumber the ERs at any time and that the buyer will receive good marketable title to the ERs upon delivery; and
- confirming that the seller has the rights and title to sufficient ERs to fulfil its delivery obligations under the ERPA.

The buyer will also want certain minimum information from the project entity as to the progress of the project. Whilst it is desirable for communication between seller and buyer to be as open as possible, the seller will want to avoid any onerous reporting requirements or to provide excessive information. Here, the differences between different types of ERs may be relevant. Under the CDM, for example, most of the project documents are publicly available through the UNFCCC website; in contrast, there may be no obligation for the public release of project information in a project generating VERs. Accordingly, reasonable clauses should be drafted to require the seller to provide the buyer with information necessary to chart the progress of the project.

5.10 Managing a shortfall in the delivery of ERs

Where ERs are sold on a forward basis in advance of their creation, there exists a risk of non-production and/or non-delivery giving rise to a delivery shortfall. The seller will be concerned to ensure that it will not incur significant penalties if the project does not perform exactly to expectation. The buyer will want to provide as much certainty as possible that shortfall will not occur and that, if it does, the buyer will not suffer any loss as a consequence. Contractual provisions to deal with a delivery shortfall may include:

- the buyer and seller agreeing to negotiate an amended delivery schedule which is fair in the circumstances;
- the right for the seller to substitute ERs sourced from other projects, either with or without the buyer's consent;
- in the event that alternative ERs cannot be sourced or are unacceptable to the buyer, an obligation on the part of the seller to pay to the buyer the cost to the buyer of purchasing replacement ERs or the market value of the shortfall (which may be premised on ER mark-to-market values or by reference to

equivalent EUA prices on the EU ETS);
- the right for the buyer to terminate the contract if the delivery falls below a specified minimum amount or if there is a persistent failure to deliver by the seller; or
- provisions dealing with any carry forward of a delivery shortfall.

While the provisions outlined above indicate the potential scope of the seller's obligations under the ERPA, they do not cover when those obligations arise. For example, some ERPAs are drafted so that the trigger for shortfall remedies only occur upon the seller's wilful default, fraud or gross negligence or where the seller has failed to act as a reasonable and prudent operator. Others include trigger provisions by reference to a "guaranteed delivery" threshold below which remedies will be available to the buyer. In the end, the final form of the ERPA will depend on the type of project, the price of the ERs and the bargaining strength of the parties.

5.11   Assignment and novation

In general, the same considerations apply to assignment and novation clauses in an ERPA as to other commercial contracts. The starting position is likely to be that assignment and novation require the consent of both parties. However, the seller may want the freedom to assign the proceeds of sale. Correspondingly, the buyer may want flexibility to allow him to onward-sell the ERs or rights under the ERPA without the express consent of the seller, particularly if he is seeking to generate maximum revenue in a fast-moving market, or if he contemplates using the ERPA as security.

5.12   Termination

ERPAs will generally include a right for one or both of the parties to terminate in the event of the default of the other party (eg material breach of contractual obligations, breach of warranty, non-payment or insolvency), or in some cases where there has been no default but a specified trigger such as an event of *force majeure* (see below) or failure to satisfy certain conditions precedent. Where such termination provisions are included, one of the main issues to be resolved between the parties is what loss (if any) the terminating party is entitled to recover on termination. For example, if the seller has no liability for delivery failure except in the case of wilful default etc (see section 5.10 above), it may well want this concept to apply also on termination. Consider also whether the ERPA should exclude liability for loss of profit and other consequential losses.

The scope of the *force majeure* provision in the ERPA is also an important aspect, as it will determine whether the parties will only be excused from their obligations for:
- natural *force majeure* events such as fires, storms etc.; or
- *any* events beyond the control of either party, including a failure of the registries system etc or other international emissions trading mechanisms.

In addition to the scope of the *force majeure* definition, the parties should consider the effect of *force majeure* on the parties. For example, can either party terminate after prolonged *force majeure* or just the non-affected party, and how will losses be allocated between them on such termination?

5.13 Resolving disputes and choice of law

By their nature, emission reduction projects involve cross-border transactions between entities that may not have had previous business contact in a rapidly developing area of law. It is therefore important to determine which legal system will govern the construction, validity and performance of the ERPA and how and where disputes will be dealt with if they arise.

Experience to date suggests that English Law (with its reputation for certainty and its "hands off" approach) is the law of choice for many ERPAs. Whatever the choice of law, both parties will want to make sure that the dispute resolution procedures will not be unduly time consuming or costly and for this reason may prefer the opportunity to use alternative dispute resolution techniques (ie negotiation, mediation) as a first option, rather than requiring every dispute to be dealt with before a court or arbitration body.

In many ERPAs the parties specify arbitration under international rules as a more "neutral" dispute resolution process. In general, it is preferable for the buyer and seller to attempt to resolve any disputes through good faith negotiations and then potentially through mediation before imposing any binding dispute settlement process. It should be noted in this context that some host country legal systems may provide that courts can overrule contractual provisions if they are against public policy. Additionally, it may not be possible to enforce a contract governed by foreign law within the host country. The buyer and seller should therefore both seek legal advice as to the enforceability of the chosen dispute resolution provisions and governing law in the host country and any implications for the CDM project.

6. Discussion of the IETA standard

6.1 Introduction

In 2002, IETA began work on the development of a standardised ERPA that could be used in the emerging CDM market (the "IETA ERPA"). The aim of the project was to improve the efficiency of trading by streamlining the contractual process. A corollary of this would be to reduce transaction costs for all those involved in the market. Version 1.0 of the IETA ERPA was launched in 2004. This was soon followed by version 2.0 in the same year. The current version (version 3.0) came about from experience gained from earlier versions and the wider CDM market and was published in September 2006.

This section focuses on the IETA ERPA with respect to the CDM, as similar standardised agreements have yet to be developed for the JI or voluntary markets. IETA has developed a similar standardised contract for the EU ETS (the Emission Trading Master Agreement or "ETMA") and some reference will be made to the ETMA in the following discussion. Generally, the IETA ERPA serves as a useful study in the identification of issues when seeking to standardise contracts in the modern emissions market.

6.2 The IETA ERPA

The first two versions of the IETA ERPA were based on a traditional contractual format, with articles providing the substance of the agreement and schedules providing project specific details and the number of CERs to be sold under the agreement. In contrast, version 3.0 of the IETA ERPA is a departure from the more traditional format, with the front end of the agreement providing a framework or shell that is fleshed out by reference to another IETA document, the "Code of CDM Terms".

The purpose of the Code of CDM Terms is to provide a standardised set of contract terms with various options allowing the parties to pick and choose the options in light of the commercial arrangements between them. Schedule 1 of the IETA ERPA indicates which options have been chosen, while Schedule 2 of the IETA ERPA completes the agreement setting out project details and commercial details such as the price and contract quantity.

By eschewing the more traditional format, the latest form of the IETA ERPA follows a new breed of contract that seeks to separate the architecture of an agreement (ie the basic contractual framework) from commercially sensitive provisions. The IETA ERPA is theoretically flexible enough to govern the relationship where parties are full project participants, as well as in situations where the agreement is limited to offtaking CERs.

6.3 The use of the IETA ERPA in the CDM market and lessons learned

The first two versions of the IETA ERPA have been adopted in the market, with their basic structure in use in a wide range of transactions. Take up of the most recent version has, however, been less successful, though it should be remembered that its publication remains relatively recent. It is perhaps too early to assess the impact of the latest version on the market. Therefore, the rest of this section looks at how version 2.0 of the IETA ERPA has been treated by those involved in CDM projects.

In contrast to the ETMA, the IETA ERPA operates in a market that is not yet liquid, and with products that are of varying quality. The EU ETS, which is the focus of the ETMA, is both a standardised platform and has participants that are – by and large – subject to similar legal and regulatory regimes. The parties to an IETA ERPA, on the other hand, may be subject to very different legal and regulatory regimes and the parties themselves may be an unknown quantity. As a result, one might expect to see more variation in the approach to IETA ERPAs than to ETMAs, and this expectation is borne out in practice.

The number of variables and unknowns in a CDM project (from post-2012 concerns to the creditworthiness of parties) has meant that the IETA ERPA (version 2.0) has been asked to cover a number of different situations. As a result, the standard form is often amended to take into account dissimilar commercial arrangements. This can create obstacles in the secondary market. Secondary Emission Reduction Purchase Agreements (SERPAs) are widely used where primary buyers onward-sell CERs. In these circumstances, sellers under the SERPAs are keen to impose back-to-back arrangements with the primary ERPA. In other words, if an event is a *force majeure* under the primary ERPA, so it should be *force majeure* under the SERPA. This principle extends beyond primary termination events. Consider, for example, options clauses. These can be structured in a number of ways. Buyers in the secondary market often contract to buy "batches" of project CERs, and each of these projects may have a different option arrangements. The identification of the option in the primary ERPA and inclusion into the SERPA can be a time-consuming and expensive exercise.

Part of the rationale for version 3.0 of the IETA ERPA is to make the identification of bespoke commercial arrangements easier to identify. If the examples given above were based on version 3.0 of the IETA ERPA, then it may be that corresponding SERPAs would be easier to draft. However, the theory must be matched by practice, and only time will tell if the latest version of the IETA ERPA will be widely accepted and used in the CDM market.

7.   Conclusion

The documents supporting emission reduction projects and allowing for the sale of ERs from those projects do have common elements that will ultimately allow a large part of such contracts to be standardised. The IETA ERPA for the CDM provides one example of this standardisation but, as noted above, its adoption has not been met with universal acceptance. However, it is foreseeable that over time only the project-specific elements of ERPA contractual documentation will need to be negotiated. In other words, only key commercial risks and issues such as price will continue to be the subject of direct negotiation. Even as regards these issues (including remedies for non-performance), standard approaches such as those espoused by the latest IETA ERPA may be adopted by buyers and sellers in the market, thereby reducing the time and costs associated with individual contractual negotiations.

Notwithstanding the development of standardised contracts, lawyers will still need to be sensitive to particular commercial arrangements. A fully standardised ISDA (International Swaps and Derivatives Association, Inc) document, for example, designed for transactions between sophisticated counterparties, will not be appropriate or relevant for many large CDM projects in host countries from which CERs are sold initially into the marketplace. The latest version of the IETA ERPA is aimed at allowing for the transfer of ERs and is able to be fine tuned for the particular circumstances of the project. Nevertheless, the IETA ERPA remains a partially standardised document. It is likely that fully standardised documents such as ISDA contracts will have an important role to play in the secondary ER market as it continues to develop.

Carbon trading – the view from the floor

Seb Walhain
Fortis

1. Introduction

1.1 The EU Emissions Trading Scheme as the cornerstone of European climate action

The Kyoto Protocol was designed to regulate greenhouse gas emissions responsible for global warming. Under the terms of the Protocol, the European Union has committed to making an overall 8% emission reduction in greenhouse gas emissions in the period 2008 to 2012 compared to the level in 1990.

In July 2003, the European Parliament passed legislation to implement a system of tradable emission permits. This European Union Emissions Trading Scheme, EU ETS, officially started on January 1 2005. The first phase of the scheme covers the three-year period 2005 to 2007. The second phase, the Kyoto period itself, runs from 2008 to 2012. Nearly 12,000 installations belonging to approximately 5,000 companies from different sectors throughout the member states are covered by the EU ETS. The EU ETS uses a simple "cap and trade" system, whereby each EU member state government allocates a number of emission allowances (EUAs) to each installation in line with their national reduction target. At the end of each year, every installation covered by the EU ETS must hold sufficient allowances to cover its actual emissions for that year. The EUAs are tradable in the EU member states, via a system of national registries. The tradability dimension facilitates emissions to be reduced where it is cheapest to do so. An EUA allows the holder to emit one tonne of CO_2. An installation for which it is too expensive to reduce emissions can, if needed, buy additional allowances on the market. Installations with cheaper abatement potential can invest in emission reductions and sell surplus allowances. This is an economically efficient and effective way of reducing overall emissions.

2. The past. The success story ...

Set up a market to achieve emission abatement ... That is the brief mission statement of the EU ETS! From a market perspective, the evolution of the EU ETS has been spectacular. Figure 1 shows the evolution of the number of EUAs traded every day. Although the rise in liquidity is spectacular, from a mere 100,000 tonnes CO_2 at its start to more than 5 million mid-2007, it is not clear if this proves the market to be sufficiently liquid.

To put the liquidity of the EU ETS to the test, the net position of the installations covered by the EU ETS is examined. Some installations have a surplus in allowances, enabling them to sell EUAs. Others have a deficit in allowances, forcing them to buy EUAs. If the market were to do nothing more than "simply" transfer allowances from companies with a surplus position to companies with a deficit, the market would "merely" need to trade about 0.5 million allowances daily... At cruise speed, the market trades more than 10 times that critical mass. This proves that the market does much more than simply transfer surpluses to deficits, but has grown to become a significant financial market used for other purposes than mere compliance needs. So, the set-up of the market has been established.

Figure 1: Evolution of the EUA market: market prices and daily traded volumes

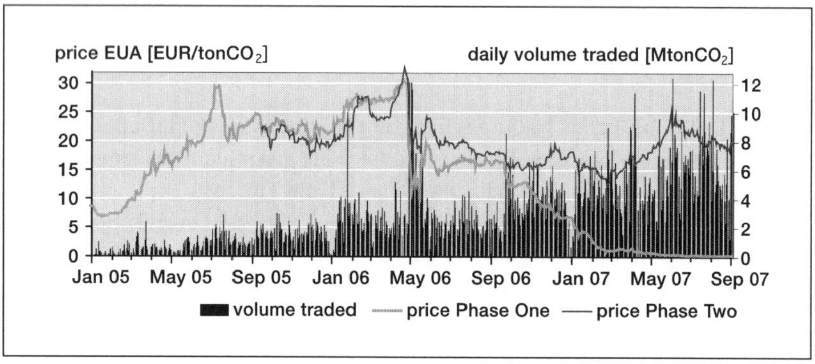

(data taken from Reuters and PointCarbon)

A second part of the ETS mission statement lies in emission abatement. In order to isolate the influence of the EU ETS on the actual emissions, one needs to answer the difficult hypothetical question of how emissions would have evolved without the EU ETS, and then compare those to actual emissions as they have been observed since the beginning of 2005.

In order to provide a partial answer to this hypothetical question, we focus on the power sector. In this sector, very short-term emission reduction potential is available, as utilities have a broad variety of plant in their portfolio. A generator with both coal- and gas-fired plants can choose which ones to use, taking into account the prices of CO_2 allowances for coal and natural gas (note that a coal-fired plants emits roughly twice as much CO_2 as a gas-fired plant). Figure 2 shows such a comparison for a generator choosing between a gas-fired unit and a coal-fired unit. If the CO_2 market value is below a certain threshold, the generator will choose to use the coal plant. If the CO_2 value is higher, the generator has an incentive to switch to the gas-fired plant, emit less CO_2 and cash in the value of the emission abatement achieved. Given the prices for coal, gas and EUAs since the start of 2005, Figure 2 suggests that without the ETS, that is, with no value for CO_2, the coal plant would have been preferred at all times. Under the ETS, however, the CO_2 market value gave a clear incentive for utilities to switch to the gas plant from March 2005 until October 2005, in June 2006 and in August until November 2006.

Using this logic for all 25 EU countries involved and the local mix of power plants, and under the premise that utilities behaved rationally for given market prices, the CO_2 price signal should have triggered fuel switching resulting in about

150 million tonnes of CO_2 emission reductions since the beginning of 2005. Hence, the ETS is responsible for emission reductions.

Figure 2: EUA prices and the incentive for utilities to switch from coal to gas

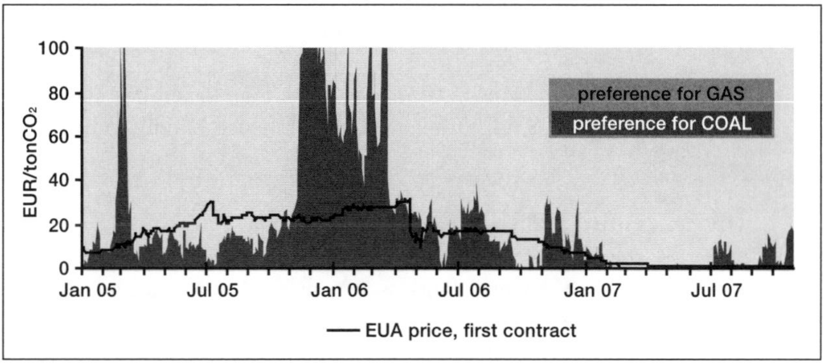

(If the EUA price is above the switch level, the utility should prefer to use the gas-fired unit. If the EUA price is below the switch level, the utility should prefer to use the coal-fired unit.)

3.   The past. The dark side and lessons learned...

The emissions of the installations covered in the EU ETS are verified annually. With the release of the verified emission reports for 2005, the EU ETS has passed its first checkpoint. Until then, the CO_2 market traded solely on forecasts. These reports were published in April/May 2006.

The first verified emission reports pointed out that the emissions in 2005 had been lower than the allocations for that year; hence 2005 was net long some 100 million allowances. But not everybody was long. The power sector, which received more than 60% of the total allowances, was short 40 million EUAs and industry as a whole was long 140 million EUAs.

Since many forecasts prior to the release of the verified emissions data estimated the market to be slightly short for 2005, the verified emission reports initiated a market correction taking prices down from above €30/tCO_2 to less than €10/tCO_2 in a couple of days, as indicated in Figure 1.

This shock was immediately confused with market failure. Market data, however, revealed that the market worked perfectly, after and even during the shock:

- The decrease in price was very logical. The verified emissions data revealed that the demand/supply was different than previously expected. The market reacted logically.
- Figure 1 shows that liquidity vastly increased during the price shock; volatility attracts traders. In March 2006, prior to the shock, the market traded about 2 million allowances daily. During the shock, liquidity increased to more than 10 million allowances for three days in a row and liquidity remained high until the market again settled to a new equilibrium. At any time before, during and after the shock, there was a market price. It was possible to buy or sell EUAs at all times.

- Last but not least, the verified emissions data was mistaken for blunt initial over-allocation. Note that we established earlier that we believe that the EU ETS has been responsible for emission abatement of at least 150MtCO$_2$. The verified emissions data merely indicates that emissions were below the cap for 2005, but says nothing on whether this difference comes from over-allocation, actual emission reductions or both.

The only "malfunction" in the market came from the error in the forecasts. The lesson to be learned is not to follow popular forecasts blindly, but to rely only on hard data.

4.   The near future. Phase II and Kyoto

Phase I of the EU ETS could be interpreted as a test for emissions trading – a test which it passed with flying colours, as demonstrated above. In a broader picture, the EU ETS should trigger a wider range of potential emission reductions. The scheme will evolve in Phase II of the EU ETS as a compliance tool within the broader Kyoto target. Geographically, the scheme is already evolving to a global scheme in encouraging emission reductions in developed and developing countries under Joint Implementation and Clean Development Mechanisms.

The Kyoto target is an emissions target on a country scale. The sectors and installations under the EU ETS represent slightly more than 40% of the EU emissions. In order to reach the Kyoto target, Phase II of the EU ETS adopted allocation plans that significantly reduce the number of allowances allocated in comparison to the first phase.

Governments are responsible for the emissions not covered under the EU ETS. If countries grant more allowances to their industrial sectors, they will simply face tougher targets for the remaining emissions. Therefore, the European Commission carefully weighed the distribution of effects between trading sectors and non-trading sectors in the assessment of the allocation plans. There is only "one shop" for emission certificates, although in different shapes and sizes. The allocations themselves do not matter that much from a macro perspective. If companies need to buy (or reduce) less because of lenient allocations, governments will simply need to buy (or reduce) more.

Furthermore, Phase II falls within the wider scope in which all countries that have ratified Kyoto will have to observe its terms. The EU countries emit about half of the emissions of all Annex I countries that have ratified Kyoto, again all looking at the same shop for emission permits.

The supply/demand balance for emission allowances in the Kyoto period from 2008 to 2012 is still unclear.

The installations covered by the EU ETS are expected to be short between 200 and 300 million emission allowances on average per year. This is based on allocations as approved by the European Commission and the expected emissions from the installations covered in the scheme.

Emissions trading becomes broader than the EU ETS in 2008, however. European governments and other Annex I countries also face emission constraints. Under business as usual, greenhouse gas emissions in Europe and Japan will exceed the Kyoto cap by about 3 billion tonnes of CO_2 equivalents in the period from 2008 to 2012. Canada faces a potential deficit of another 2 billion allowances. Canada also ratified Kyoto, but recently announced that it would not honour its obligation.

On the supply side, the Kyoto flexible mechanisms can provide some relief. In the Clean Development Mechanism and Joint Implementation, Annex I countries can invest in projects that result in additional emission abatement abroad and import the resulting credits for local use. Based on the current status of such projects, roughly 2 billion credits could be generated before the end of 2012. This number, however, is far from certain. The path from a project idea and delivery of actual reduction credits is full of risks ranging from project proposals being refused because of lack of proof of actual emission abatement up to projects delivering fewer credits than initially anticipated. Hence, the 2 billion potential supply figure perhaps needs to be viewed with one or two billion grains of salt.

When comparing the potential demand to the potential supply from Kyoto projects alone, a deficit in allowances still remains. Hence, hard emission abatement will be needed, which was the purpose in the first place.

Within the EU ETS, fuel switching from coal to gas, as described above, is again a viable candidate for swift delivery of emission abatement. For this fuel switching to take place, the CO_2 price needs to hit at least a threshold value to compensate utilities for the use of natural gas instead of cheaper, but more carbon intensive, coal. This threshold value, or switch level, depends on the ratio between coal and gas prices. Based on current forward prices for coal and gas, a CO_2 price of at least €20/tCO_2 is needed throughout Phase II to provide an incentive for switching from coal to gas.

Unfortunately for those hoping for a stable long-term CO_2 price signal, the market price tends to be volatile. The theoretical equilibrium price needed to balance supply and demand depends on underlying fundamentals such as prices for energy carriers throughout 2012, economic growth, the exact number of credits from Kyoto projects that will be available for use in the EU ETS, the impact of the inclusion of aviation, weather and its potential impact on supply and demand and post-2012 decisions for the EU ETS. These fundamentals change with time, and many are still unknown. Given the limited abatement options available on a short timescale (new investments can be triggered by a CO_2 price signal, but have no immediate effect on the actual emissions), the equilibrium price is extremely sensitive to even small changes in the fundamentals. It is our finding that changes in fundamentals are magnified in the CO_2 price needed to balance supply and demand. Assuming a mere 5% change in overall supply and demand results in a range of price forecasts from €0 to €100/tCO_2. This not only leads to an uncertain price for CO_2 but also results in persistently volatile market prices.

There is, however, also good news. Although the future may be uncertain, the present is not. Whatever analysts may say, believe or forecast, any debate with the market is futile. The market is always right. Furthermore, at all times there is a market price at which investments can be valued and at which positions in the EU ETS, either long or short, can be hedged or monetised.

5.   Long term. Turning dreams and goals to reality

With the establishment of a liquid emissions trading scheme, emission valuation is now well embedded in the EU economy. Global warming concerns are growing all over the world and are high on political agendas. Non-ETS participants and regions that have not ratified Kyoto are genuinely considering the adoption of emission trading schemes potentially compatible with the EU ETS. Companies geographically outside the EU ETS are starting to express concerns over not being able to share in the opportunities and potential rewards in emissions trading. Companies inside the EU ETS, on the other hand, express concerns over having to bear additional costs unilaterally.

Beyond 2012 and the expiry of the Kyoto Protocol, it is simply unimaginable that nothing will happen and that the world will simply stop bothering to deal with global warming and related climate issues. Since emissions trading has been shown to work and is compatible with economic activity, some form of a global cap-and-trade scheme seems a likely candidate to play a central role in combating climate change. Given the complexity and the diversity of different global regions, there are hurdles to be surmounted and compromises and sacrifices to be made. Those are political issues that have to be faced, because the alternatives for tackling global warming are simply not up to the task for the reason that none of them ensures that emissions will be reduced.

Europe has already expressed a desire to take its commitment on beyond 2012. By 2020, the European Union wants to reduce emissions to 30% below the level of 1990, compared with 8% in the Kyoto period, if other industrialised nations take on similar targets. But even without hard commitments from other countries, Europe intends unilaterally to take on a 20% reduction target.

Nature of an allowance

Martijn Wilder
Baker & McKenzie

1. Introduction

The international, regional and national frameworks that regulate the emission of greenhouse gases (GHGs), together with the emerging voluntary markets for carbon offsets, have created a suite of carbon instruments that include emissions permits, offsets and allowances, which are collectively referred to as carbon credits.

The new regulatory frameworks have also prompted the emergence of a new, cross-disciplinary area of law. This extends far beyond traditional environmental law and is partly aimed at defining the exact nature and treatment of these carbon credits in the context of existing areas of law covering property rights and ownership issues, taxation and financial services, project financing and other contracting issues.

Defining the exact legal nature of the carbon credits that exist within (and outside) the various emissions trading schemes requires this new area of law to examine both public international law (where the allowances under examination are public international law instruments, particularly the various allowances created under the Kyoto Protocol) and any domestic laws that may apply in order to determine how carbon credits will be treated in existing regulatory frameworks.

2. Defining carbon credits

The term carbon credit is used to refer to any instrument that represents a tradable right in greenhouse gas emission reductions.[1] Within this broad definition there are a range of different types of carbon credits. The nature of these different types of carbon credits varies depending on the scheme or framework under which they are created. However, in general, all carbon credits can be divided into two categories – "allowances" or "offsets".

2.1 Emissions allowances

Allowances generally represent a permit to emit one metric tonne of carbon dioxide equivalent (CO_2e),[2] granted to participants in a cap-and-trade emissions-trading scheme. Examples include EU Allowances (EUAs) which are issued or auctioned to installations that are covered by the European Union Emissions Trading Scheme (EU ETS), or the Assigned Amount Units (AAUs) which Annex I countries will be granted

---

[1]   A Beatty and E Williams, "Trends in Carbon Trading: Practical Lessons" (Paper presented at Asia-Pacific Centre for Environmental Law Conference on Crucial Issues in Climate Change and the Kyoto Mechanisms in Asia, Singapore, 2007) at 1. This paper is to be published by World Scientific Publishing in a collection of papers from the conference.

under the Kyoto Protocol if they have an emissions target assigned to them under the Protocol.[3] Allowances are first and foremost a compliance instrument – a way of setting emissions targets for countries or companies. For example, if the CO_2 emissions of an installation covered by the EU ETS exceed the EUAs it holds, then it will be fined for each tonne of CO_2 by which it exceeds its EUAs.[4] But allowances can be traded. If a company's emissions exceed the EUAs it was granted, then it can buy additional EUAs from a company that has more EUAs than it needs. This creates a market in allowances that provides greater flexibility for companies than set compliance targets, as well as a monetary incentive for companies to reduce their emissions (to avoid penalty payments and free up EUAs so that they can be sold).

Allowances are defined and administered pursuant to a formal emissions trading scheme, usually based on a treaty or statute. Table 1 outlines the features for AAUs and EUAs, the two most prominent examples of emissions allowances.

2.2 Project-based offsets

Offsets are credits given to projects that reduce the amount of CO_2e emissions released into the atmosphere (eg capturing methane from a coal mine) or that sequester CO_2e from the atmosphere (eg forestry). In both cases the amount of emissions reduced or sequestered by the project is calculated against an established baseline to ensure that the reductions are "additional" to a business-as-usual scenario (ie they would not have occurred if the carbon credits had not been given to the project). Each offset credit generally represents one metric tonne of CO_2e. Once issued to a project, these credits are able to be sold to another party which wishes to offset the emissions that it is producing through its own activities. Where offset credits are allowed to be applied for compliance purposes in an emissions trading scheme, they provide regulated entities with another avenue by which they can meet their emissions targets in addition to purchasing surplus allowances.

Project-based offset credits can be generated within or without a regulated scheme. Offset credits created within regulated schemes are generally defined under

---

2   Carbon dioxide equivalent or CO_2e is the common unit of measurement of the global warming impact of greenhouse gases. Different greenhouse gases contribute to the greenhouse effect to different degrees – that is, each greenhouse gas has a different Global Warming Potential or GWP. Although there is scientific debate over GWP values, carbon markets generally use the GWP values given in the Second Assessment Report of the International Panel on Climate Change (1995). These GWP values were accepted as the values which would be used to equate different greenhouse gases under the Kyoto Protocol when it was agreed to in 1997. The GWP for any gas is the expression of the number of carbon dioxide molecules which would need to be released in order to have the same global warming effect as one molecule of that gas. For example, using the IPCC's 1995 GWP values, methane has a GWP of 21. As such, one molecule of methane has the same effect as 21 molecules of carbon dioxide or one tonne of methane is 21 tonnes of carbon dioxide equivalent (tCO_2e).

3   Annex I countries are countries that have committed to emission restraints under Article 4.2(a) and (b) of the UNFCCC as listed in Annex I of the UNFCCC (generally developed countries and countries undergoing the process of transition to a market economy). Not all countries listed under Annex I of the UNFCCC have a target under the Kyoto Protocol. Those that do are listed in Annex B of the Kyoto Protocol, being a list of Annex I countries that have committed to a quantitative emission reduction target under Article 3.1 of the Kyoto Protocol. See M Wilder, M Willis and J Carmody, *Legal Issues Guidebook to the Clean Development Mechanism* prepared by Baker & McKenzie for the United Nations Environment Programme CD4CDM project (Roskilde, Denmark: UNEP, 2004) at 7 to 12. Available at <http://cd4cdm.org/publications.htm> (Last Accessed: June 28 2007).

4   Note that here CO_2 is used and not CO_2e, since at present the EU ETS only covers emissions of carbon dioxide and not other greenhouse gases.

Table 1: Examples of emissions allowances

Carbon credit type (Allowances)	Source of legal authority	Description
Assigned Amount Units (AAUs)	Kyoto Protocol	AAUs are issued to Annex I Parties up to the level of their assigned amount under the Kyoto Protocol. A country's assigned amount is essentially the level of greenhouse gas emissions that an Annex country is permitted to emit under the Kyoto Protocol.[5] Annex I Parties may trade AAUs with other Annex I Parties or with private entities, though to date, the number of such transactions has been very limited.
EU Allowances (EUAs)	EU ETS	Issued to private entities with compliance obligations under the European Union Emissions Trading Scheme (EU ETS) for use in meeting an emissions target under that scheme. In the EU ETS, a community-wide cap is set and each member state issues EUAs to liable firms operating in their country according to allocation plans approved by the European Commission. Firms with projected emissions that are greater than the number of EUAs they are allocated can either purchase excess EUAs from liable firms that have reduced their overall emissions (through the public exchange), purchase additional AAUs auctioned by the Commission or purchase project-based offset credits generated under the Kyoto Protocol.

5   The assigned amount for each party is calculated using its Quantified Emission Reduction and Limitation Commitment, together with the rules on which emissions are to be counted towards compliance obligations and how they are to be accounted for. Articles 3.5 to 3.8, Kyoto Protocol; See also F Yamin and J Depledge, *The International Climate Change Regime: A Guide to the Rules, Institutions and Procedures* (2004) at 120 to 21, 129 to 130.

the statute or treaty upon which the scheme is based and contracts dealing with regulated offset credits rely on the relevant statute or treaty to define the credits being traded. Examples of major statute or treaty-based offset credits and their characteristics are listed in Table 2.

Table 2: Examples of project-based offset credits

Carbon credit type (Project-based offset credits)	Source of legal authority	Description
Certified Emission Reductions (CERs)	Kyoto Protocol	Project-based credits issued pursuant to the Kyoto Protocol Clean Development Mechanism (CDM).[6] CERs are created and issued by the CDM Executive Board in respect of emission reductions from projects in developing countries that are registered under the CDM.
Temporary CERs (tCERs) and Long-term CERs (lCERs)	Kyoto Protocol	The rules regarding tCERs and lCERs[7] are designed to ensure that the credits issued to forestry projects are backed up by real-world sequestration of carbon dioxide. The provisions were developed because of the concerns about forest permanence – emissions sequestered can be released again if a forest is burnt or logged. *Temporary CERs (tCERs)* – expire at the end of the Kyoto commitment period subsequent to the one in which they were issued. On the tCER's expiry, the original purchaser becomes liable to replace it. If the original project is verified for another commitment period (ie a further five years), it can be re-issued. The renewal of tCERs from a project may continue for up to 60 years so long as the carbon remains sequestered.

---

6   Article 12, Kyoto Protocol.
7   "Modalities and procedures for afforestation and reforestation project activities under the clean development mechanism in the first commitment period of the Kyoto Protocol", Decision 5/CMP.1, 1st Meeting of the UNFCCC Conference of Parties serving as the Meeting of Parties to the Kyoto Protocol, [38] to [60], UN Doc FCCC/KP/CMP/2005/8/Add.1 (2006).

Carbon credit type (Project-based offset credits)	Source of legal authority	Description
		Long-term CERs (lCERs) – each lCER derived from a forestry CDM project remains valid for the project's crediting period. The crediting period may be a single period of up to 30 years, or a renewable period of up to 20 years that may be renewed twice giving a maximum of 60 years. Each lCER must be verified and certified every five years until the end of the crediting period. When a tCER or lCER expires and can no longer be renewed it must be replaced by a "permanent" credit such as an AAU, CER, ERU or RMU (and not an lCER or tCER).
Emission Reduction Units (ERUs)	Kyoto Protocol	Project-based credits issued pursuant to the Kyoto Protocol Joint Implementation (JI) mechanism.[8] ERUs are issued by the host country governments of JI projects, which must convert AAUs to ERUs in order to issue them to project participants.
New South Wales Greenhouse Gas Abatement Certificates (NGACs)	New South Wales Greenhouse Gas Reduction Scheme (GGAS)[9]	Project-based credits created under the Australian state of New South Wales' Greenhouse Gas Reduction Scheme (GGAS). NGACs can be generated by approved abatement certificate providers which develop projects that lead to low-emissions electricity generation, improved energy efficiency, biological CO_2 sequestration, or on-site emissions reductions not directly related to electricity consumption. A registry records the registration and transfer of NGACs. GGAS does not allow for the use of offset credits generated outside of the state of NSW.[10]

---

8   Article 6, Kyoto Protocol.
9   This scheme is administered in Australia under the Electricity Supply Act 1995 (NSW).
10   K Hamilton, R Bayon, G Turner and D Higgins, "State of the Voluntary Carbon Market 2007 Picking Up Steam", *Ecosystem Marketplace and New Carbon Finance* (July 17 2007) at 14.

Where they fall outside a regulated scheme, the right to all legal and equitable title in the abatement or sequestration action taken by the project must be legally defined and captured in a contract. These credits are often referred to as voluntary carbon credits because they are not created under a mandatory emissions trading scheme. There are two main types of voluntary carbon credits, namely Verified Emission Reductions (VERs) and non-verified Emission Reductions, which are described in Table 3.

Table 3: The two types of voluntary carbon credits

Carbon credit type (Voluntary carbon credits)	Source of legal authority	Description
Verified Emission Reductions (VERs)[11]	Contract	Contractually based credits that have been subjected to some form of third-party verification.
Non-verified Emission Reductions	Contract	Same as VERs except they have not been subjected to third-party verification.

Organised voluntary schemes, such as the Chicago Climate Exchange and the Commonwealth Government's Greenhouse Friendly programme in Australia, operate using contractual agreements and therefore anticipate the generation and transaction of contractually based credits. In such voluntary schemes, the underlying emission reductions must be verified according to approved standards and guidelines. Contractually based credits may also be created outside an established voluntary trading scheme and sold to companies or individuals seeking to offset their carbon emissions and reduce their "carbon footprint".

As voluntary carbon credits rely on contract for their legal status, it is essential that contracts which create or transact voluntary carbon credits provide a clear and comprehensive definition of the right being dealt with. The critical components of any contractual definition of emission reductions must include the following:[12]

- a reference to the physical reduction in levels of greenhouse gas emissions;
- a clear definition of the greenhouse gases to be included (generally being those under the Kyoto Protocol);[13]

---

11   Some people now use the acronym VER to mean voluntary emission reduction, which can lead to confusion. We continue to use VER to mean Verified Emission Reduction, since this is the original usage and the more accepted amongst climate change lawyers. See C Carr and F Rosembuj "World Bank experiences in contracting for emission reductions" (2007) 2 *Environmental Liability* 114 at 117; A Beatty and E Williams, "Trends in Carbon Trading: Practical Lessons" (Paper presented at Asia-Pacific Centre for Environmental Law Conference on Crucial Issues in Climate Change and the Kyoto Mechanisms in Asia, Singapore, 2007) at 3.

12   M Wilder and P Curnow. "Trading Carbon as a Commodity – Sale and Purchase Agreements for Carbon Credits" (2005) *29th Annual AMPLA Conference* (August 24 to 27 2005) at 7.

- a clear unit of measurement, usually being per tonne of CO_2e;
- reference to the particular and clearly defined project creating the reductions;
- the basis against which such reductions are occurring (ie against a pre-determined baseline); and
- a statement of the assessment methodology involved in verifying the carbon credits (this is particularly important for contractually based credits which are created pursuant to a voluntary framework – where statutory-based credits are sold, the legislative framework will establish the assessment methodology).

2.3 Voluntary carbon credits and the concern for quality

Verified Emissions Reductions emerged as an instrument for defining CO_2e emissions abatement or sequestration rights in contracts written before the rules of many international (in particular the CDM) and domestic regulated schemes had been settled.[14] The verification process for those emissions reductions was performed in line with the developing national or international regulatory standards and regulatory schemes with the intention that the VERs would be "converted" in the future for use in regulatory regimes.[15] When the rules for the CDM became established, many contracts began defining the credits being traded as CERs whereas before they had used VERs.

For buyers who did not intend to convert credits for use in a regulated scheme, third-party verification was less of a concern, and they would often buy non-verified ERs at cheaper prices than could be obtained for VERs. However, the growth in the consumer-based voluntary offset market, increasing criticism of the environmental benefits of non-verified credits[16] and the reputational risk a company faces if credits it has purchased are exposed as not being backed up by genuine emissions reductions has led to an increasing tendency amongst voluntary credit buyers to favour quality over price and purchase VERs even when they have no intention of later converting them for use in a regulated scheme.[17] VERs continue to be in high demand in markets such as the United States, where the details of anticipated mandatory emission trading schemes have not been settled as they offer the potential to be converted for use in the those future schemes.[18]

---

13 The targets established under the Kyoto Protocol cover emissions of six GHGs, which are listed in Annex A to the Protocol – carbon dioxide (CO_2), methane (CH_4), nitrous oxide (N_2O), hydrofluorocarbons (HFCs), perfluorocarbons (PFCs) and sulphur hexafluoride (SF_6).
14 C Carr and F Rosembuj "World Bank Experiences in Contracting for Emission Reductions" (2007) 2 *Environmental Liability* 114 to 117.
15 M Wilder and P Curnow. "Trading Carbon as a Commodity – Sale and Purchase Agreements for Carbon Credits" (2005), 29th Annual AMPLA Conference (August 24 to 27 2005) at 6.
16 F Harvey. "Beware the Carbon Offsetting Cowboys", *Financial Times* (April 25 2007); F Harvey and S Fidler. "Industry Caught in 'Carbon Credit' Smokescreen", *Financial Times* (April 25 2007).
17 A Beatty and E Williams, "Trends in Carbon Trading: Practical Lessons" (Paper presented at Asia-Pacific Centre for Environmental Law Conference on Crucial Issues in Climate Change and the Kyoto Mechanisms in Asia, Singapore, 2007) at 1; K Hamilton, R Bayon, G Turner and D Higgins, "State of the Voluntary Carbon Market 2007 Picking Up Steam", *Ecosystem Marketplace and New Carbon Finance* (July 17 2007) at 8.
18 New Carbon Finance, "Record volume of voluntary carbon credits offered in fast-growing US market" (August 30 2007). One example of a US company buying VERs for this reason, American Electric Power, which entered an agreement in June 2007 to purchase 4.6 million credits via the Chicago Climate Exchange for the period from 2010 to 2017, in anticipation of some form of carbon constraining mandate being placed on the company by 2010: Point Carbon, "AEP buys 4.6 million offset carbon credits" (June 14 2007).

An additional element required for the contractual definition of a VER is the process for third-party verification and the standard against which the carbon credit is being verified. In response to the increasing concern about the quality of voluntary credits there has been a proliferation in the number of voluntary carbon standards against which verification can occur.[19] Prominent standards include the Voluntary Carbon Standard and the Gold Standard, both administered by NGOs, and the Greenhouse Friendly standard administered by the Australian Government.

A key criticism levelled at VERs is that there are no central registries for VERs at the national or global levels. This gives rise to the potential for double counting or sellers offering the same credits for sale multiple times. By contrast, CERs generated under the CDM, for example, are tracked on an international registry. For companies purchasing VERs it is important that they exercise extreme care in their due diligence process for assessing sellers. A number of VER registries have emerged[20] which offer a mechanism for assisting buyers to track the history of a carbon credit, but which cannot guarantee that the credit has not been sold off-registry.

3.   **Motivations behind purchasing credits**

The nature of the carbon credit that will be involved in any given transaction depends largely on the buyer's motivation behind purchasing the carbon credit. There are four main motivations for purchasing carbon credits:

- immediate compliance with legal obligations, such as those under the Kyoto Protocol or the EU ETS;
- an anticipated requirement to comply with future legal obligations – parties may purchase credits for the purpose of complying with the legal obligation when it is imposed;
- to achieve some voluntary goal by way of voluntary compliance with voluntary targets established by virtue of social responsibility or a desire to gain experience in carbon trading in the voluntary market in order to prepare for a future where legal obligations create a carbon-constrained environment; and
- for trading and investment purposes – as with any commodity market, the carbon market has investors and speculators who aim to make money from trading carbon credits.

The motivation behind the purchase of carbon credits affects, in turn, whether the credits are created by virtue of a regulatory framework, or whether they are created and evidenced purely by way of a contractual agreement.

4.   **Legal issues concerning the nature of a carbon credit**

When dealing with carbon credits generated under regulated systems, a number of important legal issues arise from the treaty or statute upon which the scheme is based. Each scheme has its own requirements and rules, of which buyers and sellers must be

---

19   K Hamilton, R Bayon, G Turner and D Higgins, "State of the Voluntary Carbon Market 2007 Picking Up Steam", *Ecosystem Marketplace and New Carbon Finance* (July 17 2007) at 38 to 43.

20   See K Hamilton, R Bayon, G Turner and D Higgins, "State of the Voluntary Carbon Market 2007 Picking Up Steam", *Ecosystem Marketplace and New Carbon Finance* (July 17 2007) at 44 to 47.

aware when looking to trade in carbon credits intended to be used under a regulated scheme. For example, some types of projects will not be allowed to generate credits under one scheme but will be under another. The NSW GGAS system allows NGACs to be generated by forestry sequestration projects, activities that result in reduced consumption of electricity and low-emission electricity generation projects. Forestry projects under GGAS must be maintained for 100 years.[21] Under the CDM to generate CERs, forestry projects must be maintained for five to 60 years, with different types of credits being issued for forestry projects of different duration.[22] The EU ETS allows regulated installations to import a limited number of CERs in order to help them cover any shortfalls in EUAs, but will not allow any CERs generated from forestry projects, nuclear projects or hydropower projects which involve dams with more than 20MW capacity and do not comply with the World Commission on Dams' Sustainability Guidelines.[23]

In addition to the specific regulatory requirements for statute or treaty-based credits, transactions involving both regulated credits and voluntary or contractually-based credits need to be considered in the context of other existing areas of law, including in relation to ownership rights and status under taxation and financial services regulation. Contracts for the purchase and sale of carbon credits must take these key legal issues into account to ensure that title is properly passed from seller to buyer and all related contingencies are dealt with.

4.1 Property rights and ownership

The basis on which an "offset" style of credit is generated – that is, the abatement or sequestration of greenhouse gases in the atmosphere – is merely an action which in the absence of specific legislation has no inherent legal or property status. Furthermore, the ownership of the emissions reductions achieved by the project and the ownership of carbon credits which have been created from those emissions reductions can often be separated, although to attempt to use both as separate rights will not create two separate reductions in greenhouse gas emissions. As such, carbon credit transactions usually involve the transaction of the right to the underlying emissions reductions and to all carbon credits which are generated in relation to those emissions reductions.

Where a carbon credit is an "allowance" or "permit" style of credit, the legislation under which that allowance is granted may well determine the legal or property status of the relevant credit.

The Kyoto Protocol is silent on whether Kyoto credits create a property right, although they do provide rules according to which Kyoto credits can be generated and transferred.

The legal status of a particular carbon credit (including its treatment for property, tax and accounting purposes) will generally hinge on the particular domestic law of the jurisdiction in which that credit is created or held. Under some domestic legal

---

21   "Greenhouse Gas Benchmark Rule (Carbon Sequestration) 2003", Clause 5(e).

22   "Modalities and procedures for afforestation and reforestation project activities under the clean development mechanism in the first commitment period of the Kyoto Protocol", Decision 5/CMP.1, 1st Meeting of the UNFCCC Conference of Parties serving as the Meeting of Parties to the Kyoto Protocol, [38] to [60], UN Doc FCCC/KP/CMP/2005/8/Add.1 (2006).

23   Articles 11(a)(3) and 11(a)(6), Directive 2004/101/EC of The European Parliament and of the Council of October 27 2004.

systems, carbon credits can be seen as bearing some, if not all, of the characteristics of personal property. For example, a carbon credit can be viewed as an intangible type of personal property to a particular legal benefit arising from a certain action (analogous to an intellectual property right). However, in other jurisdictions carbon credits can also be regarded as having some of the characteristics of a service, a natural resource or a permit. Moreover, in most jurisdictions, there is little or no legislation dealing specifically with property rights in carbon credits, so a "first principles" analysis based on general domestic law must usually be undertaken.

The silence of both the Kyoto Protocol and most domestic laws on the nature of carbon credits in the property rights context leaves participants in the carbon market with little guidance about several key points. For example, there is no direction about who is entitled to carbon credits in the case of a dispute between different entities involved in the project which generated the credit, whether and under what conditions credits may be expropriated, what happens to credits if the holder becomes insolvent, or how credit transactions are to be executed and secured.

For project-based credits, in most domestic property regimes there is a working assumption that it is the person responsible for implementing an emission reduction project (usually the owner of the land or site on which a project is developed) who is prima facie entitled to emission reductions (and resulting carbon credits) arising from the project. This assumption can of course be negated by any local law or policy to the contrary. For example, a government may seek to claim rights over all carbon credits generated on state-owned land or by state-owned resources, which in some countries may include many key renewable energy resources, such as water and wind resources.[24]

The working assumption that the developer of the emission reduction project is entitled to the carbon credits arising from the project is borne out by the practice of Kyoto Protocol parties under the Clean Development Mechanism and Joint Implementation framework. The Kyoto Protocol and accompanying rules[25] provide that CERs and ERUs will be granted to participants in a CDM or JI project in accordance with the instructions the participants communicate to the CDM Executive Board or JI Supervisory Committee respectively. However, each participant is required to obtain a letter of authorisation from a Kyoto Protocol party. The local project participant, which must obtain an approval from the host country of the relevant CDM or JI project, is ordinarily the developer of the emission reduction project itself. Most host countries will approve the participation of the developer of the emission reduction project, and thereby impliedly consent to CERs or ERUs being

---

24   The policy of the New Zealand government in relation to carbon credits is an interesting example of how domestic policy can influence the property rights of carbon credits. The New Zealand government initially took the view that all rights and obligations under the Kyoto Protocol prima facie vest in the Crown and adopted a policy of retaining ownership over all Kyoto credits that could be generated by emissions reductions activities in New Zealand. This policy position led to significant protests from the forestry sector, which argued that it should be entitled to the property rights in the emissions reductions generated from forestry sequestration. The New Zealand government has now adopted a policy of devolving the rights to Kyoto credits through an emissions trading scheme and through the Permanent Forest Sinks Initiative. See C Streck and R O'Sullivan, *Forests and Climate Change: Will Emission Trading Make a Difference?* (to be published 2008).

25   Subsequent COP/MOP decisions and guidance from the CDM Executive Board and JI Supervisory Committee.

issued to that project developer, or to any entities to which that project developer has on-sold the CERs or ERUs.

However, third parties may still challenge the legal title of project participants to carbon credits. In addition, if a party that has entered into a forward transaction to receive a stream of carbon credits from a project becomes insolvent, the administrator and creditors will need to determine who is entitled under domestic law to receive the credits to which that entity would be entitled. For this reason, any contracts purporting to transact emission reductions or carbon credits should specifically deal with the issue of legal title, even where the relevant legal framework under which those credits are created operates on a working assumption in respect of legal title to such credits (eg the Kyoto Protocol).

In some circumstances it may be difficult to establish which entity is responsible for implementing a particular project activity and thereby at first instance entitled to the emission reductions and carbon credits created by that activity. For example, a particular project may involve a lessor of land, a lessee and a sub-lessee of the land, an owner of project infrastructure, a project manager responsible for implementing the project activity, a government granting a concession deed and a mortgagee, all of whom may consider that they have an entitlement to any emission reductions and carbon credits resulting from the project. In such projects, the appropriate "seller" of carbon credits (ie the entity prima facie entitled to the credits generated by the project) may be difficult to identify. A prudent purchaser of carbon credits from such a project would seek evidence that all of the entities with a potential claim to the credits had consented to the particular "seller" dealing with the carbon credits in the manner envisaged in the sales contract.

(a)   *Addressing uncertainty in legal title to carbon credits*

In order to deal with the risks inherent in this uncertainty around property rights to carbon credits, it is important that contracts for the purchase and sale of carbon credits clearly define the credit asset for sale in a manner that is consistent with the characteristics of a freely tradable property right. These characteristics include:

- a clearly identifiable and definable right, which exists within a clear legal or policy framework;
- clear ownership over the right, to the exclusion of all other potential claimants;
- irrevocability of transfer of title, or revocability only subject to certain pre-established criteria; and
- transferability of the carbon credit itself (including an agreed process by which such credit is deemed to be transferred).

As a matter of prudence, in contracting to transact carbon credits, the relevant documentation should also clearly establish the point at which legal title transfers from seller to buyer. In addition, for the buyer's protection, such contracts should also contain an unconditional warranty from the seller that it holds unencumbered title to the underlying emission reductions and the resultant carbon credits, upon delivery of the credits to the buyer. Although such provisions cannot prevent conflicting claims to legal title arising, they assist the buyer to establish to third parties that it is a bona fide purchaser for value, and would also enable the buyer to claim damages from the seller if the buyer's title is challenged.

(b)   ***Example: CERs within the CDM context***

A key portion of the global carbon market is constituted by the sale and purchase of Certified Emission Reductions (CERs) generated by Clean Development Mechanism projects in developing country parties to the Kyoto Protocol.

Although the Kyoto Protocol international rules both create and recognise CERs,[26] they do not directly deal with the issue of legal entitlement to greenhouse gas abatement of CERs. Nevertheless, it can be implied from the manner in which Kyoto Protocol parties have implemented the approval of CDM projects and participation therein (as discussed above) that the project proponent responsible for implementing a project which reduces greenhouse gas emissions has a prima facie legal title to the emission reductions and the CERs that flow from them, and that such CERs may be dealt with in the same way as other kinds of property.

This assumption, however, may be overridden by domestic law or contrary contractual arrangements. For example, domestic law could provide that the government holds title of the emission reductions and the resultant CERs.[27] Alternatively, domestic laws may restrict the types of entities that may become project participants. For example, the Chinese CDM regulations limit the number of agencies that may sell CERs and that a CDM project developer must be at least 51% Chinese-owned.[28]

As noted above, however, most domestic jurisdictions are also silent on the issue. Accordingly, in most domestic jurisdictions, the property developer(s) have a prima facie entitlement to the emission reductions from the project.

Notwithstanding that the developers may be entitled to the underlying emission reductions, if the project developer(s) wish to register the project under the CDM, the government of the host country has the discretion to decide which local entities may actually develop a CDM project (and thereby receive the CERs or distribute the CERs to purchasers of these credits). This is due to the fact that projects cannot be registered as CDM projects until the host country government approves the project and authorises the potential project developer as a participant in the relevant project.[29] Without such approval, the developer will not be able to receive CERs under the international rules. Experience to date has shown that most host countries have authorised project participants and the receipt of CERs.

---

26   Article 12, Kyoto Protocol.

27   Such a position has been taken by the New Zealand government, although as an Annex I country the relevant Kyoto credit is ERUs. See above n 24.

28   Article 11 of the "Measures for Operation and Management of Clean Development Mechanism Projects in China" (2005). The NDRC in the People's Republic of China has agreed in principle that a "PRC party" can include entities established in the Special Administrative Region of Hong Kong; however, it is still unclear under what circumstances this will be allowed.

29   Clarifications on Validation Requirements to be Checked by a Designated Operational Entity, 8th Meeting of the CDM Executive Board, Annex 3 at [2(a)], UN Doc CDM-EB-8 Annex 3 (2003); Modalities and procedures for a clean development mechanism as defined in Article 12 of the Kyoto Protocol, Decision 3/CMP.1, 1st Meeting of the UNFCCC Conference of Parties serving as the Meeting of Parties, Annex at [40(a)], UN Doc FCCC/KP/CMP/2005/8/Add.1 (2006).

The uncertainties within domestic laws may leave some scope for third parties to challenge legal title to CERs. Accordingly, when contracting to transact CERs it is crucial to include in the contract the types of provisions discussed above in respect of the transfer of legal title. Further prudent measures to ensure that project participants actually receive CERs from the project include:

- due diligence in order to determine whether there are other entities that could actually make competing claims to the CERs, and the likelihood of the success of such claims;
- ensuring that such entities have been consulted in respect of the development of the project and, ideally, the project developer has entered into arrangements with any entities identified as potential claimants to legal title to establish the project developer's rights to sell the CERs arising from the project;
- ensuring that the project developer purporting to be the "seller" of CERs is listed as a project participant in the project documentation and has obtained a letter of approval for the host country authorising participation in the relevant project;
- making provision for the project developer to add other participants in the project (including the purchaser(s) of CERs from the project), if this should prove necessary; and
- the provision of the allocation statement to the CDM Executive Board which instructs the Executive Board to issue the requisite quantity of CERs to the project developer's registry account or the account of the purchaser(s) to whom that entity has on-sold the CERs.

4.2   Carbon credits within existing legal frameworks

(a)   Introduction

As mentioned above, carbon credits are created by contract or by virtue of specific legislation or treaty, but they exist and are transacted in the context of other domestic legal frameworks. Such frameworks include accounting requirements, taxation, financial services and foreign investment regulation.

There are a number of salient taxation and financial services regulation issues surrounding the generation and purchase of carbon credits. As taxation and financial services regulation varies between jurisdictions, the treatment of carbon credits under such regulations will vary depending on where a credit is created and how it is transacted.

Four key questions which should be considered in any carbon credit transaction are:
- Is the sale of a carbon credit treated as a derivatives transaction under the laws by which the seller of the credit is bound?
- What are the possible foreign exchange controls that may be applied to payment for carbon credit transactions where the payment is made in a currency other than the host country currency?
- How are carbon credit transactions to be taxed under the law of the buyer and seller? and

- If the carbon credit transaction is cross-border, or the project developer is a foreign national, is the emission reduction project subject to any restrictions on foreign direct investment?

(b) *Will the sale of a carbon credit be treated as a derivatives transaction?*

The classification of the sale of carbon credits as a derivatives transaction could mean that such transactions are regulated under the financial services regulation of the host country. For example, Australian financial services laws[30] require a person to hold a financial services licence if that person deals in financial products. A financial product includes a facility designed to manage financial risk (ie avoids or limits the financial consequences of fluctuations in market prices). A "derivative" is considered to be a financial product. A derivative is an arrangement where:

- a party to the arrangement must (or may be required to) provide consideration in the future (ie any time after the moment of entry into the agreement); and
- the amount of the consideration, or the value of the arrangement, is determined by, derived from or varies by reference to, the value or amount of something else (of any nature and whether or not deliverable), including an asset, an interest or exchange rate, an index or a commodity.

Under this analysis, if a purchaser of a carbon credit in Australia used a forward contract to purchase credits on a particular date in the future for a price determined by reference to a market index on or close to settlement, then the forward will be a derivative and the purchaser may be required to hold an Australian financial services licence to enter into the trade.

Under US law, the definition of a security includes instruments such as notes, stocks, bonds and similar items, as well as documents traded for speculation or investment and any interest or "instrument commonly known as a security".[31] The definition of a security also includes so-called "investment contracts". Carbon credits would not appear to fall within any of the specific categories of instruments that are deemed securities in US law. However, the arrangement governing the sale of carbon credits may meet the definition of an "investment contract" depending on the nature and structure of the carbon credit transaction, in which case US securities law would apply and the contract would have to be registered with the SEC. Generally, an "investment contract" is defined as a "contract, transaction or scheme" whereby a person invests "money in a common enterprise and is led to expect profits solely from the efforts of the promoter or a third party".[32] An arrangement will not be an investment contract unless four elements are present:[33]

- the investment of money;

---

30   Chapter 7, Corporations Act 2001 (Cth).
31   See Section 2(1) of the Securities Act of 1933 (US) and Section 3(1) of the Securities Exchange Act of 1934 (US) for the full definition of security and list of instruments which will be considered a security for the purpose of US law.
32   *SEC v W J Howey Co* 328 US 293 (1946).
33   *SEC v W J Howey Co* 328 US 293 (1946); *United Housing Foundation, Inc v Forman*, 421 US 837, 852 (1975).

- in a common scheme or enterprise;
- with expectation of profits; and
- to come solely from the managerial or entrepreneurial effort of others.

Whether a carbon credit is a security for the purposes of UK law is governed by the UK Financial Services and Markets Act 2000 (FSMA). While carbon credits or emissions reductions are not likely to fall within the categories of regulated investments[34] which automatically trigger the application of UK securities law, certain arrangements may lead to securities law applying to a carbon credit transaction. Interests in a carbon fund established as a trust are likely to constitute units in a collective investment scheme, which are deemed securities.[35] Alternatively, if the transaction is a forward contract to purchase carbon credits, it could constitute a derivative contract, which will attract the application of UK securities law.

It is quite possible that similar requirements may apply in host countries of emission reduction projects (eg CDM host countries). If so, a market-indexed transaction could require one or both parties to hold a financial services licence or equivalent. It is important to analyse carbon credit transactions in the context of existing domestic financial services and derivatives legislation, to ensure that all applicable legal requirements in this regard are complied with.

(c) **What are the possible foreign exchange controls that may be applied to payment for carbon credit transactions where the payment is made in a currency other than the host country currency?**

Many countries regulate foreign investment into projects and transactions. For example, some countries have foreign exchange controls to restrict or limit the influx of foreign currency into a particular country.

On the other hand, many cross-border carbon credit transactions will provide that payment for delivered credits will be made in a currency other than the local host country currency. In this case, it is important to ascertain whether local law may place any restriction on the seller's receipt of funds in a foreign currency.

Even where no such foreign exchange controls apply, a seller may of course still face a foreign exchange risk that is enlivened if the seller defaults in delivery of the credits and must purchase in other currencies in the international market to honour its contractual obligations to the purchaser of carbon credits from the seller.

(d) **How are carbon credit transactions to be taxed under the law of the buyer and seller?**

In certain jurisdictions, the transaction of carbon credits may be considered the supply of a good or service and therefore subject to value-added or similar tax. In addition, the transaction of carbon credits between related companies may be subject to transfer pricing regulation.

---

34   The list of regulated investments can be found in the Financial Services and Markets Act 2000 (Regulated Activities) Order 2001.
35   Section 235 of Financial Services and Markets Act 2000.

Finally, in some jurisdictions it is possible that "participation" in an emission reduction project (even by simply purchasing CERs from such project) may lead to an analysis that an entity has a permanent establishment in the host country jurisdiction and is therefore subject to host country income tax regulation.

Some international and domestic regulation may impose specific taxes on carbon credits, or the revenues arising from the transaction of such credits. For example, in the international context the Kyoto Protocol rules require the UNFCCC Secretariat to deduct 2% of each issuance of CERs. The CERs collected through this "share of proceeds" deduction are placed in a separate account maintained by the UNFCCC Secretariat, which will be used towards assisting least developed countries to meet the costs of adaptation to climate change.[36] In the domestic context, China requires CDM project developers to pay a "sustainable development levy" based on the revenues received from the sale of CERs from the project.[37] The amount of the levy varies depending on the project type, with projects perceived as contributing directly to sustainable development in China being taxed at the lowest rate of 2%.

Such taxation considerations are clearly relevant for both sellers and purchasers of carbon credits. As the tax treatment varies between jurisdictions, a case-by-case analysis is necessary in the context of each individual transaction of carbon credits.

(e)   *If the carbon credit transaction is cross-border, or the project developer is a foreign national, is the emission reduction project subject to any restrictions on foreign direct investment?*
Finally, the domestic laws of many countries impose restrictions on foreign ownership and/or control of capital investment projects, including emission reduction projects. Indeed, many CDM host countries impose restrictions on foreign direct investment in major projects. These restrictions, however, are also jurisdiction-specific. China, for example, requires CDM project developers to be at least 51% Chinese owned.[38]

5.   Conclusion

There are a number of different types of carbon credits created by virtue of treaty or legislation (such as the Kyoto Protocol or the EU Emissions Trading Scheme), or by virtue of contracts which record transactions of voluntary emission reductions utilised to meet voluntary greenhouse reduction targets, or to offset the emissions of products and services. The nature of these carbon credits varies depending on how and where they are created and the purpose for which (and the location in which) they will be used.

There is a sparsity of regulation dealing specifically with the legal nature of, and the property rights inherent in, carbon credits. However, it is possible to analyse

---

36   Article 12.8, Kyoto Protocol; Modalities and procedures for a clean development mechanism as defined in Article 12 of the Kyoto Protocol, Decision 17/CP.7, 7th Meeting of the UNFCCC Conference of Parties [15(a)], UN Doc FCCC/CP/2001/13/Add.2 (2001). Note that at [15(b)] projects hosted by least developed countries are exempt from the share of proceeds contribution.
37   Article 24 of the "Measures for Operation and Management of Clean Development Mechanism Projects in China" (2005).
38   See text accompanying n 28.

existing legal frameworks, including property laws, financial service regulation, tax laws and foreign investment laws, to determine how the creation and transaction of carbon credits will be treated in the context of a specific transaction.

Prudent sellers and purchasers of carbon credits should turn their minds to these considerations early in the preparation of a transaction, to ensure that they understand the legal treatment of the credits which they are transacting and can accurately assess the risks and opportunities arising from the transaction.

Market contracts

Anju Sanehi
Hunton & Williams

1.   Emissions trading

Emissions trading, as a market-based alternative to the traditional "command and control" approach to realising environmental goals, has emerged over the last two decades.[1] Though the European Union Emissions Trading Scheme (EU ETS)[2] does not have the distinction of being the first trading market created by environmental regulation, it does represent a landmark in being the world's first large-scale greenhouse gas trading programme. In 2006, trading of European Union Allowances, (EUAs) – the units issued under the EU ETS – was valued at nearly US$25 billion (€19 billion), out of an estimated total carbon trading market worth US$30 billion (€23 billion).[3]

Though still a relatively immature market, subject to both regulatory and political uncertainty, the general expectation is for the continued expansion of the EU ETS. The numbers of industrial sectors and installations regulated and the gases covered are set to increase. It is designed to link in[4] with trading schemes of non-EU countries such as Norway and Switzerland and, more significantly, designed to accept carbon credits[5] and link into international emissions trading under the Kyoto Protocol.[6]

Over and above other carbon trading schemes – both voluntary and mandatory – the EU ETS shows the greatest potential for providing both the traction and the model for a global carbon trading market. It is, thus, unsurprising that standard emission trading contracts have developed most rapidly for the trading of EUAs and carbon credits from project mechanisms under the Kyoto Protocol. This chapter will thus concentrate on energy trading contracts in use in the EU ETS market.

2   What is being traded under EU ETS

The units issued under the EU ETS are EUAs, whilst the international trading scheme under the Kyoto Protocol deals in Assigned Amount Units (AAUs), Certified Emission Reductions (CERs), Emission Reduction Units (ERUs) and Removal Units (RMUs).

---

1   Most notably under the Clean Air Act Amendments 1990 controlling sulphur dioxide in the United States.
2   The EU ETS is a scheme established pursuant to Directive 2003/87/EC to trade greenhouse gas emission allowances within the European Union.
3   The World Bank "States and Trends of the Carbon Market 2007" in Cooperation with the International Emissions Trading Association – page 3 (May 2007).
4   Pursuant to Directive 2004/101/EC, commonly referred to as the Linking Directive.
5   Articles 12 and 6 of the Kyoto Protocol provide flexible mechanisms that create carbon credits – certified emission reductions and emission reduction units respectively – that are fungible with EUAs. See section 2 of this chapter.
6   Pursuant to Article 17 of the Kyoto Protocol.

Allowances such as EUAs and AAUs permit the right to emit 1tCO$_2$e, whilst ERUs and CERs (and in the future RMUs) provide *a credit* to emit 1tCO2e. Nevertheless, the commodity being traded within EU ETS and within the international trading scheme under the Kyoto Protocol is 1tCO2e and as such that commodity is fungible or interchangeable, allowing trading of these units as equal units.

As well as differences in how and by whom these units are issued, there are differences in the periods within which they can be used for EU ETS compliance purposes,[7] the permanence of the units and restrictions on use of these commodities for compliance purposes.[8] There are also price differentials between these commodities – for instance CERs and ERUs carry the risk of project performance and so trade at a discount to EUAs. Though less marked, some market commentators have also noted price differentials within commodity classes linked to provenance – so in some instances buyers have paid a premium for CERs from Gold Standard[9] projects or sought a discount for CERs from less well perceived projects such as HFC[10] projects. All these differences between the different units provide the opportunity for arbitrage and so promote trading.

3.   Who is trading

3.1   Compliance buyers
The EU ETS, as with other cap-and-trade schemes,[11] permits operators of facilities that have to surrender allowances (compliance operators) to reduce their emissions and then sell off the surplus allowances to operators that have not been able to reduce emissions or have increased their operations and so need to surrender more allowances.

Such operators may review the price of carbon against other factors such as fuel and power prices – a low power price may mean that the operator would make more money selling its surplus allowances than selling any power it produces. Such trading parties may adopt sophisticated trading strategies, to keep their carbon position balanced, such as by trading the difference between allowances and the gas/electricity spark price spread. In addition compliance operators may trade in carbon credits as they are an attractively priced alternative to EUAs in meeting compliance under EU ETS. Compliance operators are, and will continue to be, responsible for a significant percentage of trading volume.

---

7   In Phase I of EU ETS, EUAs and CERs may be used for compliance, whilst in Phase II ERUs and in some limited circumstances AAUs may also be used.
8   EU member states have differing caps on the number of carbon credits originating from projects under the Kyoto Protocol that can be used for compliance purposes.
9   The Gold Standard is a set of voluntary guidelines produced by, *inter alia*, the Worldwide Fund for Nature, seeking to ensure sustainable development.
10   Hydro Flurocarbon destruction projects.
11   Emissions trading, typically, involves the establishment of a cap-and-trade system. A regulatory body establishes a limit (cap) on a particular pollutant emitted by a group of installations for a specified period of time (a compliance period). The regulatory body allocates emission allowances to the regulated facilities. The total amount of allowances allocated cannot exceed the cap. At the end of the compliance period each facility is required to surrender an equivalent number of emission allowances to cover its emissions during the compliance period. Some entities may need to buy emission extra allowances to run their operations, whilst others, through more efficient running or a reduction in operations, may have surplus units that can be sold (trading). The theory being that those that can easily reduce emissions most cheaply will do so.

3.2   Traders

Successful trading requires liquidity and so EU ETS does not limit trading to just the regulated emitters – any person may hold allowances.[12] This presents opportunities for third parties that are not regulated by EU ETS to trade allowances. Financial traders, including investment banks, carbon funds and commodity traders, treat allowances as just another alternative asset class. Their trades are speculative and make use of the opportunities for arbitrage between compliance periods and prices of the different allowances and carbon credits.

3.3   Governments

Another significant group involved in trading are governments seeking to meet Kyoto Protocol compliance requirements. Countries that are parties to the Kyoto Protocol and that fail to meet their emission targets face, *inter alia*, suspension of trading and making up the difference in the second Kyoto compliance period, plus a penalty of 30%. Governments are mainly involved in buying Kyoto units via bespoke agreements. Some governments, such as the Belgian, Austrian and the Dutch, already have well-developed procurement programmes.

3.4   NGO or off-setters

Another category of traders that are not compliance traders is a diverse group of "voluntary" traders. These range from non-governmental organisations that purchase allowances in order to retire them, thus ensuring tighter emission reductions, to corporates seeking to offset emissions from their unregulated operations and thus achieve self-imposed carbon neutrality (either for corporate social responsibility or branding reasons) or, increasingly as climate change concerns become mainstreamed, to offer customers set-off services.

4.   Development of trading under EU ETS

Trading of EUAs commenced in 2005 with the start of EU ETS, though in fact the first forward trade occurred long before that in 2003, between Shell Trading and Nuon Energy Trade and Wholesale.[13] Most trading markets start as a spot market (one-off contracts – known as spot contracts – for the sale and purchase of a commodity at an agreed price, with delivery and payment occurring within days of the trade). Interestingly, the EU ETS developed forward trades (contracts for the sale and purchase of a commodity at an agreed price but with delivery and payment occurring some time in the future) first. Part of the reason for this is that EUAs are bankable (though Phase I EUAs are only bankable in Phase I, subsequent phases allow banking between phases) and thus encourage forward trading. Another, more practical, reason has been that since 2005, CERs have been able to be used to satisfy compliance under EU ETS; however, CERs have not been able to be transferred to national registries, as the International Transaction Log has not yet become fully functional. Accordingly, traders in CERs have had to transact forward trades.

---

12   Article 19(2) of Directive 2003/87/EC provides that any person may hold allowances.
13   Shell Press Release dated February 27 2004.

With increasing confidence in the EU ETS, traders are not only transacting spot and forward trades but also developing options and swaps and other more exotic derivatives. Some market players are even taking options on future rights to emission commodities that may be subject to a quite different regulatory regime in Phase III of EU ETS, and even on commodities that may or may not exist after (unless extended) the Kyoto Protocol 2012 expiry date.

Emissions trading over the futures market has also developed since 2005. Futures trades, carried out on a regulated electronic trading platform, utilise standardised contracts produced by the exchange, with the exchange taking on credit and performance security. EUAs and some carbon credits are being traded on the futures markets on exchanges such as the European Climate Exchange and Nord pool. However, the majority of trades remain over-the-counter and bilateral trades rather than trades over exchanges.

5.   Development of trading documentation

Though the Kyoto Protocol and the EU ETS Directive[14] set the scene for trading, there are no provisions within the Protocol or the Directive that prescribe mechanisms for trading or standard-form trading contracts. The market has been left to develop trading forms shaped by the specific risks and characteristics of trading a commodity that is a creature of regulation.

Initially, this meant bespoke agreements had to be drafted. Primary trading (purchases of CERs and ERUs direct from the CDM or JI projects) still involves bespoke emission-reduction purchase agreements that reflect the performance and credit risks related to contracting with project developers. Even within the secondary market (ie the trading of allowances or carbon credits where the seller is not the original owner), one-off trades are still documented with single-trade agreements or long-form confirmations.

However, the development of a secondary market, with significant increases in both volumes and values being transacted, has led to the development of standard-form agreements. Standard-form agreements utilise the concept of an umbrella master agreement containing standard terms and incorporating particular preferences of the parties by way of an accompanying schedule and then recording individual deal-specifics in a confirmation – see section 7 below for more detail. It is the larger trading parties, which regularly trade emissions, that use the forms, because the need for credit, legal and back-office arrangements present entry barriers for smaller parties.

The advantages of standard-form agreements are that they promote market liquidity, transparency and reductions in transaction costs. Trading entities using standardised terms also avoid detailed and time-consuming negotiations every time they enter into a transaction, and the use of consistent trading terms every time they buy and sell means their purchase terms are back-to-back with their sales terms and so minimise legal risk exposure when they sell on. However, there is more than one set of standard-form agreements and, though there have been attempts in the development of these different standard forms to harmonise the provisions, some

---

14   Directive 2003/87/EC.

key differences remain – see section 9 below.

The forms continue to undergo further amendments, in particular, to deal with the different characteristics of Phase II of EU ETS and the trading of Kyoto carbon credits. Until the new forms are agreed, parties are negotiating additional language in annexes or in confirmations to cover Phase II EUA trading and trading of Kyoto carbon credits – see section 10 below.

In addition, the potential, within the emissions market, to hedge risks by the banking of emission allowances, forward markets and derivatives is pushing development and growth towards a full-scale derivatives market and a move for documentation to accommodate options, swaps and other exotics – see section 13 below. In time, further modifications may also need to be made to the standard forms to deal with specifics related to trading into Phase III of EU ETS and any descendant of, or alternative to, the Kyoto Protocol.

6.   Main standardised forms for EU ETS trading

The first standard-form emissions trading agreements were produced in 2004 to 2005. There have been several amendments since then and the forms continue to be refined, with further amendments expected. Unsurprisingly, the first standard-form agreements were published by the international market trading organisations, which adapted their existing standard forms for trading energy. In addition, IETA, an organisation set up to promote emissions trading, produced a stand-alone standard form.

The three main standard-form emissions trading agreements are produced by:
- the International Swaps and Derivatives Association, Inc (ISDA);
- the European Federation of Emissions Trading (EFET); and
- the International Emissions Trading Association (IETA).

The trading documents produced by these organisations are commonly referred to by the name of the sponsoring organisation, and therefore as the ISDA, EFET and IETA respectively. There are other standard forms, such as the Deutscher Rahmenvertag, which is preferred by some German entities as it is negotiated in German, but the ISDA, EFET and the IETA are the three in most widespread use and are described next.

6.1   The ISDA

In terms of member firms, the International Swaps and Derivatives Association, Inc, is the largest global financial trade association. Its membership consists of major commercial, merchant and investment banks, corporations, governments and other institutions that participate in the privately negotiated or over-the-counter derivatives market.

The association has produced two ISDA master agreements, the 1992 version which is still widely used in the market, and the 2002 version which is gradually increasing in usage. Care needs to taken when negotiating emissions trades under the ISDA to determine which version the parties have used and to ensure the definitions and the calculations for replacement costs in the event of a party not complying with its obligations are as intended by the parties.

Both ISDA master agreements were originally drafted for financially settled markets, but over time have incorporated a series of commodity definitions and annexes to accommodate the particular characteristics of the physically delivered markets. To trade emissions under the ISDA master agreements, ISDA published a form-of-allowances annex to be used as Part 6 to the schedule to the ISDA master agreements. There are two versions of the Part 6 form – one published in March 2006 (which provides for forward and spot transactions only) and a version published in September 2006 (which includes options). Further versions of both forms are being drafted at the time of writing to include modifications for Phase II delivery of EUAs. The Association has also published a long-form EU Emissions Allowance Confirmation for an over-the-counter physically-settled EUA transaction for parties that have not executed the Form of Part 6 because they do not expect regularly to trade emissions.

Legal opinions on the enforceability of the ISDA master agreements in various jurisdictions can be accessed by ISDA members via the ISDA website.

Parties that already have an ISDA master agreement in place find it advantageous simply to add the allowance trading form, thus ensuring that such trading is covered by the standard provisions and agreed netting and collateral provisions that govern the trading relationship of the parties in respect of their other traded commodities. Thus it is unsurprising that financial institutions with existing ISDA portfolios, and familiarity with the ISDA master agreements, tend towards using the ISDA allowance trading form.

6.2   The EFET

The European Federation of Energy Traders comprises a group of European energy trading entities. The Federation has published two master agreements governing the trading of power and gas – the EFET General Agreement concerning the Delivery and Acceptance of Electricity[15] and the EFET General Agreement concerning the Delivery and Acceptance of Natural Gas.[16] To deal with trading of allowances, the Federation published an Allowances Appendix[17] to the EFET General Agreement concerning the Delivery and Acceptance of Electricity and a similar Allowances Appendix to the EFET General Agreement concerning the Delivery and Acceptance of Natural Gas. Neither of the EFET allowances appendices provide for options.

EFET produces legal opinions in respect of the enforceability of the EFET master agreements in the various European jurisdictions. These are available from EFET for a fee. A separate legal opinion on the EFET Allowances Appendix has not been produced.

The EFET Power and EFET Gas master agreements are widely used by the European energy majors, particularly the incumbent suppliers which already have an existing EFET portfolio and so will seek to use the EFET Allowances Appendix.

---

15   Current version 2.1, published December 20 2000.
16   Current version 1.0, published March 2006.
17   Current version 2.0, published July 20 2005.

6.3   The IETA

The International Emissions Trading Association was formed to represent the interests of a variety of players involved in the development of an active, global greenhouse gas market. The Association developed and published the Emissions Trading Master Agreement (usually referred to as the IETA or IETA ETMA).[18] The IETA utilises the familiar format of a master agreement under which the individual trades are concluded and documented by means of a schedule and confirmation. The IETA has three schedules – schedule 1 contains the definitions; schedule 2 contains an elections sheet in which the parties set out their preferences and any amendments; and schedule 3 contains a form of confirmation. The IETA does not currently provide for the trading of options but a new version is being drafted to deal with Phase II of EU ETS, and which is expected to contain provisions covering options.

Again, similar to the ISDA and EFET, the IETA contemplates the parties undertaking multiple trades over a long period until the IETA is determined by either party. To document one-off transactions, the International Emissions Trading Association also published the Emissions Allowances Single Trade Agreement for the EU Scheme.[19]

Industry-wide legal opinions in respect of the IETA are available from the IETA website.

The advantages of the IETA is that it is relatively easy to negotiate and as such is being used by a variety of financial institutions, physical players, energy majors and some trading houses. The IETA only covers emissions trading and not any other commodities and so, though it does allow for netting of multiple emission trades, a master netting agreement will be required if cross-product netting is required.

7.   Documentation architecture

Though the nomenclature may be different, the basic format of the three standard forms is similar, consisting of (i) a master agreement, (ii) schedule, annexes and election sheets to the master agreement, which contains commercial terms (referred to for convenience in this chapter as the commercial terms schedule), (iii) an emission-specific schedule (IETA), form (ISDA) or allowances appendix (EFET) (referred to for convenience in this chapter as an emissions schedule), and (iv) a confirmation. These documents interlock as follows:

- *Master agreement* – the master agreement is a pre-printed framework agreement pursuant to which individual transactions may be carried out. The master agreements contain the main standard non-commercial terms such as capacity and authority, termination, defaults, set-off provisions, credit, tax, dispute resolution, governing and change of law. In essence, the master agreement deals with the key issues that parties negotiate prior to trading and that will govern the relationship between the parties – the master, once agreed, will remain effective indefinitely, until amended or cancelled by either party.

---

18   Current version 2.1, published June 13 2005.
19   Current version 3, published 2006.

- *The commercial terms schedule* – the commercial terms schedule is also a pre-printed document, but it allows the parties to tailor the terms in the master agreement by filling in the blanks or ticking the boxes to indicate particular preferences. It is also possible to add additional provisions or make bespoke amendments to the master agreement to record the parties' particular preferences and any amendments to the master agreement without amending the text of the master agreement itself. Typically, it is the negotiation of the commercial terms schedule that is the most contentious part of agreeing to a set of standard-form documents.
- *The emissions schedule* – the emissions schedule, also pre-printed, contains provisions in respect of emissions trading and will include a second set of elections for completion specifically in relation to emissions transactions. The emissions schedule allows parties to amend the master agreement or commercial terms schedule in respect of emission transactions and to add provisions to accommodate the unique positions of the parties.
- *The confirmation* – individual transactions are recorded by means of confirmations. The confirmation, often in letter format, sets out the commercial terms of each individual transaction entered into under the master agreement, as amended by the commercial terms or emissions schedule. Confirmations will deal with delivery and payment obligations and mechanisms; administrative details and any provisions applicable to that specific trade. Though written confirmations are usually exchanged to record individual transactions, the master agreements provide for verbal agreements to be binding.

Adopting this approach means that any amendments to the master agreement can be identified and analysed by reviewing the commercial terms schedule, the emissions schedule and confirmation, rather than having to review the master agreement.

For regular trading parties that have master agreements and agreed schedules in place, conducting a trade will only require the deal-specific aspects to be considered in the confirmation, thus the process of trading becomes mechanical and consequentially quicker and cheaper.

8. Provisions specific to emissions trading

Though the standardised agreements on trading of emissions build upon the structure utilised for trading other commodities, there are significant differences that require specific provisions to be incorporated in the emissions schedule.

8.1 Allowances

The standard-form agreements all refer to the emissions being traded as "allowances". These include Kyoto units, as allowances are broadly defined as EUAs and alternative allowances so long as they are recognised under the EU ETS and so long as the type of allowance is specified in the confirmation or the emissions schedule. However, all three master agreements are currently being amended to deal with Kyoto units in a more comprehensive manner. The term "allowances" is used in the remainder of this section to refer to units traded under the standard-form agreements.

8.2   Reconciliation deadline

Installations regulated under the EU ETS must surrender sufficient allowances on April 30 of each year to cover their actual emissions in the previous year. This is referred to as the reconciliation deadline, and installations trading in order to meet their compliance obligations will need to ensure they have sufficient allowances to surrender on the reconciliation deadline. Thus, provisions in the standard form agreements seek to ensure that where a party fails to meet a delivery date, any grace period granted to effect delivery of the allowances does not override the obligation to meet the reconciliation deadline. Most emissions trading settles on December 1 every year in a further commercial effort to provide sufficient buffer to ensure that allowances are transferred in time to meet the annual reconciliation deadline.

8.3   End-of-phase reconciliation deadline/compliance period

Trading within EU ETS falls within phases. EU ETS imposes restrictions on borrowing and banking across phases. In Phase I, EUAs may be banked and borrowed forward across years, but not phases. In Phase II, EUAs may be borrowed forward across years, but not phases. EUAs can be banked over phases after the second phase. The end-of-phase reconciliation deadline or compliance period is accordingly very important to compliance traders, who must meet the reconciliation deadline, and also to other traders because if allowances cannot be "carried forward" into the next phase, they will have no value. The standard-form agreements require counterparties to specify the vintage (year of issue) or compliance periods for the allowances to be delivered. The standard-form agreements also make provision for failures to deliver or accept delivery after end-of-phase reconciliation deadlines/compliance periods.

At the time of writing this chapter, international negotiations are ongoing on whether or not to extend the Kyoto Protocol. Thus, banking and borrowing of Kyoto units beyond 2012 may not be relevant unless and until there is international agreement on whether there should be a further compliance period under the Kyoto Protocol.

8.4   Registry accounts

An allowance is an intangible asset, existing simply in the form of an electronic sequence of numbers. An allowance is traded by the physical transfer of the allowance, in the form of the electronic sequence of numbers, from one registry account to another. National registries, established under EU ETS,[20] are standardised secure electronic databases (not trading platforms) that record the issue, holding, transfer, acquisition, surrender, cancellation and replacement of allowances and that permit the reconciliation between allowances and verified emissions.

The EU ETS relies upon the proper functioning of the member state registries.

---

20   Article 19(1) of Directive 2003/87/EC.

Problems with registries represent a systemic risk that will vary from one member state to another. In addition in Phase II, the EU must meet its obligations under the Kyoto Protocol and trading under EU ETS will be constrained in that trading will also need to meet the international trading requirements of the Kyoto Protocol. Trades between the countries will be tracked via the International Transaction Log (ITL) and, in order to trade, each country must meet the Article 17 and Commitment Period Reserve (CPR) requirements. Uncertainties relating to the Kyoto Article 17 and CPR requirements and the reliability of ITL operations remain issues for trading parties, and these are being dealt with in energy contracts documentation – see section 10 below.

8.5   Excess emissions penalty

Each of the three standard forms requires the parties to specify the applicability of the Excess Emissions Penalty (EEP) or the Excess Emissions Penalty Equivalent (EEPe). The EEP, currently €40/tCO$_2$e (but which increases to €100/tCO$_2$e in Phase II of EU ETS) is a fine imposed on installations that do not surrender sufficient allowances by the reconciliation deadline.[21] The EEP is only payable by a compliance buyer but, as these buyers may be relying on timely delivery, they may seek to pass on an equivalent amount for late delivery to their sellers via the EEPe.

9.   Key differences

Entities using a particular standard form may wish to trade with entities trading under other standard forms. Differences in the standard forms introduce the potential of legal basis risk if the obligations and liabilities in any on-trade are not back-to-back with those in the contract under which the allowances are acquired. Any restriction which affects ease of trading has an effect on the liquidity of the market. In recognition of this, the three sponsoring organisations have made attempts to harmonise the trading agreements. However, differences still remain. There are procedural differences – so, for instance, where there is a failure to deliver or failure to accept allowances, the forms contain differences on whether a notice triggering the grace day does or does not have to be served. Along with procedural differences, there are some differences in commercial consequences – for instance the close-out amount calculations vary between the different forms.

However, the fact that the standard forms are not interchangeable is not merely due to incomplete harmonisation, but also because the choices or "elections" and default options such as on payment cycles mean that there will always be differences that will need to be considered when trading under the standard forms.

Unsurprisingly, the differences in the terms of the agreements and the differences in the architecture of the standard-form documents (with some elections being made in the confirmation, some in commercial term schedules and others in emission schedules) give rise to difficulties in aligning different standard-form agreements when dealing with a chain of trades.

---

21   The fine is imposed under Article 17 of Directive 2003/87/EC.

10.   Transition from Phase I to Phase II and trading under the Kyoto Protocol

At the time of writing, the standard-form agreements were being reviewed and there were ongoing discussions between the sponsoring organisations in relation to the amendments required to the standard forms to deal with the transition of EU ETS from Phase I to Phase II and the start of the first Kyoto Protocol trading period. CERs have been able to be traded since 2005 (though CERs have not actually been able to be transferred to national registries because the ITL has not been operational), but Phase II will permit the trading of other Kyoto Protocol units in EU ETS requiring various definitional changes in the standard-form agreements.

However, it is not just changes in terminology that are required prior to the alignment of EU ETS with the Kyoto Protocol international trading scheme. The Kyoto Protocol imposes eligibility requirements and constraints on the trading that will impact on cross-border trading and so present further risks that need to be reflected in the standard-form agreements. Further, there are concerns that ITL may either not be operational in time for the start of Phase II or may fail during Phase II. Again, such risks need to be reflected in the standard-form agreements. The main focus of discussion in the working groups of the three sponsoring organisations has been the consequences where a failure to deliver a credit or allowance or for a trading party to accept a credit or allowance is as a result of:

- the failure of the International Transaction Log (ITL);[22]
- a failure of the delivering party or a receiving party's registry account country to meet the initial and continuing eligibility requirements[23] under Article 17 of the Kyoto Protocol to trade; or
- the trade by the delivering party's registry account country being in breach of that country's Commitment Period Reserve (CPR).[24]

These issues are not matters that are only of concern at the start of the alignment between EU ETS and the Kyoto trading scheme as the eligibility and CPR constraints and the risk of failure of ITL may occur at any time within the compliance period. Nor are the risks only relevant to the trading of Kyoto units, because EUAs, when being traded across borders, will be treated as AAUs and so may be affected by the eligibility requirements, CPR constraints and the operation of the ITL.

The provisions under consideration, at the time of writing this chapter, to deal with circumstances where cross-border transactions are affected because the ITL or registry accounts are not operational involve the suspension of obligations of parties to deliver or accept delivery allowance until the ITL is operational or the Article 17 eligibility or CPR issues are resolved. Delayed delivery will be subject to an interest payment – a cost-of-carry adjustment. If there is no resolution by December 2012, the trade may be terminated without any payment being owed.

---

22   The ITL is the UNFCCC system for tracking trades and links the CDM registry (which houses CERs) with national registries.
23   The Kyoto Protocol requires each nation to satisfy certain eligibility criteria before international emissions trading is permitted from its territories.
24   The Kyoto Protocol imposes a cap on the level of emissions a nation may trade at any given time in order to reduce the likelihood of there being a shortfall at the end of the compliance period.

In addition, parties are agreeing in the documentation to open more than one account – normally up to four national registries (with the buyer's registries set out in order of preference), so that if one registry is inoperational the trade can be conducted in another registry. That is not a complete answer, of course, as the buyer may find that the delivery in an alternative registry to the buyer's first choice may impact on back-to-back arrangements for any onward delivery arrangements; however, it provides a greater level of control than being required to open a registry account in any registry that was operational in order to accept delivery.

Whilst the sponsoring organisations make arrangements to amend their respective forms, trading parties are incorporating specific definitions and mechanisms in emission schedules or confirmations to deal with these issues.

11.   Key provisions

As noted above, despite attempts to harmonise the three standard form agreements, differences remain, and market participants should carefully evaluate the commercial and legal aspects of each agreement, focusing particularly on critical terms relating to termination, settlement disruption, and close-out mechanics. The section below, for convenience using generalised terminology rather than the defined terms used in the agreements, provides a summary of the key provisions of the agreements. This section does not represent, in any way, a definitive exposition of the three standard-form agreements.

11.1   Primary obligations

The primary obligations contained in all three standard-form agreements are for the seller to sell and the buyer to buy the allowances. As noted above, allowances exist only as numbers in a registry account and so the three standard-form agreements provide detailed provisions on delivery arrangements into registry accounts. The seller's obligation is to deliver from any registry account unless one or more of the seller's delivery accounts are specified, in which case the obligation is limited to deliver from one of the specified accounts. The buyer must accept delivery into a nominated registry account. Where multiple accounts are listed by both parties, unless otherwise specified the parties are deemed to have set out the list of accounts in order of preference. All three standard-form agreements provide for changes to the designated accounts. The importance of having a valid registry account means all three standard-form agreements also contain provisions to ensure the parties maintain operational accounts.

Title to the allowance and all risk related to the allowance pass on delivery of the allowance into the buyer's nominated account. The buyer's obligation is to accept delivery and pay for the allowances delivered. The three standard-form agreements contain provisions allowing the parties to elect between payment options. If no election is made, the EFET automatically applies a monthly billing and payment cycle; the other two standard-form agreements require a specific election, as they do not contain any fall-back if a payment option is not selected. The IETA and EFET state payments must be made in euros (though this can be altered) and the ISDA states payments must be made in the currencies nominated by the parties.

11.2   Failure to deliver/failure to accept

Failure to deliver or failure to accept is not automatically an event of default. If, on the delivery date specified in the confirmation, the seller fails to deliver or the buyer fails to accept delivery (for instance, by not holding an account in the nominated registry), all three standard-form agreements contain a one business/banking day grace period within which the defaulting party can attempt to cure the failure. The ISDA and IETA grace day is triggered by the non-defaulting party giving notice of the grace period, whilst the EFET grace day commences automatically. The ISDA and EFET circumscribe the grace day if the reconciliation deadline is earlier – see section 8 above.

If the failure is cured within the grace period, default interest is payable on the contract allowance price of the number of allowances undelivered or unaccepted from the scheduled delivery date to the actual date of transfer. If the failure is not cured within the grace period, under the ISDA and IETA the non-defaulting party may terminate that particular transaction by giving notice – the EFET, again, contains no notification obligation. The buyer's or seller's replacement costs (or, under the EFET, the buyer's or seller's cover costs), as appropriate, will then be payable. The date of payment of such costs differs in each of the three standard-form agreements.

11.3   Buyer's replacement/cover costs

The buyer's replacement costs in the ISDA and IETA (and the buyer's cover costs in the EFET) are basically the difference between the contract allowance price and the price the buyer would have to pay in an arm's-length transaction, together with default interest. Both the IETA and EFET also allow the recovery of reasonable costs and expenses. Each standard-form agreement also provides, if specified as applying, indemnification provisions in respect of EEP or EEPe, if they have been paid by the buyer – see section 8 above and section 11.4 immediately below.

11.4   EEP and EEPe

The three standard-form agreements all contain elections on whether EEP or EEPe apply, although the circumstances where EEP and EEPe apply automatically or have to be specifically applied or disapplied differ dependent on which standard-form agreement is used and on whether EEP or EEPe is being considered. Where EEP and EEPe are applied and the buyer has been unable to buy replacement allowances by the reconciliation deadline, the seller must indemnify the buyer for any EEP or EEPe paid. The three standard-form agreements contain differing provisions on the evidence required to demonstrate that the buyer took action to mitigate loss.

11.5   Seller's replacement/cover costs

All three standard-form agreements provide that if allowances are not delivered, the seller will be compensated by payment of the difference between the contract allowance price and the price the seller would receive in an arm's length transaction together with interest (and, in the case of IETA and EFET, any reasonable incidental costs incurred by the seller).

11.6 *Force majeure*/settlement disruption event

The nature of emissions trading means events or circumstances outside the control of the trading parties, such as changes in the regulatory framework, present a significant risk. This makes the *force majeure* provisions in the standard-form agreements of particular importance.

All three standard-form agreements incorporate *"force majeure"* provisions. The ISDA master agreements differ, in that whilst the 2002 version contains provisions dealing with *force majeure*, the 1992 version does not. However, this presents no particular problem in allowance transactions, as the ISDA allowance schedule introduces the concept of a settlement disruption event which essentially mirrors the *force majeure* definitions in the IETA and EFET. All three standard-form agreements provide that during a *force majeure*, the obligations of the parties are suspended and no breach or default is deemed to have occurred during the continuation of the *force majeure*.

The suspension of the parties' obligations in the event of a *force majeure* continues until the sooner of (i) nine business days from the delivery date, (ii) a reconciliation deadline ((ii) does not apply in the IETA) or (iii) three business days prior to the end-of-phase reconciliation deadline (see section 8 on reconciliation deadline and end-of-phase reconciliation deadline). If the *force majeure* continues up to these specified periods, the IETA and EFET provide that either party may terminate all (but not less than all) the transactions affected by the *force majeure*, whilst the ISDA provides that a party may terminate the allowance transaction affected by the settlement disruption event.

The parties must elect what happens in the event of a termination for *force majeure* at the outset of the transaction. In the IETA and the EFET, the elections are not to require a termination payment, a two-way termination payment based on market quotations or a two-way termination payment based on loss suffered by the parties. The consequences of a *force majeure*/settlement disruption event under the ISDA are the same as if there was a termination event.

As has been noted above, the standard forms are in the process of being amended to incorporate specific provisions to deal with Article 17 eligibility, CPR constraints and the risk of failure of ITL. These events are dealt with as specific suspension events which have differing consequences from other *force majeure* and settlement disruption events.

11.7 Events of default/termination events

All three standard-form agreements contain the right to cancel the agreement in the event of default by one party to the agreement. The circumstances or events of default in which a non-defaulting party can terminate the agreement are set out in the master agreements. The three standard-form agreements contain differing terminology (the EFET, for instance, refers to material reasons instead of events of default) and some differences in the actual events of default or termination. However, on the whole, in common with all commercial contracts, the ISDA, IETA and EFET contain those events which, if they were to occur, would materially prejudice the position of the non-defaulting party, either because the defaulting party is failing to perform its obligations under the agreement or because it has created an increased risk to which the non-defaulting party is exposed.

The consequences on the occurrence of an event of default or termination event differ between the standard-form agreements. The ISDA termination payments differ between the two versions of the master agreement. The 1992 version provides termination payments (referred to as a settlement amount) based on market quotations or loss (as elected by the parties). The parties also elect whether the termination payment is one-way or two-way of either the loss or market quotations. Thus, the 1992 version provides four possible elections on the termination payment. The 2002 ISDA master agreement provides a two-way termination payment (referred to as the close-out amount). The IETA termination payment provides for a termination payment based on a loss or market amount, though loss is the default option. The EFET termination payment is based on loss.

11.8   Payment and physical netting

The three standard-form agreements all contain provisions in respect of both payment netting and physical netting of deliveries, though the circumstances where the netting arrangements apply automatically or have to be specifically applied or disapplied differ dependent on which standard-form agreement is used and on whether it is physical or payment netting.

Payment netting applies automatically in the ISDA (though an election must be made if the payment netting is to apply to more than one transaction) and IETA, but must be elected in the EFET. Physical netting also applies automatically in the ISDA and the IETA, whilst it must be elected to apply in the EFET. The IETA and EFET allow parties to opt-out of physical netting, but the ISDA does not. Physical netting is only possible if the delivery is on the same day between the same pair of registry accounts and is of the same type of allowance and of the same compliance period.

The EFET master agreements cover gas and power, and the ISDA covers a range of commodities and financial asset classes. Thus, both contain provisions in relation to cross-product netting. The IETA only covers allowances and so cross-product netting does not apply.

11.9   Governing law and dispute resolution

The governing law provisions of each standard-form agreement reflect its provenance. So ISDA offers English or New York law, with the parties submitting to the English courts or the jurisdiction of New York courts. IETA is governed by English law, with the parties submitting to either the non-exclusive jurisdiction of the English courts or, more commonly, selecting from a variety of arbitration options set out in the confirmation. EFET defaults to German and the exclusive jurisdiction of the German Institution of Arbitration in the case of the power contract, and in the gas contract includes a further option of choosing between English law and arbitration by the London Court of International Arbitration. Each of the standard-form agreements permits the parties to specify changes to the governing law clauses.

The standard-form agreements also contain varying arrangements as to when, and in respect of which matters, referrals can be made to expert determination.

11.10   Changes/abandonment of EU ETS

None of the three standard-form agreements contains any provisions dealing with the consequences, were there to be changes to the EU ETS. However, the ISDA does provide that monies paid (with interest) will be repaid if the EU ETS is abandoned before a delivery date. The IETA and EFET contain no provision related to such a situation.

12. Taxation, accounting, financial services and insolvency regulation

The nature of allowances, as a legal construct, raise questions as to the type of property rights there are in allowances and how such property should be treated. Though the EU has provided some level of harmonisation, traders should consider whether there are any differences between jurisdictions on how allowances are governed under taxation, accounting, financial services and insolvency regulations.

13. Development of other derivatives

The increasing sophistication of emissions as an asset class is leading to the development of more complex carbon instruments than the existing standard-form agreements for spot and forward trades. The development of structured products and emission derivatives will promote further evolution of trading documentation.

13.1 Spreads

Spreads are linked transactions that seek to provide arbitrage between differences in prices of a commodity. As has been noted above, there are significant price differences between different types of allowances and between different vintages of allowances and so there is considerable scope for increasing numbers of spread transactions.

13.2 Swaps

Emissions trading has developed as a physically settled market – that is to say there is a delivery of allowances. Swaps are over-the-counter derivative instruments that enable financial settlement. One party agrees to trade allowances at a fixed price, whilst the other party agrees to trade the allowances based on a floating price based on the average price of allowances at some predetermined time in the future – no delivery of allowances takes place, but at the date of the "delivery" the parties settle in cash the difference between the fixed and floating price. Though, due to recent large fluctuations in price, traders tend towards fixed-price forward contracts, the swap market is likely to develop as reliable sources of emissions price data develop.

13.3 Call or put options

Options are transactions that provide for the payment of a premium in return for a right or "option", but not the obligation, to purchase (in the case of a call) or sell (in the case of a put) a specified quantity of allowances at a predetermined price (the strike price). The option can be settled either by physical delivery or by cash settlement. In the latter case, the seller of the option pays the buyer the difference between the market price of the allowances on the exercise date and the strike price.

Options are a price risk-management tool, and as the price of allowances becomes less volatile and emissions price data develops, traders will be better able to determine the premium and an options market in allowances is likely to develop.

Creating a global carbon market

Anthony Hobley
Norton Rose LLP

1. Beginnings of the carbon market

More than a decade ago, 160 of the world's countries joined an international treaty – the 1992 United Nations Framework Convention on Climate Change (UNFCCC) – to establish an international legal framework to tackle the emerging issue of climate change.[1] The UNFCCC has, at the time of writing, been ratified by 175 countries including the United States.[2]

The UNFCCC creates an umbrella within which all aspects of addressing climate change can be coordinated including: mitigating and adapting to the effects of climate change; and the process of reaching scientific consensus on the causes, impacts and responses required to tackle climate change. The necessary detail beneath this umbrella is settled by the Convention's governing body, the Conference of the Parties (CoP).

The UNFCCC creates a number of soft targets, the clearest of which is that the parties take action to prevent dangerous climate change. The question "What is dangerous climate change?" leads us to a critical part of the UNFCCC framework – the International Panel on Climate Change (IPCC), an international group of scientists who examine and report on the science of climate change every five years.

The emerging scientific consensus on tackling climate change is coordinated through the IPCC process and there is now almost unanimous scientific consensus that climate change is happening and that it is a result of man-made anthropogenic emissions.[3] It has even reached the stage where senators proposing federal action in the United States no longer need to begin their speeches by stating that there is international scientific consensus that climate change is happening and results from human activities.[4]

Taking the effect and cause of climate change as read, the consensus as to what needs to be done to mitigate global warming provides the vital context for examining the emerging global carbon market and its future development. The prevailing consensus is that the risks of irreversible and potentially cataclysmic

---

1   For a more detailed overview of this process and the relevant international provisions see Hobley, A., 2002, "Is Kyoto Dead? Climate Change After Bush" 5 *Env. Liability*, p 167 and http://unfcc.int/essential_background/items/2877.php.
2   http://unfccc.int/kyoto-protocol/background/status-of-ratification/items/2613.php.
3   Copies of the third IPCC Assessment report can be downloaded in English, Arabic, Chinese, French, Russian and Spanish from: http://www.grida.no/climate/ipcc_tar/. The fourth Assessment Report of the IPCC has been available since early 2008.
4   Speech by The Honorable Amy Klobuchar, US Senator, 7th IETA Forum on the State of the Greenhouse Gat Market, Washington DC, September 26 2007.

alterations to the global ecosystem will amplify if global warming increases above 2C compared to pre-industrial temperatures. The EU, for example, believes that the principal objective of global action against climate change must be to keep global temperature increase within a 2C limit. Any additional warming above the 2C limit, however fractional, would have severe repercussions: the EU estimates that a global temperature increase of 2.5C above pre-industrial levels would be likely to cause an additional 3 billion people worldwide to suffer from water scarcity.[5]

If global temperature increases are to be restricted to within the 2C limit, then atmospheric concentrations of greenhouse gases (GHGs) need to remain well below 550 parts per million (ppm) of Carbon Dioxide Equivalents (CO₂e). Indeed, the European Union estimates that even by stabilising long-term concentrations of GHGs at around 450 ppm CO₂e there is still only a 50% chance of limiting any global average temperature increase to less than 2C.[6] Although the 2C limit is attainable, these statistics highlight the need for international discussions to move beyond rhetoric and negotiations to firm commitments.

The consensus, or whatever it becomes, is important as it forms the benchmark against which international and domestic decision-making will be made. It is an indicator of the order of magnitude of the technical and policy challenges and can be used as a guide to the specific policy tools that are required.

This point is neatly illustrated by the events that followed the agreement of the UNFCCC in 1992, when it became apparent that the issue of climate change was more serious than had been thought[7] and that more was needed than the soft and non-quantitative UNFCCC targets, which could and were being ignored in practice. The Convention took effect in 1994, but by the following year governments were already negotiating the Kyoto Protocol, which was adopted unanimously in 1997 and entered into force on February 16 2005.

The Kyoto Protocol's major feature is its legally binding targets and timetables for the reduction of GHG emissions for 38 of the world's leading economies – referred to in the Protocol as Annex I parties. These targets range from -8% to +10% of the Annex I countries' individual 1990 emissions levels "with a view to reducing their overall emissions of such gases by at least 5.2% below existing 1990 levels in the commitment period 2008 to 2012" (the "Kyoto Commitment Period"). The targets form the basis for the assigned amount of each Annex I country, which represents the amount of GHGs that each country is permitted to emit during the Kyoto Commitment Period. The assigned amount is measured in Assigned Amount Units (AAUs) – the primary Kyoto Protocol unit of accounting, each AAU representing one metric tonne of CO₂e.[8] In almost all cases, the limits, even those set at +10% of 1990

---

5   Climate Change and the EU's response, Brussels November 27 2007 http://europa.eu/rapid/
    pressReleasesAction.do?reference=MEMO/07/515&format=HTML&aged=0&language=EN&guiLanguage
    =en.
6   http://eur-lex.europa.eu/LexUriServ/LexUriServ.do?uri=CELEX:52007DC0002:EN:NOT.
7   Relevant IPCC report. See http://www.ipcc-ch/pub/sa(E).pdf.
8   The Kyoto Protocol covers the so called "six-gas basket" which covers: carbon dioxide (CO₂), methane
    (CH₄), nitrous oxide (N₂O), and three fluorinated gases, HFCs, PFCs, and SF₆. CO₂e is an internationally
    accepted measure that expresses the amount of global warming of GHGs in terms of carbon dioxide that
    would have the same global warming potential.

levels, demand significant reductions in currently projected emissions. Future mandatory targets are envisaged for "commitment periods" after 2012. The intention was that these were to be negotiated well in advance of the periods concerned.

Commitments under the Protocol vary from nation to nation. The overall 5.2% target for developed countries is to be met through cuts (from 1990 levels) of 8% in the European Union (EU 15), Switzerland, and most Central and East European states; 6% in Canada; 7% in the United States (although the United States has since withdrawn its support for the Protocol); and 6% in Hungary, Japan, and Poland. New Zealand, Russia and Ukraine are to stabilise their emissions, while Norway may increase emissions by up to 1%, recent ratifiers Australia by up to 8%, and Iceland by 10%. These numbers are the outcome of long, complex negotiations and horse trading in Kyoto. The EU has made its own internal agreement to distribute its 8% target among its member states. These targets range from a 28% reduction by Luxembourg and 21% cuts by Denmark and Germany to a 25% increase by Greece and a 27% increase by Portugal.

Commentators have speculated that major compromises, particularly to allow greater use of sinks or land use, land change and forestry (LULUCF), made at Bonn (CoP6) in July 2001 and Marrakech (CoP7) in November 2001 (which resulted in the so-called "Marrakech Accords") have effectively reduced the aggregate target to somewhere between 0.5 and 1.5%. But, even if the targeted emissions of the Kyoto Protocol are a modest goal, the aggregate target represents a radical change from the still rising trend.[9]

Perhaps the greatest legacy of the Kyoto Protocol, however, will not be those modest cuts but the principle it establishes of legally binding cuts and, importantly for the subject of this chapter, the universal norms for international emissions trading created beneath it. This principle provides a blueprint for a global carbon market (the "Kyoto Legacy"). It is this set of norms which will allow the emergence of a global carbon market, whether it grows from the top down or from the bottom up.

At one level, the Kyoto Protocol is a simple agreement. It sets legally binding targets and a timetable for their achievement by Annex I parties. Despite much misinformation to the contrary, the Protocol does not dictate how these countries should meet their targets – it provides three innovative options (described below), but it is up to each country to determine exactly how to do this.

At the political level, however, the Kyoto Protocol is a troublesome, complicated agreement, as demonstrated by the many years it took to enter into force. The Protocol's biggest challenge is to be effective against a worldwide problem in a politically acceptable way. This challenge has led to a multiplication of panels and committees to monitor and referee its various programmes. Even after the agreement was approved in 1997, further negotiations were deemed necessary to hammer out instructions on how to "operate" it in the form of the Marrakech Accords.

---

9   For a more detailed overview of this process and the relevant international provisions see Hobley, A., 2002, "Is Kyoto Dead? Climate Change After Bush" 5 *Env. Liability*, p 167 and http://unfcc.int/essential_background/items/2877.php.

There is a delicate balance to international treaties. Those appealing enough to gain widespread support are often not strong enough to solve the problems they seek to address. The UNFCCC is a case in point, despite its many valuable provisions. Yet treaties with real "teeth" may have difficulty attracting enough widespread support to be effective. In that respect, the Kyoto Protocol is also remarkable, being widely acknowledged as having some of the toughest enforcement provisions of any multilateral treaty. Only the WTO Treaty is considered to be tougher.[10]

The Protocol provides Annex I parties with a major helping hand to achieve their targets by giving them the option to use flexible or market mechanisms, the so-called Kyoto "Flexible Mechanisms", which are:

- International Emissions Trading (IET), as set out in Article 17 of the Kyoto Protocol, which allows Annex I parties who are likely to exceed their assigned amount to sell their excess AAUs to other Annex I parties to meet their reduction targets. It also allows such parties to trade credits generated by projects under the other two flexible mechanisms, CDM and JI, outlined below.
- The Clean Development Mechanism (CDM), defined in Article 12, which provides for Annex I parties (developed countries) to earn Certified Emission Reductions (CERs) by implementing projects in non-Annex I parties (developing countries) that reduce emissions or absorb carbon through accredited activities, and which assist the host countries in achieving sustainable development. The CDM is supervised by the CDM Executive Board.
- Joint Implementation (JI), defined in Article 6 of the Kyoto Protocol, which provides for an Annex I party (with a commitment inscribed in Annex B of the Kyoto Protocol) to implement an emission-reducing project or a project that enhances removals by sinks in the territory of another Annex I party and count the resulting emission reduction units (ERUs) towards meeting its own Kyoto target.

In other words, the Kyoto Protocol allows countries, if they so wish, to buy and sell GHG emissions "units" and "credits". This is the basic premise of IET. The Protocol also provides for a system of project-based emissions reductions. This allows an Annex I country to finance emissions-reducing or emissions-avoiding projects in developing nations through the CDM or in other developed countries through JI. These Flexible Mechanisms are one of the Protocol's ground-breaking features that reduce the overall costs of achieving its emissions targets. They enable parties to access least-cost opportunities to reduce emissions, or to remove carbon from the atmosphere in other countries. While the cost of limiting emissions varies considerably from region to region, the effect for the atmosphere of limiting emissions is the same, irrespective of where the action is taken.

The agreement of the detailed rules for the Flexible Mechanisms, as well as other operational aspects of the Kyoto Protocol, in the form of the Marrakech Accords was

---

10   For a detailed examination of the Protocol's enforcement mechanisms, see Depledge J, Yamin F, Chapter 12 "Compliance"; *The International Climate Change Regime: A Guide to Rules, Institutions and Procedures*, CUP 2004.

the result of long negotiations of the UNFCCC CoP. The Protocol and Marrakech Accords define a common currency based upon one metric tonne of CO_2e in the form of interchangeable or "fungible" units or Kyoto Units: AAUs, ERUs, CERs and Removal Units (RMUs). The Marrakech Accords also complete the process of defining broad operating rules, procedures and design principles for setting specific rules for the Flexible Mechanisms. These include the following key components:

- seller liability, that is, units once issued are non revocable;
- freedom to transfer, that is, no regulatory restrictions on transfers;
- clear definitions of units;
- absence of restrictions on participation;
- international carbon accounting rules;
- determination of baselines;
- monitoring;
- verification; and
- design and operating parameters of registries.

The significance of the Marrakech Accords is that they provide the detailed international framework or norms upon which the emerging global carbon market is based and can continue to develop. By adopting these common principles and building blocks, Annex I parties can design domestic and regional emissions trading schemes that will support international emissions trading with other Annex I parties within the Kyoto framework.

2.   The genesis of emissions trading

The principles and norms of emissions trading now established at the international level and within the EU as part of the EU Emissions Trading Scheme (EU ETS, discussed below) were not invented or conjured up in Kyoto in 1997. They were learnt the hard way over nearly three decades of practical experience in the United States, which culminated in the US sulphur dioxide (SO_2) Acid Rain Program (ARP) being enacted into US federal law in November 1990 by the Clean Air Act Amendment.

To begin with, emissions trading emerged as an ad-hoc instrument to bring some flexibility into a system where permitted levels of total emissions were fixed by pre-existing performance standards.[11] But, confronted by the problem that existing legislation blocked the location of new activities and even the growth of certain businesses, the authorities had to do something to reduce the burden of this self-imposed scarcity by allowing specific forms of exchange. These early forms of exchange were as far from today's SO_2 emissions markets as a Stone Age barter economy is from today's global financial markets.

So the early markets were characterised by restrictions on the ability to trade freely and transfer emissions rights. This, together with uncertainty over the status of property rights and high transaction costs, largely explains why the number of

---

11   See Klassen and Nentjes, 1997 "Creating Markets for Air Pollution Control in Europe and the USA" *Environmental and Resource Economics* 10(2): 125 to 146.

trades (and hence economic efficiency) was initially low, notwithstanding that much-needed flexibility had been introduced into the system.

By contrast, the SO_2 ARP introduced a US-wide emissions trading scheme for electricity producers based on an institutional framework for a genuine market in emissions allowances with minimum regulatory restrictions or other market interference by the authorities. In 2002 more than 11 million SO_2 allowances were transferred between unrelated parties.[12]

Many of the design elements or norms of the SO_2 ARP are the same norms on which both IET and the EU ETS are based. Furthermore, the same norms are also being incorporated in state and national GHG emissions trading schemes emerging in Australia, Canada, Norway, and many US states.

The fact that many emerging trading schemes as well as major schemes such as the EU ETS are built around these norms will, from a legal and technical perspective, make it much easier for them to link. Hence a global carbon market – whether top down, bottom up or indirectly linked through a commonly recognised currency such as CERs – is a genuine prospect.

3.   Global leadership of the European Union

Since the end of the 1990s, the European Union has committed itself to playing a global leadership role in the fight against global warming. After the US federal government decided to withdraw from the Kyoto Protocol, the European Union used all its diplomatic power to keep other countries (especially Russia) to their word and, eventually, succeeded in persuading enough countries to sign.

The European Climate Change Programmes (ECCP), launched in 2000, provides the road map for EU initiatives to combat global warming. It is a stakeholder structure under which the European Commission debates with industries and NGOs and prepares new cost-effective measures to fight climate change. Through the ECCP, around 30 measures have been identified and implemented, including the EU Emission Trading Scheme (EU ETS) and its link to the CDM and JI project mechanisms, the directive on the promotion of electricity from renewables and the voluntary agreement with car producers to reduce CO_2 emissions from cars.[13] The EU Emissions Trading Directive 2003/87/EC (the Directive) was agreed on July 22 2003 and came into force on October 25 2003. The Directive had sailed through the EU legislative process in almost record time, being less than 44 months from the Green Paper on March 8 2000.This was due to a number of reasons. There was, at the time, a unique coalition between business, green NGOs and governments on the issue. Business wanted to pre-empt any chance of command and control legislation or a carbon tax, and the green NGOs saw an opportunity to have binding climate change legislation with caps on industry sooner rather than later. Those who designed the Directive were also very clever. They produced a Directive which provided an overarching European framework for an EU-wide GHG emissions allowance trading scheme, but left the politically difficult issues to member states (ie the setting of

---

12   See www.epa.gov/airmarkets/trading/so2markets/transtable.html.
13   http://ec.europa.eu/environment/climat/eccp.htm.

targets and allocations of allowances). One can only speculate that if this had not been done, the Directive might still be grinding its way through the EU legislative machinery.

The EU ETS is currently the largest cap-and-trade scheme of its kind in the world and the first international scheme of its kind to limit CO_2 emissions through a cap and trade mechanism. It not only draws heavily on the norms established in the United States and tested so effectively in the SO_2 ARP, but also on lessons learnt from the voluntary GHG Emissions Trading Scheme which became operational in the United Kingdom in 2002. The EU ETS was designed in such a way as to be both compatible with the Kyoto Protocol and at the same time independent of it. It started three years before the Kyoto Commitment Period and continues after the Kyoto Commitment Period in five-year rolling phases. However, during the Commitment Period it is intrinsically linked to the Kyoto Protocol and the system of international carbon accounting on which the international system is based. The EU ETS and the Kyoto system share the same Registry System and each EU Allowance is (from 2008) created from an AAU; it is in fact a "tagged" AAU. This means that any movements of EU allowances from one member state to another will automatically true up with that country's holdings under the Kyoto system. In effect the EU ETS brings IET down from the sovereign-state level to the private-entity level. It does this across 27 countries, 25 of which are Annex I parties with Annex B targets under the Kyoto Protocol.

The EU ETS currently covers CO_2 emissions from 10,500 installations in the 25 EU member states, including power stations, oil refineries and the cement, ceramics, pulp and paper, and glass manufacturing sectors. In 2008, the Scheme will expand to cover all 27 member states.

A critical aspect of the EU ETS is that it has no sunset clause. Apart from one exception[14] it would require new legislation at the EU level to end it and this is highly unlikely, given the scientific consensus discussed earlier in this chapter. In fact, in 2005 ECCP II began focusing on the potential for linking the EU ETS with other emissions trading schemes and thus creating an efficient global carbon market.

The EU ETS began on January 1 2005 with an initial three-year "learning by doing" or "calibration" phase to run from 2005 to 2008. It will then run continuously in rolling five-year phases starting with 2008 to 2012. The EU has already indicated carbon emission reduction targets to 2020. Also, under current proposals the EU ETS is due to be expanded by January 2011 to include the aviation sector, one of the fastest growing carbon emitters.

Under the Scheme, an operator of a relevant installation can only emit CO_2 if it holds a site-specific GHG permit. It is this permit which sets requirements for monitoring and verification of the site's CO_2 emissions and, critically, requires the operator of the installation to surrender allowances equal to the installation's verified emissions. If the operator fails to do so, it will have to pay a penalty of €40 (rising to

---

14   The one exception is if civil society and government lose faith with the market-based approach to tackling climate change and fall back on command and control of tax. This is unlikely, as both of these approaches have significant downsides compared to market-based approaches.

€100 from 2008) for each metric tonne of CO_2 emitted for which it has failed to surrender an allowance. For many installations, such as power stations, this could easily mount up to many millions of euros.

The target for each installation is effectively set by the allocation of allowances given to that installation at the beginning of each compliance year (which runs from January to December). Each member state is responsible for developing these allocations in the form of a National Allocation Plan (NAP). These NAPs have to be prepared in accordance with criteria laid down in Schedule III to the Directive and must be approved by the EU Commission. This had led to a significant number of NAPs being rejected by the EU Commission and the member states having to reduce their allocations (quite drastically in some cases).[15]

The Directive was quickly followed by the Linking Directive (2004/101/EC) which came into force on November 13 2004. The Linking Directive amends the Directive to enable member states to allow operators to use credits obtained through Kyoto mechanisms (CERs and ERUs) to comply with their obligations under the EU ETS. In effect, it links the EU ETS directly to the other Kyoto mechanisms.

This linking means that the price of CERs from CDM projects and ERUs from JI projects are driven by the carbon price signal in Europe. This is currently the case even if the buyers are buying for non-EU ETS use, for example government buyers buying for their international obligations under Kyoto. The price is not the same as CERs and ERUs have some different characteristics from EU allowances and, if being bought on a primary basis, have a particular project risk profile not seen with EU allowances.

For a more detailed treatment of the EU ETS, see the previous chapter.

4. **Lessons learnt from the "learning by doing" phase of the EU ETS**
The pre-Kyoto "calibration" phase of the EU ETS, extending from 2005 through to 2007, is intended to provide the experience and to establish the institutions (mainly, allowance registries, monitoring, reporting, verification and compliance procedures) to ensure that the period coinciding with the first Kyoto Protocol commitment period of 2008 to 2012 will be a success.

One consequence of this has been a near-zero price of CO_2 as the trial period draws to a close, due to over-allocation and a prohibition on banking from the trial period to the "real" 2008 to 2112 period. Although that prohibition may be judged by some as a technical mistake, there were good political reasons for making that decision – essentially to contain any teething problems within the trial period and not to complicate achievement of the EU's attainment of its Kyoto obligations.

The dramatic price-fall during Phase I shows that the market mechanism is working perfectly: sending the appropriate price signal in light of the overallocation of allowances in EU ETS Phase I. Since allowances cannot be "banked" or carried over from EU ETS Phase I to Phase II (which commenced on January 1 2008), the effects

15   For example, The European Commission reduced Bulgaria's NAP by 37.4%. For a full summary of NAPs, see http://europa.eu/rapid/press Releases Action.do?reference=IP/07/1614&format=HTML&aged=O&language=EN&guiLanguage=en.

of the overallocation of allowances for Phase I will not be carried into Phase II and the system will get a fresh start.

There are indeed already strong indications that Phase II of the EU ETS from 2008 to 2012 will be robust and effective. The aggregate EU cap for Phase II ETS 2008 to 2012 is about 9% lower than the Phase I cap and some 6% lower than 2005 emissions. With continuing economic growth, no-one doubts that this cap will be challenging and that it will encourage emission reductions and other forms of climate-friendly behaviour. The European experience with carbon trading is being closely followed by other countries around the world, in particular in the United States where legislators are looking at setting up cap-and-trade schemes which may or may not be directly linkable to the EU ETS.

According to the most recent analysis of the EU ETS published by the Carbon Markets Association (CMA), the second-period price is unlikely to fall to zero: EUAs can be banked from the 2008 to 2012 period into the post-2012 period, and the cap for the post-2012 period will be even lower. The argument that the EU ETS will be flooded with Kyoto credits (under the provisions of the Linking Directive) and the price taken to zero at the end of the second period is not, at the time of writing, reflected in the Phase II price, nor by the price of CERs.

This positive sentiment on the future prospects of the EU ETS generating a price for carbon that sends signals to reduce emissions is echoed in a recent report issued by New Carbon Finance. The report suggests that the EU ETS will most likely be "short" in the period 2008 to 2012 with a demand in the region of 1.3 billion over the period and for the global Kyoto market supply of CDM/JI credits to be broadly equivalent to demand in the same period.[16]

Indeed, some countries are complaining that their Phase II allocations are too low, potentially squeezing their economies. This is particularly the case for the member states of Central and Eastern Europe, which have launched legal proceedings against the Commission. The challenges concern technicalities relating to the European Commission's review and revision of the caps proposed by these member states. These legal proceedings in the European Court of Justice do not challenge the EU ETS itself, and the member states concerned will continue to participate in the EU ETS. Similar challenges were brought in the first period and they were resolved in a manner that did not bring the EU ETS to a halt.

In fact it can be seen that markets have done a relatively good job of predicting the Phase II constraint, as evidenced by the prices for Phase II EUAs which have fluctuated at around €20 (+ or – €5) since those futures were first introduced in late 2005. This price is sufficient to have an abatement effect on emissions and it has provided the lead times needed for capital investment in carbon reducing technology. It is also worth making the point that, although EUA prices for the 2005 to 2007 and 2008 to 2012 periods have exhibited considerable volatility, that volatility is no greater than that readily seen in the price of other commodities such as power, gas, oil and freight. Furthermore, the emissions market has already developed a range of trading instruments to manage price volatility, including futures, forwards and derivative instruments.

---

16   New Carbon Finance, EU ETS "Deep Dive Analysis", June 2007.

The result has been that the cost of carbon emissions is no longer free in Europe: it has a price. An equally important development is that the carbon price signal in Europe "succeeded in stimulating emissions abatement both within Europe and especially in developing countries".[17] The value of global emissions trading tripled in 2006 to $30.1 billion, 81% of which was in the EU, according to 2007 World Bank figures.

5.   A global carbon market?

Is there currently a global carbon market? There is probably not at the time of writing a coherent and fully integrated global carbon market. However, there is clearly an emerging global carbon market made up of different parts. These are the framework of IET under the Kyoto Protocol covering 36 OECD and Economies in Transition, the EU ETS (which is embedded into IET for 25 of these 36 countries), the Kyoto Project Mechanisms of CDM and JI, some national schemes formally linked to the EU ETS (eg in Norway), and some national and sub-national schemes not linked (eg the New South Wales ETS). There are also emerging schemes such as the Regional Greenhouse Gas Initiative (RGGI) in the US north-east States and AB32 in California. There is also the increasingly likely prospect of some form of federal cap-and-trade scheme in the United States within the next three to four years.

What does all of this look like at the moment? One way of viewing the carbon market is to picture it as a sun. Currently, the red hot core of this sun is the EU ETS, which sets a carbon price across Europe and to some extent globally. This is surrounded by a slightly cooler, but still hot, layer which comprises the project mechanisms of the Kyoto Protocol, in particular CDM. Around this is a cooler outer layer made up of the emerging voluntary market, which may or may not emerge as another part of the regulatory market.

Then there are other emerging trading schemes (as discussed above) orbiting this sun, but which are not yet linked to it. It seems that many of these emerging trading schemes may recognise CERs from CDM projects and this raises the interesting prospect of CERs forming a commonly recognised currency between such schemes.

6.   Linking trading systems

Establishing linkages between different trading schemes – either unilateral or bilateral – currently seems the most promising way to establish a global GHG certificate market and come closer to a global price of GHG abatement. The global "carbon economy" is today based on a mix of international treaties and decisions and regional and domestic schemes, as well as sub-domestic schemes. In order to make a global carbon market a reality, proper linkages have to be established between these instruments, in order to enable exchanges of the "currencies" or "commodities" traded in them. Systems in the making or already in existence include the California state proposals, the Canadian Large Final Emitter System, the RGGI, the New South Wales Abatement scheme, the Norwegian emissions trading scheme, and the Chicago Climate Exchange.

---

17   Stated by the World Bank in its report "State and Trends of the Carbon Market 2007".

Economists and lawyers, however, have been forthright in spelling out the major legal obstacles to linking that are currently to be found in different international commitments behind the different schemes and in constitutional restrictions with respect to sub-domestic schemes. Three design elements have emerged as the major potential obstacles to linking: the presence or absence of an absolute cap on emissions; different rules on credit generation and recognition; and differences in penalty regimes.

In 2006, senior European Commission officials spent time in the United States exploring the political possibilities of intergovernmental top-down linking with a US cap-and-trade system which would drive demand around the world by creating a more deeply liquid market. At present, it is envisaged that there may be no direct price link but that, to use a phrase employed by the CMA, which lobbies for the effectiveness of market-based solutions on climate change, "a window of opportunity" should be left open for some form of linkage, most likely through the global Kyoto currency of CER credits from the CDM, the most transparent, robust credit market in the world.

It is therefore worth looking in greater detail at the status of the current legislation in the United States, the world's largest developed economy and by far its biggest per capita emitter. There are currently more than a dozen climate change or climate related bills circulating in the US House and Senate. However, a recent proposal by Senators Lieberman and Warner has attempted to reconcile language from these disparate bills into one single act. The "Lieberman–Warner America's Climate Security Act of 2007" (the "Bill") has been released for comments and will be finalised soon.

The Bill would require reductions to 2005 levels by 2012; 10% below 2005 by 2020; 30% below 2005 by 2030; 50% below 2005 by 2040; and 70% below 2005 by 2050. It would cover electric power, transportation and industry (including producers of iron/steel, aluminium, cement, lime, adipic acid, nitric acid, ammonia, pulp, nitrous oxide, hydrofluorocarbons, perfluorocarbons, sulphur hexafluoride, other GHGs, or importers of products containing GHGs). This represents approximately 80% of US emissions.

The Bill would also create a Climate Change Credit Corporation to auction and/or distribute allowances and a Carbon Market Efficiency Board to monitor the economy and trading system. Allowances would be "freely" allocated to different sectors, with some reserves for new entrants. Free allocation would be scaled down to zero over time, with auction amounts increasing in tandem. Some 8% of allowances for 2012 will be allocated in recognition of pre-enactment action; this will scale down to 0% by 2020.

The Bill envisages unlimited trading and banking, and allows 15% borrowing with five years as the default term of the loan; 15% of allowances may be offset, and credits and offset rules would be promulgated no more than two years after the Bill passes. In addition, 15% of allowances may be purchased on foreign GHG trading markets certified by the EPA.

To address concerns on international trade competitiveness, the Bill allows for the President to decide if countries such as India and China have not made the necessary steps to address their GHG emissions, and then importers may be required to submit allowances equal to the value that would be required domestically.

Analysis of the current proposals suggests that the North American carbon markets could rival the EU ETS by 2015 in terms of value of transactions. However, with little in the way of concrete scheme rules in place at the present time, trading activity will pick up only gradually on the back of pre-compliance trading and the voluntary market.

However, it is clear that much political progress still needs to be made. At the federal level, President Bush is more than likely to veto any cap-and-trade bills. The earliest a federal bill could be signed is therefore early 2009, when a new President takes office. It would then take at least two years before such a bill could be fleshed out and implemented. At the state level California's proposals do not bite effectively until 2012; and the RGGI East Coast states scheme, whilst coming into effect in 2009, will, on the basis of projections, create only a relatively weak demand until 2015.

In the event that a federal scheme does not materialise, state-level initiatives will very likely become the norm. New Carbon Finance has calculated that the currently proposed state-level programmes could generate the need for around 130Mt/yr of annual emissions reductions by 2015. According to their analysis of the current rules of both the Californian and the RGGI state-level schemes, demand will first come from California and from RGGI states only after 2014. By 2015, the Californian market could reach a traded value of around $3 billion, and the wider state-level market a traded value of some $7 billion. This is in contrast to RGGI's value, which is predicted to remain weak until around 2015.[18]

The influence of common standards for monitoring, verification and credit generation in emissions trading is uncertain so far, as different standards are in existence; but its influence is likely to grow in order to achieve fungible credits. Although standardisation does not have any binding force on regulators or emitters directly, references to common standards within different schemes will create a higher degree of transparency and facilitate the development of linkages. Agreeing on common standards may be an important element in the linking processes.

Most commentators do not expect any US federal cap-and-trade scheme which does eventually emerge to be integrated into the IET system under the Kyoto Protocol. The smart money is on the two existing side by side. The hope, however, is that the US scheme will incorporate enough of the norms of the IET system to make the two compatible. However, if any US scheme contains a price cap provision such a link may prove difficult. In addition, it is clear that US prices are likely to be lower than EU prices and will not represent an equivalent effort. As such, the most important outcome is that the EU ETS, which has proved highly successful, maintains a steady price and is not destabilised by any new trading systems in the United States. It would also be advisable for a delay in any linkage, so that the US system's performance (and pricing) can be monitored.

---

18   New Carbon Finance, North American "Deep Dive", October 2007.

7. Creating a global market after 2012

Where does this leave the development of a truly global carbon market? It is true to say that the outlook has shifted dramatically in a relatively short period. As recently as 18 months before the time of writing, the US Federal Government would not even acknowledge climate change as a serious global issue requiring action. That has changed, and even the current Bush administration acknowledges that climate change is an issue which needs to be acted upon. But the United States is still at a stage where state-level initiatives compete with those that are beginning to emerge at the federal level. It is probably fair to say that the international position and role of the United States will not become clear until a new administration takes over the levers of power in Washington.

With no effective US international leadership on climate change, the EU continues to set the pace for the creation and completion of a global carbon market. In January 2008, the European Commission set out several Proposed Directives which represent the Energy and Climate Change Package that lays out the EU's future climate strategy in order to enhance the conditions for reaching a new global agreement to follow on from the Kyoto Protocol's first commitments after 2012.

The Commission proposes that the EU pursue, in the context of international negotiations, the objective of a 30% reduction in GHG emissions by developed countries by 2020 (compared to 1990 levels). Furthermore, the EU makes a firm unilateral commitment to achieve a 20% reduction of GHG emissions by 2020, through the EU ETS and other climate change policies and actions (eg tough renewable energy targets, in the context of energy policy). The approach allows the EU to demonstrate international leadership on climate issues. It has given a signal to industry that the ETS will continue beyond 2012 and will encourage investment in emission reduction technologies and low carbon alternatives.

The 13th COP/MOP in Bali, Indonesia, took place in December 2007. It opened with a standing ovation for the Australian delegation who, under the new Labour government, had just ratified the Kyoto Protocol, so leaving the United States as the only developed nation not to have ratified it. At the eleventh hour, during all-night negotiations, it also finally agreed a road map towards an agreement in Copenhagen in 2009 with a clear process for negotiation (with regular meetings). Critically, the Bali road map includes the United States and is to be negotiated through a combination of the UNFCCC and Kyoto Protocol processes. There is no prospect of other fora taking it over.

The Commission suggested before Bali that an agreement in itself would be sufficient to trigger the European Union's commitment to a 30% target (although the actual wording of that commitment suggests that more is needed – that other states must be making an appropriate level of commitment).

The eight elements of the Commission's road map suggested before Bali are:
- A shared vision of an objective based on a maximum 2C rise in temperatures.
- Binding commitments for developed countries for 30% reductions "or similar levels". This is clearly a precondition for the EU target to rise to 30%, but perhaps not all countries must be as high as 30%. It seems likely that the EU will leave itself room for manoeuvre and does not expect the United States to

accept an immediate target.

- Flexible commitments for developing countries based on carbon intensity. The objective is to curtail emissions rather than impose absolute reductions, but more effort will be expected of high-income developing countries such as South Korea (to ensure fairness with lower-income EU states such as Romania). These flexible commitments will mainly involve energy efficiency, renewables and sustainable development targets. It is essential, of course, that flexible commitments are binding and enforceable. The Commission does not see binding targets on developing countries emerging until a post-post-Kyoto deal circa 2030. LDCs (least developed countries) would be completely omitted from binding obligations.

- The continuing development of the global carbon market, including the continuation of the CDM and the existence of hard caps to create demand for CERs. The Commission is looking for increased geographical spread of CDM projects through the provision of technical assistance to countries that are struggling, or would struggle, to establish the necessary national administrative processes. Linking to other national and regional schemes also falls within this element of the road map. The Commission's discussions with California and RGGI are well advanced, notwithstanding that a number of compatibility-related issues remain unresolved (such as the price cap of the RGGI scheme).

- Adaptation – to reflect growing scientific evidence that impacts are already affecting economic, socio-cultural and ecological systems.

- Inclusion of global aviation and global shipping (maritime).

- Technology transfer – in particular enabling (formal) processes for technology transfer and mapping these out in greater detail.

- Deforestation – a vital component, but the key issue of how to link it to emissions trading markets makes it a long-term play. The key to forestry is the concept of avoided deforestation and creating tradable and permanent carbon credits in avoided deforestation projects.

There is certainly a sense that the world outside Europe is fast catching onto the European free-market model. In July 2006, Singapore's Minister for the Environment and Water Resources, Yaacob Ibrahim, commented that his country was well placed to become a hub for environmental financing and trading of carbon credits, given its inherent expertise in financial services and its place as the world's third-largest centre for oil trading.[19] The Singapore-based Asia Carbon Group set up an electronic platform in 2003 to conduct auctions of CERs, and Asia Carbon eventually aims to establish a global carbon exchange – a "seller exchange" focused on Asian project developers. However, in the absence of caps in its developing world neighbours such as China, and therefore a paucity of demand for carbon on any Singapore exchange, Europe, and in particular London, is likely to remain the hub for the global carbon market for the foreseeable future.

---

19   See app.mewr.gov.sg/press.asap?id=CDS3996.

The scale of the climate challenge will require a profound transformation, including in those sectors that cap-and-trade markets cannot easily reach. These include: public and private investment in research and development for new energy efficient technologies and diffusion; economic and fiscal policy changes; programmatic approaches to decouple economic growth from emissions development; and the removal of distortional subsidies for high-carbon fuels and technologies.

In the meantime, carbon is integrating itself into the global economy through a new breed of structured financial-service products being offered to investors through the London offices of major US investment banks such as Merrill Lynch. Such products include principled notes that link to underlying commodities, such as EU allowances being traded in the EU ETS prices, or carbon-inspired index products that allow an investor access to a set of companies that may benefit from a low-carbon economy. The result is that the investor is not buying the right to emit a metric tonne of carbon, but rather what he or she is buying is linked to the price of carbon. How far these sorts of ingeniously structured financial product will integrate the price of carbon into the global economy is uncertain. However, on the basis of the rapid spread of similar products in different commodities markets, they may prove to be a decisive factor in turning the world's economy into one based on an ever-present financial incentive for carbon saving.

Accounting and taxation

Iain Calton
Helen Devenney
Sarah Nolleth
Deloitte

1. Accounting for emission rights

1.1 Introduction

Accounting for greenhouse gas emissions remains a challenge, and market participants continue to wait for clear guidance from accounting standards setters. Formative efforts on the part of those standards setters have so far proven unsuccessful. The International Financial Reporting Interpretations Committee (IFRIC) initially took on this task, and issued IFRIC 3, Emission Rights. Unfortunately, considerable pressure from both the business community and European politicians, who objected to the financial statement consequences of applying that interpretation, led to its withdrawal by the International Accounting Standards Board (IASB) within a year of its issue.

As a consequence of this lack of guidance, companies are currently adopting a range of accounting treatments. This chapter first considers the story to date, current developments in accounting for emissions, and the respective accounting consequences. The various taxation implications of emission rights are then considered in the second part of the chapter. This chapter is not aimed at providing accounting guidance nor any opinion on the accounting applied in practice, but it simply aims to provide a description of some of the more commonly applied accounting treatments. Market participants and others are, therefore, advised to seek professional guidance from their accountant and/or auditor.

1.2 The European market for emissions allowances

The European Union (EU) established a cap-and-trade emissions programme as a market-based response to the emissions reduction targets established by the Kyoto Treaty. With effect from January 1 2005, carbon-emitting entities were allocated allowances (known generally as "EUAs") through a complex allocation process, with the mandate that they subsequently manage their overall emissions against these initial allocations. Companies emitting more than their allotted amounts must either purchase additional allowances through the EU Emissions Trading Scheme (ETS), or pay a fine. Companies emitting less may sell their excess allowances. This provides companies with a direct financial incentive to curtail emissions levels. Consequently, the ETS has become an active market for buying and selling emissions allowances (generally under forward contracts providing for the delivery of allowances in the future). Meanwhile, the United Nations (UN) has established its own programme to encourage emissions reductions by companies operating in developing countries. Following a structured process with various "audit" checkpoints, such entities may receive Certified Emissions Reductions (CERs) from the UN. These also have market value, as the European Union is willing to accept either CERs or EUAs in satisfaction of an entity's yearly compliance obligation under the EU ETS. Although there is considerable market interest in CERs, the market is less liquid and more opaque than the EUA market, simply because there are additional operational, legal, and regulatory hurdles involved in applying for, and ultimately receiving, CERs through the UN programme.

1.3   Accounting considerations

Since companies may either hold allowances, or forward contracts to acquire allowances in the future, it is necessary to consider the accounting consequences for both scenarios. The first requires revisiting the content of IFRIC 3 (now withdrawn by the IASB) referred to above; the second raises issues regarding the application of the IASB's financial instruments standard, International Accounting Standard (IAS) 39, Financial Instruments: Recognition and Measurement.

(a)   *Accounting for allowances held*

IFRIC noted the lack of accounting guidance for a cap-and-trade emissions rights scheme and the lack of market consensus on an appropriate accounting treatment, and it concluded that it should develop an interpretation. In December 2004, IFRIC issued its final interpretation, IFRIC 3, effective for financial reporting periods beginning on or after March 1 2005, which dealt with the accounting for an operational cap-and-trade emission rights scheme.

The consensus in the interpretation was that a cap-and-trade scheme gives rise to:

* an asset for allowances held;
* a government grant for the value of the allowances on the date of receipt; and
* a liability for the obligation to deliver allowances equal to emissions that have been made at the reporting date.

IFRIC 3 concluded that emissions allowances, whether issued by government or purchased in the market, are intangible assets to be accounted for in accordance with IAS 38, Intangible Assets, as follows:

* On initial recognition, allowances issued for less than their fair value should be measured at fair value, with the difference between the amount paid and fair value reported as a government grant, in accordance with IAS 20, Accounting for Government Grants and Disclosure of Government Assistance. This grant should be recognised as deferred income and subsequently recognised in income, on a systematic basis over the compliance period for which the associated allowances are issued, regardless of whether those allowances continue to be held or are sold. An entity may subsequently choose to measure them under either the cost or revaluation model in IAS 38.

- As the entity actually emits greenhouse gases (GHGs) or carbon equivalents, a liability should be recognised for the obligation to deliver allowances equal to those actual emissions. This liability is a provision within the scope of IAS 37, Provisions, Contingent Liabilities and Contingent Assets, and is required to be measured at the best estimate of the expenditure required to settle the present obligation at the balance sheet date. This will usually be the present market price of the number of allowances required to cover emissions made up to the balance sheet date.

Many market participants had reservations about the different bases for measuring and presenting changes in the component assets and liabilities of the proposed accounting model. During the consultation period on IFRIC 3, the main area of concern was around the fact that, under IAS 38, changes in the market value of intangibles (ie emissions allowances held) are recognised in equity. However, the change in the value of the emissions obligation is recognised through profit and loss. Additionally, where allowances are allocated for less than the fair value, under IAS 20, the difference is accounted for as a government grant.

As a deferred credit is not a liability under the IFRS framework, it is inappropriate for it to be re-measured during the year to reflect changes in the value of allowances. IFRIC noted the concerns arising from the mixed measurement model, and asked the IASB to propose an amendment to IAS 38 to permit emission allowances traded in an active market to be measured at fair value with changes in value recognised through profit or loss.

Noting that amendments to IAS 20 and 38 might not be finalised for some time, and concluding that the need for timely guidance to prevent divergent practices outweighed the disadvantages of the IFRIC 3 model, IFRIC issued IFRIC 3. It did note that changes might be necessary to the interpretation in the event the IASB amended IAS 20.

On issuance of IFRIC 3, the European Financial Reporting Advisory Group (EFRAG) issued negative endorsement advice. EFRAG recommended that the European Commission not endorse IFRIC 3 for use in Europe, as it did not meet all of the requirements of the Regulation (EC) no 1606/2002 of the European Parliament and of the Council on the application of international accounting standards because:

- *"it is contrary to the 'true and fair principle' set out in Article 16(3) of the Council Directive 83/349/EEC and Article 2(3) of Council Directive 78/660/EEC; and*
- *it does not meet the criteria of understandability, relevance, reliability and comparability required of the financial information needed for making economic decisions and assessing the stewardship of management."*

The IASB withdrew IFRIC 3 "with immediate effect" at its meeting in June 2005, stating: *"... the Board observed that in developing IFRIC 3, the IFRIC had appropriately addressed how existing Standards apply to emission rights. The Board also reaffirmed its view that IFRIC 3 is an appropriate interpretation of existing IFRSs."*

The IASB also directed IFRIC to discontinue discussion of possible amendments to IAS 38, stating that: *"[the] Board also decided that because developing a coordinated approach [would] require the amendment of one or more standards, it would be more appropriate and efficient for the Board to reconsider the accounting for cap and trade emission right schemes itself, rather than ask the IFRIC to continue its work on developing amendments to the relevant Standards."*

In the absence of definitive guidance, there are a number of different IFRS accounting treatments being considered, and the challenge for companies is to decide which method is appropriate and acceptable.

There are a number of different views under IFRS currently being reflected in the marketplace. The approaches most commonly adopted can be summarised as follows:

View 1

Follow IFRIC 3 in its entirety, on the basis that IFRIC 3 is consistent with current endorsed IFRSs, specifically IAS 38, IAS 20, and IAS 37.

View 2

Recognise the intangible asset initially at fair value, together with a government grant in line with IFRIC 3, but recognise a provision on the following basis:

- to the extent that the entity holds a sufficient number of allowances, the provision should be recognised based on the carrying value of those allowances (ie the cost to the entity of extinguishing their obligation);
- to the extent that the entity does not hold a sufficient number of allowances, the provision should be recognised based on the market value of emission rights required to cover the shortfall; and
- in light of the penalty that the entity will incur if it is unable to obtain allowances to meet obligations under the scheme, and it is anticipated that the penalty will be incurred (note that the obligation to deliver allowances must still be fulfilled).

View 3

No asset or deferred income is recognised when the allowances are initially received as IAS 20's accounting policy choice of recognising the grant at nominal amount is applied (nominal amount being zero in this case). Allowances granted to an entity are used to offset any liability arising as a result of carbon emissions. Hence, no entries are required so long as the entity holds sufficient allowances to meet its emission obligations. Where the entity has no allowances or a shortfall in allowances to meet its emission obligations, a provision should be made for the best estimate of the cost to be incurred to meet its emission obligation, that is, at the present market price of the number of allowances required to cover the shortfall at the balance sheet date (eg for the cash cost of obtaining allowances to meet its obligation at market value).

(b)   ***Accounting for forward contracts to acquire allowances***

A full analysis of the potential implications of the derivatives accounting rules under IAS 39 is beyond the scope of this chapter. However, a brief summary is useful.

EUA forward contracts may qualify for treatment as derivatives within the scope of IAS 39, unless they are for the fulfilment of the entity's own emissions obligations (and thereby qualify for what is known as the "own use" exemption from IAS 39). Companies which use forward contracts more actively to enter into both purchases and sales, so as economically to optimise the ultimate cost of emissions allowances used to meet their obligations, or for purely speculative purposes, will find that the own-use exemption cannot be applied so the derivatives accounting rules under IAS 39 will require fair value accounting treatment.

1.4 Where does that leave us?

The consequence of there being various acceptable accounting treatments for emission rights is that the effect on the different components of financial reports (ie balance sheet, profit or loss or cash-flow statements) will be different depending on which treatment is adopted. This could have significant implications not only for financial performance reported in the profit or loss account, but also on how a company may decide to manage its participation in the ETS. A company will therefore need to explain its accounting policy to the market to ensure that the impact of its emission rights accounting on financial performance is understood. The market may expect accounting for emissions rights to be comparable across the sector, but in practice a company's choice of accounting policy may affect its profit or loss (or equity where the entity's policy is to revalue allowances in equity) quite differently, particularly where it is not only an emitter but also a trader. It is essential that such differences and the reasons for these are intelligible to investors and other stakeholders alike.

Given the lack of consistency in this area, accounting for emissions allowances will undoubtedly be a focus of the IASB at some point in the future, but for now the project is on hold pending completion of other more urgent topics. Until this specific issue is addressed, we are likely to continue to see divergent accounting treatments.

2. Direct taxation implications of emissions rights

2.1 Background

The direct tax implications of emission allowances will depend upon the local tax law and the accounting treatment adopted by the company in question, which as noted above may vary due to the lack of guidance in this area.

There are various differences between how emission allowances are taxed in different jurisdictions, for example in relation to the qualification of the allowances for tax purposes (eg as intangible assets or stock), and the deducibility of penalties. In addition, it is possible that there may be a difference in treatment between companies which hold allowances for use in their own trade (ie to surrender to cover their annual emissions) and entities which trade allowances with a view to making a profit.

Some countries, such as Hungary, have established specific rules for the trading of emissions allowances, whilst other countries, such as the United Kingdom, have chosen to rely on the principles in established tax law. In countries where there have been no specific guidelines, taxation is likely to follow the accounting treatment.

It is beyond the scope of this chapter to cover in detail the tax implications in each individual country and the comments below focus merely on the UK tax treatment of emission trading schemes.

There is no specific UK tax legislation regarding the direct tax treatment of emission trading schemes and, in contrast to a number of other countries in the European Union, the UK tax authorities have not published any specific guidance in this area. Accordingly, in the absence of any specific rules it is necessary to follow general tax principles. Prima facie, the direct tax implications of emission allowances should follow the accounting treatment, and any associated credits or charges to the profit and loss account should be taxable or deductible accordingly, subject to any specific rules to the contrary.

In the absence of specific law or guidance, the taxation commentary in this chapter is based on the accounting position described above and current practical experience. It should be noted that in the absence of legislation, HM Revenue & Customs (HMRC) may take a position contrary to the comments below and it is therefore always advisable to seek up-to-date advice specific to the scenario in question.

Following on from the previous section, it is clear that there are currently a number of different alternatives under IFRS for how to account for emissions allowances and the tax implications of all three given views are considered below. Some UK companies involved in this sector may report under UK GAAP, although the accounting and tax implications of this are beyond the scope of this chapter. Since the accounting position is still currently unclear, there is additional uncertainty for companies as to how they will be taxed in this area.

2.2   UK direct tax treatment

(a)   *Capital or revenue?*

One of the fundamental principles in UK tax law is determining whether items are taxed as capital or revenue items.

One possible accounting treatment (Accounting Views 1 and 2 above) is to recognise the allowances as intangible fixed assets on the balance sheet. There is a specific intangible fixed assets regime for taxation purposes, although it is questionable whether the allowances will meet the definition under these rules. This definition states that assets must be "acquired or created by the company for use on a continuing basis in the course of the company's activities". Since allowances are likely to be acquired and utilised within 12 to 18 months, the current view is that they may not be considered to be held "for use on a continuing basis" such that this regime would not apply. Some companies, however, may be able to argue that they fall within this regime (eg if they intend to hold the assets for longer than 12 to 18 months). In this case, they may be able to elect to receive tax deductions at a rate of 4% per annum in the cost of the allowances (which may be nil if allocated free of charge).

Similarly, the current view is that it is unlikely that the allowances will be classed as capital assets under general tax principles since the widely cited definition, which comes from *Atherton v British Insulated and Helsby Cables Ltd* [1925] 10TC155, states that capital expenditure is made "with a view to bringing into existence an asset or an advantage for the enduring benefit of a trade".

Accordingly, the current view is that it is likely that the tax treatment of expenditure relating to allowances in the United Kingdom will be dealt with under revenue principles, that is, when any expense or income is reflected in the profit or loss account.

(b)   *Revenue expenditure*

Assuming that the revenue principle approach to emissions trading schemes is followed, it is likely that any related charges or credits to the profit and loss account will be treated as trading income or expense. In order to be tax deductible, any expense in relation to the allowances must be incurred "wholly and exclusively" for the purposes of trade. The timing of relief is then likely to be dependent upon the accounting treatment adopted.

(c)   *Initial recognition of emissions allowances*

In the United Kingdom, the most likely tax treatment is that direct tax should only arise on the initial allocation of emissions allowances if there is a credit or debit to the profit and loss account under the accounting treatment adopted. Under the accounting treatments discussed above, to the extent the allowances are allocated free of charge, there should be no impact to the profit and loss account and therefore it is unlikely that there will be any tax impact.

To the extent that allowances are auctioned, the cost paid to purchase the allowances which is recognised in the profit and loss account should be deductible from trading profits, assuming the allowances are to be used wholly and exclusively for the purposes of the trade. (Most countries allocated allowances free of charge in Phase I, but some countries chose to auction a small percentage of their allowances, such as Hungary (2.4%) and Ireland (0.75%); and the United Kingdom has indicated that it plans to auction approximately 7% of allowances in Phase II.)

(d)   *Subsequent release of deferred income*

Under Accounting Views 1 and 2, a liability in the form of deferred income is recognised in respect of the difference between the amount paid for the allowances and their fair value. This balance is then released to the profit and loss account over the compliance period (whether the intangible asset is held or sold). The credits arising in the profit and loss account as a result of this should be chargeable to tax as part of the trading profits of the company.

(e)   *Recognition of liability for emissions allowances*

Under Accounting Views 1 and 2, a liability for emissions is recognised resulting in a debit to the profit and loss account. This charge should be tax deductible for tax purposes if it is incurred wholly and exclusively for the purposes of trade and is calculated on a specific basis. Under Accounting View 2, if the entity holds insufficient allowances, a provision should be recognised based on the market value of emission rights required to cover the cost of the shortfall and any penalties that may be incurred. In this case any provision for penalties is likely to be non deductible (see below).

Under Accounting View 3, a liability for emission allowances should only be recognised when there is a shortfall in allowances to meet emissions obligations. This charge should be tax deductible, provided it is incurred wholly and exclusively for the purposes of the trade and is specifically calculated. As for Accounting Views 1 and 2, any provision for penalties is likely to be non-deductible.

(f) Purchase of allowances

If allowances do not fall to be taxed under a capital regime for direct tax purposes, as discussed above, the purchase of allowances will be treated as a revenue expense. Consequently, companies purchasing allowances should receive tax relief on any costs incurred as part of the purchase provided they are incurred wholly and exclusively for the purposes of the trade.

(g) Sale of allowances

Any profit or loss generated (according to the accounting treatment) on the sale of allowances should be taxable or tax deductible for trading purposes provided any losses are incurred wholly and exclusively for the purposes of the trade.

There is no specific transfer pricing legislation in relation to the trading of emission allowances and transactions between related parties will therefore be subject to the general arm's length principle contained in the UK's transfer pricing rules, which follow the OECD Transfer Pricing Guidelines.

(h) Penalties

If a company fails to surrender sufficient allowances to cover the emissions generated, it will be subject to penalties. Although there is no specific guidance in this area, for UK tax purposes punitive penalties received by a company in respect of non-compliance are generally not deductible for direct tax purposes. It is worth noting that this position is not consistent between EU member states. Accordingly, companies may find the effective cost of paying penalties to be different in various countries, depending on whether these countries currently allow a direct tax deduction for penalties arising from the EU ETS. Currently, countries where such penalties are likely to be deductible, depending upon the specific circumstances, include France, Germany and Austria.

(i) Overall UK direct tax implications

It is possible that a net tax charge could arise under Accounting Views 1 and 2 if a company holds more allowances than required, assuming those allowances are issued free of charge or at less than market value. This scenario will result in an excess of deferred income being released to the profit and loss account in the period compared with the charges made to the profit and loss account in respect of the emissions made. Accordingly, if a company expects to utilise fewer allowances than it has been allocated, it may be an advantage to adopt Accounting View 3, which does not require the recognition of deferred income and should result in a nil tax charge.

If an entity has a shortfall in allowances, under Accounting Views 1, 2 and 3 a liability should be set up for the value of the additional allowances required, which should be tax deductible provided it has been calculated on a specific basis. This may result in a net tax deduction with regard to emissions allowances if a greater number of allowances than that issued by the government is required.

(j)   *Voluntary purchase of allowances*

Due to the increasing profile for many companies of their corporate and social responsibility agenda and the desire to be "carbon neutral", a number of businesses which are not included within an Emission Trading Scheme are considering the option of purchasing allowances from the market. The tax implications of this activity are again uncertain, particularly as to whether these are revenue or capital items and whether they are incurred wholly and exclusively for the purposes of the company's trade. It is likely that companies may be able to argue that the cost of purchasing allowances is a revenue expense if, in a similar way to advertising, it is aimed at attracting business but has no material lasting effect. However, HMRC may argue that companies are aiming to enhance the goodwill of the business such that this is capital expenditure. Since allowances are being purchased voluntarily rather than as a result of a legal obligation, whether the expense is likely to meet the "wholly and exclusively" test will depend upon the purpose of expenditure and whether this includes a non-business purpose. For example, HMRC may argue that this is due to the altruistic nature of the business and hence should be non-deductible; however, if the company can show that the purchase was to boost the morale of the employees and attract business, these costs are likely to be deductible.

3.   **Stamp duty**

The rules for imposition of stamp duty and other transfer taxes differ between jurisdictions. Therefore, any potential liability will depend on the initial country where the allowance is issued and the countries where the trade is deemed to take place, as well as the form of the transfer. We would recommend a review of the relevant agreements be carried out to determine whether any transfer taxes will be payable on the trade.

4.   **VAT**

The European Commission has attempted to introduce a common VAT treatment within the European Union for emissions allowances; however, VAT is still an area with potentially substantial risks for entities engaged in emissions trading. Managing this VAT position, especially where cross-border trades are carried out, is critical to ensure companies do not face an unwelcome VAT cost.

4.1   **Initial issue of allowances**

The issue of allowances by national authorities within the European Union should not be liable to VAT. Allowances are issued free of charge by national authorities; therefore, recipients do not pay a consideration for the allowance. In any case, it is arguable whether issuers of allowances carry out a business activity for VAT purposes. Clients should therefore not expect to be liable on allowances initially issued, but must be aware that VAT, in some form, is likely to arise once allowances are traded.

4.2 How should trades be treated for VAT?

(a) *Background*

The supply of an emission allowance, where the recipient is capable of using the allowance, is considered to be a supply of a service subject to VAT at the standard rate (the treatment of "non-deliverable" trades is discussed below). Therefore, trades between counterparties in the same country are usually liable to local VAT, which should be recoverable by the recipient through its VAT returns. Some exceptions exist; for example, trades on certain exchanges are zero-rated and this is discussed in more detail below.

The correct VAT treatment of cross-border emissions trades is not as straightforward. From a policy perspective, the ideal position is that recipients of cross-border trades should be required to self-account for any VAT due, in the same way as recipients of advertising and similar services. This allows recipients to account for and recover VAT in their own country without needing to seek refunds of VAT from tax authorities in other countries.

If these rules did not apply, then the supply would be deemed to take place where the supplier is located and recipients would be charged VAT in the country where their supplier is based. Businesses established in the European Union are able to recover VAT incurred in another EU jurisdiction by making a claim under the EC 8th Directive. At a practical level, however, this often involves time delays and substantial compliance costs. Although a similar refund system exists for making VAT refunds to non-EU businesses, the availability of refunds depends on whether the non-EU country in question has a reciprocal arrangement with the EU member state in which VAT has been incurred. Without such agreements the non-EU businesses will find they are unable to recover EU VAT and this can increase the cost of transactions with EU businesses by up to 25%.

(b) *Agreed position in the European Union*

To provide more certainty around this matter, the European Commission agreed to give guidance on the VAT treatment of EU emission allowances. Specifically, it was agreed that these services would fall within the scope of Article 56 (previously Article 9(2)(e)) of the EU VAT Directive, meaning that the service is deemed to take place in the country where the business recipient is located. There has been no amendment of European VAT legislation, although a note of the agreement is shown on the Commission's website.

The result of this is that non-EU businesses trading with EU counterparties should not incur EU VAT. Where a recipient of an allowance is established in the European Union, then VAT on cross-border trades should be accounted for in the recipient's home country, by the mechanism of a self-supplied "reverse charge". The self-assessed VAT can then be recovered by the recipient, usually on the same VAT return as it is declared, provided it was incurred as part of a taxable business activity.

(c) *Is this the end of the story?*

Whilst the agreement was an important step towards achieving a common approach, in practice there have been a number of difficulties in implementing a single agreement across the EU. Set out below is a list of the main "pitfalls" – practical issues and further risks to be aware of when considering the correct VAT position.

(i)   *Implementation throughout European Union*
Despite the agreement at a European Commission level, tax authorities have taken varying approaches to issuing guidance on the subject at an individual country level. The United Kingdom issued a Business Brief in October 2004 confirming adoption of the EU agreement, and Belgium and Germany were also quick to issue formal guidance. However, in some EU member states the agreement has been acknowledged only informally whilst in others no guidance has been provided at all. Even though the standard EU position should still apply across the member states, it may not be wise for traders to rely on this without checking that it has been implemented locally.

(ii)   *Trades outside the European Union*
There is a risk that traders will incur a foreign VAT cost on trades of any emissions allowances with counterparties in non-EU countries. Tax authorities outside the European Union are clearly not required to follow the view of the European Commission, and may require VAT (or an equivalent tax such as Goods and Services Tax) to be charged on trades. In this case there is a high risk that the foreign VAT would be an irrecoverable expense for businesses not located in that jurisdiction. The local VAT (or equivalent) tax rules need to be investigated at an early stage to avoid any anticipated profits being wiped out by an unexpected tax charge.

(iii) *Force of attraction rules*
A number of EU member states have "force of attraction" VAT rules, which apply where foreign entities have branches in that state. Such member states include Belgium, Germany, Spain and Sweden. When a supply is made by a foreign entity to a recipient within one of those member states, the supply is deemed to take place in that state for VAT purposes, by virtue of the branch operation. Instead of allowing the recipient to self-account for VAT, the supplier would need to account for VAT in the country where its branch and its customer are based.

Importantly, these rules apply regardless of whether the branch is connected to the supply in any way. Therefore, any traders with foreign branches should be particularly aware of these rules, as they may face an unexpected VAT liability in these member states.

(iv)   *Application to trades of other credits/allowances*
The agreed European Commission approach applies only to trades of EUAs and does not specifically cover other greenhouse gas allowances, such as CERs or Emission Reduction Units gained through Clean Development Mechanism or Joint Implementation projects. In the United Kingdom, HMRC has recently issued guidance to confirm that trades of these other allowances should also be subject to the agreed treatment for EUAs (ie subject to VAT in the country of receipt).

HMRC's application appears to be a sensible extension of the agreed EU position on cross-border EUA trades. Whilst we would expect that other EU member states would apply the same principle to trades of other greenhouse credits and allowances, there is no unified EU position, and therefore traders again face a technical risk that some member states may seek to impose VAT on trades made by suppliers from that country.

(v)   *Is the trade a financial supply?*

Given the fast-moving pace of the emissions market, it is also possible that the agreement will not cover all types of emissions trades. In particular, given an impending shift towards derivative trading, it is possible that trades will constitute exempt financial supplies for VAT purposes. The European Commission's agreed position is based on the assumption that trades are a supply of a right that may be used by the purchaser. As the trade is deemed "to be capable of physical delivery" for VAT purposes, the supply is non-financial.

This view may not be correct, however, for some types of trades. For example, we imagine that certain derivatives trades would not be capable of leading to an actual transfer of emissions allowances. Where this is the case, the trade would be an exempt supply of financial services (or outside the scope of VAT with or without credit when traded cross-border). This may result in traders needing to restrict their VAT recoveries, as businesses are unable to recover VAT incurred in relation to exempt supplies.

(vi)   *Terminal markets trades*

Specific rules apply within the United Kingdom for trades made on certain recognised exchanges. The VAT (Terminal Markets) Order 1973 allows zero-rating for trades of commodities ordinarily dealt with on specified markets, subject to meeting certain conditions. A number of exchanges in the United Kingdom have sought agreement from HMRC that their emissions trades will be zero-rated under these rules. There has been no amendment to the legislation, so it is necessary to check the rules case by case.

Whilst zero-rating of such trades is a favourable result for trades on these exchanges within the United Kingdom, it is important to note that this treatment does not automatically extend to other parts of the European Union. Whilst a supply may be zero-rated in the United Kingdom, a foreign supplier or recipient would still be obliged to charge or self-account for foreign VAT as normal. Traders on these exchanges, taking advantage of zero-rating under the terminal market rules, must take care to ensure the conditions of zero-rating are met, and also be aware of foreign VAT when dealing with foreign trades.

4.3   Summary

The intended position within the European Union is for recipients of emissions trades not to be charged VAT on cross-border trades. This position is ideal, as it enhances the liquidity of the market.

Despite this, there are many VAT pitfalls that confront businesses. These issues must therefore be carefully considered when assessing proposed trading activities and when drafting or reviewing contracts for emissions trades.

5. Environmental taxes and credits

Although this chapter focuses on the accounting and tax implications of emissions trades, no commentary on tax in relation to climate change would be complete without mention of the growing number of tax measures that have been introduced to achieve various environmental objectives. In particular, some governments have introduced new environmental taxes to discourage environmentally unfriendly behaviours whilst others have introduced tax credits to encourage environmentally responsible behaviour.

5.1 Environmental taxes

Whilst these taxes often have a common underlying theme, there is no common approach even within the European Union and each tax needs to be looked at on a case-by-case basis.

From a legal perspective, it is important to be aware of the environmental taxes that apply to company transactions (eg fuel- or waste-based contracts, or sales/purchases of businesses that have significant environmental tax compliance obligations) and consider whether appropriate registrations and reporting procedures have been arranged. Environmental taxes have specific documentation requirements that must be complied with and failure to meet these requirements can result in material financial exposures.

By way of illustration, the most prominent environmental tax in the United Kingdom is the Climate Change Levy (CCL), which has been in place since 2001. This tax is levied on sales of coal, gas, power and similar fuels to business and industry. This tax was introduced as a way to manage CO_2 emissions, but also with a view to "protect the competitiveness of UK firms"; however, in practice, some businesses have been caught by technicalities in the rules and have suffered unexpected tax liabilities. For example, some exemptions and reliefs from CCL only apply if appropriate certificates are obtained from the recipient prior to the supply taking place. Failure to collect certificates at the appropriate time has exposed suppliers to multi-million pound CCL bills. Careful attention to these matters when drawing up contracts can be useful in determining responsibilities for providing certificates and liabilities for any under-declared CCL.

5.2 Environmental tax credits

A number of countries have introduced, or are considering the introduction of, tax incentives to encourage investment in alternative or renewable fuels and electricity generation to help combat climate change.

In the United Kingdom, there are various tax incentives for expenditure on energy-efficient plant and machinery and duty differentials on certain biofuels (although the duty differentials are due to be replaced with the Renewable Transport Fuel Obligation mechanism by 2010).

One of the most attractive countries from this perspective is the United States, which has introduced a mixture of investment- and production-based tax credits designed to stimulate capital investment in the alternative and renewable fuels industries. These credits include (i) production-based credits for renewable and alternative energy sources, including wind, geothermal, biomass, the production of synthetic coal, and the gasification of coal among others, and (ii) investment-based credits for capital investment in certain other types of renewable energy property such as solar electric facilities. The credits are designed to try to level the economics for alternative and renewable fuels when compared with the integrated profitability of crude derived fuels.

In addition to the United States, most other petroleum-importing or petroleum-producing countries in the world provide similar economic and/or tax incentives for the production or investment in alternative and renewable fuels, including China, India, Russia, Australia and Indonesia.

Until such time as there is clarity, consistency and international consensus as to the accounting and tax aspects of measures intended to protect against climate change, this will remain a relatively high-risk area for compliance. Businesses are advised to consider scenarios on a case-by-case basis and to seek local and specific advice where appropriate.

The authors would like to thank Pat Concessi, Julian Dené, Trang Hoang, Ross Howard, Jason Moore and Brian Murrell for their kind assistance in the preparation of this chapter.

Corporate social responsibility and climate change

"This report of my death was an exaggeration"[1]

Angela Delfino
Dewey & LeBoeuf
Mike Wallace
Wallace Partners
Paul Q Watchman
Dewey & LeBoeuf

---

1.   Introduction

After a few troublesome years of criticism, stagnation and premature obituaries,[2] corporate social responsibility (CSR), far from dead, is in good health and very much alive.

CSR recently featured at the UN Global Compact Leaders Summit, where corporate leaders stated their commitment to making the 10 Global Compact principles more effective and emphasised the importance of climate action. The first Annual Review of the UN Global Compact,[3] which analysed the extent to which companies have implemented the 10 Global Compact principles in the areas of human rights, labour and the environment, concluded that (i) the majority of the survey respondents have policies in place relating to the principles; and (ii) 63% of respondents participated in the Global Compact to increase trust in the company. In addition, the Principles for Responsible Investment Report on Progress[4] was released. According to this report, 80% of investment manager signatories to the Principles for Responsible Investment, which includes more than 200 institutional investors representing more than US$9 trillion in assets, are conducting at least some shareholder engagement on environmental and social governance issues, while 82% of asset owners are doing so.

In the Heligendam Summit, G8 governments committed "to promote actively internationally agreed corporate social responsibility" and appealed to business leaders to improve the transparency of their performance with respect to CSR, recognising their importance in world markets and as fundamental globalisation players. As a result of the G8 Summit, the OECD has been given the task of providing a framework for a high-level dialogue with emerging economies and CSR.

---

1   The text of a cable sent in 1847 by Mark Twain from London to the press in the United States after his obituary had been mistakenly published.
2   Alina Ward and Craig Smith, *Corporate Social Responsibility at a Crossroads: Futures for CSR in the UK to 2015* (London: IIED 2006), p 26.
3   The Global Compact, *UN Global Compact Annual Review* (New York: UN Global Compact Office 2007).
4   PRI, *PRI Report on Progress* (New York: UN Global Compact Office 2007).

Two groundbreaking reports, by Goldman Sachs and McKinsey & Co, show that an increasing number of business leaders see corporate responsibility as a way to compete successfully and to build trust with stakeholders and that sustainability front runners in a range of industries can generate higher stock prices.

The report released by Goldman Sachs[5] showed that among the six sectors covered – energy, mining, steel, food, beverages and media – companies that are considered leaders in implementing environmental, social and governance (ESG) policies to create sustained competitive advantage have outperformed the general stock market by 25% since August 2005. In addition, 72% of these companies have outperformed their peers over the same period.

The survey prepared by McKinsey[6] concludes that more than 90% of CEOs are doing more than they did five years ago to incorporate environmental, social and governance issues into strategy and operations; that for 72% of CEOs corporate responsibility should be embedded fully into strategy and operations; and that for 59% of CEOs corporate responsibility should be embedded into global supply chains.

CSR is now an industry in its own right and a flourishing profession and many business schools now offer CSR courses. In general, CSR as part of the wide sustainability movement is thriving. Since its official launch on July 26 2000, the UN Global Compact has grown to over 3,300 "active" business participants which are publicly committing to CSR-related actions. On our desks lie numerous CSR reports from all industry sectors. The CorporateRegister.com, the largest online directory of company issues, CSR, sustainability and environment reports, currently[7] features 16,181 reports from 4,201 different companies across 105 countries. In 2007, 2,445 reports were produced and, as of March 2007, 86% of the FTSE100 had produced a corporate responsibility report.[8] Also, the proliferation of CSR reports or CSR sections in annual reports is happening at the same time as CSR ratings and rankings grow.

Does quantity imply quality? We know that it does not necessarily do so. CSR has yet to find consensus as to its object, methodologies and goals. Most CSR reports are still empty of substantive and quantitative content. A logical and coherent framework for CSR activities, and most importantly a strategic one, are often missing from these publications.

What is CSR? A form of risk evaluation? A source of business opportunity and improved competitiveness? A form of insurance? A public, government or investor relations exercise? Greenwash? Philanthropy? A distraction? A threat? CSR has had different meanings attributed to it in different contexts. Also CSR has multiple sub-agendas, each associated with a different theme: "business and human rights", "business and tax avoidance" and "business and environment", to name just a few.

What is the purpose of CSR reports? Are they an element of a company's transparency and accountability? A form of engagement with its stakeholders? A collection of huge volumes with nice and glossy pictures? "Eco-pornography"? And what

---

5   Goldman Sachs, GS Sustain (London: Goldman Sachs 2007).
6   McKinsey, Shaping the New Rules of Competition: UN Global Compact Participant Mirror (McKinsey 2007).
7   As of end of February 2008.
8   CorporateRegister.com.

about all the sudden carbon and climate concerns? Are they affecting the CSR agenda?

This chapter attempts to provide our view on the above questions. Section 2 analyses the concept of CSR and how climate change issues are affecting it. Section 3 then discusses types of instruments that companies use to enhance their internal governance. We use a classification proposed by the European Commission and divide the section in three subparts: responsible management, investment and consumption. Section 4 discusses the activity of reporting climate change; section 5 discusses climate change reporting in four different sectors of activity: banking, oil and gas, insurance and shipping. Section 6 provides insights of CSR practices around the world. Subsequently, section 7 discusses the effectiveness of, and the business case for, CSR. Finally, section 8 addresses some questions for the future.

Our general aim goes beyond each of the topics addressed in the different sections of this chapter. We try to find out how climate change is affecting CSR, the new trends in CSR arising because of climate change reporting, and how businesses and investors should regard and prepare for the future.

2.   CSR and the impact of climate change

2.1   CSR

The 1950s are generally accepted as the beginning of the modern academic debate on corporate social responsibility. Howard Bowen, perhaps the founding father of CSR, defines the concept as "the obligations of businessmen to pursue those policies, to make those decisions, or to follow those lines of action which are desirable in terms of the objectives and values of our society".[9] This trend was followed until the 1970s.

In contrast to this 1950s idea of CSR reflecting the objectives and values of society, the 1970s highlighted the capacity of a business to respond to its environment. Corporate social responsiveness or CSR2 dealt with how companies should and could adapt to specific societal needs.[10] Almost simultaneously there emerged the concept of corporate social performance (CSP)[11] dealing with outcomes of CSR.

In the 1990s, Wood[12] revised the CSP model and divided it into: principles of corporate social responsibility (including legitimacy, public responsibility and managerial discretion); processes of corporate social responsiveness (such as environmental assessment, stakeholder management, and issues management); and outcomes of corporate behaviour (ranging from social policies to social impacts). After Wood's model, other authors have added to the analysis the economic and environmental outcomes to social outcomes.

The consideration of the social, environmental and economic responsibility

---

9   Howard Bowen, *Toward Social Responsibilities of the Businessman* (New York: Harper and Row 1953).

10   Robert W Ackerman and Raymond A Bauer, *Corporate Social Responsiveness* (Reston, VA: Reston Pub. Co 1976) and William C Frederick, "From CSR1 to CSR2: The Maturing of Business-and-Society Thought", Working Paper (Katz Graduate School of Business, University of Pittsburgh 1978).

11   Philip L Cochran and Steven L Wartick, *Corporate Governance* (Morristown NJ: Financial Executives Research Foundation 1988) and S Prakash Sethi, *Up Against the Corporate Wall: Modern Corporations and Social Issues of the Seventies* (Englewood Cliffs: Prentice-Hall 1974).

12   Donna J Wood, "Social Issues in Management: Theory and Research in Corporate Social Performance", *Journal of Management*, vol 17(2) (1991), pp 383 to 406.

became common and was stimulated by concepts such as the triple bottom line approach[13] and corporate sustainability, which gained acceptance in the 1990s.

During the 1980s and the 1990s, the stakeholder theory also represented an important contribution to the CSR discourse, because it challenged the stockholder paradigm defined by Milton Friedman (1970) that considers the maximisation of financial returns to stockholders as the primary if not the only responsibility of a company. According to the stakeholder theory, the effective management of a company depends on the consideration of the legitimate interests of *all* stakeholders defined as "anyone who has a stake in or claim on the company".[14]

Also, the concept of corporate citizenship (CC)[15] likens companies to citizens and claims rights and duties for companies towards society in general.

Another critical perspective is corporate accountability that emphasises that corporations are answerable in some way for the consequences of their actions. Because of their influence on public and private life, companies become more accountable to the whole of society. One of the means of accountability is the creation of transparency through reporting on non-financial performance and the engagement with stakeholders in general.[16]

Outside the academic context, CSR has been defined, divided or confused with "business ethics", "triple bottom line", "sustainability", "corporate accountability", "corporate responsibility", "corporate stewardship", "responsible entrepreneurship", "business and sustainable development", "environmental social governance" and "responsible competitiveness" among others. Although causes for the different definitions cannot be easily found, perhaps these relate to competition among CSR players and the different interests involved in the "CSR game" – greenwashing, rebranding, or simply the effort to find the most appropriate word for a yet undefined concept.

Despite any agreed definition of CSR, which we do not intend to provide, some elements are well established, including the voluntary and the unenforceable nature of CSR. This does not mean that there is no law governing CSR. There is legislation regarding instruments whose adoption remains voluntary (eg the EMAS[17] legislation), in which case, a company subjects itself voluntarily to legislation. There are also CSR-related instruments which were previously voluntary (eg market disclosure and directors' duties).[18]

---

13 John Elkington, *Cannibals with Forks: The Triple Bottom Line of 21st Century Business* (New Society Publishers 1998).

14 R Edward Freeman and David Reed, "Stockholders and Stakeholders: A New Perspective on Corporate Governance", *California Management Review*, vol 25(3) (1983), pp 88 to 106.

15 Alyson Warhurst, *Corporate Citizenship and Corporate Social Investment: Drivers of tri-sectors partnerships* (Sheffield: Greenleaf 2001); Jorg Andriof and Malcolm McIntosh, *Perspectives on Corporate Citizenship* (Sheffield: Greenleaf 2001); André Habisch et al, *Social Capital and Corporate Citizenship* (Berlin: Logos 2001), McIntosh et al, *Living Corporate Citizenship* (Harlow: Financial Times Prentice Hall 2003).

16 Zadek et al, *Building Corporate Accountability* (London: Earthscan 1997).

17 Council Regulation (EC) No 761/2001 of March 19 2001, allowing voluntary participation by organisations in a Community eco-management and audit scheme (OJ L114, 24.4.2001, p 1).

18 In December 2007, Sweden announced that all 55 state-owned companies in Sweden have to file an annual sustainability report based on the Global Reporting Initiative (G3) before the March 31 each year from 2009.

2.2   CSR and climate change

The potential financial implications of climate change are receiving growing attention and recognition from investors, shareholders, consumers and other stakeholders, thus encouraging companies to identify, assess and disclose the implications of climate change on their operations. Non-financial implications of climate change reporting are also growing. This is due to the enactment of new legislation and to the fact that climate change is also becoming a reputational and strategic issue for companies.

Short-term and long-term climatic changes and the need to focus on adaptation measures as well as mitigation have also come to the attention of certain companies.

All these considerations are reflected in recent CSR reports.

In a survey conducted by the GRI and KPMG Global Sustainability Services,[19] it was found that almost all the companies which were part of the survey reported on climate change in their sustainability reports and that they reported more on opportunities than on the financial risks deriving from climate change.

Opportunities were amply reported, mostly in the area of emissions trading and carbon credits (irrespective of whether or not they were based in Annex I countries of the Kyoto Protocol). Other opportunities were also reported, for example low-emission and energy-efficient products.

The reduced reporting on risks (except in respect of savings from improvements in energy efficiency and reduction in emissions) may be due to the understanding that risks go beyond current business planning horizons, or that risks have not been fully identified or, most importantly, quantified.

According to the latest report produced by CorporateRegister.com,[20] climate change has become a key component of CSR reports and the dominant issue in CSR and corporate sustainability. Of the Global FT500 companies that issue stand-alone financial or CSR reports, almost nine out of 10 include information on their climate change strategy and 78% of the reports include greenhouse gas emissions data[21] alongside broader information on companies' climate change policies. However, fewer than half of the reports including greenhouse gas emissions data provided external assurance to verify reporting figures, and only half of the reports include commitments to reduce emissions.

CSR seems to be changing because of climate change considerations and it appears that the increased awareness of climate change has resulted in an increase in CSR reporting. Companies of all sizes and from all industries are suddenly talking about carbon. It is an important business concern in terms of activity planning, and it presents more business opportunities than perhaps any other environmental issue. The disclosure of carbon-related matters may in fact be a good thing for the business of a company.

19   Global Reporting Initiative and KPMG's Global Sustainability Services, *Reporting the Business Implications of Climate Change in Sustainability Reports* (Amsterdam: Global Reporting Initiative and KPMG's Global Sustainability Services 2007).

20   CorporateRegister.com, *Corporate Climate Communications Report 2007* (London: CorporateRegister.com 2008).

21   63% of the reports align with the GHG Protocol. 54% of the reports in the study include a GRI contents index, with the majority – 33% – including a G3 contents index.

However, while climate change communication is becoming commonplace, there is a definite lack of balanced reporting. Discussion of opportunities is more prevalent than self-assessment or the recognition of risks. This trend has a distinct parallel with the communications witnessed during the "dot-com" boom and the explosion in the "organic foods" market. An important differentiator, however, is that carbon emissions can and are being quantified. In fact, there is growing consensus around a few global standards for measuring and reporting carbon emissions. These are addressed in section 4.

Once a degree of consensus is agreed on metrics, better information on climate change and perhaps other environmental indicators will start being disclosed for the benefit of all. This should result in a standard, which should then allow for verification through auditing. In turn, this fact should increase trust in CSR.

3. Types of CSR instruments

The instruments that companies use to enhance their internal sustainability governance or that are used by stakeholders to induce responsible corporate behaviour may be categorised in three areas in accordance with the European Commission:[22] socially responsible management, which includes codes of conduct, management systems, and reporting; socially responsible investment (eg SRI funds and indexes); and socially responsible consumption, based on instruments for social and environmental labelling. These are discussed in turn next.

3.1 Socially and environmentally responsible management

Codes of conduct are "formal statements of principles that define standards for specific company behaviour".[23] Their purpose is to serve as internal management tools that influence the behaviour of companies themselves, as well as subsidiaries, contractors or suppliers, and to inform customers and the public in general. Codes usually refer to areas such as the environment, human rights and corporate behaviour in respect of consumers, customers, competitors or employees.

Management systems are internal tools for the integration of certain values within normal operations of a company and establish procedures and specifications used in the management of an organisation. Management systems which originally focused on quality processes (eg ISO 9000 and AA(AccountAbility)1000 Assurance Standard) are now being applied in other fields such as the environmental (eg ISO 14000 and EMAS) and occupational health and safety (Social Accountability (SA 8000), IL-OSH 2001 and OHSAS 18000). There are ongoing negotiations within the ISO framework on a new International Standard on Social Responsibility. To be known as ISO 26000,[24] the standard is expected to be a guidance document not intended for certification. Although management systems are voluntary in nature, those linked with third-party certification schemes have an effective compliance mechanism, because certificates awarded are dependent on compliance.

---

22   European Commission, *ABC of the Main Instruments of Corporate Social Responsibility* (Luxembourg: Office of Official Publications of the European Communities 2004).

23   *Ibid*, p 7.

24   The guidance standard will be published in 2010.

Reporting is a tool for "communicating the accounted for and assessed social and environmental activities, either to consumers or to rating systems used by the investment community".[25] Reporting is the object of the next section.

Corporate citizenship activities include a variety of initiatives such as donations, sponsoring, or the establishment of foundations and exemption of staff for volunteering activities.

3.2   Socially and environmentally responsible investment

Socially responsible investment (SRI) is an instrument that "links the access to capital of publicly listed companies to the financial targets of investors as well as to their social, environmental and ethical considerations".[26] Unlike socially responsible management tools, SRI is an instrument used by fund managers and individual investors, which influences companies via their investment decisions. According to the European Commission, SRI works either directly, through shareholders that directly influence a company's orientation towards socially responsible behaviour through dialogue, pressure on management, and voting rights in shareholder meetings,[27] or indirectly through the selection of assets for their portfolios on social and environmental grounds (social/ethical screening).

(a)   Dow Jones Sustainability Indexes

The Dow Jones Sustainability Indexes (DJSI), the first global indexes tracking the financial performance of sustainability-driven companies, focus on meeting the financial markets' demands for rational and investable indexes to benchmark the performance of investments in sustainability companies and funds. DJSI account for issues such as corporate governance, climate change, supply chain standards, human capital development, and labour practices.

(b)   FTSE4Good

The FTSE4Good Index Series was designed to measure the performance of companies that meet corporate responsibility standards, and to facilitate investment in those companies. FTSE4Good already demands high environmental standards; but since January 1 2008, criteria have been raised to include CO_2 emissions and climate change. All in the index must meet certain criteria in the areas of policy and

---

25   AccountAbility, *Mapping Instruments for Corporate Social Responsibility* (AccounAbility 2003), p 7.
26   RARE, *Corporate Social Responsibility: Integrating a Business and Societal Governance Perspective* (RARE 2005), p 37.
27   According to the Ceres Report, Douglas G Cogan, *Corporate Governance and Climate Change* (Ceres 2006), p 16: "In 2004 and 2005 over two dozen global warming shareholder resolutions were filed with companies – more than triple the number of filings in 2000 and 2001". In accordance with the same source, some resolutions received the highest voting support levels ever – a direct result of pension funds, labour funds and other institutional investors increasing their interest and involvement in the climate change issue. According to the Institutional Shareholder Services a record 1,169 shareholder resolutions on corporate governance issues were proposed in 2007. A record 23% of those were withdrawn by shareholders after companies agreed to adopt new policies or to discuss the issues. A total of 43 global climate resolutions were filed by Trillium Asset Management, Calvert mutual funds, the SEIU and the North Carolina State treasurer with energy, auto, home-building and financial companies. Shareholders withdrew one-third of the resolutions after companies made their climate change commitments (Edward Iwata, "Boardrooms Open up to Investors", *USA Today*, September 6 2007).

governance, marketing and strategy, disclosure and performance; however, companies have been classified in "High Operational Impact", "Medium Operational Impact", and "Additional High Product Impact" reflecting the level of associated greenhouse gas (GHG) emissions. In the early stages of implementation of the new climate change criteria, FTSE will allow flexibility in respect of disclosure, reflecting the fact that no single methodology is yet accepted as the single global standard.

(c) **Merrill Lynch Carbon Leaders Europe index**
Another example is the Merrill Lynch Carbon Leaders Europe index (MLCX) launched in October 2007 by Merrill Lynch Global Research in partnership with Trucost. The MLCX, the first of its kind, is an index based primarily on the carbon footprint of a company.

The MLCX Global CO_2 Emissions Index is based on contracts established under the European Union Emissions Trading Scheme and under the Kyoto Protocol. The MLCX Global CO_2 index (MLCXCO2E) gives investors exposure to both schemes, weighting them by their relevance in the global emissions market. In addition, the European Union Allowance and Certified Emissions Reduction markets can also be accessed individually through the MLCX EUA Index (MLCXEUAE) and the MLCX CER Index (MLCXCERE), respectively.

(d) **SRI funds**
According to Carbon Counts 2007, the Trucost Carbon Footprint Ranking of UK Equity Investment Funds,[28] a quarter of so-called SRI funds sold in the United Kingdom have a higher carbon footprint than their more mainstream rivals. However, the carbon footprints of the funds analysed varies hugely, the most carbon-intensive fund having a footprint almost 10 times as large as the least carbon-intensive fund. Additionally, of the 185 funds reviewed, the three with the lowest footprints were all SRI funds.[29]

Although the conclusions of the study are significant, it should be said that the definition of SRI investment is very broad, and in general SRI mandates do not yet specifically target carbon emissions reduction. However, the same study makes reference to the fact that the SRI industry is experiencing increased demand for products that specifically address climate change. Another important conclusion of this study is that carbon intensity does not correlate with performance.

3.3 Socially and environmentally responsible consumption
Social and ecological labels are market-based instruments aimed at influencing purchasing decisions of customers, retailers, traders and end consumers in favour of products that have socially/environmentally favourable characteristics (eg energy efficiency), and that were responsibly manufactured (eg in respect of labour standards) or traded (eg by granting fair product prices).[30] Labels bring

---

28   Trucost, Carbon Counts 2007, *The Trucost Carbon Footprint Ranking of UK Equity Investment Funds* (London: Trucost 2007).
29   Prudential Ethical Trust, Axa Ethical and Sovereign Ethical.
30   See above at note 22, p 38.

demand into the process of making businesses more sustainable, at the same time serving as business instruments for marketing and thereby creating competitive advantage.

(a)   *Carbon Trust*

Carbon Trust is a private company set up by the UK government, which aims at the development of clean technologies and the reduction of carbon emissions by different organisations. It has already launched a carbon reduction label to provide a measure of a product's carbon footprint across its lifecycle from source to store to disposal.

4.   Reporting climate change

As previously mentioned, almost every company in the FTSE100 now produces a corporate responsibility report.[31] Although 80 FTSE100 companies have identified climate change as a business risk, only 38 of those have targets for emissions reduction. According to the latest study of environmental disclosure in the statutory Annual Reports and Accounts of FTSE All-Shares Companies produced by Trucost to the Environment Agency, climate change and energy use were mentioned by 61% of companies; absolute CO_2 emission levels were disclosed by 15 companies, and 37 provided some figures for energy; and five companies reported on CO_2 in quantitative terms (Emap, Johnson Matthey, Invensys, Scottish Power, and Scottish and Southern Energy).[32]

Corporate and social responsibility reporting is very dynamic, and measuring and publicising social and environmental performance are undoubtedly powerful means of influencing corporate behaviour in all sectors of activity. It is even being encouraged by governments.[33] Nevertheless, the majority of companies have yet to provide the consistent and comprehensive reporting that allows investors and other stakeholders to make meaningful comparisons between companies and to analyse the financial implications of climate change.

Specific weaknesses in corporate disclosures have been pointed out in relevant literature and include the focus on historical rather than future performance and the use of different greenhouse gas emission methodologies and reporting standards.

Since they are only voluntary, CSR and climate change reporting initiatives do not create legal relations between the company issuing the report and third parties. There are generally no offences under civil or criminal law of providing false or misleading information in a CSR report as there are with annual accounts reports and listing particulars. For this reason, there are no sanctions – despite existing laws on misleading advertising – to impose on errant or dishonest company directors or officers.

However, despite not being directly enforceable, the above principles set a benchmark and represent a different type of liability – responsibility – and may have

---

31   See above at note 8.
32   Trucost and Environment Agency, *Environmental Disclosures* (Bristol: Environment Agency, 2007), p 5.
33   *Ibid* with respect to the United Kingdom.

important consequences, mostly reputational.[34] In addition, the increasing disclosure of quantified data begins to raise the performance bar for non-reporting companies. It is the absence of any data that is beginning to "raise a red flag" on overall corporate governance. What message is being sent when sector peers are measuring and reporting in quantified terms, while a single company makes no public statement on the issue at hand?

But what to say about reporting initiatives and methodologies? In the scope of climate change, five, of different natures, are worth mentioning: (i) securities filings; (ii) the Global Reporting Initiative (GRI); (iii) the Carbon Disclosure Project (CDP); (iv) the Greenhouse Gas Protocol Initiative; and (v) the California Climate Action Registry.

4.1   Disclosure

(a)   Securities filings

Under US law, the registration and sale of securities and related disclosure requirements is regulated under the Securities Act of 1933.[35] Further, with the Securities Act of 1934,[36] publicly-traded companies must periodically disclose certain information to the public. These disclosure goals have been furthered by regulations promulgated under the Securities Acts of 1933 and 1934. They are commonly referred to as Regulation S-K. In particular, pursuant to SEC Regulation S-K, publicly traded companies are required to disclose environmental information on at least a quarterly basis. For example, Regulation S-K Item 101 requires a detailed description of a business, including among other matters the material effects of complying or failing to comply with environmental requirements on capital expenditures and earnings, among others.[37]

The climate of increased risk management and disclosure in the United States fostered by the Sarbanes-Oxley Act (S-OxAct) of 2002[38] and its implementing regulations has increased the call for more reliable environmental disclosure. Two requisites of the S-OxAct and its implementing regulations are worth mentioning. First,

---

34   *Kasky v Nike* was a legal case in the United States that went all the way to the Supreme Court and that has implications for how companies approach and communicate their CSR policies. In order to deal with a controversy on working conditions and human rights in its supply chain, Nike launched a PR and advertising campaign. As a result, in 1998 Marc Kasky sued Nike under California's unfair competition and false advertising laws, alleging that the company's claims were misleading. The case ended with a settlement stipulating that Nike would pay US$1.5 million to the Washington, DC-based Fair Labor Association.

35   15 U.S.C. §§ 77a *et seq.*

36   15 U.S.C. §§ 78a *et seq.*

37   17 C.F.R. §229.101. Other relevant SEC environmental disclosure requirements include: Reg S-K, Item 103, which requires a detailed disclosure of legal proceedings, including disclosures on at least a quarterly basis of pending environmental legal proceedings or proceedings known or contemplated which are material, involve 10% of current assets or more, or monetary sanctions of US$100,000 or more (17 C.F.R. §229.103); and Reg S-K, Item 303, which requires disclosure in the Management's Discussion and Analysis of Financial Condition and Results of Operation (MD&A) section of reports of environmental contingencies that may reasonably have a material impact on net sales, revenue, or income from continuing operations (17 C.F.R. §229.303).

38   15 U.S.C. §§7201 *et seq.* On the relevance of Sarbanes-Oxley in the environmental disclosure arena, see for example Andrew N Davis and Stephen J Humes, "Environmental Disclosures after Sarbanes-Oxley", *The Practical Lawyer* vol 50 no 3 (2004), p 19 and Gregory Rodgers, *Financial Reporting of Environmental Liabilities and Risks after Sarbanes-Oxley* (Hoboken, NJ: John Wiley & Sons, Inc 2005).

a corporation's chief executive officer (CEO) and chief financial officer (CFO) must certify, in a company's 10-Q and 10-K reports, and periodically ensure that a company has put in place an internal management system, including "disclosure controls and procedures", that guarantees that information that must be disclosed under Securities Exchange Commission (SEC) regulations, and that such information is accumulated and communicated to corporate management.[39] Secondly, under Section 906 of the S-OxAct, which further imposes criminal sanctions, CEOs and CFOs must provide additional certifications with each additional periodic report containing financial statements filed with the SEC, stating that the report complies with the Securities Exchange Act requirements and that the information provided in the periodic report fairly presents the financial condition and results of operations of the company.

The disclosure requirements under the Securities Acts of 1933 and 1934 have not yet been amended to address specifically the demands placed on companies by climate change regulation and litigation. None the less, the requirements of Regulation S-K have potential application to climate change matters.[40] Furthermore, the S-OxAct puts ongoing pressure on management to account for and disclose any material aspect of climate change risk that can fairly be said to be quantifiable.[41]

(b)   *The Global Reporting Initiative*

The Global Reporting Initiative (GRI),[42] covers the social, environmental and economic footprint of an organisation and a wide range of specific CSR issues. It has its origins around 1997 to 1998, when the non-profit group Ceres started a "Global Reporting Initiative". In 1999 UNEP joined as a partner and in 2000 the GRI's first Sustainability Reporting Guidelines were released.

The GRI aims at transparency, accountability, reporting and sustainable development. The GRI network promotes these aims based on a plethora of principles and indicators through a Sustainability Reporting Framework, at the core of which are the Sustainability Reporting Guidelines. Other components in the Reporting Framework are Sector Supplements and Protocols.

The current Sustainability Reporting Guidelines (GR3)[43] consist of Reporting Principles, Reporting Guidance, and Standard Disclosures (including Performance Indicators).

Specifically on climate change, the new GR3 guidelines at the end of 2006

---

39   Moreover, under Section 302 of the S-OxAct, both the CEO and the CFO must sign a certification statement to be attached to the company's 10-Q and 10-K reports saying that each report filed with the SEC meets all requirements of the Securities Exchange Act, and that the information contained in the report "fairly presents in all material aspects" the financial condition and results of operations of the company. Also, they must certify that they have reviewed the report; that there are no untrue statements of material facts or omissions necessary to make the report not misleading; and all significant deficiencies and material weaknesses in the design and operation of internal control over financial reporting have been disclosed.

40   Jeffrey A Smith and Matthew Morreale "Disclosure Issues" in Michael B Gerrard (ed.) *Global Climate Change and US Law* (Chicago: ABA 2007), pp 453 to 496.

41   Recently, the New York Office of the Attorney General filed a petition with the SEC to compel five energy companies to quantify their carbon costs in their 10-K disclosures. Also, see Beth Young, *Whose Carbon Footprint is Too Big for Their Corporate Boot?* (Portland: The Corporate Library 2008).

42   www.globalreporting.org/Home.

43   www.globalreporting.org/ReportingFramework/G3Online/.

included a new core indicator: EC2 – Financial implications and other risks and opportunities for an organisation's activities due to climate change.

(c) **Carbon Disclosure Project**

The Carbon Disclosure Project (CDP) was established to conduct research into carbon markets and economics to provide an insight for investors on the risks and opportunities presented by climate change, and for company managers on the views of shareholders on climate change issues. As such, it represents a vital source of information on essential investment and management considerations that would otherwise be difficult to obtain because of the uncertain nature of future exposure to climate change liabilities. The CDP has been operating for seven years and there are now more than 250 institutions signed up, which collectively manage in excess of US$45 trillion of assets.[44]

4.2   Measurement and inventory

(a)   **The Greenhouse Gas Protocol (GHG Protocol)**

The GHG Protocol initiative is the result of a partnership between the World Resources Institute (WRI) and the World Business Council for Sustainable Development (WBCSD). It is an international GHG accounting tool, which is used by governments and businesses for the quantification and management of GHG emissions.

It comprises two modules: The Corporate Accounting and Reporting Standards and the Project Accounting Protocol and Guidelines.

While the latter is an accounting tool for quantifying the GHG benefits of climate change mitigation projects, the Corporate Accounting and Reporting Standards provide standards and methodologies for companies and other organisations to inventory and report all of the GHG emissions they produce. It also aims at providing companies with information that can be used to build effective

---

44   The CDP was launched on December 4 2000. The first cycle of the project (CDP 1) involved sending a letter and questionnaire to the FT500 largest companies in the world on May 31 2002. This letter was signed by 35 institutional investors who collaborated to provide an efficient mechanism for disclosure of this information. In the CDP 1 report, 71% of corporations responded and 45% answered the questionnaire in full. The CDP 2 information request was signed by 95 institutional investors with assets of US$10 trillion. 86% of corporations responded and 60% answered the questionnaire in full. The CDP 3 information request was signed by 155 institutional investors with assets of more than US$21 trillion. 89% of corporations responded and 71% answered the questionnaire in full. The CDP4 information request was signed by 225 institutional investors with assets of more than US$31 trillion. The information request was sent to 2,180 companies and more than 940 answered the questions. From the FT500 sample, 91% of corporations responded and 72% answered the questionnaire in full. The CDP 5 information request was signed by more than 280 institutional investors, with assets of more than US$41 trillion. The information request was sent to 2,400 companies. The CDP 5 report reveals that response rates for the FTSE 250 companies were much higher (61% answered the questionnaire, up from 36%) in comparison to the previous year). 92% of FTSE 100 companies answered the questionnaire, the highest response rate of all indices surveyed globally, and 69% provided quantified data on direct emissions under Scope 1 of the GHG Protocol. Total Scope 1 emissions reported by FTSE 350 companies amounted to more than 466 million tonnes of CO_2. Carbon intensities of sectors varied widely when direct emissions were compared with indirect emissions under Scope 2, which amounted to more than 96 million tonnes of CO_2. More companies attempted to provide estimates for Scope 3 emissions. However, there were inconsistencies in boundaries for indirect emissions under Scope 3, which includes supply chains, business travel, and products in use. (Source: Carbon Disclosure Project available at www.cdproject.net/aboutus.asp and Trucost available at www.trucost.com/pressreleases/CDP5.html.)

GHG-emission management and reduction strategies.

The WRI/WBCSD GHG Protocol Corporate Standard is commonly referred to as the world's leading standard and has been explicitly adopted by ISO[45] as its organisation-level GHG accounting and reporting standard.

Unlike other GHG programmes, the WRI/WBCSD GHG Protocol does not require emissions information to be reported to WRI or WBCSD. In addition, while this standard is designed to develop a verifiable inventory, it does not provide a standard for how the verification process should be conducted.

(b)   The California Climate Action Registry

The California Climate Action Registry is a voluntary registry for GHG. The purpose of this registry is to help companies and organisations with operations in California to establish GHG emissions baselines against which any future GHG emission reduction requirements may be applied. The California Climate Action Registry has developed a General Protocol and additional industry-specific protocols (cement, forestry, and power and utility). These provide guidance on how to provide inventories of GHG emissions for participation in the scheme: what to measure, how to measure, the back-up data required, and certification requirements. The Registry requires the reporting of only CO_2 emissions for the first three years of participation. The reporting of the remaining five GHGs covered in the Kyoto Protocol (CH_4, N_2O, HFCs, PFCs and SF_6) is required after three years of participation.

(c)   Other reporting mechanisms

Two important publications from Ceres[46] of January and October 2006 should be referred to at this point since they are useful in framing reporting. In *Managing the Risks and Opportunities of Climate Change: A Practical Toolkit for Corporate Leaders*, a climate change strategy is recommended and structured in three phases: assessment, implementation, and disclosure and engagement. In the first, the measurement, benchmarking and inventory of GHG (step 2) remits to the WRI/WBCSD GHG Protocol and in the third, the public disclosure of assessments and implementations in annual financial reports and corporate responsibility reports (step 9) suggests securities filings and GRI guidelines.

In *Using the Global Framework for Climate Risk Disclosure*, Ceres recommends a harmonised disclosure via existing reporting mechanisms. The study therefore compares GRI, CDP and SEC 10-K reporting provisions and requirements and attempts to harmonise individual requirements.

GRI and CDP have also been working closely together so that their work is harmonised and mutually supportive. The main aim is to ensure that CDP questionnaires and the GRI indicators are closely aligned and are in fact complementary. Also both CDP and GRI highlight the WRI/WBCSD GHG Protocol as providing the preferred framework for reporting.

---

45   ISO 14064-1 Greenhouse Gases — Part 1: Specification with Guidance at the Organisation Level for Quantification and Reporting of Greenhouse Gas Emissions and Removals.

46   Ceres is a network of investors, environmental organisations and other public interest groups working with companies and investors to address sustainability challenges.

Hopefully, this emerging consensus should, over time, improve consistency and comparability between corporate GHG emissions reports. However, agreeing a reporting protocol is only the beginning, since investors and companies must be able to incorporate and make sense of it.

There are still many formats of GHG reporting being produced by companies, with the majority of data being self-reported and based on internal surveys, estimates and broad operational assumptions. Even within sectors there is a lack of consistent, timely and comparable reporting. Accordingly, the variations in reporting and sector studies leave the market and stakeholders questioning the standards by which the accounting is occurring and the overall credibility of the reporting.

The market has produced its own solution in its demand for, and hence the proliferation of, rating and ranking organisations. There are dozens of entities ranking, rating, judging and measuring all or some components of CSR performance. While the methodologies appear to be very rigorous, the end result is still an opinion based primarily on unverified data. To simplify the complicated and opaque methodologies being employed, the resulting performance measure is often presented as alphabetical grades or numerical rankings with one, two, or even three significant digits.

As to measurement and inventory, the GHG Protocol is becoming a commonly agreed standard. However, difficulties still remain as to the quantification of emissions and most importantly as regards the determination of the price of carbon. Also, very few studies exist that refer to carbon efficiency, to total emissions over a certain period of time, or which compare and contrast the performance of each company based on turnover.

5.   Banking, insurance, oil and gas and shipping

In general, climate change awareness and its reflection in CSR policies has dramatically increased in the last few years. In the authors' experience, the major goal in the banking, insurance, oil and gas, and shipping industries has been to assess risks, profile companies, improve energy efficiency and achieve carbon neutrality. However, we are far from achieving adequate climate change reporting. In a study released in August 2007, the Association of Chartered Certified Accountants (ACCA) examined the sustainability reports produced by 42 UK-based companies, all working in high-impact or medium-impact sectors such as aviation, chemicals, electricity generation and construction. The study concludes that even companies with a good reputation for sustainability reporting are failing to report adequately on their impact on climate change.[47] Our attention is, however, given below to the banking, insurance, oil and gas, and shipping sectors.

5.1   Banking

Due to their strategic role in lending and project finance, banks are well positioned to set an example in relation to facing climate change challenges. A contribution can

---

47   According to the study, no single company was found to be reporting evenly across all the key climate change issues – especially those relating to product impacts and initiatives to reduce carbon emissions. 57% disclosed short- or medium-term emissions targets, but only 43% produced targets.

be made through the financing of "green" and renewable energy projects, by research and development of clean technologies and by acting as intermediaries in the carbon market. In addition, banks have been positioning themselves to assist companies in generating carbon credits from Clean Development Mechanism and Joint Implementation projects.

CSR reports from banking institutions have been increasingly focused on climate change and emissions reduction. Commitments to reduce the carbon intensity of business have been registered in the majority of banks with international projection, such as HSBC and ABN AMRO. Banks have achieved this commitment at least in part by minimising emissions at source, by implementing energy-efficiency measures and by increasing the purchase of energy from renewable sources. HSBC recently went "carbon-neutral" and launched an environmental efficiency programme worth £45 million over the next five years, aimed at reducing its environmental impact. HSBC is also launching a Climate Change Fund that will apply the quantitative models used by hedge funds to shares in companies combating climate change.

In March 2007, Bank of America Corporation announced a US$20 billion initiative to support the growth of environmentally sustainable business activity to address global climate change. Bank of America's 10-year initiative encourages the development of environmentally sustainable business practices through lending, investing, philanthropy and the creation of new products and services.

In May 2007, Citi announced that it will direct US$50 billion over the next 10 years to address global climate change through investments, financings and related activities to support the commercialisation and growth of alternative energy and clean technology among the clients and markets it serves, as well as within its own businesses and operations. In February 2008, Citi together with JPMorgan Chase and Morgan Stanley announced the formation of the "Carbon Principles", which are climate change guidelines for advisors and lenders to power companies in the United States.

Nevertheless, under the Climate Risk Disclosure by the S&P 500, published in January 2007,[48] four of the 12 companies with the worst disclosure of risk analysis and emissions management were in the banking sector. In line with the findings in this study, many banks stated that strategic analysis of climate risk, emissions management and corporate governance pertaining to climate change had little to do with their business.

Under another very important report by Ceres,[49] evidence is found that many banks are responding to climate change, with many European banks being in the forefront and many US banks following closely behind. For example, the Ceres report highlights that banks have issued nearly one hundred research reports on climate change and related investment and regulatory strategies (more than half of them in 2007 alone); 85% of the surveyed banks responded to the latest CDP report; 60% of

---

48   Ceres and Calvert, *Climate Risk Disclosure by the S&P 500* (Boston: Ceres 2007), p 18.
49   Douglas G Cogan, *Corporate Governance and Climate Change: The Banking Sector* (Boston: Ceres, 2008). The report assessed 40 of the world's largest banks and focuses on how corporate executives and board directors are addressing the governance systems that will be needed to minimise climate risks while maximising investments in solutions that mitigate and help society adapt to climate change.

the surveyed banks have set some type of greenhouse gas reduction target for internal operations; and 72.5% of the surveyed banks have reported on their financial support for alternative energy projects. However, according to the CERES report, climate change is not a governance priority yet, and only a few of the surveyed banks are formally calculating risk in their loan portfolios. Also, only Bank of America has announced a specific target to reduce the rate of greenhouse gas emissions associated with the utility portion of its lending portfolio.

5.2   Oil and gas

Climate change concerns have been increasingly reflected in the policies and CSR reports of oil and gas companies to the point that reports are now mainly focused on climate change.

Some companies are looking at climate change as a source of new business opportunities. Major oil and gas companies have been undertaking voluntary reductions of GHG emissions for almost a decade and investing in alternative energy technologies. Oil and gas companies operating in Europe have been complying with the EU Emissions Trading Scheme and going to great lengths to report on this issue.

To mention just two examples: in 2007, ConocoPhillips announced its support for a mandatory federal policy to cap greenhouse gas emissions and committed US$150 million towards alternative fuels research. Royal Dutch Shell has invested more than US$1 billion since 1998 to develop alternative energy technologies and has established Shell Renewables and Shell Hydrogen as business units. The company has set a long-term target to hold its GHG emissions from its facilities at least 5% below 1990 levels through to 2010. It also has extensive experience with GHG emissions trading.[50]

5.3   Insurance

Like the banking sector, the insurance industry provides an interesting case study, since a difference can be established between the activities of the businesses it secures and its own activities.

Insurers have been particularly affected by the effects of climate change and if scientific predictions come true they may suffer enormous losses. Due to climate change, insurance companies have created innovative products and policies to manage potential risks and cover for the damage caused by variations in the intensity and frequency of extreme weather. According to a recent report by F&C, however, the response of the insurance industry, has been "patchy with some companies seeing climate change as a core of their future strategy and others hardly aware of it".[51]

Key issues for insurers in respect of climate change are: undertaking, capital adequacy, pricing, and risk research; loss reduction, claims processes and repairs; new products and services (new market opportunities, renewable energy technologies, carbon markets and investment products); and the value of investment portfolios.

---

50   Andrew Logan and David Grossman, *ExxonMobil's Corporate Governance on Climate Change* (Boston: Ceres 2006), p 5.
51   REO and F&C, *In the Front Line: The insurance industry's response to climate change* (London: F&C 2007), p 4.

In terms of emissions, however, insurance companies are not major GHG emitters compared with industrial firms.

To mention a few examples, major insurance companies such as AIG have set targets to reduce their greenhouse gas emissions and support the carbon market. In 2006, AIG became the first US insurance company to adopt a corporate climate change policy to seek ways for AIG and its clients to cut greenhouse gas emissions. In December 2006, R&SA became the first UK insurance company to achieve carbon neutrality. The insurance industry has also contributed to the climate change debate. For example, in 2006, Lloyd's launched the 360 Risk Project on Climate Change aimed at understanding the risks that climate change poses.

5.4   Shipping

Is there a structural difference between land-based industries and the shipping industry in terms of CSR? This is one of the questions dealt with in a report by Det Norske Veritas.[52] Until now, CSR has not been high on the agenda of the maritime industry. However, in the authors' experience, awareness of CSR issues in the shipping sector has increased in recent years, in relation to issues such as marine and air pollution, shipbreaking, crewing, labour conditions and the accountability and transparency of shipping companies.

Yet consideration of climate change within CSR policies and reports has not been regarded as relevant to the same degree as in other sectors.

One of the explanations for this fact may be that enunciated in the Det Norske Veritas report. Whereas companies and industry associations in land-based industries largely lack international organisations defining industry-specific performance levels, the shipping industry does have organisations adopting global rules and guidelines. Nevertheless, further to the advantages of adopting CSR practices that exist for all industries, arguments remain for the adoption of CSR practices by shipping companies. Such arguments include: governmental failure to secure enforcement of shipping rules; the fact that international regulation often takes on a least-common-denominator character; shipping companies' increasing need to be able to communicate with customers using CSR-terminology and to demonstrate supply chain responsibility; and the fact that the image and reputation of the shipping industry is not as strong as before. In particular, some consideration of the impact of shipping in terms of CO_2 emissions may also serve as preparation for a legislative future, for example in the European Union, when CO_2 emissions will be regulated.

5.5   Sectors combined

Table 1 below provides a snapshot of the four sectors discussed in this section.[53] The total number of companies represents the companies currently contained in Trucost's data collection. The sources of the quantified data are:

---

52   Det Norske Veritas, *Corporate Social Responsibility and the Shipping Industry* (Project Report), 2004.
53   According to the CorporateRegister.com study referred to at note 20 above, 71% of reporters in the oil and gas sector, 50% in banks and finance, and 44% in the insurance sector include a specific section on climate change. The report also states the correlation between the importance accorded to climate change within a sector, and the impact a sector may be regarded as having in climate change.

- Environmental/CSR disclosure – the company has voluntarily reported useful quantified data in this report;
- Derived from ENV/CSR – the company has voluntarily reported data, but it requires additional analysis and calculation to standardise it in global terms.
- Annual Report disclosures – the company has reported environmental data in its financial reports;
- Derived from Annual Report – the information in the financial statements required additional analysis to produce standardised information;
- Other – the company received and responded to the Data Verification Sheet with additional information; and
- Derived from previous year – the company reported information from an earlier year that was then adjusted for the current financial year.

Table 1: Climate change awareness in different sectors

Sector	Total number of companies	1 Env/ CSR disclosures	2 Derived from Env/CSR	3 Annual Report disclosures	4 Derived from Annual Report	5 Other	6 Derived from previous year
Monetary authorities and credit intermediation	272	12	16	1	2	5	6
Insurance carriers and related activities	160	2	13	0	0	5	6
Oil and gas extraction	74	6	2	0	0	5	0
Water transportation	36	2	5	0	1	0	1

While there is a significant increase in CSR reporting across all sectors, the results of Trucost's analysis demonstrate the low level of quantified data that is being reported to the market. In addition, the source of the data also provides a perspective on the level or quality of disclosure. In essence, the companies that fall under "1 – Environmental/CSR disclosure" could be regarded as the most transparent, because this voluntary information was provided in the most useful and comparable form. In addition, companies under "5 – Other" could be viewed as providing yet another level of transparency given that they have responded to a direct request for information. However, there is growing recognition of the increasing financial implications of environmental issues – whether through regulation, shifting consumer choice, or simple resource efficiency. Thus, a few leading companies are meeting the need to communicate credible and material information to shareholders by including this data in company annual reports.

6.   CSR around the world

Reporting rates are highest in Europe, followed by Japan.[54] with the United States showing the lowest rates of reporting among comparable companies.[55] According to EIRIS, progress in Europe can be explained by a more mature socially responsible investment market, a history of pressure from campaigning non-governmental organisations and a strong regulatory environment.[56] Academic studies offer explanations for this phenomenon on the basis of existing social democratic traditions in the European Union against more individualistic and libertarian strands of political thought in the United States.

In an important paper,[57] Cynthia Williams and Ruth V Aguilera review existing literature on the comparison of legal and institutional factors shaping CSR across the globe. The paper analyses differences in management and consumer behaviour.

One of the most interesting studies quoted by Williams and Aguilera is a study by Matten and Moon,[58] who have proposed a conceptual framework of "explicit" versus "implicit" CSR. They define "explicit CSR" as that seen in the United States, where companies volunteer to address important social and economic issues through their CSR policies in significant part because of less stringent legal requirements (in comparison with Europe) in such areas as healthcare provision, employees' rights and environmental protection. In contrast, in Europe and in the United Kingdom in particular, responsibility for these issues is undertaken as part of a company's legal responsibility, and thus CSR is "implicit" in the way the company does business.

Another study[59] points to institutional factors that explain differences in CSR

---

54   A study, commissioned by the International Finance Corporation and conducted by the environmental research organisation Trucost – Trucost, *Carbon Counts Asia 2007: Carbon Footprints of Asian Investment Funds* (London: Trucost 2007) – provides the first comprehensive review of greenhouse gas emissions by Asian companies. The study analyses the carbon intensity of the MSCI Asia ex-Japan index and 90 individual investment funds in Asia. The report concludes that Asian listed companies are more carbon intensive than their peers in other regions of the world and that investors in Asian Equity funds are therefore more exposed to carbon risks.

55   According to the CorporateRegister.com study referred to at note 20 above, Australasia, Japan and Europe are the leading regions in the disclosure of climate change. Japanese CSR reports have a slight edge over their European counterparts while North American reports are lacking climate change disclosure. The study also reports that Japanese companies are taking climate change disclosure very seriously. Most Japanese reports include a specific section on climate change and demonstrate management commitment on the issue. All Australasian reports include climate change performance data.

56   EIRIS, *The State of Responsible Business: Global corporate response to environmental, social and governance (ESG) challenges* (London: EIRIS 2007). According to this study, on matters of environmental management and innovation, Japanese companies dominate, with European firms close behind.

57   Cynthia Williams and Ruth V Aguilera, *Corporate Social Responsibility in a Comparative Perspective*, unpublished paper, 2007.

58   Dirk Matten and Jeremy Moon, "Implicit" and "Explicit" CSR. A Conceptual Framework for Understanding CSR in Europe, *ICCSR Research Paper Series* no 29, Nottingham University (2004):

59   Ruth Aguilera et al, "Corporate Governance and Corporate Social Responsibility: A Comparative Analysis of the UK and the US", *Corporate Governance: An International Review,* vol 14 no 3, (2006), pp 147 to 157. See also C A Williams and J Conley, "An Emerging Third Way?: The Erosion of the Anglo-American Shareholder Value Construct", *Cornell International Law Journal,* vol 38 no 2 (2005), pp 493 to 555.

reporting between the United Kingdom and the United States: (i) differences in the composition of institutional investors in the two markets, with a higher percentage of institutional investors in the United Kingdom being pension funds and insurance companies with longer time-horizons for investment than the mutual funds that have dominated in the United States; (ii) the encouragement of "soft law" instruments in the United Kingdom by the highly influential Cadbury Commission in the area of institutional investor engagement with portfolio companies; and (iii) the encouragement of attention to CSR issues by the Institutional Shareholders Committee, which represents more than 80% of institutional investment in the United Kingdom.

Specifically on climate change, the lower level of climate change issues in CSR reporting may be due, on the one hand, to weaker public awareness and acceptance of climate science and, on the other, to limited national public policy action on climate change.

Research on comparative consumer attitudes towards CSR is less developed, and there is less literature than on comparative managerial work. However, studies evidence that US consumers are mostly concerned with corporate economic responsibilities, agreeing with such statements as business must "maximise profits" and "control their production costs strictly",[60] as opposed to emphasising companies' legal, ethical and philanthropic responsibilities.

But what about other countries? And what should be the role of multinational corporations?

Corporate and social responsibility still means a developed-world agenda. CSR concepts and methodologies have their origins in developed countries. For example, the European Commission has a specific CSR agenda. The latest communication from the Commission on CSR is entitled "Implementing the Partnership for Growth and Jobs: Making Europe a pole of excellence on CSR".[61] It announces backing for a European alliance of enterprises for CSR, which aims to promote and encourage CSR.

International companies have helped in bringing social and environmental concerns (ethical codes of conduct, environmental certification, non-financial reporting and strategic community investment) to less developed countries. However, there are still doubts over the relevance of developed-world methodologies to less developed countries. CSR in Europe and the United States have been shaped by specific business conditions and social expectations, which broadly derive from shared traditions such as political democracy, corporate philanthropy and social solidarity. They are a product of ideological conditions and stringent legal expectations such as consumer rights, financial transparency, corporate governance and environmental protection, a critical media and a well-developed non-governmental sector.

Many less developed countries lack domestic regulatory pressures, strong institutions, consumer and employee lobbying, competitive corporate sectors and robust legal systems. According to the GRI, Latin American companies make up a

---

60   Cynthia Williams and Ruth V Aguilera, at note 57 above, p 44.
61   This Communication was published in 2006. It follows a Green Paper from 2001, a Communication from 2002 and subsequent initiatives in the field.

mere 4% of the 728 companies that issue corporate responsibility reports.[62] Moreover, many low-income individuals and micro-enterprises may not be able to afford long-term planning.

The challenge facing less developed countries is to take the best from CSR models and adapt them for their own developmental needs (eg the promotion of inclusive economic growth and the participation of civil society and governments).

7.   Legitimacy and effectiveness

CSR has been discussed both in a narrow and in a broad sense. In the narrow sense, CSR is about building responsible behaviour into processes and product decisions and operations relating to the company's business activities. It includes efforts to make corporate processes more sustainable (eg sustainable resource management in raw material extraction; the greening of sourcing decisions, of production and of distribution processes; fair trade practices and consumer information; and compliance with labour standards) and to improve the ecological and social properties of the products or services themselves (eg research, innovation, product development and the introduction into the product range of more environmentally friendly or socially sustainable products).

In the broader sense, CSR also encompasses a societal commitment that goes beyond immediate business activities (corporate citizenship). It covers the promotion of sustainable consumption (eg by means of pricing and marketing) and cooperation in creating the socio-ecological framework conditions governing production (or the sustainability alignment of companies' influence on legislative processes and industry norm-setting as well as on general patterns of perception and interpretation).[63]

How effective are corporate social responsibility instruments? To what extent do they really contribute to sustainable development? What are the prerequisites for CSR activities to achieve material impacts in the social (including business) and environmental realm? CSR initiatives can manage the negative impacts of companies on the communities of which they are a part, as well as those beyond their communities and core business operations. As long as such initiatives are adequately assessed and tailored, external parties may profit both directly and indirectly. Therefore, from the perspective of societal stakeholders, CSR can be viewed as a specific form of socio-economic relationship and of societal governance in general.[64]

On the other hand, is there a business case for CSR? Multiple reasons have been posited to justify CSR's business case – moral obligations, sustainability, licence to operate (every company needs implicit or explicit permission from governments, communities and other stakeholders to do business) and reputation (improving the company's image, strengthening brands, increasing morale, and raising stock

---

62   Brazil may be an exception. The EXAME Sustainability Guide 2007 ("Guia EXAME de Sustentabilidade 2007") shows that the existence of performance targets in respect of social and environmental issues is an irreversible trend for companies. For example, the guide reports that 40% of Brazilian companies have a GHG inventory and 32% have targets for the reduction of such emissions.
63   See above at note 26, p 18.
64   See above at note 26, p 23.

value).[65] Other reasons, correlated or independent, have also been pointed out: human resources (CSR attracts, retains and motivates employees), risk management and reduction of costs, access to capital, and innovation and competitive advantage. As to climate change risks, the following have been conceptualised: regulatory exposure, physical exposure, competitive exposure, reputational (including litigational) exposure and technological and business opportunities.

CSR should not be seen as a cost, a constraint, or a charitable deed. Instead, it should be seen as an investment in a strategic asset and as a distinctive capability.

However, CSR should be dealt with carefully. An uncoordinated CSR approach, disconnected from a company programme, that neither makes a meaningful social impact nor strengthens the firm's long-term competitiveness should be avoided. Such an approach constitutes a lost opportunity.

Each company must therefore select CSR "causes", which are coordinated with its particular business. Other social and environmental agendas should be left to other companies in different industries, NGOs or government institutions. As claimed by Porter and Kramer,[66] "the essential test that should guide CSR is not whether a cause is worthy but whether it presents an opportunity to create shared value – that is a meaningful benefit for society that is also valuable to the business".

Also, as stated by Mallen Baker,[67] CSR, innovation and marketing describe a range of possible activities, which in different circumstances and depending on the judgement in the selection of which actions to take, may be beneficial or detrimental to business. The business case, therefore, is for a course of action and not for some broad general concept of a type of activity. In the words of the author, "it is a sign of the immaturity of the CSR movement that we still believe it is an 'it' that you either do or you don't, rather than a discipline containing choices, dilemmas, benefits and catastrophes".[68]

Climate change is increasing the business and the societal case for CSR – in particular, climate change opportunities, but also climate change risks. Also, climate change provides not only legitimacy for CSR as a business instrument but also developing its effectiveness as a reporting measure.

There is still a long way to go in terms of quantification and, most importantly, consistency and aims of reporting. This presents a formidable challenge for all market participants, but also an opportunity for leaders to demonstrate a new level of transparency.

8.   The future

While businesses have only recently woken up to the potential financial risks resulting from lack of accountability, they remain uncertain as to what to do about them. A substantial part of CSR activity has been cosmetic, rather than strategic or

---

65   Michael E Porter and Mark R Kramer, "Strategy & Society: The Link Between Competitive Advantage and Corporate Social Responsibility", *Harvard Business Review* (HBR.org December 2006).
66   See above at note 65, p 8.
67   Mallen Baker, "So what's the Business Case for Corporate Social Responsibility?" (ClimateChangeCorp.com, August 15 2006).
68   *Ibid.*

operational in substance. CSR must be discussed at the highest level of a company as part of an overall strategic plan, and executive managers must educate and engage their boards of directors.

There is also a need to develop harmonised standards, and metrics or other measurements that usefully describe the relevant issues.

It should be acknowledged that there remains a degree of scepticism about CSR, because companies are not benevolent agents, but self-interested organisations. Perhaps climate change will convince the sceptics since, in this case, governments are leaving significant market failures unaddressed.

CSR is also raising the issue of fiduciary duties for trustees, in particular in the area of climate change and the fiduciary's role.[69] Does a fiduciary have a legal right or responsibility to consider climate risk and to act based on knowledge of such risk? According to a report of a workshop held at the Harvard University John F. Kennedy School of Government, fiduciaries have legal authority and may have an obligation to address climate risk.[70] Many pension funds and asset management companies, such as CalPERS, CalSTRS, F&C and Hermes, are in fact already acting to analyse the issue of climate change, raise awareness, encourage corporate disclosure, and press for improved corporate strategies to address climate risk.

Probably more than any other environmental issue, climate change requires urgent attention and concern, and radical measures. It represents a new category of risk and opportunity for individuals, companies and investors alike. Even more than other environmental and social issues, climate change challenges our acquired notions of time and space and poses many regulatory and CSR challenges. An interesting example is a new CSR trend being adopted by the Co-operative Bank, which, in 1992, was one of the first organisations to launch an ethical business policy. Rather than merely canvassing customers about the issues they would like to see influence its business practice and products, it has actively encouraged them to lobby UK Members of the Parliament, in particular on the issue of climate change legislation.

9   Conclusion

CSR is a difficult topic to address. This is due to several factors: the current lack of consensus on what it means; the multiple modes in which CSR can appear; the distinct perceptions of CSR by different sectors of activity; and the meaning of CSR in different countries and particular areas of the globe.

Additionally, the nature of CSR is changing. Multiple underlying causes can be pointed out, climate change being one of them. This is why, concomitantly with a renewed interest in the topic, CSR is discussed in this book.

---

69   An interesting concept in respect of fiduciary duties is the one of "universal ownership". "Universal ownership" is a term coined by Bob Monks and Nell Minow in a book of 1995 entitled *Corporate Governance* to describe an institutional investor owning such a wide range of asset classes distributed among economic sectors that the organisation effectively owns a slice of the broad economy. The universal owner hypothesis is reinforced by steps taken to integrate CSR issues into investment decision making.

70   Ceres, *Sustainability and Risk: Climate Change and Fiduciary Duty for the Twenty-First Century Trustee* (Boston: Ceres, 2004).

On the occasion of the launch of CDP5, Simon Thomas, Chief Executive of Trucost said: *"The dramatic increase in both the number and quality of responses to the CDP5 demonstrates just how much climate change has risen up the corporate agenda and shows once again that the CDP exerts a powerful and cumulative effect on the disclosure of emissions data."*

How is climate change affecting CSR? First, there is more reporting; then, in relation to CSR reporting, there are more perceived business opportunities; thirdly, the nature of CSR is changing, as disclosed information is being progressively quantified. There are still, of course, many difficulties in measurement and in terms of the "show me the numbers" challenge (which is also an external cause to CSR); but extensive work is being done on the matter.[71]

In any event, businesses and investors should prepare for the future, since an inability to measure accurately is not an excuse for inaction. Reputation, the risks of litigation and regulation, as well as the ability better to plan operations constitute further incentives.

There are still the views of the pessimist reminding us that we are still missing the basics of environmental accounting on the liability side and accurate carbon counting. While everyone is highly confident on carbon reporting, there are only bits and pieces of accurate and useful disclosure available. There is also a "witch hunt" mentality around the issue of "corporate disclosure" among investors who are not really willing to measure or change their own investing habits.

On the other hand optimists proclaim a paradigm shift in CSR, and in fact another death for it. CSR is now very restricted and should be replaced by the concept of "sustainable development".

As an old sailing saying states, while in the beginning of a storm, the pessimist complains about the wind and the optimist waits and expects it to change, the realist adjusts the sails.[72] Then, whether a company is considered to be socially responsible or not, ultimately rests with how it is perceived by its stakeholders.

Environmental Data Analysis was provided by Trucost. Trucost is an environmental research company that enables companies, institutional investors and governments to understand the environmental impacts of business activities in financial terms. Since 2000, Trucost has analysed the environmental performance of more than 4,200 companies worldwide using its unique methodology. Trucost's models and tools allow measurement of greenhouse gas emissions and other environmental impacts of companies from the world's major investible indexes (including MSCI World Developed, MSCI Europe, FTSE All Share, Russell 1000 and S&P 500).

---

71   Even in the case of labelling it is difficult to analyse energy use and GHG emissions across a product lifecycle, as it is required in existing label schemes.

72   The sentence is generally attributed to William Arthur Ward.

Corporate transactions

John Bowman
Dewey & LeBoeuf
Simon Read
Pinsent Masons LLP

With the proliferation of climate change laws around the world, carbon issues are increasingly having impacts on corporate transactions, often with highly significant consequences. Indeed, a failure to consider fully the potential carbon liabilities of a company could result in the acquisition of a business quite different from what the purchaser envisaged.[1] It is therefore important for any person involved in affected transactions to have an understanding of climate change law if they are to achieve a satisfactory result.

It is necessary to consider carbon issues in transactions relating to a range of different types of companies. Those most likely to be affected are companies that have installations that directly emit greenhouse gases, such as electricity generators, companies that supply such companies, such as oil and gas companies, and companies that manufacture greenhouse gas emitting products, such as automobile manufacturers. However, other companies are also likely to be affected, including those that use large amounts of electricity,[2] which will be exposed to increases in the cost of carbon, those that supply parts or equipment to industries likely to be directly affected, and those that are likely to be affected by results of climate change such as increased frequency of severe weather events. Climate change could have profound effects on each of these types of company. However, it is equally clear that climate change issues may be relevant in less obvious cases – for example, the acquisition of a commercial property portfolio of office buildings which cannot be adapted to the challenges of climate change or meet the green requirements of tenants.

The major difficulty for lawyers advising on transactions with carbon issues is the uncertainty surrounding the legislative environment. Some countries, for example the United States, are expected to introduce within the next few years laws designed to mitigate climate change. However, the form of these laws remains uncertain. Even in those countries that have introduced climate change legislation there is still little long-term certainty. For example, EU policy is still highly subject to political influences, in particular allocation volumes and procedures under its Emissions Trading Scheme (the EU ETS). Major cuts in allocations, or increased use of auctioning of allowances could incur significant costs for carbon-regulated installations. It is

---

[1]   See for example the Carbon Disclosure Project 4 "Electric Utilities 265" report, which found that only six of the 25 electric utilities surveyed had assets in excess of their liabilities if a cost of $22 per tonne of carbon dioxide emitted was internalised.

[2]   See for example the United Kingdom's proposed Carbon Reduction Commitment (www.defra.gov.uk/environment/climatechange/uk/business/crc/index.htm).

therefore very difficult for persons looking to invest in companies that will be subject to legislation to determine the potential carbon liabilities and assets, and therefore value, of that company. In addition to carbon regulation doubts, the inherent uncertainty surrounding the effects of global warming creates further uncertainty for the future of those companies, such as insurance and agricultural companies, likely to be affected by extreme weather events and other effects. The quantification of risks therefore presents considerable difficulties for advisors on corporate transactions.

This chapter will consider how climate change issues may impact on each stage of a transaction, from the due diligence stage through to drafting the contractual documents.

1.   Types of transaction

Carbon issues can arise in any type of corporate transaction. The typical transaction in which such issues will arise will be in the acquisition of a greenhouse gas emitting business, with different issues arising depending on whether the acquisition is of the business's shares or assets.

Other types of transaction may also entail a consideration of carbon issues. Joint venture arrangements have become common in the climate change sector, such as between investment banks and project developers. In addition, carbon issues are likely to be increasingly significant in preparing for any stock market listing or other share offering.

2.   Due diligence

Due diligence is the legal and administrative process carried out at the outset of a transaction to identify the key issues both in relation to the target business as well as in relation to the transaction itself. In an ideal world, access would be granted to all relevant documents, information would be provided punctually, and there would be no limit either on the time or resources available. However, due diligence is more often compromised by the constraints imposed on each of these, in particular the investor's budget and timetable.

It is therefore important at the start of any due diligence exercise to determine exactly what the goals are and how these are to be achieved. Typically these depend on the nature of the investor and may, for example, be limited to those issues likely to affect the target's right to operate or liabilities above a certain threshold. This latter limitation is likely to cause considerable difficulties, because, for the reasons set out above, it may not always be possible accurately to quantify climate change risks.

Identifying carbon issues in a transaction will form part of the ordinary due diligence procedure. Accordingly, under the principle of *caveat emptor*, the onus on obtaining appropriate information will rest with the purchaser through inspection of available documents, pre-acquisition questionnaires and using warranties to obtain additional disclosure. It is therefore important to determine at the outset what issues may be relevant and how to identify these, albeit that the vendor may be unwilling to respond to requests for information or be unable to do so because the potential transaction is of a confidential nature and the only employees aware of it may be at a very senior level.

Sections 2.1 to 2.11 below provide a discussion of issues that should be considered as part of a due diligence exercise.

2.1 Permits[3]

It is becoming increasingly accepted that emissions of greenhouse gases should be subject to permit, rather than a right to be enjoyed. Indeed, the former viewpoint is crystallised in EU law under the EU ETS Directive,[4] which not only establishes the mechanisms of the Emissions Trading System, but also requires all participants to obtain a permit authorising the emission of greenhouse gases,[5] although at this stage not all greenhouse gases or industrial sectors are covered. Nevertheless, it is reasonable to assume that whilst the scope of the EU ETS is expanding, more countries are adopting climate change legislation and scientific opinion is increasingly supporting the view that the emission of greenhouse gases impacts upon the rights of others, the right to emit greenhouse gas will continue to erode.

Accordingly, it is important to determine whether the target company requires a permit to emit greenhouse gases. It may be the case that a permit is required for each greenhouse gas-emitting installation operated by the company. Each such permit should be reviewed to ensure that it allows the installation to operate at the levels anticipated by the purchaser. In addition the review should consider whether there are any onerous obligations and when the permit expires.

It is also important to consider who holds the permit. This is crucially important in determining whether the right to operate will continue after the ownership of the installation has transferred to the purchaser. For example, under the EU ETS the obligation to hold a permit is on the operator of an installation rather than the owner of the installation. It will not necessarily be the case that the two are the same, for example if the installation is operated by a subsidiary or has been subcontracted to a third party. Where the permit is not held by the selling party, consideration will need to be given to how the installation is to be operated after the completion of the transaction, which may, for example, entail entering into a separate agreement with a third-party operator.

Of course, whether a transfer of permit is necessary will also depend on the structure of the transaction. For example, under a sale of shares, no express transfer of permit will be required, unless the permit or legislation expressly provides otherwise. Under a sale of assets, on the other hand, the identity of the operator is likely to change and so transfer of the permit will be required. This will need to be considered in advance of completion for each installation, as it may take some time for the transfer to be effected and this may need to be done before the installation can be operated under the new owner.

---

3   This section is a discussion of greenhouse gas permits generally and does not necessarily relate to permits issued under the EU ETS. The EU ETS Directive (see notes 7 and 8) sets out basic conditions that must be included in each permit. However, it is possible that the scope of permits, either under the EU ETS or in other jurisdictions, may expand to include additional restrictive conditions.

4   Directive 2003/87/EC of the European Parliament and of the Council of October 13 2003 establishing a scheme for greenhouse gas emission allowance trading within the Community and amending Council Directive 96/61/EC.

5   *Ibid* – Article 4.

The obvious risk with failing to identify issues with greenhouse gas permits is that the business may not have a right to operate or that it may lose this right to operate upon completion if the permit is not properly transferred. Any permit may alternatively contain conditions that have significant effects on the ongoing operations or are likely to require future expenditure.

2.2 Emission credits[6]

As discussed in other chapters in this book, fungible and liquid emission credits are key to any market-based mechanism designed to mitigate climate change. Under a typical cap-and-trade scheme[7] (such as the EU ETS), emission credits will be created up to a certain limit and these can be freely traded.

It is important to determine how many emission credits the business is holding and is going to hold at the time of completion. In addition, not only is it important to consider how many credits are held, but also the type of credits that are held. Under the EU ETS, CERs and ERUs may be surrendered in place of an EUA[8] and as such are generally considered interchangeable. However, there are certain characteristics which are unique to each, for example CERs and ERUs from certain types of projects, such as land use, land use change, and forestry (LULUCF) projects, cannot currently be used for compliance with the EU ETS.[9] Furthermore, CERs and ERUs can only be used up to a certain percentage of a regulated installation's compliance requirements. If the holdings of CERs and ERUs exceed these maximum limits, EUAs will need to be surrendered in their place. Accordingly, the nature of the credits held will also need to be considered to determine whether expenditure is going to be required for the company to comply with its obligations.

Under the EU ETS the majority, if not all, emissions have, to date, been allocated to regulated installations free of charge. It is possible that other cap-and-trade systems will also operate on this basis.[10] It will be necessary to consider allocation histories and anticipated future allocations to consider whether the free allocation will be sufficient to meet expected emissions. If the anticipated allocation is less than the expected emissions, either because emissions have risen or because allocations are to be reduced from a business-as-usual scenario, additional credits will need to be purchased.

2.3 Emissions

In association with considering the number of emission credits held, it is necessary to consider the historical and projected emissions of the business to ascertain

---

6 "Credits" is used in this chapter to connote units traded under greenhouse gas emission mitigation schemes, and includes, but is not necessarily limited to, EUAs, CERs and ERUs.
7 "Cap and trade" is the term used to define a scheme in which total emissions are capped and then the participants in the scheme trade the rights actually to make those emissions. The alternative "baseline and credit" schemes are not generally favoured.
8 The ability to use credits from the Kyoto Protocol project mechanisms was facilitated by the Linking Directive (Directive 2004/101/EC of the European Parliament and Council of October 27 2004 amending Directive 2003/87/EC establishing a scheme for greenhouse gas emission allowance trading within the Community, in respect of the Kyoto Protocol's project mechanisms).
9 Article 11a(3) of the Linking Directive.
10 The primary alternative to free allocations is the distribution of allowances through auctioning.

whether the holdings will be sufficient. Obviously, if projected tonnage of carbon dioxide emitted is higher than the number of credits held, additional credits will be required. Failure to surrender sufficient credits to meet actual emissions is likely to incur a penalty. Under the EU ETS this is currently set at €100 per tonne of emissions above the number of credits surrendered, with the obligation to surrender the required number of credits not being expunged by the fine.

It may also be prudent to consider the company's approach to verification to ensure that it complies with recommended practices.

2.4   Trading activities

Related to the company's holdings of credits and its actual and projected emissions is the trading activity that it has undertaken. Of particular relevance are those trades that have been entered into, but are not settled at the time of completion of the transaction. Such trading is common in emission credits, with trading often being undertaken on a forward basis with delivery on December 1 of any particular year. Clearly, any unsettled forward-trades need to be taken into account when determining the total emission credit-holdings of the company. Conversely, the company may have entered into a bad bargain with respect to the credits, if it was trading for more than mere compliance purposes, with the result that the credits may subsequently have to be sold at a loss.

Additionally, the business may also have participated in Clean Development Mechanism (CDM) or Joint Implementation (JI) projects, or entered into an Emission Reduction Purchase Agreement with the expectation of a future delivery of CERs or ERUs. Such credits will also need to be taken into account.

2.5   Capital expenditure

In order to comply with climate change regulations, it may be necessary for companies to invest in cleaner technologies to reduce their greenhouse gas emissions. Such expenditure is likely to be treated as capital expenditure (CAPEX) for accounting purposes. Operational expenditure (OPEX) may also be required if operating such technologies incurs some ongoing costs. For example, the installation of carbon capture technologies would be CAPEX with the ongoing energy costs to run the technology being OPEX. Both should be considered in the due diligence process.

2.6   Audits and voluntary offsetting

As in other areas of environmental due diligence, it is possible that some form of climate change audit will have been carried out by the seller, either to assess potential compliance programmes, such as investment in cleaner technology, or for voluntary purposes, in an effort to enhance the business' branding and corporate social responsibility position. Either way, an examination of any such audit report should be carried out to obtain a fuller picture of the company.

It is common for a wide range of companies,[11] beyond those that are directly affected by climate change laws, to carry out assessments of their operations for the

---

11   For example, Avis and HSBC have undertaken internal carbon initiatives.

purposes of reducing their "carbon footprint" and potentially offsetting their emissions by purchasing credits. Such assessments are often carried out by specialist companies, which also provide the offset credits. The main purpose of this is for brand enhancement, but it may also be for the purpose of offering clients "carbon-free" products.[12] It is important to consider the veracity of any claims made by the company on the basis of these assessments. For example, there have been criticisms that a number of the projects invested in by offset providers do not satisfy additionality requirements.[13] Furthermore, some of the issues associated with bona fide offsets are not well understood, such as double counting, and it may be that certain claims are being incorrectly made through such unawareness.[14]

Although such issues may not incur any monetary losses directly and therefore not necessarily exceed the reporting thresholds for the due diligence exercise, they do have the potential to adversely affect the image and goodwill of the company. It does not seem companies that have made such false claims have necessarily yet suffered in this regard, for incorrect claims of carbon neutrality are arguably no worse than no claims at all. However, as public awareness of these issues increases, negative impacts on company image are likely to increase.

2.7 Tax

Trading in emission credits is likely to incur tax liabilities.[15] To the extent that it is not covered in the general tax due diligence, this should be considered.

2.8 Litigation

Almost all due diligence exercises will include some consideration of current litigation against the company. Any climate change litigation (which is discussed in the chapter entitled "Climate change litigation" below) will also need to be considered and, where necessary, appropriate protection sought.

In addition to the existing litigation against the company, it is also prudent to consider the nature of the company and general litigious trends. For example, a company that manufactures products that emit greenhouse gases may be at risk of being sued at some stage in the future, even if no action is at that point under way, which could have serious implications for future profits and therefore value of the company. Ascertaining accurately the prospect of such litigation and any liabilities that may follow is likely to be almost impossible. Nevertheless, it is an important issue to be considered.

Whether existing litigation will have adverse effects for the purchaser will depend to a large extent on the nature of the transaction. If the structure is for the purchase of the shares of a target company, any ongoing litigation will attach to those shares and so any liabilities from such litigation will need to be considered as

---

12   For example, easyJet offer customers the opportunity to offset the carbon emissions caused by their flights.
13   See for example "The Inconvenient Truth about the Carbon Offset Industry", Nick Davies, *The Guardian*, June 16 2007.
14   See for example "Rhodia Profits from Double Counting of Carbon Credits", *ENDS Report 390*, July 2007.
15   See the chapter on "Accounting and taxation" above.

part of the transaction. However, if the purchase is of assets only, or of shares in a hive-down company, the litigation liability will attach to the seller and so will not be the responsibility of the purchaser on completion. An exception to this would be if the litigation was directed in some way at the assets being acquired.

2.9 Contractual commitments

Again, the contractual commitments of a business will be a key part of any due diligence exercise. Contracts which raise climate change related issues should also form part of the exercise. Some of these will be straightforward commercial contracts, for example for the provision of climate change related consultancy services. Other contracts may, for example, relate to climate change projects, such as joint venture agreements with project developers. Each of these contracts should be reviewed to consider potential legal risks and opportunities presented by the company.

Other contracts may not have such obvious climate change risks, for example because they are affected by the effects of climate change rather than climate change legislation and policy. Nevertheless, these will still need to be considered and reported on where the risk is material. An example would be an insurance company that has not properly factored in climate change risks, such as adverse weather events, into its contractual arrangements and therefore leaves itself potentially heavily exposed.

2.10 Legislation/policy

As was discussed above, one of the main difficulties in determining legal risk in relation to climate change is the lack of certainty over legal and policy developments. A number of the issues discussed above depend to a certain extent on laws that may or may not yet be in place, or whether there will be relevant carbon laws in place after 2012. Of course, this is the situation in almost all areas of law as laws very rarely stand still. However, climate change laws are highly significant in this regard as they have the potential to incur large liabilities or capital expenditure requirements on companies across a range of sectors without necessarily offering any defences or safe harbours.

The most obvious example would be the introduction of a cap-and-trade emission trading scheme. If the scheme does not provide for free allocations, but for auctioning, any company obligated under that scheme will immediately incur significant compliance costs. The Carbon Disclosure Project found that introducing a price of carbon at $22 per tonne would result in 19 of the 25 electric utilities it surveyed having higher operational costs than their total value.[16] Some of these costs would of course be passed on to consumers. Nevertheless, companies with higher carbon efficiency would be considerably more competitive in such an environment, with companies with low carbon efficiencies likely to struggle. The result would be that the introduction of such laws would have a significant effect on the value of the investment in such an affected company. It is therefore crucial to consider the developing legislative climate when considering the overall exposure to climate change risks.

16   See note 1 above.

It may also be necessary in this regard to consider any plans the investor has for the future business of the asset it is intending to purchase. For example, if an investor were to invest in a CDM project development company with the aim of expanding into new jurisdictions, legislative developments in those jurisdictions should also be considered. Indeed, the Chinese government introduced a taxation system which taxed the proceeds of CDM projects, the rate of taxation being determined by the type of project. HFC-23 reduction projects,[17] as an example, attract a tax of 65% of income generated. As a result, CDM projects using this methodology are considerably less profitable than previously. The introduction of this law would have significantly impacted on any planned development of HCFC-22 facilities in China and could therefore have impacted on the perceived value of an investment in the above scenario.

2.11 Reporting risk

Reporting risk, which is an area of increasing importance, addresses the risks arising out of traditional environmental and other areas of due diligence in corporate acquisitions. It will be of particular importance to a buyer in a share acquisition. In addition to scrutinising the financial impacts from the environmental risks of the target in the course of traditional environmental due diligence, the buyer should also address the financial impact from the risks associated with misstatements in corporate financial statements arising from unrecognised, misclassified or improperly valued environmental liabilities and impairments.[18]

Failure to do so may result in adverse financial consequences for the buyer, which may even exceed those of the environmental risk itself. For instance, in transactions involving public companies the buyer may be subject to investigations by regulatory authorities for prior misstatements made by the seller. Similarly, the cost and time it takes to rectify the seller's environmental financial reporting may be substantial. Furthermore, unlike long-term environmental risks that may never materialise, the impact of financial reporting risk can crystallise before completion or soon after it, quite independently of the corresponding environmental liability.

Although the idea of financial due diligence is more developed as a concept in relation to broad environmental law, it will apply equally to reporting on climate change issues affecting a company's performance. To consider fully the scope of this risk, buyers will need to expand the scope of traditional due diligence to assess financial reporting compliance of the seller, review the seller's documented accounting policies and procedures, and assess the operational effectiveness of the seller's internal control over financial reporting of carbon matters.[19]

---

17   HFC23 is a greenhouse gas with a high greenhouse gas potential (11,700 times greater than carbon dioxide). It is a by-product in the production of HCFC22, a refrigerant. Destruction of HFC23 is a common project with high rewards for low cost (because up to 11,700 credits could be created from each tonne of HFC23 burnt).

18   Environmental Disclosure Due Diligence (ED3)™ – The Next Step in Environmental Due Diligence – p 7.

19   *Ibid*, p 10.

3. Vendor disclosure[20]

In certain corporate transactions the onus of providing information rests with the vendor rather than the purchaser. The typical situation in which this would be the case is in an offering document which a company would use to attract equity investors. Such documents require the disclosure of information necessary to enable potential investors to make an informed decision over the value of their investment. Disclosure will also typically be required on an ongoing basis for companies listed on stock markets, as investment in such shares is intended to be fluid and therefore prospective shareholders require up-to-date information on the company's position. As climate change can have serious implications on the financial position of companies, the disclosure of risk associated with climate change is increasingly becoming an issue of concern.

The first key issue is determining whether disclosure of carbon risks is likely to be appropriate. This will depend greatly on the economic sector in question, but utilities, car manufacturers, insurance companies, and industries that supply these sectors are more likely to face disclosure requirements than other sectors. However, disclosure may also be required by companies with high-value consumer-facing brands even though climate risk may not be as high.

In the United States, under the rules of the Securities Exchange Commission (SEC), a company should consider information to be material, and therefore appropriate and necessary to disclose, if it is information for which there is "a substantial likelihood that a reasonable investor would attach importance in deciding to buy or sell the securities registered".[21] Under this principle, it could be argued that the costs of climate change legislation in the United States are currently too speculative to force disclosure. After all, the costs and opportunities for companies will depend dramatically on which of the numerous legislative proposals eventually become law. However, it is becoming increasingly the case that investors already consider carbon risks to be material and are seeking such disclosure. For example, the Carbon Disclosure Project (CDP), which is backed by nearly 300 institutional investors with assets under management of more than $41 trillion, is having considerable influence on publicly traded companies to measure their greenhouse gas emissions and disclose the data in a public and standardised format.[22]

The immediate risk for most companies is from climate change related legislation, regulation, and litigation, and associated issues such as renewing existing environmental permits, the creation of emissions trading schemes, and taxes on fuels. The longer-term risk is exposure to the direct physical effects of climate change. For example, a company with facilities located on a floodplain, in an area exposed to rising sea levels, dependent on rainfall to supply or replenish water reserves, or with a workforce that is exposed to an increased incidence of disruptive climatic events could, depending on the exact nature of its business, face significant climate risks. While some companies may not be exposed to these risks directly, they

---

20   See also "A Flawed Prospectus? Disclosure Requirements for Environmental Information", Angela Delfino et al (2007) 13 *Journal for European Environmental & Planning Law*, 195 to 212.
21   17 C.F.R. §240.12b-2 (Exchange Act); 17 C.F.R. §230.405 (Securities Act).
22   www.cdproject.net/.

may nevertheless be exposed to volatility in the price of their raw materials because of vulnerability higher up in their supply chain.

Companies will also need to consider the potential disruptions on operations caused by climate change. More frequent and intense extreme-weather events such as floods, hurricanes or droughts could all have significant effects on operations in many sectors of the economy. Similarly, companies facing increased difficulty and cost in obtaining insurance to guard against these risks could also face a duty to disclose. Furthermore, following on the recent rise of climate change litigation in the United States, pending regulation or litigation related to GHG emission-intensive processes is also an obvious climate risk that would merit disclosure. While in some cases quantifying these risks may be impractical, at the least some companies in sectors such as coal mining or petroleum refining should consider including statements in management's discussion and analysis (see the discussion of Item 303 of Regulation S-K below) to the effect that there are broad climate-related trends affecting the business, such as increasing climate change litigation.

The EU ETS, the obligatory national emissions inventories under the Kyoto Protocol, and state-level monitoring requirements in the United States (such as California's Climate Action Registry,[23] or the Regional Greenhouse Gas Initiative (RGGI)[24] requirement for inventories in the utility sector) are all advancing expectations related to corporate GHG emissions monitoring. As a result, many companies in the metals, minerals, coal, oil and automotive sectors will be aware of their emissions and their exposure to legislative developments. For other types of company, the combination of social pressure and possible business risk means that consideration and quantification of carbon issues is likely to become increasingly more common.

Converse to the risks posed by climate change, some companies are likely to gain from climate change, be it through the use of project-based mechanisms (CDM or JI), or the fact that their product is a low-GHG substitute for an existing product. Such prospects, to the extent that management is developing substantial plans involving capital expenditures to realise them, would also constitute material information of interest to investors.

The next key issue will be determining how to disclose these issues appropriately. Disclosure requirements in US law arise under regulations created by the SEC under the Securities Act of 1933 and the Securities Exchange Act of 1934.[25] However, the particular form of disclosure is governed by Regulation S-K.

Under Item 101 of Regulation S-K, a company must disclose the impacts that complying with environmental laws and regulations is having, and may have, on profitability, capital expenditure, and its general business environment. Both definite and contingent environmental issues that arise out of existing legislation and rules must be disclosed. Furthermore, the Financial Accounting Standards Board (FASB) issued a statement more than 30 years ago that codified the obligation of companies

---

23   www.climateregistry.org/.
24   www.rggi.org/.
25   See Securities Act Rules, 17 CFR § 230 et seq, Exchange Act Rules, 17 CFR § 240.0-1 *et seq*, Regulation S-K, 17 CFR § 229.10 *et seq*.

to report potential losses.[26] Since the SEC regards the FASB as the authoritative self-regulating body of the accounting profession, the obligation to disclose climate risks (as opposed to only disclosing definite climate-related losses) is clear. Risks that can be reasonably quantified and are reasonably probable are subject to disclosure requirements.[27]

Item 103 of the Regulation requires companies to disclose litigation that could materially affect it. In particular, Item 103 requires a heightened standard of disclosure for environmental matters.[28] Since many GHG-intensive industries rely on a variety of state and federal pollution permits and face the possibility of new permitting regimes for carbon, litigation or the threat of litigation is a serious issue for disclosure.

Finally, Item 303 of Regulation S-K requires the management of a public company to provide a "Discussion and Analysis".[29] The SEC has generally encouraged broad disclosure on the part of companies of trends and upcoming issues facing the company in order to provide investors with a holistic understanding of the conditions their investments face.

Beyond SEC requirements there is also a great deal of voluntary disclosure in the United States, as discussed above in the context of the CDP. There are, however, other reasons beyond the CDP that might encourage companies to disclose climate risks in advance of strict requirements. Several companies have already experienced direct shareholder activism on climate issues. Another factor that could motivate voluntary disclosure is a preference amongst global companies to establish global reporting standards. Furthermore, the more advanced requirements for environmental disclosure under EU and UK law[30] may result in reporting requirements in the United States and other countries being brought up to the same level as a matter of convenience or best practice.

In sum, there are a variety of areas where climate risk could raise disclosure requirements for companies – in different sectors of the economy, and in different aspects of business operations. The requirements of securities law to make full material disclosure of known or reasonably possible risks, particularly where quantifiable, puts the onus on companies to analyse their vulnerability to climate change and make appropriate disclosure in their quarterly and annual reports.

4. Drafting the contract

In drafting an agreement between parties, it will be important to properly allocate the carbon assets, liabilities and risks in accordance with the commercial agreement, which will typically be determined by the results of the due diligence exercise. The carbon terms will, of course, also be determined by the structure of the transaction and will need to fit into the rest of the agreement (eg with respect to capping

---

26 Financial Accounting Standards Board, Statement of Financial Accounting Standards No 5; Accounting for Contingencies (March 1975), available at www.fasb.org/pdf/fas5.pdf.
27 *Ibid* at para 8.9.
28 Instruction 5 to Item 103, 17 C.F.R. § 229.103 (2006).
29 17 C.F.R. § 229.303 (2006).
30 For example, the EU Accounts Modernisation Directive and the UK Companies Act 2006 have each increased the need for public companies to disclose information on environmental issues and policies (including policy effectiveness, and relationships with suppliers).

warranty claims). The terms of the contract will therefore vary greatly from transaction to transaction, but a number of common issues are likely to arise, as set out next.

4.1   Transfer of permits and allowances

The transfer of the relevant permits will be necessary on a sale of assets if the company is going to be able to continue to operate after completion. Depending on the timetable of the transaction, in particular where there is little or no time between signing and completion, this may have to be considered before the contracts are signed. For example, under the legislation implementing the EU ETS into English law, the transferor and the transferee may agree a date with the UK Environment Agency on which the transfer is to be effective. Since this must be in the future, and adequate time must be given to the Environment Agency to consider the application and to effect the transfer administratively, and it is an offence to carry out prescribed operations without a permit, it is essential to consider the transfer prior to completion.

Where there is a gap between the signing of the contract and completion, it may be necessary to include a provision as to how this transfer is to be managed. Since this is a "right to operate" issue, it is likely to be paramount to the buyer and so he should seek to obtain control over this process. The seller on the other hand will have some interest in transferring the permit as there is no benefit in keeping it, and it may incur certain liabilities by doing so if the terms of the permit are not met. Although it will be in the interests of both parties to effect the transfer, the procedure and responsibilities of each party should be clearly set out in the agreement. For example, it should be made clear who is to be responsible for preparing the application, what input the other party should have, and the dates that this should be done by.

In the case of a share acquisition, it is unlikely that any action to transfer permits will be required since the identity of the permit is not likely to change. The main exceptions to this will be where the operator and permit holder is a third party and the appointment of that third party is to cease on completion and where the legislation requires action on the change of control of the permit holder.

The transfer of emission credits will also need to be considered. There is likely to be more flexibility in how this can be dealt with, in particular because the credits need not necessarily be held by the operator of the installation, at least not until they need to be surrendered for compliance purposes. Again, the specific mechanism for transfer should be dealt with in the contract. It is likely that any trading system, like the EU ETS, will involve electronic, rather than physical assets. Accordingly, it will be necessary to include in the contract details of the accounts between which the credits are to be transferred. It may be necessary to specify accounts in more than one national registry to mitigate system failures within the national registries.

A buyer should seek to ensure that this transfer is effected on the day of completion, or even as a condition precedent to completion. This is so as to minimise the risk of the transfer being delayed after completion, with the risk of costs being incurred as a consequence. The seller, on the other hand, should have no qualms about transferring the allowances on or shortly after completion, but should seek to resist any penalties for failing to transfer as a result of registry failures or other events beyond its control.

Much more care is likely to be required in drafting contracts in which there is to be an ongoing relationship between the parties, such as in joint venture agreements or in service agreements. In such arrangements, it may be necessary to dedicate a schedule or even a separate agreement to the rights over carbon between the parties.

Although the terms of such agreements will be determined by the negotiations of the parties, there are likely to be certain common issues, such as precisely defining each party's rights and obligations. A typical example of a relationship where these issues will be relevant is in an agreement for the operation of a power plant between the plant's owner and a third party. In this instance, the third-party operator is likely to be the obligated entity in terms of complying with the emissions caps, but the owner may want to retain rights over emission credits for trading purposes. In such arrangements, it will be important to set out the mechanism for the transfer of the credits to ensure that it is timely, but without imposing undue restrictions on the operator. The operator will, however, want adequate credits to meet its obligations, and will want assurances prior to the deadline for surrendering credits that it is to receive sufficient allowances to meet its obligations. This may be achieved, for example, by allowing the operator access to the plant owner's registry accounts or periodic transfers of credits from the plant owner to the operator.

4.2   Warranties

Warranties serve two purposes in any corporate transaction. First, they offer a degree of contractual protection. Second, and perhaps most significantly, they can be used to obtain information about the target company during the due diligence exercise. Warranties in relation to climate change issues are no different.

With the evolution of climate change laws and the spread to an ever increasing range of sectors, it is becoming increasingly important for legal advisors to develop a suite of climate change warranties from which to select the most apposite for that particular transaction. It is generally considered bad practice to include irrelevant or unnecessary warranties in any first-draft sale-and-purchase agreement, and this is particularly true of specific areas such as climate change.

The basic suite of warranties should broadly cover the issues covered in the due diligence exercise, which are discussed above. Those issues that are determined not to be relevant, either because of the nature of the business or through information obtained through due diligence, have no need to be covered in the warranties.

One of the key issues in the negotiation of warranties is whether any particular warranties will be limited to the awareness of the seller and, if so, how awareness is defined. The seller will want such a limitation to guard against warranting information of which it has no knowledge. Furthermore, the seller will want the breadth of knowledge to be as narrow as possible, limited solely to the actual knowledge of the seller, which may for example be certain senior personnel involved in the transaction or the board of a parent company on the sale of a subsidiary.

Limiting the warranties in this way may significantly hinder their effectiveness, since most knowledge is likely to be with the employees of the target company that are involved in the day-to-day operations of the business, particularly in large companies. The buyer should therefore seek absolute warranties that are not subject to knowledge, or alternatively that the seller be deemed to have the knowledge of all the employees of the company and its professional advisors. With respect to climate change issues, warranties relating to holdings of emission credits are likely to be easier for the seller to verify than those relating to day-to-day operations such as anticipated greenhouse gas emissions or required expenditure, and the seller will be more likely to offer such warranties without qualification.

Where warranties are agreed to be subject to the seller's awareness, it is important for the buyer to seek to ensure that such awareness is deemed to be broad enough to include individuals that have knowledge of climate change issues. Such individuals should be listed, either generally or specifically in the agreement. It is therefore likely to be necessary for the buyer to carry out investigations to determine exactly which individuals should be named.

4.3 Indemnities

In certain instances, it may be desirable for the buyer to seek an indemnity from the seller for a particular climate change liability. Of course, the likelihood of a buyer successfully obtaining an indemnity will depend on the negotiating position of the parties and their appetite for assuming risk. Generally, indemnities are most common in situations in which the anticipated liability would flow from the activities of the seller prior to completion and the extent of that liability cannot be readily quantified prior to completion. As a result, situations in which an indemnity may be used are:

- Insufficient emission credits – where it is not certain whether sufficient credits are held to meet anticipated emissions, an indemnity may be an appropriate way in which to allocate risk between the parties. As compensation is paid on a pound-for-pound basis, the party giving the indemnity should seek to ensure that it maintains some control over the way in which the shortfall in credits is rectified. For example, that party may wish to maintain control over the emissions account and trading activities after completion until the date on which the credits are surrendered. The risk of not obtaining such control is that the party benefiting under the indemnity may simply seek compliance in the most convenient way possible, and not necessarily the most cost effective.

- Breaches of greenhouse gas permit – if there is a known breach of a greenhouse gas permit, either for failing to surrender sufficient credits or for some other breach, the buyer should seek an indemnity from the seller for the costs it incurs for both bringing the company into compliance and as a result of the breach itself, for example fines issued by the relevant regulatory authority. The latter costs may not be covered by the indemnity to the extent the breach occurs after completion, because of the general rule that a person is not permitted to enforce an indemnity which covers its own criminal activities. It may, however, be possible to claim under the indemnity against the seller if the breach originally occurred prior to completion but continued after completion until the enforcement action.

- Civil claims against the company – a buyer of a company may also seek an indemnity from the seller if there are actual or threatened claims against the company. A summary of such claims and the likelihood of their success is discussed elsewhere in this book and may include claims such as those being made against automobile manufacturers and oil and coal companies. The seller may seek to resist such an indemnity on the basis that such claims are inherent to the particular nature of the business and as a result the buyer should be the party to assume this risk. However, where such claims represent a significant potential liability for the company, the buyer may counterargue that such inherent liabilities reduce the value of the company and therefore the purchase price should be reduced accordingly.

Even after the parties have agreed to an indemnity, as with indemnities generally, a number of issues are likely to be contentious before the final terms can be agreed. In particular, the buyer and seller are likely to have widely convergent attitudes towards the time limit for bringing a claim, the trigger point for bringing a claim, and the conduct of the company in relation to the claims against it following such trigger point. In these regards, the terms of the climate change indemnities are likely to follow the terms of any other general indemnities agreed.

However, one issue that may be of concern in the drafting of indemnities relating to carbon issues is that of *contra proferentum*, meaning that where there is ambiguity in the language of a contractual clause, the ambiguity will be interpreted by the court against the person seeking to rely on it. This principle can normally be overcome by careful drafting. However, in the case of climate change indemnities this may cause particular difficulties, in particular where the indemnity relates to issues not yet determined at the time of the agreements, such as future legislative development. Great care will need to be taken in the drafting of such provisions.

4.4 Other contractual risk-allocation mechanisms

In some circumstances, such as those where the ability of the seller to pay any claims under an indemnity or warranty is uncertain, mechanisms other than warranties and indemnities may be sought by the buyer (or in certain circumstances the seller). These include, for example, a reduction in the purchase price or the setting up of a retention fund or escrow accounts. Such mechanisms can also be used in the allocation of climate change risks.

4.5 Ongoing relationships

A number of corporate transactions in the climate change sector involve an ongoing relationship between the parties, such as the creation of special purpose vehicles or joint ventures for climate change related projects. The rights and obligations of the respective parties are likely to be the key driver of such arrangements and so will be agreed commercially. Nevertheless, these issues will need to be dealt with in the agreement.

5. **Looking ahead**

There is no doubt that climate change issues are now an inherent consideration in a wide range of corporate transactions. As the number of jurisdictions possessing climate change laws increases, along with the range of industrial sectors covered by that law, the impact of climate change on corporate transactions is set to increase. Although this is currently mainly limited to the direct effects of climate change legislation on a company's behaviour and performance, if a carbon-constrained economy were to become a reality, understanding a company's carbon profile would be crucial if its true value is to be ascertained. It is therefore also crucial that these issues are considered and properly understood if the rights and obligations, and risks and opportunities, of the parties are to be appropriately and correctly allocated.

As a result, it is not only those lawyers that have identified themselves as climate change specialists that will need to be familiar with the laws in this area. All transactional lawyers should be familiar with the basic principles of climate change law if they are to be able to identify and properly react to issues that may be present in a particular transaction. The task now is to ensure that the understanding of these climate change issues is properly integrated into the way that lawyers manage corporate and finance transactions.

The authors would like to thank the kind assistance of Edan Rotenberg in the preparation of this chapter, specifically in relation to the US legal aspects.

Competition

Peter Crowther
Lucie Fish
Dewey & LeBoeuf

---

1. Overview

The EU competition rules are contained in Chapter I of Title VI, which is entitled "Rules on Competition". The most important provisions are Articles 81 and 82 EC, which deal respectively with anti-competitive agreements and the abuse of a dominant position, and Articles 87 to 89 EC, which are concerned with state aid.

The most important bodies involved in the development and enforcement of the competition rules are the European Commission's Competition Directorate, as well as the national competition authorities which apply both EC and national competition law. By and large, national competition rules within the European Union mirror EC competition law. Accordingly, for the purpose of convenience in this chapter, reference is made only to the EU competition rules. The European Commission and national competition authorities have wide-ranging powers to enforce competition law. These rules include the right to request information, to conduct investigations, and to impose fines.

The EU competition rules apply fully to carbon trading, and indeed as described below the European Commission has already had the opportunity to review the compatibility of certain arrangements with the EU state-aid rules.

2. Article 81 EC

2.1 General principles

Article 81(1) EC provides:

"The following are prohibited as incompatible with the common market: all agreements between undertakings, decisions by associations of undertakings and concerted practices which may affect trade between Member States and which have as their object or effect the prevention, restriction or distortion of competition within the common market, and in particular those which:

(a) directly or indirectly fix purchase or selling prices or any other trading conditions;

(b) limit or control production, markets, technical development, or investment;

(c) share markets or sources of supply;

(d) apply dissimilar conditions to equivalent transactions with other trading parties, thereby placing them at a competitive disadvantage;

(e) make the conclusion of contracts subject to acceptance by the other parties of supplementary obligations which, by their nature or according to commercial usage, have no connection with the subject of such contracts."

Any agreements or decisions prohibited pursuant to Article 81(1) EC are, unless exempt, automatically void.

Article 81 EC provides for the possibility of exemption in the case of agreements, decisions or concerted practices which contribute to improving the production or distribution of goods or promoting technical or economic progress, while allowing consumers a fair share of the resulting benefit.

Accordingly, undertakings[1] involved in carbon trading must not enter into anti-competitive agreements within the meaning of Article 81 EC and, as is clear from the above-quoted text, Article 81(1) EC applies to agreements, decisions and concerted practices. Not only are legally binding agreements caught, but also informal understandings, "gentlemen's agreements", decisions and recommendations by trade associations and other types of informal contact. However, a finding of an agreement requires that it must be established that a concurrence of wills exists.[2]

It has long been established that Article 81 EC can apply not only to horizontal agreements,[3] that is to say agreements between firms that operate at the same level of the market, but also to vertical agreements, that is to say agreements between firms that operate at different levels of the market. Accordingly, Article 81 EC would apply to agreements between installations, as well as between installations and traders.

To be caught by Article 81(1) EC, agreements must have the object *or* effect of restricting competition. The most serious infringements of Article 81(1) EC have as their object the restriction of competition. Where parties enter into agreements of this kind, it is not necessary to prove that they will have anti-competitive effects. Within this category are horizontal "cartel" agreements, such as price fixing, market sharing and customer allocation, as set out in Article 81(l)(a) to (c) EC itself. Such agreements can expect to attract heavy fines. Vertical agreements that fix retail prices or that stipulate a minimum retail price are also considered to have as their object the restriction of competition, as are vertical agreements that impose export bans on distributors. Again, it can be expected that fines will be imposed in such cases.

Agreements that do not have as their object the restriction of competition may infringe Article 81(1) EC if they have an anti-competitive effect. A market analysis is needed to determine whether there is an infringement. The Commission has published Horizontal Co-operation Guidelines[4] that endeavour to explain how Article 81 EC applies to agreements of this nature, and Guidelines on Vertical Restraints.[5]

There must be an effect on inter-state trade before Article 81 EC can apply. The EC authorities take a wide view of the meaning of "effect on inter-state trade": the question is whether the agreement could have an actual or potential, direct or indirect effect on trade between member states. The fact that the parties to an agreement come from the same member state does not mean that their agreement cannot affect inter-state trade.[6]

---

1   Broadly, any natural or legal person that carries on an economic activity.
2   Case T-41/96 Bayer AG v Commission of the European Communities [2000] ECR II 3383.
3   Cases C-56 and 58/64 Consten and Grundig v Commission [1966] ECR 299, [1966] CMLR 418.
4   OJ [2001] C 3, p 2, [2001] 4 CMLR 819.
5   OJ [2000] C 291, p 1, [2001] 5 CMLR 1074.

2.2   Agreements of minor importance

Article 81(1) EC does not apply to "agreements of minor importance", except in the case of restrictions by object, discussed above. This arises from the *de minimis* doctrine established by the European Court of Justice (the ECJ) in *Volk v Vervaecke*,[7] as well as informal guidance produced by the Commission. The latest Commission Notice (the Notice) was published at the end of 2001.[8]

The *de minimis* market-share threshold for agreements between competitors is set at 10%, and at 15% for agreements between non-competitors. In cases where it is difficult to classify the agreement as either an agreement between competitors or an agreement between non-competitors, the 10% threshold is applicable. A 5% *de minimis* threshold applies in respect of networks of agreements producing a cumulative anti-competitive effect. The Commission takes the view that agreements will not be restrictive of competition if the market shares do not exceed these thresholds during two successive calendar years by more than two percentage points.[9]

2.3   Exemption: Article 81(3) EC

An agreement or "category of agreements" that infringes Article 81(1) EC can nevertheless be exempted under Article 81(3) EC provided that certain conditions are met. The distinction between agreements and categories of agreements anticipates the availability of both "individual exemption", for agreements notified to the Commission on a case-by-case basis, and "block exemption", for particular types of agreement defined on a generic basis in Commission regulations.

To benefit from *individual* exemption under Article 81(3) EC, an agreement must satisfy four requirements, two positive and two negative. The two positive requirements are first that the agreement must contribute to an improvement in the production or distribution of goods or the promotion of technical or economic progress, and second that consumers will get a fair share of the resulting benefit. The two negative requirements are first that the agreement does not impose on the undertakings indispensable restrictions, and second that it will not afford them the possibility of substantially eliminating competition. The Court of First Instance (CFI) and the ECJ have stressed on a number of occasions that all four requirements must be satisfied if an agreement is to benefit from exemption, for example in *Metropole Television SA and others v Commission*.[10] The burden of proof is on the applicant undertakings to prove that the agreement satisfies each of the four conditions.

2.4   Application to carbon trading

To our knowledge, Article 81 EC has not yet been applied to carbon trading in any member state. That said, it is obvious that industry participants must be mindful of the extensive reach of Article 81 EC, which catches all forms of collusive and restrictive practices. In the Commission's own words:

---

6   Case 77/160 *Vacuum Interrupters* OJ [1980] L 383, p 1, [1981] 2 CMLR 217.
7   [1969] ECR 295, [1969] CMLR 273.
8   OJ [2001] C 368,, p 13.
9   *Ibid* at paras 7 to 9.
10   T-528/93 *Metropole Television SA v Commission* [1996] 5 CMLR 386 at para 93.

"The Commission has no view on what the price of allowances should be. The price is a function of supply and demand as in any other free market. Market intermediaries quote prices for allowances offered or bid for. Should distortions occur, competition law would be applicable as with any other market."[11]

One particular issue that will need to be addressed is how the trading market will in practice operate, to avoid unintentional infringements of Article 81 EC, for example by the exchange of competitively sensitive pricing information.

Second, it remains to be seen whether operators will form trading pools. It is clear, however, that Article 81 EC will be capable of applying to such pools. Trading pools must not facilitate anti-competitive collusion between pool members.

3.   Article 82 EC

Article 82 EC provides:

"Any abuse by one or more undertakings of a dominant position within the common market or in a substantial part of it shall be prohibited as incompatible with the common market in so far as it may affect trade between member states.

Such abuse may, in particular, consist in:

(a) directly or indirectly imposing unfair purchase or selling prices or unfair trading conditions;

(b) sharing markets or sources of supply;

(c) limiting production, markets or technical development to the prejudice of consumers;

(d) applying dissimilar conditions to equivalent transactions with other trading parties, thereby placing them at a competitive disadvantage;

(e) making the conclusion of contracts subject to acceptance by the other parties of supplementary obligations which, by their nature or according to commercial usage, have no connection with the subject of such contracts."

Article 82 EC does not contain an exhaustive list of matters that fall within its scope and has been applied to many practices not specifically mentioned in it.

Whereas Article 81 EC is concerned with agreements, decisions and concerted practices which are harmful to competition, Article 82 EC is directed towards the unilateral conduct of dominant firms which use their market power in an exploitative or anti-competitive manner.

3.1   Dominant position: market power

Article 82 EC applies only where an undertaking has a "dominant position". Complex economic analysis is involved in making a determination on whether an undertaking is dominant, and legal advisers will often need expert advice from economists in order properly to prepare an action or defence under Article 82 EC.

The Court, in *United Brands Co v Commission*,[12] laid down the following test:

"The dominant position thus referred to in this article [Article 82 EC] relates to a position of economic strength enjoyed by an undertaking which enables it to prevent effective

---

11   Questions and Answers on Emissions Trading and National Allocation Plans, MEMO/05/84, 08.03.2005.
12   Case 27/76 [1978] ECR 207, [1978] 1 CMLR 429 at para 65.

competition being maintained on the relevant market by affording it the power to behave to an appreciable extent independently of its competitors, customers and ultimately of its consumers."

Dominance can exist only in relation to the supply or acquisition of a particular class of goods or services. It is therefore necessary to ascertain the relevant product or services market,[13] and then establish whether the undertaking "dominates" this particular market or markets.[14] If this is found to be the case, the "dominant" undertaking has a "special responsibility" not to distort competition.[15]

At this stage, it is not easy to foresee how an entity might acquire dominance in the carbon trading market and, in practice, Article 82 EC is likely to be of less relevance than Article 81 EC.

Perhaps the most likely exception to that would be if a dominant trading platform were to emerge. The Commission has over a number of years been developing a doctrine of "essential facilities", whereby a dominant undertaking which both owns and controls a facility or infrastructure to which competitors need access in order to provide services to customers cannot refuse access to such competitors or grant them access only on terms less favourable than those it gives to its own operations. The essential facilities doctrine, which has antecedents in US antitrust law, can be seen as a natural consequence of the judgment in *Commercial Solvents*, which held that a refusal to supply a customer downstream in the market, where that refusal would be to the advantage of the supplier's own downstream activity in that market, could amount to an abuse. The essential facilities doctrine can also be discerned in subsequent judgments of the ECJ and CFI such as *Télémarketing*[16] and the *Magill*[17] case.

Limits to this doctrine have subsequently been established: in *Tierce Ladbroke v Commission*[18] the CFI said that a refusal to supply could not fall within the prohibition:

"... unless it concerned a product or service which was either essential for the exercise of the activity in question, in that there was no real or potential substitute, or was a new product whose introduction might be prevented, despite specific, constant and regular potential demand on the part of consumers ..."

The judgment in *Oscar Brönner*[19] confirmed the trend in *Ladbroke*. Specifically on the question of whether access to the distribution system could be considered essential (or, in the language of the judgment, "indispensable"), the ECJ said that it would be necessary to establish that it would not be economically viable to create a second distribution system with a circulation comparable to that of the existing scheme.[20]

---

13   In the following discussion "product market" will be used to denote both types of market.
14   Case 6/72 *Europemballage Corpn and Continental Can Co Inc v Commission* [1973] ECR 215, [1973] CMLR 199 at para 32.
15   Case 322/81 *Michelin v Commission* [1983] ECR 3461.
16   Case 311/84 [1985] ECR 3261, [1986] 2 CMLR 558.
17   [1989] ECR 1141, [1989] 4 CMLR 749. See also for example the Commission decisions *London European – Sabena* OJ [1988] L 317/47, [1989] 4 CMLR 662 and *British Midland Airways Ltd v Aer Lingus plc* OJ [1992] L 96/34, [1993] 4 CMLR 596.
18   Case T-504/93 [1997] ECR II 923, [1997] 5 CMLR 309.
19   Case C-7/97 [1998] ECR I 7791, [1999] 4 CMLR 112.
20   *Ibid* at para 131.

4. State-aid rules: Articles 87 to 89 EC

4.1 Introduction

State-aid policy is the third main pillar of EC competition law. Article 87(1) EC states:

> "Save as otherwise provided in this Treaty, any aid granted by a Member State or through State resources in any form whatsoever which distorts or threatens to distort competition by favouring certain undertakings or the production of certain goods shall, in so far as it affects trade between Member States, be incompatible with the common market."

4.2 Elements of state aid

The state-aid rules will apply where aid: (i) is granted by a member state or through state resources;[21] (ii) confers an advantage to the recipients; (iii) favours certain (selected) undertakings or the production of certain goods; (iv) distorts or threatens to distort competition; and (v) affects trade between member states.

4.3 The concept of state aid

Article 87(1) EC refers to "aid granted by a member state or through state resources in any form whatsoever". The concept of state aid is not therefore defined by reference to its form or objective, but rather by reference to its effect.[22] The concept has been interpreted broadly, going beyond mere subsidy, and comprises many different forms of financial assistance and commercial advantage. It covers not only affirmative benefits, such as investment grants[23] and loans at reduced rates of interest,[24] but also actions which reduce charges a company would otherwise be required to pay, such as debt write-offs,[25] preferential fiscal treatment,[26] preferential energy tariffs that are not commercially justified[27] or tax exemptions.[28] Given its scope, incentive payments and tradable allowances will constitute state aid.[29]

4.4 Selective advantage

The state aid must involve selective financial assistance to a particular firm or industrial sector, favouring one firm or sector over another. In order to assess whether an advantage has been conferred to certain undertakings, the Commission has developed the "market economy investor" principle. The Commission will examine whether the terms on which funds are provided go beyond those that a private investor, operating under normal market economy conditions and having regard to the information available and foreseeable developments at that time,

---

21 "State resources" refers to public or private bodies designated or established by the state and which use resources which belong to or are controlled by the state – Case C-72-73/91 *Sloman Neptune Schiffahrts AG v Seebetriebsrat Bodo Ziesemer* [1993] ECR I 887 at para 19.

22 Case C-173/73 *Italy v Commission* [1974] ECR 709.

23 Case 730/79 *Phillip Morris v Commission* [1980] ECR 2671, [1981] 2 CMLR 321.

24 Case 323/82 *Intermills v Commission* [1984] ECR 3809, [1986] 1 CMLR 614.

25 *Rover Group* OJ 1989 L25/92 and Case C-294/90 *British Aerospace and Rover v Commission* [1992] ECR I 493, [1992] 1 CMLR 853.

26 Case C-387/92 *Banco Exterior de España* [1994] ECR I 877, [1994] 3 CMLR 473.

27 Joined Cases 67/85 and 68/85 *Van de Kooy v Commission* [1988] ECR 219.

28 Commission Notice on the application of the state aid rules to measures relating to direct business taxation, OJ 1998 C384/3, 10.12.1998.

29 State aid N416/2001 *United Kingdom, emission trading allowance* OJ C 88, 12.4.2006, p 16.

would find acceptable when providing funds to a comparable private undertaking.[30] The ECJ has also held in this regard that it is necessary to establish whether the recipient has received an economic advantage which it would not have obtained under normal market conditions and which improves its financial position.[31]

4.5 Market distortion

Actual proof of anti-competitive distortion is not required; its potential presence is sufficient.[32] According to the Court's jurisprudence, almost all selective aid will have the *potential* to distort competition, thereby satisfying the requirement in Article 87(1) EC. Only aid to firms supplying products or providing services in which there is no cross-border trade, such the water industry or in healthcare, will fall outside the scope of Article 87 EC.

4.6 Derogations

Article 87(2) EC provides that three types of aid are *automatically* compatible with the common market: (i) social aid granted to individual consumers; (ii) aid to make good damage by national disasters or exceptional occurrences, and (iii) aid granted to certain areas of Germany affected by its division following World War II. In practice, Article 87(2) EC categories rarely arise.

Article 87(3) EC allows the Commission *discretion* to permit other aids which: (i) promote economic development of areas of abnormally low standard of living or serious unemployment; (ii) promote an important project of common European interest or to remedy a serious disturbance in the economy of a member state; (iii) facilitate development of certain economic activities or of certain economic areas, where such aid does not adversely affect trading conditions; or (iv) promote culture and heritage conservation. In addition, under Article 87(3)(e) EC, the Commission may propose other categories of aid for endorsement by the Council.

Derogations to Article 87(1) EC are permissible if they are both necessary and commensurate with Community objectives. The Commission has over the years developed detailed policy guidelines for determining whether aid can be cleared under Article 87(3) EC. Of particular relevance in this context are the Guidelines on state aid for environmental protection (discussed in detail below).[33]

4.7 Exemptions

Pursuant to Article 89 EC, the Council can adopt regulations in the field of state aid and, in particular, exempting aid from notification. In 1998, the Council adopted a block-exemption enabling Regulation under which the Commission is entitled to issue block exemptions in respect of certain categories of non-sector-specific or "horizontal" aid (the Block Exemption Enabling Regulation).[34]

---

30   Case 234/84 *Belgium v Commission (Meura)* [1986] ECR 2263, [1988] 2 CMLR 331.
31   Case C-39/94 *SFEL v La Poste* [1996] ECR I 3547 at para 60.
32   Joined Cases 296 and 318/82, *Netherlands and Leeuwader Papierwarenfabriek v Commission* [1985] ECR 809.
33   Commission Guidelines on state aid for environmental protection, OJ 2008 C82/1, 01.04.2008
34   Council Regulation (EC) No 994/98 of May 7 1998 on the application of Articles 87 and 88 EC to certain categories of horizontal state aid, OJ L 142, 14.05.1998, pp 1 to 4.

Further to the Block Exemption Enabling Regulation, the Commission has adopted a number of block exemptions for state aid for employment,[35] regional aid[36] and training aid.[37] Two others are particularly worthy of mention:

- *De minimis* block exemption:[38] The Commission Regulation on the application of Articles 87 and 88 EC to *de minimis* aid (the *de minimis* Block Exemption) defines cases where aid will not have an appreciable impact on competition or trade and thus be exempt from notification (see below). The *de minimis* Block Exemption exempts aid granted to any one enterprise not exceeding €200,000 over any three-year period. The recipient firm has a duty to inform the member state about any other aid received during the preceding three years.
- **Small and medium-sized enterprises (SMEs) block exemption:**[39] The Commission Regulation on aid to SMEs exempts certain categories of aid granted to SMEs which fall below certain prescribed ceilings, concerning the aid intensity and total project costs, together with the total amount of gross aid.

The Commission has published for consultation various drafts of a proposed general block exemption regulation for state aid (the draft GBER).[40] The draft GBER will simplify and consolidate certain existing block exemption regulations due to expire on June 30 2008. In addition, the Commission proposes to integrate three types of aid that have so far not been exempted: environmental aid, aid in the form of risk capital, and research and development aid for large enterprises.[41]

5.   **State-aid procedure – Article 88 EC**

The Commission is responsible for the enforcement of state-aid rules and has wide-ranging powers to investigate examples of aid[42] and to order member states to recover such aid. Article 88 EC and the Procedural Regulation (No 659/1999) deal with Commission procedure.[43]

---

35   Commission Regulation (EC) No 2204/2002 of December 12 2002 on the application of Articles 87 and 88 of the EC Treaty to state aid for employment (expires June 30 2008), OJ L 337, 13.12.2002, pp 3 to 14.

36   Commission Regulation (EC) No 1628/2006 of October 24 2006 on the application of Articles 87 and 88 of the EC Treaty to national regional investment aid, OJ L 302, 1.11.2006, pp 29 to 40.

37   Commission Regulation (EC) No 68/2001 of January 12 2001 on the application of Articles 87 and 88 of the EC Treaty to training aid (expires June 30 2008), OJ L 10, 13.01.2001, pp 20 to 29, as amended by Commission Regulation No 363/2004 of February 25 2004, OJ L 63, 28.02.2004, pp 20 to 21.

38   Commission Regulation (EC) No 1998/2006 of December 15 2006 on the application of Articles 87 and 88 EC to *de minimis* aid, OJ L 379 of 28.12.2006.

39   Commission Regulation (EC) No 70/2001 of January 12 2001 on the application of Articles 87 and 88 EC to state aid to small and medium-sized enterprises (expires June 30 2008), OJ L 10, 13.01.2001, pp 33 to 42; as amended by Commission Regulation No 364/2004 of February 25, OJ L 63, 28.02.2004, pp 22 to 29 and Commission Regulation (EC) No 1857/2006 of December 15 2006 OJ L 358, 16.12.2006, pp 3 to 21.

40   Invitation to submit comments on the revised draft general block exemption of the Commission in the state aid area, 28.02.2008.

41   Commission FAQ, MEMO/07/151, 24.04.2007.

42   Commission Directive 2006/111/EC of November 16 2006 on the transparency of financial relations between member states and public undertakings as well as on financial transparency within certain undertakings, OJ L 318, 17.11.2006, pp 17 to 25.

43   Council Regulation (EC) No 659/99 OJ L 83/1, 27.03.1999, pp 1 to 9 and Regulation (EC) No 794/2004 OJ L 140, 30.04.2004, pp 1 to 134 lay down detailed rules for the application of Article 88 EC.

5.1   Notification

Member states are required to notify the Commission of any proposals to grant state aid before it is put into effect. Both individual aids and general aid schemes must be notified.

The notification must be made in sufficient time to allow the Commission to assess the proposal and the aid must not be implemented before this assessment is complete.[44]

It is not possible for the recipient of the aid to make the notification, although in appropriate cases the Commission may enter into informal discussions with recipient companies.

5.2   Failure to notify

A failure to notify and obtain advance Commission approval for a state aid makes aid automatically unlawful. State aid paid unlawfully is subject to recovery with interest, and aggrieved competitors may also bring actions for damages before the national courts.

5.3   Decision of the commission

In assessing whether aid can be deemed compatible with the common market, the Commission balances the positive impact of the aid in reaching an objective of common interest against its negative side effects, such as distortion of trade and competition. The State Aid Action Plan has formalised this balancing exercise in what has been termed a "balancing test".[45] The balancing test is structured as follows:

- Is the aid measure aimed at a well-defined objective of common interest?
- Is the aid well designed to deliver the objective of common interest?
  - Is state aid an appropriate policy instrument?
  - Is there an incentive effect, namely does the aid change the behaviour of undertakings?
  - Is the aid measure proportional, namely could the same change in behaviour be obtained with less aid?
- Are the distortions of competition and effect on trade limited, so that the overall balance is positive?

5.4   Procedure

The Commission is required to determine one of three outcomes within two months of notification:[46] it may (i) find that the measure does not constitute aid; (ii) find that the measure constitutes aid but is compatible with the common market, or (iii) initiate a formal investigation procedure.[47] Where the Commission has not made a decision within the relevant period, the aid shall be deemed to have been authorised by the Commission.[48]

The Commission is obliged to open the formal investigation procedure should it have difficulty in determining the compatibility of aid with the common market.

---

44   *Ibid* at Article 3.
45   State Aid Action Plan, OJ C 37, 03.02.2001 at paras 11 and 20.
46   See n 43 at Article 4(5) although the period can be extended with the consent of the Commission and the member state concerned. The two-month period does not apply if the preliminary examination was initiated on a complaint by a competitor or *ex officio*.
47   See n 43 at Articles 4(1) to (5).
48   *Ibid* at Article 4(6).

The Commission can then: (i) decide that the measure does not constitute aid; (ii) take a "positive" decision that the aid is compatible with the common market; (iii) take a "conditional" decision (ie the Commission may request certain changes or specify certain restrictions); or (iv) take a "negative" decision that the aid shall not be put into effect.[49]

If a member state does not comply with a Commission decision within the stated time, the Commission or – in principle – another member state may take the matter directly to the ECJ.

6 Application to carbon trading

By virtue of the Emissions Trading Directive (2003/87/EC),[50] the Commission must ensure that National Allocation Plans (NAPs) concluded under the EU ETS comply with the state-aid rules, while at the same time achieving their intended environmental benefits.

According to the EP Guidelines (see below), the Commission may consider environmental aid as falling within the exemption articulated in Article 87(3)(c) EC, namely, "to facilitate the development of certain economic activities or certain economic areas" or, in respect of specific projects, Article 87(3)(b).

6.1 EP Guidelines

Article 6 EC requires that environmental policy objectives are integrated into Commission policies, in particular with a view to promoting sustainable development.

The Commission first adopted Guidelines for environmental protection in 2001. These set out the way in which the Commission intended to assess state aid for environmental protection.[51] The current Guidelines were adopted on January 23 2008 (the EP Guidelines) and entered into force on April 1 2008.[52]

The EP Guidelines state that the primary objective of state-aid control in the field of environmental protection is to ensure that state-aid measures will result in a higher level of protection than would occur without the aid and that the positive effects of the aid outweigh its negative effects in terms of distortions of competition, taking account of the "polluter pays" principle (the PP principle).[53]

The PP principle is set out in Article 174 EC and establishes the requirement that the costs of measures to deal with pollution should be borne by the person responsible for causing the pollution. In general terms, the PP principle militates against the granting of state aid in the absence of the internalisation of environmental protection costs.[54]

The EP Guidelines state that aid for environmental protection will primarily be

49   *Ibid*, at Article 6.
50   Directive 2003/87/EC of the European Parliament and of the Council of October 13 2003 establishing a scheme for greenhouse gas emission allowance trading within the Community and amending Council Directive 96/61/EC, OJ L 275, 25.10.2003, pp 32 to 46.
51   Commission Guidelines on state aid for environmental protection, OJ 2001 C32/3, 03.02.2001.
52   Commission Guidelines on state aid for environmental protection, OJ 2008 C82/5, 01.04.2008.
53   *Ibid* para 6.
54   *Ibid* at para 8. The internalisation of costs requires that all costs associated with the protection of the environment should be included in a company's production costs.

justified under Article 87(3)(c) EC.[55] As described above, exemptions from Article 87(1) EC are interpreted narrowly and only permissible if they are both necessary and proportionate. The EP Guidelines also set out the application of the balancing test (described at 5.3 above) to environmental aid (described further below).

The EP Guidelines also identify specific measures for which state aid may, under specific conditions, be compatible under Article 87(3)(c) EC. Of particular relevance here is the treatment of aid involved in tradable permit schemes (described further below).[56]

The EP Guidelines also deal with aid in the form of reductions in or exemptions from environmental taxes.[57]

6.2   Pre-EU ETS emission trading schemes

(a)   *Introduction*

Prior to the adoption of the Emissions Trading Directive, the Commission considered certain national emission trading schemes notified under the state-aid rules.[58] The early national schemes provided the Commission with valuable learning experience.

The Commission formulated the view that an emission allowance was equivalent to an intangible asset (the value of which would subsequently be determined by an allowance market) and that the allocation by the state of a free allowance conferred an advantage on the recipient company; by opting not to sell that allowance, the state had deprived itself of a revenue stream, and so the advantage had therefore been funded by state resources; and, because the advantage had been provided only to certain sectors or companies, it was selective.[59]

(b)   *UK ETS*

The closest scheme to the EU ETS is generally considered to be the United Kingdom's emissions trading scheme (the UK ETS).[60] The UK ETS was voluntary and involved the payment of financial incentives so as to attract participants. Once a participating entity had proved an actual emissions reduction, it would receive a payment (per tonne of reduced CO_2) and a corresponding allowance which could then be traded.

The United Kingdom did not regard the incentive payment and tradable allowance as free benefits, as both were conditional upon the recipient's meeting of specified targets, and effectively the "price" paid for a "service".

The Commission disagreed and considered both the incentive payments and the tradable allowance to amount to state aid for the purposes of Article 87(1) EC.[61] The

---

55   *Ibid* at para 12.
56   *Ibid* at paras 55 to 56. The criteria set out in point 55 form the basis for the Commission's assessment of situations arising during the trading period ending on December 31 2012.
57   *Ibid* at para 57.
58   State aid N653/1999 *Denmark, CO₂ quotas* OJ C 322, 11.11.2000, p 9; State aid N416/2001 *United Kingdom, emission trading allowance* OJ C 88, 12.4.2006, p 16; State aid N35/2003 *Netherlands, trading scheme* OJ C 227, 23.9.2003, p 8.
59   *Ibid.*
60   Angus Johnston "Free Allocation of allowances under the EU emissions trading scheme: legal issues", *Climate Policy* 6 (2006) 115 to 136, at p 117.
61   State aid N416/2001 *United Kingdom, emission trading allowance* OJ C 88, 12.4.2006, p 16. See also, IP/01/1674, 28.11.2001.

Commission stated:

"... the State allocated a number of transferable emission permits free of charge. The State thus provides these companies with an intangible asset for free, which can be sold on a market. This advantage distorts competition between companies. Companies able to make a profit from the allowances can use the profit for their business competing with other companies not having access to such a scheme. This can affect trade between Member States."[62]

In the event the Commission concluded that the scheme was compatible with the common market under Article 87(3)(c) EC.

The Commission did note, however, that the UK ETS differed significantly from the proposed mandatory EU ETS. As mentioned above, the EU ETS is based on the "polluter pays" principle without financial incentives, and imposes penalties in respect of emissions in excess of allowance holdings. The Commission suggested that this might lead to market distortions in the future and that the UK ETS should be revisited following the adoption of the EU ETS.

(c)   ***The EU ETS – National Allocation Plans***

Since the adoption of the Emissions Trading Directive, the Commission's focus has shifted to National Allocation Plans drawn up by member states.

A NAP will stipulate a member state's quota of tradable emission allowances for the relevant Phase of the EU ETS, and detail the methods by which the quota will be allocated to eligible companies and installations. The EU ETS periodically obliges individual member states to draw up a NAP detailing its tradable scheme. As a general point, it is noteworthy that NAPs submitted to the Commission have been far from uniform: member states have adopted different approaches as regards the basis for initial allocations, rewards for early action, allocation to new entrants and, to some extent, the scope of installations covered by the scheme.[63]

The Emissions Trading Directive does not provide a safe harbour from the application of the state-aid rules. In fact, Article 11(3) of the Emissions Trading Directive specifically obliges member states to consider Articles 87 and 88 EC.

(d)   ***Commission assessment***

The Emissions Trading Directive requires the Commission to assess NAPs in accordance with criteria specified in its Annex III. Criterion 5 of Annex III (non-discrimination between companies or sectors) states:

"The plan shall not discriminate between companies or sectors in such a way as to unduly favour certain undertakings or activities in accordance with the Treaty, in particular Articles 87 and 88 EC."

In January 2004, the Commission confirmed that normal state-aid rules would apply.[64]

---

62   State aid N416/2001 *United Kingdom, emission trading allowance*, p 9, para V1(b).
63   State aid aspects in the implementation of the Emission Trading Scheme, B. Renner-Loquenz EC C.P.N. 2005, 1 (Spr) 16 to 18.
64   Communication from the Commission on guidance to assist Member States in the implementation of the criteria listed in Annex III to Directive 2003/87/EC establishing a scheme for greenhouse gas emission allowance trading within the Community, COM/2003/0830 at para 47.

(e)   State aid considerations

Article 87(3)(c) EC explicitly recognises that state aid can be an effective tool for achieving objectives of common interest. The Commission will seek to ensure that state-aid measures will result in a higher level of environmental protection and that the positive effects of the aid outweigh the negative in terms of competition distortion.

The EP Guidelines state that the overall effect on environmental protection will be positive if the number of permits granted by a member state is lower than the expected needs of the undertakings. Where allowances granted to an undertaking do not cover the totality of expected needs of the undertaking, the undertaking will be incentivised either to reduce its pollution (thus contributing to the improvement of the level of environmental protection) or buy supplementary allowances on the market (thus effectively paying compensation for its pollution).[65]

Pursuant to the EP Guidelines, tradable permit schemes must fulfil the following conditions:

- the scheme must be designed to achieve environmental objectives over and above the mandatory Community scheme;
- the allocation must be transparent, based on objective criteria and the total amount of tradable permits or allowances granted to each undertaking for a price below their market value shall not be higher than its expected needs;
- the allocation methodology must not favour certain undertakings or certain sectors, unless this is justified by the environmental logic of the system itself or where such rules are necessary for consistency with other environmental policies; and
- in particular, new entrants shall in principle not receive permits or allowances on more favourable conditions than existing undertakings operating on the same markets.

The Commission will further assess the necessity and the proportionality of state aid involved in a tradable permit scheme according to the following criteria:

- the choice of beneficiaries must be based on objective and transparent criteria, and allowances must be granted in principle in the same way for all competitors in the same sector/relevant market if they are in a similar factual situation;
- full auctioning must lead to a substantial increase in production cost for each sector or category of individual beneficiaries; and
- the substantial increase in production costs cannot be passed on to customers without leading to important sales reductions.

(f)   Challenges to NAPs

In the event of a successful challenge, unlawfully granted aid must be recovered by the member state.[66] There are two potential avenues of challenge.

---

65   See n 33 at para 55.
66   See Case 52/84 *Commission v Belgium* [1986] ECR 89.

(i)   *Before the Commission*

Interested parties, including any member state and any person or undertaking whose interests may be affected by the granting of state aid, and in particular the beneficiary of the aid, competing undertakings and trade associations, may inform the Commission of any alleged unlawful or alleged misuse of aid. The Commission is then obliged to examine such information without delay.[67]

Such a challenge was launched by EnBW, a power producer and network operator in Germany, in June 2004. EnBW filed a complaint with the Commission aimed at nullifying the Commission's decision to accept the German NAP. EnBW objected specifically to the provision that allowed operators to transfer allowances from an existing installation to a new installation provided it was of the same kind. EnBW argued that this amounted to illegal state aid because it allowed operators to phase out its nuclear installations in favour of fossil fuel installations, whilst at the same time refusing to permit EnBW to transfer allowances between installations. Although this claim was ultimately declared inadmissible by the CFI, it demonstrates the potential activism of market participants.[68]

(ii) *Before national courts*

Another possibility is that of judicial review before the national courts of a member state. National courts may enforce the requirement that member states must notify state aid and may not implement such aid in the absence of a notification.[69] Further, a national court may make a reference to the ECJ under Article 234 EC for the interpretation of the relevant EC law.

(g)   ***Environmental tax reductions/exemptions***

Reductions in or exemptions from environmental taxes granted to undertakings in particular sectors will, prima facie, be considered illegal state aid. The EP Guidelines state that where such measures are conducive to environmental protection, the Commission will take the view that they are acceptable, subject to certain conditions and for a limited period of 10 years.[70]

---

67   Procedural Regulation, Article 20.
68   Case T-387/04 *EnBW Energie Baden-Württemberg v Commission*, OJ C 140 of 23.06.2007, p 23.
69   Article 88(3) EC.
70   See n 33 at paras 151 to 158.

Carbon regulation in the United States

Steven Ferrey
Suffolk University Law School
Courtney A Queen
Dewey & LeBoeuf LLP

1.   The power connection for carbon

Greenhouse gas (GHG) regulation in the United States is a story of the electric utility industry. Technologically, the offending GHGs are a function of modern society's use of energy – particularly combusting fossil fuels for electric power production.[1] Power is derived from burning gaseous, liquid and solid fossil fuels to create electric power. This releases copious quantities of CO_2 into the environment.[2] Yet despite the emphasis now in the United States on the reduction of GHG emissions, electric power demand is continuing to increase.[3] Most countries are using fossil fuels, not renewable power resources, to satisfy this exponential increase in demand.

All forecasts by the US Department of Energy, the International Energy Agency and independent forecasters agree that GHG emissions will increase exponentially, not decrease, in the foreseeable future.[4] Why is this? The construction of power generation facilities is increasing as population growth and development continue. Unabated, this exponential increase in power demand will tip the global environmental thermostat to runaway global warming levels.[5] The logical conclusions are:

- the electric power sector is the key battleground in the fight against global warming; and
- substitute renewable energy technologies are appropriate alternative choices in these environments.

---

[1]   About 75% of the anthropogenic sources of carbon in the atmosphere results from the combustion of fossil fuels, while 25% is the result of deforestation and the resultant inability of the biosphere to assimilate and reprocess this chemical compound. Regarding global climate change, shifting land-use patterns, leading to increased commuting and other transportation-related emissions, are suspected by many researchers to be as significant as industrial emissions. The destruction of carbon dioxide sinks, such as forested areas, reduces the amount of carbon dioxide that can be stored, causing the remaining bare land to release less water into the atmosphere. This reduces annual rainfall, which increases local temperatures by a significant amount. In addition, stripped land releases back into the atmosphere more easily the heat that it would otherwise store. These factors upset climate balance.

[2]   The amount of carbon released per unit of usable energy decreased each time as human populations moved from wood to coal as the dominant CO_2-releasing fuel in the late nineteenth century, and again moved from coal to oil in the mid-twentieth century, and will move toward natural gas in the future. See Steven Ferrey, *The Law of Independent Power* § 2.1 (25th ed 2007).

[3]   See, for example, International Energy Agency, *World Energy Outlook 2004* (2004), available at www.iea.org/textbase/nppdf/free/2004/weo2004.pdf.

[4]   US Department of Energy, Energy Information Administration, *International Energy Outlook 2007* Ch 7 (2007), available at www.eia.doe.gov/oiaf/ieo/emissions.html [hereinafter "International Outlook"].

[5]   United Nations Environment Programme, Intergovernmental Panel on Climate Change, *Climate Change 2007: The Physical Science Basis, Summary for Policy Makers* 17 (2007), available at www.ipcc.ch/SPM2feb07.pdf.

Since the Industrial Revolution, emissions resulting from combusting fossil fuels for mechanical and electrical energy have poured into the atmosphere.[6] GHGs are those gases of most concern: carbon dioxide (CO_2), nitrous oxide (N_2O), methane (CH_4), sulphur hexafluoride (SF_6), hydrofluorocarbons (HFCs), and perfluorocarbons (PFCs).[7] Notably, the most prevalent GHG is water vapour. It, alone, is the unregulated GHG.

The molecule-by-molecule global warming impact of many of these secondary and less prevalent GHGs is significantly greater than CO_2.[8] Because they are released in smaller quantities, however, and/or have shorter residence times in the atmosphere before they dissipate, CO_2 is the most troubling GHG and therefore receives the greatest policy focus.[9] The GHGs in Table 1 are displayed in descending order of their impacts on the environment, which is a function of quantities released, their heat radiation properties, and their residence time in the atmosphere.

Table 1: Key facts about greenhouse gases

GHG	Global warming potential [CO_2=1]	Residency time [years]	Amount of US total GHG release [%][10]
Carbon dioxide (CO_2)	1	100	85
Methane (CH_4)	21	12	11
Nitrous oxides (NOx)	310	120	2
Hydrochlorofluorocarbons (HFCs)	140–11,700	Varies	< 1
Chlorofluorocarbons (CFCs)	6,500	Varies	< 1
Sulphur hexafluoride (SF_6)	23,900	Varies	< 1

CO_2 is the main by-product of fossil fuel combustion and therefore results from any energy production that uses oil, coal, natural gas or other solid waste fuels. Some 98% of anthropogenic CO_2 emissions are from combustion of fossil fuels, and 84% of energy-related US GHG emissions are attributed to CO_2.[11] More than one-third of CO_2 emissions are attributable to the electric power sector. The sheer amount of CO_2

---

6   Pew Center for Climate Change, *Global Warming Basics* (2007), available at www.perclimate.org/global-warming-basics.

7   In 2000, anthropogenic activities emitted 320 million tonnes of methane and 33 TgN (teragrams of elemental nitrogen) of N_2O into the atmosphere. These levels are rising at a rate of about 4% per year. United Nations Environment Programme, Intergovernmental Panel on Climate Change, *Climate Change 2001: Working Group I: The Scientific Basis* § 4.2 (2001), (hereinafter WG1 Full Report) available at www.grida.no/climate/ picc_tar/wg1/index.htm.

8   US Environmental Protection Agency, EPA 230-R94-014. *Inventory of US Greenhouse Gas Emissions and Sinks: 1990–1994 ES-2* (1994).

9   *Ibid.*

10   *Ibid.*

11   US Department of Energy, Energy Information Administration, *Emissions of Greenhouse Gases in the United States* (2005), available at www.eia.doe.gov/oiaf/1605/ggrpt/carbon.html.

12   See "Residency Time" in Table 1; *see also* Ray Purdy, "The Legal Implications of Carbon Capture and Storage Under the Sea", 7 *Sustainable Dev. L. & Pol'y.*, Am. U. 22, 22 (2006).

emitted into the environment is enormous and persists for 100 years.[12] US energy-related CO_2 emissions in 2006 amounted to 5,877 million metric tonnes.[13] Global CO_2 emissions are rising at the rate of approximately 10% per year internationally.[14] Despite the emergence of, and attention to, renewable energy sources, forecasters do not see the international mix of power generation sources changing appreciably over the next several decades.[15] The percentage of fossil fuels in the mix – and thus the potential sources of GHGs in the power sector – is forecast to remain relatively constant. The International Energy Agency in Paris predicts that, by 2030, world demand for energy will have grown by 59% and fossil fuel sources will still supply 82% of the total, with non-carbon renewable energy sources supplying only 6%.[16]

Clearly GHGs in the twenty-first century are about power generation.[17] The single-point nature of power plants' emissions, and the exploding demand for electricity, make electricity generating plants a logical choice for the regulation of GHG emissions in the United States.

2.   Voluntary domestic carbon regulation

The United States has a handful of national voluntary programmes. With the passage of the Energy Policy Act of 1992, Congress authorised a voluntary programme to encourage the public to report achievements in reducing GHG emissions. Beginning in October of 1994, the US Department of Energy issued guidelines on the voluntary reporting of emissions reductions and carbon sequestration.[18] This programme, though, only offers an opportunity to report annual GHG emissions and record projects that reduce emissions or increase carbon sequestration, but it does not provide a mechanism or monetary incentives to reduce carbon emissions.

The Chicago Climate Exchange (CCX) was among the first to create a voluntary, legally binding, multi-sector reduction and trade programme that provides true monetary incentives. CCX is currently the single voluntary emissions trading system for all six GHGs and has almost 300 members from various sectors worldwide.[19] For CCX members who choose to participate in CCX's binding commitment to meet annual GHG emission-reduction goals, the programme provides an opportunity to capitalise on the burgeoning carbon market.

CCX issues Carbon Financial Instrument (CFI) contracts, each representing the equivalent of 100 metric tonnes of CO_2, as the tradable commodity. The CFI contracts are either "Exchange Allowances" based on a member's emission baseline and an overall reduction schedule, or "Exchange Offsets" generated by certain types

13 US Department of Energy, Energy Information Administration, *US Carbon Emissions from Energy Sources: 2006 Flash Estimate* (May 2007), available at www.eia.doe.gov/oiaf/1605/flash/pdf/flash.pdf.
14 *Ibid.*
15 Clark Gelling, Electric Power Research Institute, presentation at Aegis Conference, July 25 2007.
16 International Energy Agency, *World Energy Outlook 2004* (2005), available at www.iea.org/textbase/nppdf/free/2004/weo2004.pdf.
17 For detailed coverage of the power industry law and regulation, see generally Steven Ferrey, *The Law of Independent Power* (25th ed 2007).
18 US Department of Energy, *Voluntary Reporting of Greenhouse Gas Emissions under Section 1605(b) of the Energy Policy Act of 1992: General Guidelines* (Oct. 1994), available at www.eia.doe.gov/oiaf/1605/1605b.html.
19 Chicago Climate Exchange, *History* (2007), available at www.chicagoclimatex.com/content.jsf?id=1.

of offset projects.[20] CCX members that reduce emissions below the target levels can sell or bank their surplus allowances.

Participation in the trading system requires that members agree to surrender their CFI contracts to meet the emission reduction requirement.[21] To meet the requirement, members follow a schedule for reducing emissions that is to be carried out in two phases. Phase I (2003 to 2006) required members to commit to reduce to at least 1% below the 1998 to 2001 baseline,[22] for a total reduction of 4% by 2006. Phase II (2007 to 2010) requires members to commit to an annual reduction schedule of an additional 2%, resulting in an overall reduction commitment of 6% below baseline.[23]

CCX's offsets programme allows members and other entities that do not have significant GHG emissions to register offset projects.[24] CCX will issue traditional CFI contracts to offset providers or offset aggregators "for eligible projects on the basis of sequestration, destruction or displacement of GHG emissions". An offset provider is defined as an owner of an offset project that registers and sells offsets on its own behalf. An offset aggregator is defined as an entity that serves as the administrative representative, on behalf of offset project owners, of multiple offset-generating projects. Offset aggregators register and sell offset projects involving less than 10,000 metric tonnes of CO_2 equivalent per year.

CFI contracts are issued by CCX according to standardised rules for projects involving agricultural methane, landfill methane, agricultural soil carbon, forestry, renewable energy, coalmine methane, and rangeland soil carbon.[25] Other types of projects, such as energy efficiency and fuel switching, are approved by CCX on a project-by-project basis.[26]

Another voluntary programme is the Western Climate Initiative (WCI). In a regional effort to address climate change, the governors of Oregon, Washington, California, Arizona, New Mexico, and Utah, as well as the premiers of British Columbia and Manitoba, signed an agreement establishing the Western Climate Initiative.[27] In August 2007, WCI announced the establishment of its regional, economy-wide goal to reduce GHG emissions to 15% below 2005 levels by 2020.[28] To

---

20   *Ibid.*
21   *Ibid.*
22   *Ibid.* The Phase I baseline is the average annual emissions from 1998 to 2001.
23   *Ibid.* The Phase II baseline is the average annual emissions from 1998 to 2001 or the single year of 2000.
24   Chicago Climate Exchange, *CCX Offsets Program* (2007), available at www.chicagoclimatex.com/content.jsf?id=23.
25   *Ibid.*
26   *Ibid.*
27   The original agreement was signed in February 2007 by Governors of Arizona, California, New Mexico, Oregon, and Washington. In May 2007, the state of Utah and the Canadian provinces of British Columbia and Manitoba joined WCI. The states of Kansas, Colorado, Wyoming and Nevada, the Canadian provinces of Ontario, Quebec and Saskatchewan and one Mexican state, Sonora, will participate in WCI as observers. See Cathy Cash, Western Region Plan to Reduce GHG Emissions has Energy Suppliers Waiting for Specifics, *Electric Utility Week* at 20 (NY: McGraw-Hill Publishers, August 27 2007).
28   Western Climate Initiative, Press Release: Western Climate Initiative Members Set Regional Target to Reduce Greenhouse Gas Emissions (August 22 2007), available at www.westernclimateinitiative.org/ewebeditpro/items/O104F13013.pdf. See also The Pew Center on Climate Change, *Regional Initiatives: Western Climate Initiative* (June 2007), available at www.pewclimate.org/what_s_being_done/in_the_states/regional_initiatives.cfm?preview=1.

help reach this goal, WCI member states and provinces have committed to unveiling a multi-sector market-based mechanism, such as a load-based cap-and-trade programme, by the end of August 2008.[29]

The metrics for establishing this regional goal are based on: (i) aggregate GHG emissions and the goals of WCI partners that have already established a 2020 goal[30]; (ii) emissions inventories from states or provinces, where available; (iii) gross emissions estimates (across all sectors) for the six GHGs reported to the UN Framework Convention on Climate Change;[31] and (iv) load-based emissions estimates for the electricity sector.[32]

Table 2: State and provincial goals for GHG reductions[33]

	Short term (2010 to 2012)	Medium term (2020)	Long term (2040 to 2050)
Arizona	Not established	2000 levels by 2020	50% below 2000 by 2040
British Columbia	Not established	33% below 2007 by 2020	Not established
California	2000 levels by 2010	1990 levels by 2020	80% below 1990 by 2050
Manitoba	6% below 1990	6% below 1990[34]	Not established
New Mexico	2000 levels by 2012	10% below 2000 by 2020	75% below 2000 by 2050
Oregon	Arrest emissions growth	10% below 1990 by 2020	>75% below 1990 by 2050
Utah			Will set goals by June 2008
Washington	Not established	1990 levels by 2020	50% below 1990 by 2050

New entrants making comparable efforts to reduce GHG emissions are encouraged to join WCI. WCI members consider several factors when determining whether to admit a new state or province. Such factors include whether the

---

29   *Ibid.* See also Cathy Cash, Western Region Plan to Reduce GHG Emissions has Energy Suppliers Waiting for Specifics, *Electric Utility Week* at 1 (NY: McGraw-Hill Publishers, August 27 2007).

30   An important facet of the regional, economy-wide goal is its consistency with the pre-existing emission goals of WCI members. See Table 2, below.

31   These six GHGs include: carbon dioxide (CO_2), methane (CH_4), nitrous oxide (N_2O), hydrofluorocarbons (HFCs), perfluorocarbons (PFCs), and sulphur hexafluoride (SF_6).

32   Western Climate Initiative, *Statement of Regional Goal* (Attachment A: Metrics used to Establish WCI Regional Goal) 3 (August 22 2007), available at www.westernclimateinitiative.org/ewebeditpro/items/O104F13006.pdf.

33   Western Climate Initiative, *Statement of Regional Goal* 4 (August 22 2007), available at www.westernclimateinitiative.org/ewebeditpro/items/O104F13006.pdf.

34   Manitoba has not yet established a formal goal for 2020, but expects to meet or do better than its short-term goal. *Ibid.*

proposed entrant: has adopted an economy-wide reduction goal and developed a comprehensive plan to reach that goal; has agreed to adopt GHG tailpipe standards for passenger vehicles; and is participating in the Climate Registry.[35]

To achieve the new regional GHG emissions-reduction goal, WCI is committed to limiting emissions that contribute to climate change from all sources of GHGs, including but not limited to stationary sources, energy supply, residential properties, commercial and industrial activities, transportation, waste management, agriculture, and forestry.[36] Eventually, WCI's plan to curb emissions will focus on power plants and vehicles. Implementing the WCI plan will probably restrict the continued development of coal-fired power generation facilities because it will otherwise be difficult to meet the emission reduction goals. In developing its market approach, WCI members are engaging in discussions with leaders in the Regional Greenhouse Gas Initiative and may consider some variety of incentives, standards and regulations similar to the approach California has taken to combat climate change.[37]

3.   The Regional Greenhouse Gas Initiative

To fill the vacuum left by the United States' refusal to participate in the Kyoto Protocol, many states have taken direct regulatory action.[38] Beginning in April 2003, Governor George Pataki of New York initiated the effort by inviting neighbouring states to participate in a regional cap-and-trade emissions programme. On December 20 2005, seven states, namely Connecticut, Delaware, Maine, New Hampshire, New Jersey, New York and Vermont, entered into an agreement to implement the Regional Greenhouse Gas Initiative (RGGI).[39] Since that time, Massachusetts, Maryland, and Rhode Island have agreed to sign the RGGI Memorandum of Understanding (MOU) (collectively, RGGI states).[40] The principal goal of the MOU is for RGGI states to:

"... commit to propose for legislative and/or regulatory approval a CO_2 Budget Trading Program (the 'Program') aimed at stabilising and then reducing CO_2 emissions within the Signatory States, and implementing a regional CO_2 emissions budget and allowance trading program that will regulate CO_2 emissions from fossil fuel-fired electricity generating units having a rated capacity equal to or greater than 25 megawatts."[41]

The market-based design of the RGGI MOU is a cap-and-trade programme. "Cap-

---

35   Western Climate Initiative, *Statement of Regional Goal*, above note 36, at 2.
36   *Ibid.*
37   *Ibid.*
38   For example, Massachusetts, prior to joining any formal agreement, had enacted its own regulations to reduce CO_2 emissions from 1997 to 1999 by 10%. 310 Mass. Code Regs. § 7.29 (2007).
39   Regional Greenhouse Gas Initiative, Memorandum of Understanding (December 20 2005), available at www.rggi.org/docs/mou_final_12_20_05.pdf.
40   Massachusetts and Rhode Island were originally given the status of observing states. In January 2007, both agreed formally to join RGGI as signatory states. Maryland, a predominantly coal-powered electricity generating state in contrast to the other RGGI states, also subsequently joined RGGI in 2006. State of Mass., Press Release: Governor Patrick Signs Regional Pact to Reduce Greenhouse Gas Emissions (January 18 2007), available at www.mass.gov/ ?pageID=pressreleases&agId=Agov3&prModName=gov3pressrelease&prFile=reduce_greenhouse_gases01 1807.xml; State of R.I., Press Release: Lt. Gov. Roberts Calls for Rhode Island to Join Regional Greenhouse Gas Initiative (January 23 2007), available at www.ri.gov/press/view.php?id=3423; State of Md., Press Release: Governor O'Malley Takes Steps to Fight Global Warming, Climate Change in Maryland (April 20 2007), available at www.gov.state.md.us/pressreleases/070420.html.
41   RGGI MOU, above note 42, at 2.

and-trade systems operate by capping the amount of CO_2 emissions allowed, distributing CO_2 emissions allowances to sources up to the cap, and requiring each covered source to have sufficient allowances to cover its CO_2 emissions at the end of each compliance period."[42] This is a supply-side initiative: "CO_2 emission allowances will be allocated to, and traded among, fossil-fuel-fired electricity generators within the region that supply electricity to the grid."[43]

The RGGI Staff Working Group (SWG) finalised the Draft Model Rule (Model Rule) in January of 2007. The Model Rule is a product of over two years of work by the SWG and it is the foundation upon which the RGGI states will base their individual model rules. The Model Rule will be used by each state as a starting point for obtaining regulatory or legislative approval of its cap-and-trade programme.

The RGGI MOU sets the start date for the programme as 2009. At that time, CO_2 emissions from power plants in the region will be capped at current levels[44] and the cap will remain in place until 2015. RGGI states would then begin the process of incrementally reducing emissions, with the goal of achieving a 10% reduction by 2019.[45] By 2020, the programme is expected to reach an emissions reduction of approximately 35%.[46]

One significant aspect of the Model Rule is its requirement that each state reserve a minimum of 25% of that state's allowances for "consumer benefit or strategic energy purpose[s]".[47] Depending on the market for allowances, this could leave states with millions of dollars in an open-ended fund. Consumer benefits could range from using the money to supplement consumer electricity bills or funding state-run energy efficiency programmes, to putting the money back into the state coffers.

In reaction to the "consumer benefit or strategic energy purpose" requirement, power producers lobbied states to auction only the minimum of 25% and to allocate the remaining shares to power producers based on their historical or future energy production levels without charging for these allocations.[48] It is unprecedented in US environmental regulation that the allocations for emissions are auctioned to pre-existing already-built and operating emission sources.[49] Forcing power producers to

---

42   Edna Sussman, "New York Addresses Climate Change with First Mandatory US Greenhouse Gas Program", N.Y. St. B. J. 43, 44 (May 2006).

43   Heddy Bolster, "The Commerce Clause Meets Environmental Protection: The Compensatory Tax Doctrine as a Defense of Potential Regional Carbon Dioxide Regulation", 47 B.C. L. Rev. 737, 744 (2006) (citing to RGGI MOU, above note 42).

44   The regional base annual CO_2 emissions cap will be equal to 121 million short tonnes. RGGI MOU, above note 42, at 2.

45   Regional Greenhouse Gas Initiative, Press Release: States Reach Agreement on Proposed Rules for the Nation's First Cap-and-Trade Program to Address Climate Change 2 (August 15 2006), available at www.rggi.org/docs/model_rule_release_8_15_06.pdf.

46   *Ibid.*

47   Regional Greenhouse Gas Initiative, Model Rule §§5.3(a) to (b) (January 5 2007) [hereinafter RGGI Model Rule], available at *www.rggi.org/docs/model_rule_corrected_1_5_07.pdf.*

48   One power producer, National Grid, has advocated auctioning 100% of the allowances and then having the state use the money to supplement consumer rates. These generators propose that the costs spent on allowances by the utilities will be passed along to the consumer, resulting in higher retail prices for consumers.

49   Roman Kramarchuk, "All Out Auctions?", *Environmental Finance* 45, 45 (March 2007) (noting that EPA auctions only 1% of total SO_2 allowances and this does not include any auction to pre-existing sources, which are freely allocated to electric power generators), available at www.environmentalmarkets.org/galleries/default-file/Kramarchuk%20ef3marketview_p45.pdf.

pay for all of their allowances could also create a competitive disadvantage for in-state producers if neighbouring states' generators are given allowances without charge. Power producers also expressed their concerns about how this new expense will affect long-term power contracts that they have signed. The cost of CO_2 allowances was not factored into any of these existing contracts and generators producing under these long-term deals fear that they will not be able to adjust the contract price to account for them. Whether the contract allows pass-through price adjustments may depend on the individual contract.

Several RGGI states, including Maine,[50] Massachusetts,[51] Vermont,[52] and New York,[53] have adopted uniform rules to implement the RGGI programme, while other RGGI states remain in the drafting and comment period. Many RGGI states have announced that 100% of their allowances will be auctioned, including New York, Massachusetts, Maine and Vermont. This contrasts with the requirement in the MOU that at least 25% of the allowances be auctioned to generate revenue for "consumer benefit or strategic purpose[s]". These states have realised that instead of allowing the value of "freely" allocated allowances to affect the price at which electricity is sold – thereby giving power producers the windfall – the state could capture the windfall by auctioning off all of the allowances, simultaneously requiring that the proceeds be directed toward public benefits.[54,55] Under this scenario, in theory, existing electric power plants emitting carbon during their operations may not be successful bidders for these allowances and therefore could be short of the necessary allowances to continue operations.

---

50   Me. Rev. Stat. Ann. tit. 38, § 580 et seq. (2007). Maine's Regional Greenhouse Gas Initiative Act of 2007 (LD 1851) was passed by the Maine Legislature and enacted June 18 2007, available at www.janus.state.me.us/legis/LawMakerWeb/summary.asp?ID=280024997.

51   310 Mass. Code Regs. § 7.00 Appendix B and § 7.29 (2007).

52   Vt. Stat. Ann. 30 § 255 (2007). Vermont receives the majority of its power from Vermont Yankee nuclear power plant and Hydro-Québec, two power producers with very low carbon output. Since Vermont will still have a significant amount of allowances allotted to it, the state could end up selling the allowances to out-of-state power producers.

53   New York Draft Model Rule Part 242, available at www.dec.ny.gov/regulations/36588.html.

54   New York Draft Model Rule Part 242. § 242-5.3(a). The proceeds from this auction will then be used for "energy efficiency and clean energy technology purposes… the promotion of energy efficiency measures, promotion of renewable or non-carbon-emitting energy technologies, and stimulation or reward of investment in the development of innovative carbon emissions abatement technologies with significant carbon reduction potential". This account will be managed by either the New York Department of Environmental Conservation (DEC) or an agent assigned by the DEC. The draft rule specifies that the 100% allowance auction is to be used for "energy efficiency and clean energy technology purposes", defined to mean the "promotion of energy efficiency measures, promotion of renewable or non-carbon-emitting energy technologies, and stimulation or reward of investment in the development of innovative carbon emissions abatement technologies with significant carbon reduction potential".

55   Vt. Stat. Ann 30 § 255(c)(2) (2007). The Vermont rule indicates that 100% of the CO_2 allowances in the state will be auctioned and the proceeds from the sale will be allocated to one or more trustees acting on behalf of consumers. The account will be managed by trustees, appointed by the Public Service Board, to provide the maximum long-term benefit to Vermont electric consumers. Auction goals and procedures are also loosely outlined in New York's draft rule. See New York Draft Rule § 242-5.3(a)(3), available at www.dec.ny.gov/regulations/36588.html. The DEC envisions an "open and transparent allowance auction", which will be held once each year. Other stated objectives of the DEC include creating a liquid allowance market by minimising entry and exit barriers, allowing any financially qualified individuals or entities to bid on allowances, and designing the system so as to not act as a barrier to investment in new generating facilities. See also Me. Rev. Stat. Ann. tit. 38, § 580-B(7) (2007). Maine requires the Department of Environmental Protection to allocate 100% of the annual CO_2 emissions allowances for public benefit to produce funds for carbon reduction and energy conservation.

In general, however, electricity generators have a variety of options to comply with RGGI, including reducing emissions through efficiency measures, instituting newer technologies, and changing fuel sources. Generators that implement such measures can then sell their excess allowances or purchase additional allowances from other qualifying power producers.

Because the price of implementing these measures is often high, RGGI has also created an offsets programme to offer power producers flexibility in meeting the cap limitations. "Offsets" under RGGI are emissions reductions that come from sources other than fossil-fuel-fired electricity generators that are subject to the emissions cap under RGGI. The offsets programme awards offset allowances for approved offset projects that were realised on or after the date of the MOU.[56] Power producers can use offset allowances to comply with the cap requirements.

The initial offset projects that can be approved under the offsets programme include: (i) landfill methane capture and combustion; (ii) sulphur hexafluoride (SH_6) capture and recycling; (iii) afforestation (transition of land from a non-forested to forested state); (iv) end-use efficiency for natural gas, propane and heating oil; (v) methane capture from farming operations; and (vi) projects to reduce fugitive methane emissions from natural-gas transmission and distribution.[57] As expressed in the RGGI MOU, RGGI states have agreed to continue to cooperate on the development of additional offsets projects.

Importantly, offsets cannot be created by the installation of renewable resources. At first blush, this would seem to be counterintuitive and at cross-purposes with other policies. Twenty-eight states award renewable energy credits for the installation of eligible[58] renewable energy electric generation facilities.[59] In addition, 16 states also authorise a tax on retail utility bills that creates a renewable energy trust fund used to make grants, loans or otherwise provide incentives to renewable energy projects.[60] Furthermore, 80% of the states allow eligibly defined smaller renewable energy projects to enjoy the net metering of their electricity when sold back to the host electricity supplier, thus effectively allowing these entities to sell wholesale power at retail rates.[61]

However, no credit is allowed for any project that has an electric generation component unless the project sponsor transfers legal rights to the credits to the regulatory agency.[62] The RGGI scheme does not contemplate that renewable energy projects may create offsets for programme compliance. Despite controversy over this

---

56   RGGI MOU, above note 42, at 4.
57   *Ibid.*
58   There is significant variation in what is an eligible renewable energy technology in each of the states. While certain wind and solar technologies seem to qualify everywhere, the eligibility of various biomass, landfill gas, hydroelectric and other facilities varies significantly. See Steven Ferrey, Sustainable Energy, Environmental Policy, and States' Rights: Discerning the Energy Future Through the Eye of the Dormant Commerce Clause, 12 *N.Y.U. Envtl. L.J.* 507, 646 tbl. 3 (2004).
59   For a detailed discussion of these programmes, see *ibid* at 529. See also Steven Ferrey, "Renewable Orphans: Adopting Legal Renewable Standards at the State Level", 19 *Electricity Journal* 52 (March 2006).
60   See Ferrey, "Sustainable Energy, Environmental Policy, and States' Rights: Discerning the Energy Future Through the Eye of the Dormant Commerce Clause", above note 61, at 523.
61   For a discussion of net metering and its legal and policy implications, see Steven Ferrey, "Nothing But Net", 14 *Duke Envtl. L. & Pol'y. F.* 1 (2003); see also Steven Ferrey, "Net Zero: Distributed Generation and FERC's MidAmerican Decision", 17 *Electricity Journal 33* (October 2004).
62   RGGI Model Rule, above note 50, § 10.3(d)(2).

point, it was believed by the RGGI states that renewable energy projects do not themselves diminish CO_2 emissions. Renewable projects do not generate CO_2 emissions, but whether they displace other CO_2-emitting power generation sources, indirectly through substitution, remains in dispute. This debate turns on issues of reliability and the location of the renewable resource.

As a whole, renewable resources are not eligible for offset allowances. Moreover, the Model Rule disallows offset allowances for any offset project that receives funding or other incentives from renewable energy trust funds,[63] or any credits or allowances that would be earned from any other mandatory or voluntary GHG programmes.[64] These measures are quite restrictive considering that renewable energy credits in many states are expected to trade at higher rates than RGGI offsets or credits. Therefore, the RGGI scheme stands conspicuously apart from other carbon schemes and even from the renewable energy incentive programmes that the RGGI states may have otherwise adopted and implemented.

Most offsets eligible under the Model Rule are created by dealing with agricultural resources, such as afforestation and methane capture. Afforestation projects, unless insurance against biomass loss is purchased for the forest, receive credits equal only to 90% of their absorption of CO_2 to account for possible loss of forest mass over time due to fire, pest or other causes.[65] In addition, to ensure permanent forest use, a restrictive conservation easement is required for forest projects that create credits.[66] For some RGGI states, the in-state agriculture opportunities are minimal.

In addition, the Model Rule implies, albeit with some ambiguity, that energy conservation projects can qualify to generate offsets. The avoidance of burning fossil fuels due to end-use efficiency on the consumers' side of the meter appears to be an eligible offset project. Nonetheless, the question of whether the reduction of CO_2 emissions directly relates to "combustion" remains unanswered.

For example, fossil-fuel-burning efficiency improvements to the combustion device itself – the furnace or boiler – may qualify as an offset project. Going one step further, it is less transparent whether the installation of building thermal efficiency measures – which saves CO_2 emissions by making the building retain heat more efficiently, and thus requires less operation of existing fossil-fuel-burning equipment even if the equipment itself is not made more efficient – could qualify as an offset project. Moreover, it is unclear whether one could go even a step further to make electricity-using appliances on the customer side of the meter more efficient, and, where there is fossil-fuel-fired generation in the regional electricity mix, claim a proportionate reduction in the dispatch and operation of such equipment and resultant diminution of CO_2 emissions, from such reduced fuel burning.

No credits can be awarded for projects that are required by any local, state or federal law, regulation, or administrative or judicial order.[67] Thus, retrofits, efficiency

---

63   *Ibid.* § 10.3(d)(3).
64   *Ibid.* § 10.3(d)(4).
65   *Ibid.* § 10.5(c)(4)(iii).
66   *Ibid.* § 10.5(c)(6)(i).
67   *Ibid.* § 10.3(d)(1).

improvements, or emission reductions required by regulation or embodied in permits or consent decrees will not create saleable offset credits. Therefore, voluntary reductions of CO_2 emissions at an existing large power plant will not create a saleable offset unless the unit proactively gets out in front of the curve of progressively tightening regulatory mandates to achieve, verify, register, and receive a saleable offset credit prior to such reduction being included in its emission permit limits. Once created, this credit should be valid until the renewal period discussed below.

To ensure that the majority of the emissions reductions occur within the power production sector, the MOU places limits on the use of offsets and the issuance of additional offsets to moderate offset price impacts.[68] In particular, RGGI initially allows offset projects anywhere in the United States if the average price of an emission allowance remains below $7 per tonne.[69] In each compliance period, each generator will be allowed to cover up to 3.3% of its emissions using offset allowances, which is roughly equal to half of that generator's emissions reduction obligation.[70] Therefore, some of the reduction would have to come from actual reductions at the facility. If allowance prices rise above $10 per tonne, RGGI will allow sources to cover up to 10% of their emissions with offsets, and will allow offset projects outside the United States as well as allowances from the EU Emissions Trading Scheme (EU ETS) and the Kyoto Protocol's Clean Development Mechanism (CDM). This would allow the full reduction to come from purchasing offsets on the market, rather than making actual reductions at the generation facility. If allowance prices rise above $10 per tonne, then the compliance period will be extended by one year, for a maximum compliance period of four years.[71] This mechanism will give sources more time to reduce their emissions and may enable allowance prices to fall.

The purpose of these "circuit breaker" provisions is effectively to suspend the rules of the programme during those periods when the market-based cap-and-trade system results in trading allowances at politically controversial prices. In other words, when the market works to reflect short supply of allowances, the definition of what can be counted and traded, both in geographic and percentage dimensions, is liberalised to allow regulated entities greater flexibility to document compliance. The decision to include EU ETS and Kyoto CDM project credits as eligible currency is curious. Since EU ETS credits are given away without charge by EU countries to their industries as part of the political process, this effectively works as an income and welfare shift from US power generation owners to EU industries. Moreover, since there has been a problem with overestimation of Kyoto CDM offsets,[72] this purchase is not without some interesting implications.

Offsets credits that are created have a lifetime of 10 years, with the possibility of renewal; afforestation projects create credits with a 20-year lifetime, with a possible

---

68   Regional Greenhouse Gas Initiative, *Memorandum of Understanding in Brief* (December 12 2005), available at www.rggi.org/docs/mou_brief_12_20_05.pdf.
69   *Ibid.*
70   RGGI MOU, above note 42, at 5.
71   Pew Center on Global Climate Change, *Q&A: Regional Greenhouse Gas Initiative* (2007), available at www.pewclimate.org/what_s_being_done/in_the_states/rggi/rggi.cfm.
72   Purdy, above note 14, at 23 to 24.

renewal up to 60 years.[73] All emissions from those covered units – electric generators of 25 megawatts (MW) and larger – must be verified by independent entities accredited by the state.[74] Since each state will administer its own carbon allocation, allowances and offset accounting, failure to comply with state requirements could result in the regulated entity's credits being restrained or confiscated. The Model Rule indicates that when a regulated entity's emissions exceed its CO_2 allowance budget, the state can deduct from the entity's compliance account future allowances (beyond the current control period) equal to three times the number of the entity's excess emissions. If the regulated entity has insufficient CO_2 allowances to cover three times that amount, it must immediately thereafter transfer sufficient allowances into its compliance account. This treble penalties scheme (3:1 loss of allowances) raises interesting challenges when there is a transfer in ownership during or shortly after the non-compliance period. Would a failure to transfer the necessary allowances obligate a new owner who is not responsible for the prior non-complying period of operation?[75]

4. California's Carbon Regulation

California has taken the most aggressive approach of all the states to curb emissions. Its landmark legislation establishes a comprehensive programme of regulatory and market mechanisms with the goal of achieving cost-effective and quantifiable GHG emissions reductions. Pursuant to the California Global Warming Solutions Act of 2006 (commonly referred to as Assembly Bill 32 or AB 32), the state is required to reduce its aggregate GHG emissions to 1990 levels by 2020.[76] This equates to an eventual estimated 25% reduction from business-as-usual levels.[77] AB 32 charges the California Air Resources Board (CARB) with the responsibility for developing and implementing a plan to meet this challenging emissions-reduction goal. In carrying out the regulatory development and enforcement of the state-wide emissions limit and mandatory reporting, CARB works with Governor Schwarzenegger's Climate Action Team, chaired by the Secretary of the California Environmental Protection Agency and composed of representatives from numerous state agencies, which performs state-wide climate change planning.

In addition to charging CARB with the responsibility for establishing by January 1 2008 a state-wide GHG emissions cap for implementation in 2020, based on 1990 emissions levels, AB 32 further requires CARB to:

- adopt by January 1 2008 regulations that require mandatory reporting and verification for significant GHG sources and to monitor compliance;
- adopt a plan by January 1 2009 for achieving emissions reductions from significant GHG sources via regulations, market mechanisms and other actions;

---

73   RGGI Model Rule, above note 50, § 10.3(e)(2).
74   *Ibid* § 10.6. There are provisions to attempt to avoid conflict of interest situations between verifiers and owners of projects that might employ their services.
75   RGGI Model Rule, above note 50, § 6.5(d)(1).
76   The California Assembly passed Assembly Bill 32, signed into law by Governor Schwarzenegger on September 27 2006.
77   Michael J. Bradley & Associates briefing, *Climate Change Briefing: California Global Warming Solutions Act of 2006 Summary* (Brian Jones, ed, August 2006).

- adopt rules and regulations by January 1 2011 to achieve the maximum technologically feasible and cost-effective GHG reductions, including provisions for using both market mechanisms and alternative compliance mechanisms;
- evaluate several factors – prior to imposing mandates or implementing market mechanisms – including but not limited to: impacts on California's economy, the environment, and public health; equity between regulated entities; electricity reliability; conformance with other environmental laws; and whether the rules will disproportionately impact low-income communities;
- adopt a list of discrete, early action measures by July 1 2007 that can be implemented before January 1 2010.[78]

AB 32 specifically recognises that a market-based system can be used in conjunction with regulatory and other strategies to meet California's economy-wide goal of reducing emissions. To assist CARB in fulfilling its charge, the Governor created the Market Advisory Committee (MAC) to advise CARB on the development of a state-wide plan to reduce GHG emissions. MAC is composed of national and international experts in environmental policy, regulatory affairs, economics, and energy technologies.[79] MAC's primary objective was to design a mandatory cap-and-trade programme to achieve cost-effective emissions cuts across all sectors.[80] MAC employed a systems approach and examined how a cap-and-trade programme might interact with other measures such as regulations, performance-based standards, price subsidies, and tax credits.[81] In its Final Report, "Recommendations for Designing a Greenhouse Gas Cap-and-Trade System for California", issued on June 30 2007, MAC concluded that a cap-and-trade programme is fully compatible with other regulatory programmes being introduced in the state and that such a market-based system could contribute significantly to meeting the emissions target in AB 32.[82]

MAC's Final Report includes several important recommendations. First, the California cap-and-trade programme should eventually incorporate all major GHG-emitting sectors in the state. The greatest attention should be given to the electricity, industry, buildings, and transportation sectors as the main contributors of emissions.[83] The programme's scope, however, should be expanded over time so that it covers as many sectors, sources and gases as possible to enable the state to meet its overall emissions-reduction goal. To that end, MAC recommends that CARB adopt mandatory reporting requirements for all sources likely to be subject to a GHG emissions cap.[84]

---

78 Cal. Air Res. Bd., *AB 32 Fact Sheet – California Global Warming Solutions Act of 2006* (September 25 2006), available at www.arb.ca.gov/cc/factsheets/ab32factsheet.pdf.
79 Cal. Envtl. Prot. Agency, Press Release: Expert Advisors Release Final Cap-and-Trade Report: Recommendations Intended to Complement California's Ongoing Efforts to Reduce Emissions (June 29 2007).
80 Market Advisory Committee to the Cal. Air Res. Bd., *Recommendations for Designing a Greenhouse Gas Cap-and-Trade System for California* iii (June 30 2007) available at www.climatechange.ca.gov/policies/market_advisory.html.
81 *Ibid.*
82 *Ibid.*
83 *Ibid* at iv.
84 *Ibid* at 79.

Second, the cap-and-trade programme should use a combined approach with regard to the distribution of allowances. MAC recommends the initial scheme of freely allocating some share of allowances and auctioning the other share of allowances. The percentage of allowances auctioned off should increase over time.[85] MAC encourages the state to retain the flexibility freely to allocate some of the allowances in a manner that stabilises the price impacts and manages competitiveness among power California producers.[86] Free allocation of allowances should be determined by environmental performance standards and the auction should be designed to promote voluntary early reductions.[87]

Third, the cap-and-trade programme should recognise offsets generated by sources within and outside of California's borders. The inclusion of emission reductions by sources not typically covered in the traditional programme can be used to reduce costs and help meet the 2020 emissions reduction target. MAC recommends the use of stringent criteria to ensure the quality of the approved offsets projects.

Fourth, California's cap-and-trade programme should be linked to similar policy initiatives in other jurisdictions to promote a "global greenhouse gas market".[88] MAC recommends creating linkages to other mandatory GHG emissions reduction programmes, especially those with strong compliance requirements and enforcement strategies to ensure long-lasting positive climate change impacts.

Fifth, because the quantity of California's imported electricity generated from coal is significant, California's cap-and-trade programme should take a "first-seller approach" to capping emissions associated with electricity. Under this approach, the entity that first sells electricity within the state must meet the compliance obligation established under the cap-and-trade scheme.[89] For power generated in California, the owner or operator of the in-state power plant is considered the first seller and would be required to meet the emissions cap. For imported power, the first seller is typically an investor-owned or municipal utility or wholesale power marketer that sells electricity to a load-serving entity or large end-user. The out-of-state entity under this approach would also be required to meet the emissions cap.[90]

This MAC recommendation represents a significant departure from the original scheme. Originally, California intended to regulate GHGs from the utility sector by regulating all load-serving entities (LSEs), or retailers of power. Legally, all of these LSEs are located in-state or at least doing business in-state, and regulation is imposed at the retail level. It is clear that state regulatory agencies have jurisdictional authority over retail power markets within their state.

If this MAC recommendation is implemented, however, it will shift the control upstream to regulate power wholesalers at the first seller transaction. With the restructuring of California's electric market in 1998 and the subsequent restructuring

---

85   California Environmental Protection Agency, Press Release: Expert Advisors Release Final Cap-and-Trade Report: Recommendations Intended to Complement California's Ongoing Efforts to Reduce Emissions 2 (June 29 2007).
86   Ibid.
87   Ibid.
88   Ibid.
89   Ibid at iv.
90   Ibid.

in 2001 due to an electric energy crisis, most of the power retailed in the state first goes through a wholesale power marketer. Thus, many of these first sellers are now outside the state, and regulating first sellers causes the state to regulate the wholesale transaction. Wholesale power transactions are the exclusive province of federal regulators under the Federal Power Act in the United States.[91]

Therefore, this decision on point-of-regulation is more than just a cosmetic or policy choice. It has significant legal ramifications. While MAC's recommendation would make the point-of-regulation parallel to that of RGGI, it raises legal issues, especially for a state such as California that imports wholesale power from many other states.

The California scheme covers all load-serving entities, including municipal LSEs.[92] Electric generators are required to meet a CO_2 emissions level no greater than that achievable by a combined-cycle gas-fired generator.[93] Any new contracts for a term of five years or more for the procurement of baseload generation must comply with a performance standard of emitting no more than 1,100 lbs CO_2/MWh of power generation.[94] "Baseload" generation is defined as generation that is designed and intended to operate an at annualised capacity factor of 60% or greater.[95]

Roughly half of California's electric sector GHG emissions result from electric power imports from out-of-state, which stem predominately from coal-fired power plants.[96] The impact of California's new emissions limitations will thus significantly restrict the attractiveness of coal-fired generation for California. While California has little in-state coal generation, various California LSEs, particularly the Los Angeles Department of Water and Power, import significant coal-fired power from various other states.[97] This legislation will have a significant impact on such LSEs.

---

91   16 U.S.C. § 824(a) (2000).

92   California is home to the largest municipal utility in the nation, the Los Angeles Department of Water and Power (LADWP), serving a multimillion-person consumer base. LADWP is among the most dependent California LSEs on both power imports from out of state, and coal-fired high-GHG power. See Seth Hilton, "The Impact of California's Global Warming Legislation on the Electric Utility Industry", 19 *Electricity Journal* 10, 13 (November 2006).

93   See Cal. Pub. Util. Code §§ 8340-8341 (2007). This legislation targets only electric generation. §§ 8340 to 8341 govern all new long-term energy commitments and establish a "greenhouse gas emissions performance standard". This is specific to the electric power role in meeting AB 32 goals. The GHG emissions standard creates a specific level of permissible emissions and prohibits new construction, new long-term power contracts, and any major plant investment that will not meet the performance standard. This prohibits load-serving entities from entering long-term power contracts with out-of-state producers which do not meet California's stringent new emissions standard. California's Public Utilities Commission (PUC) has set the GHG emissions performance standard at the equivalent of the emissions from a combined-cycle natural gas plant.

94   *Ibid.* This is a level that conventional coal-fired electric generation will not be able to meet, generating about 1,770 lbs. CO_2/MWh. See Hilton, "The Impact of California's Global Warming Legislation on the Electric Utility Industry", above note 95, at 14.

95   Cal. Pub. Util. Code § 8340(a) (2007).

96   Order Instituting Rulemaking to Implement the Commission's Procurement Incentive Framework and to Examine the Integration of Greenhouse Gas Emissions Standards into Procurement Policies, No. 06-04-009, D.07-09-017, 2007 WL 2579525, at *3 (Cal. Pub. Util. Comm'n. September 6 2007). Three-quarters of California's power imports come from the Southwest, and involves much coal-fired power, as opposed to the other quarter that is imported through the Northwest. Al Alvarado and Karen Griffin, Cal. Energy Comm'n., Revised Methodology to Estimate the Generation Resource Mix of California Electricity Imports: Update to the May 2006 Staff Paper 1 (April 12 2007).

97   See Hilton, "The Impact of California's Global Warming Legislation on the Electric Utility Industry", above note 95, at 13. The three major investor-owned utilities import 3% to 15% of their total supply in the form of out-of-state coal-fired power. The Los Angeles DPW imports half of its power from these sources. *Ibid.*

Pursuant to AB 32, utilities are required to "account for greenhouse gas emissions from all electricity consumed in the state, including transmission and distribution line losses from electricity generated within the state or imported from outside the state".[98] The California scheme thus impacts all in-state and out-of-state generation used to serve California's electric load.[99] It does not distinguish the geographic source of power generation, and covers the liberal flow of power into California from other states.

5.   California and RGGI compared

California's carbon regulation system is different from RGGI in that the carbon compliance obligation of the former under its original design is placed on load-serving entities, rather than generators of power.[100] As noted above, California adopted recommendations from MAC to shift its point of regulation to load-serving entities in the retail power market, rather than first sellers in the wholesale power market. This is a distinction of whether regulation covers the generator of the power or the distributor of the power. RGGI regulates the first sellers of power, while California at least initially, but not subsequently, under MAC recommendations decided to regulate load-serving entities that retail power, but is now reconsidering. As it stands, California is regulating at the retail level and RGGI is regulating at the wholesale level.

Load-serving entities are distributors of retail power, such as utilities or retail suppliers. LSEs have an entire portfolio of power generation resources that they can optimise for purposes of compliance. If LSEs are the point of regulation, they are only required over their entire power generation inventory to meet the carbon emission standards. They can average high-carbon sources with lower-carbon sources. They can continue to purchase carbon-rich generation, and compensate by adding renewable energy resources or other low-carbon generation, to achieve the requirements averaged over their entire retail portfolio of power generation resources.

By contrast, the RGGI scheme requires each generator to comply individually at the point of generation or first sale, penalises high-carbon generating resources, and does not allow any optimisation among portfolios of generation. In RGGI, each individual generator is responsible for compliance. For RGGI compliance, renewable energy projects do not qualify.

---

98   "This requirement applies to all retail sellers of electricity, including load-serving entities as defined in subdivision (j) of Section 380 of the Public Utilities Code and local publicly owned electric utilities as defined in Section 9604 of the Public Utilities Code." Cal. Health & Safety Code § 38530(b)(2) (2007).

99   The bill sets a firm limit on GHG emissions in California by requiring the Air Resources Board to determine California's GHG emission level in 1990 and then issue regulations causing GHG emissions to be reduced to that level by 2020. AB 32 also requires comprehensive GHG reporting by major sources of GHG emissions. Market-based compliance mechanisms are also discussed in the legislation, but left to the discretion of the Air Resources Board. While this regulates all significant sources of GHGs, because electric power production accounts for about 20% of GHG emissions in California, electric generation has become the primary target for regulation. This scheme can be contrasted with RGGI, which only regulates CO_2 emissions within the electric power sector, and then only focuses on part of that sector.

100   The RGGI system governs only the original power producers, whereas the California bill governs any load-serving entity, defined as "every electrical corporation, electric service provider or community choice aggregator serving end-use customers in the state".

RGGI only regulates CO_2 and only regulates the electric power sector, and then only part of that sector. California regulates all greenhouse gases. RGGI allows steep penalties for those with insufficient allowances, but does not criminalise these failures as does California. Finally, California's programme does not go into effect until 2012, whereas RGGI has a programme start date of 2009.

6.   Final thoughts

Anthropogenic carbon emissions are connected to the decision of humankind to exploit power resources. About one-third of such emissions in the United States and other industrialised countries emanate from the production and use of electric power. There is a direct link between greenhouse gas emissions and electric power production levels and technologies.

Although not an early leader, the United States will eventually regulate carbon. In the interim, certain states have taken the early lead in implementing carbon regulatory programmes. While there are modest voluntary reduction and trading programmes administered through the Chicago Climate Exchange and the Western Climate Initiative, the 10 Eastern states in RGGI and California are the leaders in the United States on regional carbon regulation.

Some of these US initiatives regulate all carbon-containing gases, while others focus on CO_2. Some regulate all emissions sources, while others target only power plants, and only larger power plants. This creates a disconnect in terms of regulatory reach and coverage, implementation dates, programme goals and requirements, points of regulation, which GHGs are covered, compliance deadlines, means of allowance distribution, and how offsets can be created and traded.

This results in an extremely complex *mélange* of programmes and legal requirements. As with any regulatory programme, there will be relative benefit to those who are able to understand the legal nuances of programme requirements, identify where strategic opportunities lie, and get out in front of the regulatory curve. In the largest economy in the world, with almost one-quarter of all global power generation resources, this is a big wave which will leave winners and losers in its legal curl.

Climate change litigation

Jose A Cofre
Nicholas Rock
Paul Q Watchman
Dewey & LeBoeuf

1.   Introduction

Certain societies and jurisdictions are regarded as being more litigious than others. Whilst differences in "litigation culture" contribute to this to some degree, essentially it is recognised that certain legal systems and their respective judicial infrastructure lend themselves to class actions and organised civil suits, whereas other jurisdictions (with national legal systems) are less geared towards the use of litigation for seeking the same kinds of redress. Addressing climate change impacts is in some countries led by individuals, public interest groups and others by lobbying to influence policy and legislative change in order to achieve reform. In other countries, litigation is more commonly used as a tool for reform to influence climate change policy. In these countries, the objectives of climate change litigation from the point of view of the plaintiff environmentalist probably have less to do with actually asking the courts to formulate climate change policy of itself, and more to do with seeking to attract public attention through the commencement of court proceedings, in order to increase pressure on governments to respond and implement suitable policies and legislation addressing global warming.

A lawyer advising on issues surrounding emerging climate change litigation requires an understanding and awareness of the sources of potential claims, the varied legal bases on which they may be made and the risk-management measures that may need to be implemented in order to mitigate the risk of exposure to potentially large-scale and costly claims which might also have adverse reputational consequences on public and private sector parties alike. The object of this chapter is not to provide detailed summaries of the latest judgments in the United States and elsewhere which deal with climate change issues. Instead, examples of the key cases to date will be used where appropriate, in order to illustrate the primary sources of climate change litigation (see section 3). Whilst we have, where possible, cited examples of climate change litigation from around the world, the substantive legal analysis in this chapter focuses on common-law legal systems (although civil law conclusions may be drawn generally).

2.   What is climate change litigation?

The US government's decision not to ratify the Kyoto Protocol to the United Nations Framework Convention on Climate Change (the "Kyoto Protocol") and the perceived reluctance of the US Congress to act on climate change has sparked frustration within civil society[1] and this has led to the first major wave of climate change litigation.[2] However, climate change litigation is a global matter, with claims also being brought in differing forms in Europe, Africa and Australasia largely in response to a perception that governments are not doing enough to deal with climate change. Accordingly, while this state of affairs exists, the potential for many more claims worldwide arising out of damage to properties and communities as a result of floods, severe and catastrophic weather events, and climate change generally is significant.

Although debate still exists, the science of climate change is becoming increasingly robust, and civil society increasingly believes that human activities and the emission of certain gases into the atmosphere can lead to serious consequences for the environment, property and human health.[3] This belief leaves governments or corporations (particularly those considered to contribute to climate change with operations in multiple jurisdictions), prone to litigious action which, once commenced, raises a multitude of legal challenges of which both plaintiffs and defendants alike must be aware. These challenges include the scope and breadth of the potential causes of action that can be alleged, the issue of legal standing in courts and tribunals, justiciability and judicial competence, expert evidence, the challenge of the science of causation and the question of appropriate remedies.

There is no one convenient definition that encapsulates the meaning of the term "climate change litigation". However, broadly speaking, on the basis of the emerging global warming liability claims worldwide impacting on the public and private sectors, climate change litigation can be described as litigation which arises from:

- a cause of action where climate change is the alleged causal factor in the context of a civil wrong, tort or delict such as negligence or nuisance, which has led to an alleged liability (liability litigation);
- an administrative law claim against a public authority challenging any action, inaction, breach of statutory duty or constitutional law or other failure properly or fairly to regulate or take into consideration greenhouse gas (GHG) emissions in the authority's decision-making processes (administrative law litigation); and
- other ancillary legal causes of action arising out of growing public awareness of climate change matters. These can include alleged breaches of advertising regulations and standards in the course of making claims in respect of climate change, or alleged failure by companies, their directors or officers to adequately report climate change and other environmental impacts affecting company performance which can lead to shareholder derivative actions, or other regulatory action (consequential litigation).

The three broad categories of climate change litigation identified above (liability,

1   Richard Dahl, "A Changing Climate of Litigation", *Environmental Health Perspectives* 115(4) April 2007 at A205.
2   TO Maiden and EM McLaughlin, "Climate Change Litigation: Trends and Developments" *Daily Environment Report*, Vol 10 No 63, April 3 2007 at 2.
3   For example, it is now commonly believed that gases such as carbon dioxide, methane, nitrous oxide and halogenated compounds produced through human activities are contributing to global warming and an "enhanced" greenhouse effect.

administrative law and consequential) have been defined for convenience and for the illustrative purposes of this chapter only. It should be understood that, given the inherent uncertainties and complexities in litigation, there can be overlap between these categories and thus hybrid types of climate change litigation can develop.[4]

The objectives of climate change litigation tend to be either (i) to seek compensation for harm to the environment, property or human health caused by global warming (in the case of liability litigation arising from an allegation that climate change is the cause of the damage complained of); or (ii) in the case of all three forms of litigation identified above, to prevent or reduce global warming (eg by challenging government acts or omissions relating to climate change), by way of judicial review or by petitioning for the disclosure of corporate behaviour which can have an impact on climate change.

3.   Sources of climate change litigation

In this section we explore some of the key case law to date which informs the rest of the chapter in relation to the specific common legal themes that arise in climate change litigation and disputes. The different sources of litigation are considered having regard to the three broad categories of climate change litigation identified in section 2 above, and the specific legal issues arising out of the case law to date are further considered in sections 4 and 5.

3.1   Liability litigation

Liability litigation comprises any proceeding, action, claim or dispute in public, private or international law, in which it is alleged that climate change is the causal connection to the alleged damage or loss for which compensation is sought. Whilst it is possible in principle for individuals to sue corporate defendants in tort for damage resulting out of GHG emissions,[5] out of the three broad categories of climate change litigation, liability litigation is probably the most difficult for plaintiffs to succeed – for example, because of the complex issues of standing, justiciability, forum and causation which commonly arise. These key legal issues are considered in more detail in sections 4 and 5 below.

Importantly, the primary "testing ground" for liability litigation to date has to a large extent been in US courts. Notwithstanding that such liability litigation is possible and indeed foreseeable in the United Kingdom and other European jurisdictions, such claims have so far been considered to be "unlikely to succeed" under English law[6] and in Europe, partly for the reasons that unlike in the United States, there is: (i) little or no recourse to contingency fee arrangements in most of Europe (although conditional fee agreements are available in the United Kingdom); (ii) the levels of damages awarded are generally far lower than in the United States

---

4   For example, some of the legal issues which arise in liability litigation can also arise in administrative law litigation (most notably, causation).

5   David A Grossman, "Warming Up to a Not-So-Radical Idea: Tort-Based Climate Change Litigation" 28 *Columbia Journal of Environmental Law* 1 (2003).

6   David Williams, Director of Claims, Axa Insurance as cited in "UK Climate change litigation unlikely", *Post Magazine*, March 22 2007, Timothy Benn Publishing Limited.

(where levels of damages are often decided by juries); and (iii) there are general restrictions on claimants becoming joined in a multi-party litigation or class actions (such as the requirement for a group litigation order[7] in the United Kingdom), whereas in the United States claimants may "opt in" at any time.[8] Notwithstanding the above, there have been examples of liability litigation in non-US jurisdictions causing significant costs to be incurred by defendants, despite plaintiffs not yet ultimately succeeding. Specific examples of potentially relevant legal bases of liability litigation follow, with reference (where applicable) to some of the key case law to date.

(a)   The law of nuisance

Nuisance can be categorised as either public or private under common law, or otherwise statutory.

Private nuisance relates to a real and unreasonable interference with a private right to use and enjoy land. Under English law, what is "unreasonable" will be judged in relation to the average man and not according to "elegant or dainty modes and habits of living".[9] The damage which is said to have been caused, or which is predicted to be caused by climate change (such as coastal erosion, flooding and building damage, displacement of peoples, reduction in crop yields or catastrophic weather events)[10] would need to be held to be unreasonable interference. However, in addition to this, a plaintiff would need to prove that a neighbouring landowner's contribution to global warming directly caused harm or damage to his or her land, and this would seem an almost insurmountable hurdle given that climate change impacts affect the world at large and there is to date no scientific method of attributing specific regional climate change impacts to any one particular emitter.[11]

Public nuisance, on the other hand, because it relates to the unreasonable interference in the health, property or comfort of the public at large, does not require the same proof of a causal link with users of any particular parcel of land. The interference with the land must be generally "unreasonable" for an action to succeed. Private individuals can generally only commence proceedings in their own name in respect of a public nuisance if certain conditions are met. In England and Wales, this will include a requirement that the individual suffered some particular, direct or substantial damage over and above that sustained by the public at large. In all other cases, proceedings must be commenced by the relevant public representative such as an attorney-general, on behalf of the public. In addition, an action in private nuisance will require specific evidence on causation as it relates to the specific region in which the land is located. This may not necessarily be required in an action for public nuisance, given that the action relates to the public at large such that aggregate impacts to the wider region would be considered. In nuisance

---

7   See the English Civil Procedure Rules, Pt 19.10. The relevant test in England and Wales is that a group litigation order will be granted where claims give rise to "common or related issues of fact or law". This has been interpreted strictly by the judiciary with the result that such orders are rare.

8   Paul Clarke, "The end of God?", 157 New Law Journal 416 (March 23 2007).

9   Walter v Selfe (1852) 19 LTOS 308.

10   J Smith and D Shearman, "Climate Change Litigation: Analysing the law, scientific evidence & impacts on the environment, health & property" (2006) Presidian Legal Publications at 10.

11   Grossman n 6 above at 52.

generally, multiple defendants can be joined and held liable for nuisance where their collective actions caused harm or injury, even if they would not individually have caused a nuisance.[12]

Recent decisions by the Southern District of New York in *Connecticut v American Electric Power Company, Inc*[13] and the Northern District of California in *California v General Motors Corp*[14] even cast considerable doubt on the present viability of public nuisance claims alleging contributions to global warming, based on non-justiciability issues predicated on the doctrine of the separation of powers (see section 4.3 below). Notwithstanding this, nuisance remains a popular cause of action in climate change related suits. On February 26 2008 the Native Village of Kivalina (the governing body of the Inupiat village in Alaska) filed a complaint for damages in the US District Court in San Francisco against 19 large oil, gas and energy companies for damages associated with global warming allegedly caused by the defendants' actions. The claims for relief are centred on public and private nuisance, civil conspiracy and concert of action.

Lawyers acting for claimants in a nuisance action will need to consider the hurdles associated with linking specific allegations of harm and damage with the actions of the defendant(s). The question of remedies is also an important one. For example, a court will be unlikely to consider itself competent to require a GHG emitting company to reduce or abate emissions below the level permitted by licences or permits they may have[15] and indeed, the defence of "statutory authority" may be available in certain jurisdictions.

(b)   *The law of negligence (fault and the duty of care)*

Generally, at common law, in order to establish a claim in negligence, a plaintiff must prove that: (i) the defendant owed a duty of care to the plaintiff; (ii) that duty of care was breached; (iii) the defendant's breach of the duty of care caused the injury or damage suffered by the plaintiff; and (iv) the injury or damage suffered was foreseeable, and not too remote a consequence of the breach of the duty. Also, there is generally a requirement of unreasonableness in negligence claims. These necessary elements of negligence can be difficult for plaintiffs to establish. For example, most GHGs are emitted with lawful authority, either by way of licence or concession from the relevant regulator. It will usually be difficult to argue that an installation's emission of GHGs was "unreasonable" if it was lawful in this sense.

Categories of negligence can change over time in accordance with social needs and so too can the persons legally bound to exercise a duty of care.[16]

---

12   See Smith n 11 above generally and *Pride of Derby and Derbyshire Angling Association Ltd v British Celanese* [1953] Ch 149.
13   406 F.Supp.2d 265 (S.D.N.Y.2005)
14   F.Supp.2d (N.D.Cal.Sep.17, 2007).
15   Note that this position will vary depending on the jurisdiction. For example, in some civil-law countries such as Belgium, meeting the statutory conditions of a permit is considered a minimum step and mere compliance will not act as a defence to free an operator from liability. See Faure et al, "International Liability as an Instrument to Prevent and Compensate for Climate Change" [2007] *Symposium: Climate Change Risk* Vol 26A/43A:123 at 153.
16   Michael Kerr, "Tort Based Climate Change Litigation in Australia" Australian Conservation Foundation, March 2002 (www.acfonline.org.au) and see *Chandler v Crane Christmas & Co* [1951] 2KB 164 at 192.

Notwithstanding this, establishing a duty of care will be a significant hurdle for claimants in any negligence-based climate-change liability litigation. It will depend on the facts of each case whether the relationship between the claimant and defendant is one where a duty of care is owed. Generally, the question turns on whether it is considered reasonably foreseeable that a defendant's acts or omissions would be likely to cause the harm complained of by the claimant.[17] The challenges associated with proving causation present a particularly difficult burden for claimants in climate change litigation and this issue is considered in more detail in section 4.6 below.

Tort-based climate change litigation can also occur in civil jurisdictions,[18] even though the common law concept of a "duty of care" will not necessarily arise specifically in such jurisdictions. There are reports of climate-change liability litigation actions now being planned in certain European civil law jurisdictions, including one such action in France against European automobile manufacturers claiming damages for the deaths of around 15,000 people during the European heatwave of August 2003.[19]

In the EU context, it is also important to appreciate what effect emerging legislation may have on future causes of action based on future negligence or fault relating to climate change matters. For example, Directive 2004/35/CE on environmental liability (the Environmental Liability Directive or ELD)[20] applies to environmental damage caused by any occupational activities listed in Annex III,[21] including any imminent threat of such damage occurring as a result. Liability is strict unless damage to protected species and natural habitats is caused by activities which fall outside Annex III, in which case liability will arise only where an operator is at fault or negligent.[22] Notably, "environmental damage" is defined to include, among other matters, damage to protected species, natural habitats, water damage and land contamination which creates a significant risk of adverse effects to human health. This limits the potential scope of the ELD as regards climate change matters, but by no means rules it out having regard to the complex and uncertain state of the science of causation and the potential damage being attributed to global warming.

(c) *Product liability law and climate change*
Suits founded on product liability grounds are another potential source of liability

---

17   As scientific knowledge develops, the legal question of whether it was reasonably foreseeable that certain actions would cause or contribute to global warming or its knock-on effects may gradually be answered differently by the courts. However, claimants will usually also be required to demonstrate that the specific harms complained of (eg: flooding due to hurricane or fires due to heatwaves) were a reasonably foreseeable consequence of the defendant company's actions and this is an even more difficult hurdle.

18   The European Group on Tort Law has reported on the Principles of European Tort Law: European Group on Tort Law, *Principles of European Tort Law* (2005). Generally, a strict liability approach is used where activities create a foreseeable and highly significant risk of damage even when all due care is exercised in its management.

19   James Kanter, "Business of Green: Fighting climate change one lawsuit at a time", *International Herald Tribune*, August 16 2007.

20   Council Directive 2004/35/CE, 2004 O.J. (L 143) 56.

21   These activities include, among others, operations subject to permits issued under the Integrated Pollution Prevention and Control Directive.

22   Article 3(1)(b). For further commentary see Faure et al, n 19 above at 148.

litigation of which business and lawyers must be aware. Product liability claims may arise in the context of climate change in two main circumstances:

- in the traditional sense, whereby manufacturers of products are sued for alleged contribution to climate change on the basis of ineffective or defective designs; or
- where manufacturers of certain products are alleged not to have adapted their product lines to take into account extreme weather conditions due to climate change, such that the products are defective or not fit for purpose.

If a business manufactures, sells, or otherwise distributes products or any component parts of products, it may be subject to a variety of different claims for product liability if the product causes bodily injury or property damage. Product liability litigation in the traditional sense relies on establishing the presence of a "defect" which makes the product unreasonably dangerous, as well as a duty under tort, contract or consumer protection legislation to warn or inform consumers about the possible harmful effects of the particular product and to foresee the potential detrimental effects the products may have. The defect must be proven to be a proximate cause of any harm alleged. Unreasonably dangerous products could be held to be so where:

- the product departs from its intended design, irrespective of the care undertaken by the business in its manufacture (otherwise known as a manufacturing defect);
- the product has a design defect such that a safer, reasonably alternative design is available; or
- the product may be found to have a "warning defect" when its foreseeable risks could have been mitigated through reasonable warnings or instructions, the lack of which make the product dangerous.

The question of whether a product liability suit could be successful in the climate change context has been considered by various authors,[23] who generally conclude that at present it may be difficult for a court to hold that a duty of care exists in the first place not to manufacture products which contribute to climate change.[24] For example, traditionally, environmentalists have argued that harm to property, the environment or human health arises from the design of certain engines and engine components (namely that the alleged production of significant amounts of greenhouse gases caused climate change, and the engine manufacturers knew of the danger but disregarded it). However, the success of such a claim will depend on how the court balances the risk of harm with the particular product's benefits. Indeed, the test for a "design defect" varies between jurisdictions from a "consumer expectations" test to a

---

23   Such as Smith and Shearman see n 11 above.
24   A duty to warn is perhaps unlikely to be held to arise in the manufacture of products that produce GHG emissions for the reason that this is a given with products such as motor engines or other machinery. However, a duty to warn may exist where a particular product is susceptible to breakdown or to damaging the environment, humans or property if exposed to extreme weather conditions such as flooding or heatwaves.

"risk-utility" test. The common thread is that a product must be shown to be unreasonably dangerous. In the climate change context, this will again invariably turn to the question of causation, and whether among other things, the product in question could have caused the climate change damage complained of.

Given the obvious limitations to a climate change suit on product liability grounds, it is interesting to note the way in which automobile manufacturers targeted by environmentalists have been legally challenged in public nuisance, personal injury and in other consequential litigation[25] where a product liability claim might theoretically have been commenced. For example, in *California v General Motors Corp*,[26] it was alleged that the vehicles produced by the defendant companies accounted for more than 20% of human generated CO_2 emissions in the United States. As discussed later in this chapter, this case was dismissed on non-justiciability grounds. In 2002 the District Court of Tokyo ruled that the Japanese government could be held liable for the asthma of certain plaintiffs alleging a failure properly to build and manage Tokyo's roads. In the same case, the court dismissed claims against automobile manufacturers (that car exhaust and resulting pollution caused their ailments). The plaintiffs are reported to have agreed to a court-mediated settlement in 2007 whereby a one-off payment of ¥1.2 billion was paid to the plaintiffs and a further ¥3.3 billion paid to support a five-year health plan along with ¥12 billion payments from government authorities to support medical programmes for patients.[27] Importantly, whilst the allegations in these cases centred upon the impacts of a product (ie car motors), product liability claims must point to breaches of a mix of tort, contract and consumer protection regulation, whereas other liability litigation causes of action such as nuisance or negligence do not necessarily impose such hurdles.

(d)   ***Human rights***
Human rights are another area of the law that have been used by plaintiffs attempting to seek redress for damage caused by climate change. International environmental claims based in human rights can arise under specific regional and international declarations, conventions and agreements. "Environmental" human rights claims are usually framed in relation to rights to life, property, personal security and health as opposed to environmental grounds alone and, as such, in the context of climate change, causation will be an important element in demonstrating that a human right was infringed due to any specific weather event or state of affairs arising from climate change. In this regard, the general consensus is that there is no international human right to be free of pollution, global warming or climate change *per se*.[28] However, the existence and violation of a related human right (such as the right to life, right to

---

25   For a consideration of other automobile-related consequential litigation, see section 3.3(a) of this chapter.
26   F.Supp.2d (N.D. Cal. Sep. 17,2007).
27   See www.straitstimes.com/Latest%2BNews/Asia/STIStory_149228.html (website last accessed on January 21 2008).
28   See, for example, Sumudu Atapattu, "The Right to a Healthy Life or the Right to Die Polluted?: The Emergence of a Human Right to a Healthy Environment under International Law", 16 *Tul. Envtl. L.J.* 65, 74 to 78 (2002).

personal property, security and the right to physical and mental health)[29] has been legally argued in the context of an alleged link to property damage or the deterioration of human health and global warming. It is important to note that, in this context, the usual remedies arising out of human rights-based causes of action in international fora can be declaratory at best, with little prospect of being awarded damages or compensation in the international courts.

Damages are more likely to be awarded, however, within national jurisdictions for human rights breaches leading to actual damage and harm. A recent example of human rights issues intermingling with environmental damage in the national context arises out of the decision of the Federal High Court of Nigeria on November 14 2005 to order the complete cessation of gas flaring in the Niger Delta by the Nigerian National Petroleum Corporation (NNPC) and six oil companies.[30] The gas flaring was alleged to contribute to greenhouse gas emissions and to produce toxic gases impacting on human health. The plaintiffs, eight individuals each living in different communities impacted by gas flaring, were held to have had their "fundamental rights to life and dignity of human person" violated under the Nigerian Constitution, the African Charter on Human and Peoples Rights and the Nigerian Environmental Impact Assessment Act 2004. Importantly, the court granted declaratory relief to the effect that the rights to life and dignity of human person also include a right to a "clean, poison-free, pollution-free and healthy environment". It also ordered legislative action to amend the gas flaring provisions in the Associated Gas Re-Injection Act 2004 in order to make the legislation consistent with the human rights provided for under the Nigerian Constitution.[31]

Another example of climate change litigation based on human rights is that of the petition filed with the Inter-American Commission on Human Rights by the Inuit Circumpolar Conference, claiming that climate change policy in the United States was in violation of the Inuit and other Arctic indigenous people's human rights.[32] Whilst the petition was ultimately rejected on evidentiary grounds, it largely challenged US energy policy and lack of regulation on GHG emissions which were alleged to be causing subsidence due to permafrost melting, causing destruction to homes, roads and other structures, and violating a host of human rights as a result.[33] Whilst the US government would not have been bound by any decision given the Commission's lack of enforcement powers, any recognition by the Commission that (i) the US government's acts or omissions had caused climate change, and (ii) the

---

29   All of which are described in different ways in certain international agreements.
30   Motion exparte, *Barr et al v Shell Petroleum Development Company of Nigeria et al*, No FHC/CS/B/1256/2005 (Nigerian F.H.C.). The plaintiffs sued on behalf of themselves and representing the Rumuekpe, Imiringi, Gbarain, Eremah, Akala-Olu, Idama, Iwherekan and Eket Communities in Nigeria, and the named defendants also included Total/Fina/ELF Limited, Nigerian Agip Oil Company Limited, Chevron/Texaco Nigeria Limited, Mobil Producing Nigeria Limited, and the Nigerian attorney-general.
31   Federal High Court of Nigeria, Benin Judicial Division, Order dated November 14 2005.
32   Petition to the Inter-American Commission on Human Rights Seeking Relief From Violations Resulting from Global Warming Caused by the Acts and Omissions of the United States (December 7 2005). The petition was rejected by the Commission in December 2006 on the basis of insufficient evidence of harm and, as at the time of writing, no new petition has been filed.
33   The specific violations in the petition include the right to life and preservation of health and wellbeing, rights to privacy, residence and protection of the home, rights to property, rights to culture, and the right to one's own means of subsistence.

climate change had led to human rights violations, would arguably have established a precedent encouraging further climate change and human rights claims to be made, in various courts, tribunals and other fora. The position of minorities, displaced peoples (such as the people of Indonesia, Sri Lanka and Thailand[34] after the December 2004 tsunami) and indigenous peoples is also relevant in the context of the US Alien Tort Claims Act 28 U.S.C. §1350 (ATCA), which is considered in more detail in the next sub-section.

(e)   **US Alien Tort Claims Act**

The Alien Tort Claims Act is another international regime[35] which has been considered in relation to climate change grievances. It allows non-US citizens to bring claims against US and foreign corporations and government officials in the US courts on the basis of torts that violate treaties or customary international law.[36] It has been argued that if a plausible claim can be made that GHG emissions violate human rights or threaten genocide, contrary to a treaty or customary international law, then the US courts may award damages to such plaintiffs in ATCA claims.[37] However, it has also been argued that the idea that individuals[38] have an international human right of some description that is violated by GHG emissions, and that such a right should be vindicated in human rights litigation, is not a normatively attractive concept,[39] consistent with the commentary on human rights above, that there is no generally recognised "environmental" human right as such.

There are few claims which have so far addressed environmental matters under ATCA.[40] However, of relevance to peoples and communities displaced due to rising sea levels in the small island states in the Pacific Ocean (which has been well documented),[41] is the fact that the US courts have held that despite ATCA's scope being limited to violations of the law of nations,[42] non-state actors, including private individuals can access justice under ATCA,[43] particularly in circumstances where

---

34   The countries affected by the 2004 tsunami included India, Indonesia, Sri Lanka, Thailand, Burma, the Maldives, Malaysia, Tanzania, Bangladesh and Kenya. See Henry W McGee, "Litigating Global Warming: Substantive Law in Search of a Forum" Vol XVI *Fordham Environmental Law Review* 371 (2005) at 381.

35   Among many such international regimes which are not discussed in detail in this chapter. For example, for commentary on causes of action for rising sea temperatures, sea levels and reduced ocean alkalinity under the United Nations Convention on the Law of the Sea (UNCLOS) see William CG Burns, "Potential Causes of Action for Climate Change Damages in International Fora: The Law of the Sea Convention" (2006) *McGill International Journal of Sustainable Development Law and Policy* Vol 2(1) March 2006 27. For commentary on petitions made to the UNESCO World Heritage Committee on the basis of climate change, see Amsterdam International Law Clinic, "Analyses of Issues to be Addressed, Climate Change Litigation Cases" (2007) *Milieu Defense* at 31.

36   Eric A Posner, "Climate Change and International Human Rights Litigation: A Critical Appraisal", University of Chicago Law School, Public Law and Legal Theory Working Paper No 148 (January 26 2007).

37   Rosemary Reed, "Rising Seas and Disappearing Islands: Can Island Inhabitants Seek Redress Under the Alien Tort Claims Act?", 11 *Pacific Rim Law & Policy Journal* 399 (2002).

38   Such as, for example, the Tegua people in Vanuatu or those displaced by the 2004 tsunami.

39   Posner n 37 above at 4.

40   Reed n 38 above at 409.

41   For example, the population of Tuvalu is decreasing as people are forced to leave the country as a result of rising sea levels. See Kathy Marks, "SOS: Pacific islanders battle to save what is left of their country from rising seas", *The Independent*, August 21 2007 available at environment.independent.co.uk/climate_change/article2773149.ece. See also generally: Reed, n 38 above.

42   28 U.S.C. § 1350 (1996).

43   See *Kadic v Karadzic*, 70 F.3d 232, 239 (2d Cir. 1995).

individuals with a common grievance are acting in concert. In these circumstances, the courts will generally hold such plaintiffs to be acting as a state and therefore subject to the same standards of conduct as a state[44] in bringing a claim. Also, whilst environmental human rights violations have not been heard under ATCA, it is clear that the courts are potentially prepared to hear such cases. In *Beanal v Freeport-McMoRan Inc*,[45] the plaintiff claimed, among other things, that the destruction of the environment of the indigenous peoples of Irian Jaya, Indonesia, was causing cultural genocide. This claim was dismissed with prejudice, on the technical basis that the plaintiffs could not sufficiently particularise their claim of cultural genocide.

In light of the above, at least for the purposes of ATCA, plaintiffs and defendants alike will need to understand how a climate change claim alleging human rights breaches needs to be particularised having regard to the complex legal issues which arise in liability litigation in particular.[46] In all cases, because ATCA relates to tortious acts, plaintiffs will always have the burden of establishing causation in relation to the specific climate-change-related tort, whether it be in nuisance, negligence or otherwise.

3.2 Administrative law litigation

Governments are under increasing scrutiny by civil society in relation to how they regulate, or fail to regulate GHG emissions. This is particularly so for those governments which have ratified the Kyoto Protocol and implemented consequential laws and policies in order to regulate GHG emissions. With new regulatory regimes come new opportunities for plaintiffs to challenge governmental decision making, and to lobby governments in public consultation exercises associated with law making and administration.

(a) Planning and permitting appeals

Various challenges have been commenced internationally in relation to the governmental approval of projects which produce or encourage the production of GHG emissions and therefore allegedly contribute to global warming. These projects and related governmental decisions are more at risk of challenge, given that proof of standing in administrative proceedings is a less onerous burden than in claims where damages are being sought. This is because administrative claims will be distinguished from private law actions[47] on the general basis that governments are accountable to the public, and at common law the test for standing for judicial review is whether the applicant has a "sufficient interest" in the decision or power to which the challenged decision relates.[48]

In the United States, case law has arisen primarily in relation to claims under the National Environmental Policy Act 1969 (NEPA) or otherwise equivalent state

---

44   Reed n 38 at 409.
45   *Beanal v Freeport McMoRan Inc*, 969 F. Supp. 362 (E.D. La 1997).
46   See Section 4 of this chapter.
47   See, for example, the summary judgment in *Friends of the Earth v Mosbacher* (previously Watson), 2005 WL 2035596 (N.D. Cal 2005) (Unreported) and the commentary in Smith n 14 above at 72.
48   This is the position in England and Wales under the Section 31(3) of the Supreme Court Act 1981.

legislation known as "little NEPAs", which require governments to consider and analyse the environmental impacts of major governmental actions. The reach of NEPA can be very broad and the characterisation of "governmental actions" can range from formulating new rules and standards, to granting rights of way or funding fossil fuel projects.

In *Border Power Plant Working Group v Department of Energy*,[49] the plaintiff challenged a decision to grant rights of way for transmission lines connecting new Mexican and US power plants onto the US electricity grid. In particular, the challenge was in respect of the Department's failure to prepare an Environmental Impact Statement (EIS), and failure to analyse the environmental impacts of CO_2 emissions. Whilst the court ordered an EIS to be prepared, the EIS contained only three paragraphs on the CO_2 impacts of the transmission lines and concluded that the project's impacts on global warming would be "negligible".[50] Whilst potentially seen as a hollow victory for the plaintiffs, the case is important in demonstrating that NEPA extends to considerations of the global warming impacts of federal actions.[51]

Multiple other US cases have arisen out of challenges to governments for failing to consider climate change impacts in respect of projects, or in relation to the setting of efficiency standards.[52]

The US courts do not, however, have a monopoly on this kind of litigation. Planning and permitting appeals in the context of climate change have also been seen in other countries. In *Australian Conservation Foundation v Minister for Planning*,[53] the Victorian Civil and Administrative Tribunal held that the minister, in deciding to allow an amendment to a planning scheme the effect of which would allow the expansion of a coalmine, was required to consider the indirect impacts of greenhouse gas emissions resulting from the burning of coal at a power station. That is, the downstream impacts of producing coal had to be a relevant consideration.

In *Gray v The Minister for Planning*,[54] a law student challenged the validity of a grant of planning permission for a coalmine in Anvil Hill, New South Wales, on the basis that the proponent failed adequately to prepare an environmental assessment in conformance with the environmental assessment requirements (EAR) issued by the director-general of the Department of Planning as part of the planning process. In particular, one of the EARs required an assessment of air quality impacts, including a detailed GHG assessment. Whilst the environmental assessment prepared by the proponent did assess GHG impacts, it did not include any

49   260 F.Supp.2d 997 (S.D. Cal. 2003).
50   Justin R Pidot, "Global Warming in the Courts – An Overview of Current Litigation and Common Legal Issues" *Georgetown Environmental Law & Policy Institute* (2006) at 12, available to view as at January 28 2008 at www.law.georgetown.edu/gelpi/current_research/documents/GlobalWarmingLit_CourtsReport.pdf.
51   *Ibid.*
52   *City of Los Angeles v National Highway Traffic Safety Administration*, 912 F.2d 478 (D.C. Cir. 1990) – dealing with climate change impacts of the Corporate Average Fuel Economy Standards; *NRDC v Abraham*, 355 F.3d 179 (2d Cir. 2004) – in respect of air conditioner efficiency standards; *and Montana Environmental Information Center and Environmental Defense v EPA*, No. 06-1059 (D.C. Cir. 2005) – in relation to consideration of coal gasification technology to reduce GHG emissions of a new coal-fired power plant.
53   *Australian Conservation Foundation v Minister for Planning* (2004) LGERA 100.
54   *Gray v The Minister for Planning* [2006] NSWLEC 720 a decision of the New South Wales Land and Environment Court on November 27 2006.

assessment of the indirect impacts GHG emissions created by the burning of the 105 million tons per annum of coal by end-users. The court held that the indirect impacts of GHG emissions resulting from burning the coal extracted from the Anvil Hill mine have a "real and sufficient link" to the proposed project and that therefore the assessment of indirect impacts was a relevant consideration in administrative law, which, when not considered, rendered the grant of planning permission invalid.

There are various other planning cases in New Zealand and Australia, both state- and federal- based, in which claimants have had varying success in proving that the original decision makers have failed to take into account downstream carbon emission impacts in granting development consent for coal projects in accordance with relevant statutory instruments.[55] Interestingly, there is also case law where the consideration of climate change impacts has been used as a sword by proponents of renewable energy projects, in order to defend appeals against the grant of development consent for such projects.[56] In *Taralga Landscape Guardians Inc v Minister for Planning and RES Southern Cross Pty Ltd*,[57] the Land and Environment Court of New South Wales held that conditions imposed by the Minister for Planning for a wind farm approval subject to limiting conditions as to number and location of wind turbines be deleted from a planning consent. The reason for the deletion of such conditions was that the benefits of wind power and renewable energy outweighed any private disadvantages to the local community in relation to visual amenity, particularly in recognition of the fact that it is known that the energy industry is itself a major emitter of GHG emissions worldwide.

In England and Wales, with the introduction of the Planning Policy Statement: Planning and Climate Change published on December 17 2007, the question of climate change impacts of certain developments will arise more frequently in planning appeals and public local inquiries. Indeed, it was recently submitted that a proposed highway linking the city of Lancaster to a major motorway was contrary to emerging policy areas of sustainable development and climate change by the increase of CO_2 emissions which would result from the construction and use of the highway.[58] In this case, the Secretary of State nevertheless approved the development, citing an overriding public need for the highway.[59]

The message for developers of projects which may directly or indirectly create GHG emissions is that all administrative procedures should be thoroughly checked

---

55   *Greenpeace New Zealand Incorporated v Northland Regional Council and Mighty River Power Limited* (2006) NZHC 1212, a decision of the High Court of New Zealand; *Wildlife Preservation Society of Queensland Proserpine/Whitsunday Branch Inc v Minister for Environment and Heritage* [2006] FCA 736, a decision of the Federal Court of Australia on June 15 2006; and *Xstrata Coal Queensland Pty Ltd v Queensland Conservation Council* [2006] AML 207/2006 ENO208/2006, a decision of the Queensland Land and Resources Tribunal on February 15 2007.

56   See *Genesis Power Limited v Franklin District Council* (2005) NZRMA 541; *Environmental Defense Society v Auckland Regional Council and Contact Energy Limited* (2002) 11 NZRMA 492; and *Meridian Energy Ltd and Ors v Wellington City Council* (2007) No W31/07 (Environment Court).

57   *Taralga Landscape Guardians Inc v Minister for Planning and RES Southern Cross Pty Ltd* [2007] NSWLEC 59.

58   Heysham-M6 Link, Lancashire County Council Planning Application Reference: 11/05/1584, Proof of evidence: Climate Change submitted for the Environmental and Sustainable Transport Alliance (ESTA) in local planning inquiry July 10 to August 10 2007.

59   The Secretary of State used her call-in powers to decide on the application. SoS Decision Letter dated February 7 2008. See www.lancashire.gov.uk/environment/env_highways/roads/heysham/ (as at February 29 2008) for more information.

and all environmental assessments carried out and appropriately disclosed, working closely with the relevant decision maker. Whilst legal challenge on the grounds of inadequate assessment of such projects is still possible and likely to produce both delay and irrecoverable costs, generally speaking where the administrative defect is remedied, and appropriate assessment is subsequently carried out, such projects are more than likely to be approved absent some obvious and significant threat to the environment due to increased GHG emissions.

(b) *Challenges to governmental action or inaction in relation to the regulation of climate change matters*

(i) *Alleged governmental breaches of duty*

At the time of writing, perhaps the most significant decision of this kind is that of the US Supreme Court in *Massachusetts v Environmental Protection Agency*, 127 S. Ct. 1438 (2007), in which the court held that the US Environmental Protection Agency (EPA) had the authority under the US Clean Air Act 1963 to regulate emissions of CO_2 and other greenhouse gases from new motor vehicles, and that the EPA could not decline to promulgate such emissions standards based on policy considerations not included in the Clean Air Act itself. In that case, a group of private organisations and states challenged the EPA's denial of a rulemaking petition seeking to compel the EPA's regulation of CO_2. The Clean Air Act provides that the EPA administrator must prescribe "standards applicable to the emission of any air pollutant from ... new motor vehicles", which, in the administrator's judgment, "cause, or contribute to, air pollution which may reasonably be anticipated to endanger public health or welfare".[60]

The EPA gave two reasons for denying the rulemaking petition, both of which were ultimately rejected by a narrowly divided Supreme Court. First, the EPA concluded that it lacked statutory authority to issue regulations addressing global climate change because Congress had previously considered and rejected establishing binding emissions limits for greenhouse gases when amending the Clean Air Act.[61] Based on both this "political history" and the EPA's belief that imposing emissions limitations on greenhouse gases would have significant economic and political repercussions, the EPA concluded that greenhouse gases were not included within the intended definition of "air pollutants" under the Clean Air Act. The court found, however, that the Clean Air Act's "sweeping definition" of "air pollutant" as "*any* air pollution agent or combination of such agents, including *any* physical, chemical ... substance or matter which is emitted into or otherwise enters the ambient air",[62] clearly granted the EPA the statutory authority to regulate emissions of greenhouse gases from new motor vehicles.[63] Because Congress had never manifested any intention to curtail the EPA's power "to treat greenhouse gases as air pollutants", Congress's failure to create exacting and specific greenhouse gas

---

60   41 U.S.C. § 7521(a)(1).
61   126 S.Ct. at 1450.
62   42 U.S.C. § 7602(g).
63   127 S. Ct. at 1459 to 1460.

emissions limitations could not be relied upon as evidence of the intended meaning of § 202(a)(1) of the Clean Air Act.[64]

The court also considered and rejected the alternative argument that, even if the EPA possessed statutory authority, it had properly exercised its discretion under § 202(a)(1) to reach a "judgment" that regulation of greenhouse gases would be "unwise".[65] Although § 202(a)(1) conditions the EPA's regulation of emissions on its determination that such emissions contribute to air pollution that "may reasonably be anticipated to endanger public health or welfare", the EPA's "judgment" could not be based on impermissible factors "divorced from the statutory text",[66] In responding to the petition for rulemaking under § 202(a)(1), the EPA's reasons for action or inaction in regulating greenhouse gases were limited to those authorised by statute.[67] Thus, the EPA could avoid taking further regulatory action "only if it determines that greenhouse gases do not contribute to climate change or if it provides some reasonable explanation as to why it cannot or will not exercise its discretion to determine whether they do so".[68] The EPA's "judgment" under § 202(a)(1) to regulate or refrain from regulating greenhouse gases *must* be based on an examination of "whether sufficient information exists to make an endangerment finding".[69] The sundry underlying rationales offered by EPA in support of its determination that regulating greenhouse gases would be "unwise" such as by potentially limiting the US President's ability to engage in international climate change negotiations, overlap with voluntary Bush Administration climate change initiatives, or reluctance to engage in an "inefficient, piecemeal approach to address the climate change issue" – were inapposite inasmuch as those rationales "have nothing to do with whether greenhouse gas emissions contribute to climate change".[70]

The Supreme Court's decision in *Massachusetts v EPA* has paved the way for a multitude of judicial and administrative challenges seeking to compel the EPA to regulate greenhouse gas emissions in permits authorising construction of power plants. However, because the nature of climate change does not fit neatly within the current Clean Air Act construct, it is questionable whether litigation based on the Clean Air Act will ultimately prove effective in addressing greenhouse gas emissions in the US.[71] At least one US court has used *Massachusetts v EPA* as authority to uphold the validity of state regulations limiting greenhouse gas emissions from motor vehicles. In *Green Mountain Chrysler*

---

64   *Ibid* at 1460 to 1461.
65   *Ibid* at 1460 to 1451.
66   *Ibid* at 1462.
67   *Ibid.*
68   *Ibid.*
69   *Ibid.*
70   *Ibid* at 1463. In his dissent, Justice Scalia disagrees with the majority's analysis in this regard by arguing that when EPA "makes a judgment whether to regulate greenhouse gases, that judgment must relate to whether they are air pollutants that 'cause, or contribute to, air pollution which may reasonably be anticipated to endanger public health or welfare'" (127 S.Ct. at 1473). "But the statute *says nothing at all* about the reasons for which the Administrator may *defer* making a judgment – the permissible reasons for deciding not to grapple with the issue at the present time" (*Ibid* (emphasis original)). "Thus, the various 'policy' rationales … that the Court criticizes are not divorced from the statutory text, … except in the sense that the statutory text is silent, as texts are often silent about permissible reasons for the exercise of agency discretion" (*Ibid*).
71   See for example *Sierra Club v EPA and Prairie State Generating Company, LLC*, No 06-3907, F.3d, 2007 WL 2406857 (7th Cir. Aug 24 2007).

Plymouth Dodge Jeep v Crombie, the federal district court in Vermont concluded that the *Massachusetts v EPA* decision "recognized for the first time the phenomenon of global warming and its potentially catastrophic effects on our environment".[72]

The hallmark of *Massachusetts v EPA* may be less about the existing regulatory authorities and more a recognition, by the highest court in the United States, of a compelling need to regulate greenhouse gas emissions.

(ii)   Claims against export credit agencies

In the United States, non-governmental organisations (NGOs) and the city of Boulder, Colorado, have challenged the Export-Import Bank of the US (EIB) and the Overseas Private Investment Corporation (OPIC)[73] on the basis that they provided funding for overseas fossil fuel projects in the order of $32 billion and did not properly assess the contribution by these projects to global warming and climate change, contrary to the requirements of the National Environment Policy Act 1969. Importantly, in holding that the plaintiffs had standing, the court ruled that they had shown a reasonable likelihood that emissions from the projects would harm their specific interests and that there was a causal connection between the defendants' funding and the projects themselves. The court also held that it would be difficult to argue that GHG's do not contribute to global warming.

The German export credit agency, Euler Hermes AG, was challenged in a freedom of information action by Germanwatch and others[74] on the basis that Hermes had not disclosed information relating to the contribution to climate change made by projects funded by the German taxpayer. The Berlin Administrative Court ruled that the export credits providing financial support to projects such as coal power plants and mining, did contribute to climate change and did affect the environment. However, it is important to note these findings were made in the context of the freedom of information appeal before the court.

One of the most recent cases against an export credit agency is the judicial review proceedings commenced in the English High Court by established NGOs WWF and Corner House Research against the UK Export Credit Guarantee Department (ECGD) on August 16 2007[75] in respect of Royal Dutch Shell's Sakhalin 2 oil and gas project off the eastern coast of Russia. Whilst climate change is not directly the issue of concern – in this case, it is the alleged damage to the environment and western Pacific grey whales of the Sakhalin 2 project – the judicial review relates to an alleged failure by the ECGD properly to address and consider the environmental impact assessment before making a decision that it would offer approximately £500 million in guarantees to the Sakhalin 2 project, conditional on the ECGD being satisfied about the project's environmental impacts.[76] The ECGD maintains it has not yet

---

72   *Green Mountain Chyrsler Plymouth Dodge Jeep v Crombie,* Nos. 2:05-CV-302, 2:05-CV-304, F.Supp.2d, 2007 WL 2669444, *90 (D. Vt. Sept 12 2007).

73   Greenpeace was also a claimant in *Friends of the Earth v Mosbacher* (previously Watson), 2005 WL 2035596 (N.D. Cal 2005) (Unreported).

74   *Bund für Umwelt und Naturschutz Deutschland e.V. and Germanwatch e.V. v Republic of Germany,* represented by the (Federal Ministry of Economics and Labour (BMWA)

75   *R (WWF and Corner House Research) v Secretary of State for Business, Enterprise and Regulatory Reform,* filed August 16 2007, High Court of Justice, Queens Bench Division, Administrative Court.

offered any guarantee to cover the project.[77] However, it is clear from this, and many other NGO suits, that judicial review is fast becoming a tool to address government action and inaction in the global sphere, a trend set to continue in relation to multi-jurisdictional climate change matters.

(iii)   *Other administrative appeals arising out of new GHG emissions regulatory and trading regimes* Whilst the focus of this chapter is on emerging climate change litigation characterised by claims and challenges revolving around alleged damage caused by global warming in the traditional sense, it would be remiss not to consider the increasing litigation arising out of emerging regulatory measures aimed at climate change. As governments seek to implement carbon caps, environmental taxes and other economic quota systems in an attempt to regulate emissions, businesses are increasingly faced with accounting for the cost of carbon within legal regimes which, can lead to litigation manifesting itself not only from a liability perspective, but also from a regulatory standpoint.

For example, teething problems and disputes revolving around newly introduced quota systems are not new. In Europe, the EC Milk Quota regime, which began in the early 1980s, was a result of the failure of the European Community to deal with inherent problems in the dairy sector, in particular the supply–demand imbalances associated with high excesses of milk products and their impacts on pricing, in turn impacting on the Common Agricultural Policy.[78] Similarly, the EU Emissions Trading Scheme (ETS), which is currently the world's largest emissions trading scheme, commenced in 2005 and brought with it a significant regulatory burden on electricity generators, steel manufacturers, aluminum operations, pulp and paper, refineries, and combined heat and power (CHP) plant operators, to name a few. With this burden to account for carbon emissions, has come a high level of litigation, which can be categorised as administrative law litigation.[79]

In the United States, one of the newly emerging emissions trading schemes being introduced by nine north-eastern states[80] is the Regional Greenhouse Gas Initiative

---

76   See Judicial Review Application available on: www.thecornerhouse.org.uk/summary.shtml?x=556012 as at August 30 2007.

77   Ed Crooksand and Michaeal Peel, "WWF Pursues Sakhalin Judicial Review" *Financial Times*, August 16 2007.

78   Dr Charles Trotman "*The Development of Milk Quotas in the UK*" (1996), Sweet and Maxwell at 19. The Common Agricultural Policy has its legal framework in the Treaty of Rome, which came into effect in 1958. The Council of Agricultural Ministers adopted the Council Regulations 856/84 and 857/84 establishing a quota system in March 1984. The aim was to bring milk production and consumption back into market balance by pegging production within the European Community to 1981 production levels plus 1%. It was up to member states to choose between 1981, 1982 or 1983 as the best reference year from which to make calculations. Each member state was then allocated a quota to be distributed to eligible milk producers. Any overproduction above the allocated quotas was subject to a levy which paid for the costs of disposal of overproduction. Unsurprisingly, a flood of applications for judicial review emerged, challenging (among other things) quota allocations, levies and compensation for periods where producers were barred from production.

79   For example, proponents appeal against, or otherwise challenge, decisions of state-based regulators, primarily in relation to allocation methodology decisions. In the United Kingdom these are largely paper-based appeals made jointly to the Department for Business Enterprise and Regulatory Reform (DERR) and the Department for Environment, Food and Rural Affairs (DEFRA).

80   The ratifying states are Connecticut, Delaware, Maine, Massachusetts, New Hampshire, New Jersey, New York, Rhode Island and Vermont.

(RGGI). RGGI will cap CO_2 emissions from electric power plants, allow for the trading of allowances, and create a mechanism for encouraging other projects that will reduce CO_2 emissions in order to create additional allowances, much like the Kyoto flexible mechanisms of Clean Development Mechanism and Joint Implementation. Whilst the issuance of the final RGGI Model Rule[81] in August 2006 and the signing of the Memorandum of Understanding (MOU) by the participating states have not been "appealable"[82] events, the formulation of state laws and regulations necessary to implement the RGGI Model Rule could bring with it potential litigation,[83] relating to the various key elements of an emissions trading system. Of particular importance is the fact that each state may distribute its quota of emissions allowances as it sees fit, and may choose its own allocation methodology, whether it be free allocations, or auctioning. The fact that there is state-based discretion over allocations means the risk of EU ETS copy-cat litigation under the RGGI regime is real. Also, as RGGI is implemented in each state, there is the potential for lobbying and challenge of governmental decision making generally, thereby increasing the scope for judicial review.

In summary, judicial review in respect of allocation-based regimes is set to increase worldwide as new climate change regulation and emissions trading regimes become more mainstream. Such judicial challenges are not new and, at least in Europe, have not always been limited to emissions trading regimes.

3.3 Consequential litigation

This category includes any proceeding, action or claim which, whilst not directly relating to the causal effects of global warming, a government's ability or willingness to regulate GHG, or other climate change matters, seeks to bring corporations and others to account with regard to ancillary matters which relate to climate change in the general sense. Many of these actions arise primarily as a result of increased public awareness as to the detrimental effects of climate change to the environment, property and human health and, in the case of corporations, an awareness by investors and shareholders of the impact of environmental and climate change matters on financial performance. The scope for litigation in this area is significant. Some examples of climate-change-related corporate activities that could potentially come under scrutiny include:[84]

- marketing fossil-fuel-consuming or emitting products;
- taking preventive measures in jurisdictions where GHG emissions are regulated, but omitting to do the same in other countries where they are not;
- holding out a company's operations as being "green", "carbon neutral" or similar where the actual state of affairs does not match up to the claim and in turn misleads consumers, investors or the public;

---

81 The RGGI Model Rules agreed in September 2006 are to be implemented and adopted by the participating states uniformly (with some scope for variation) by legislative process.
82 Aladdine Joroff, "The Regional Greenhouse Gas Initiative: An American Response", 38(3) *Trends* January/February 2007.
83 *Ibid.*
84 The list here has been adapted from David Hunter and James Salzman, "Negligence in the Air: The Duty of Care in Climate Change Litigation" 155 *University of Pennsylvania Law Review* (June 2007) at 134.

- issuing or promoting misinformation about climate change and global warming, which a company knows, or ought reasonably to know, is false;
- wrongfully withholding information from investors or the public which would increase knowledge and understanding on climate change, its causes and its impacts; and
- destroying climate-change-related documents.

Specific examples of actual and potential actions falling broadly into the category of consequential litigation are discussed below.

(a)   Advertising standards

Companies which make claims in advertisements relating to good climate change practices and "green" initiatives run the risk of breaching advertising standards if such claims cannot be substantiated. There has been an increase in corporations publicising GHG reduction targets,[85] which could also potentially impact on advertising and risk misleading the public and, importantly, shareholders if these claims are not properly qualified. Also, companies offering carbon-offsetting schemes, or carbon-neutral product lines are at risk if such offsetting schemes fail to meet required standards of integrity and authenticity. Whilst not always strictly taking the form of litigation in the traditional sense,[86] complaints are adjudicated by the relevant agency to determine whether they are misleading. In many jurisdictions there are other enforceable statutory regimes[87] regulating corporations and businesses for misleading or deceiving others in the course of business or providing false statements about the provision of any goods or services.

Some examples of adjudications carried out by the UK Advertising Standards Authority (ASA) in relation to "green" claims regarding climate change include:[88]

- In a television advertisement for the Toyota Prius, the following claim was made: "What if all cars were like the Prius? With its hybrid synergy drive technology, it emits up to one tonne less CO_2 per year..." On-screen text stated "1 tonne of CO_2 less than an equivalent family vehicle with a diesel engine. Average calculated on 20,000km a year. Toyota Prius CO_2 emissions: 104 g/km". It was held by the ASA on June 6 2007 that the advertisement breached various TV advertising standards, including misleading advertising, evidence, implications, environmental claims and comparative advertising on the basis that the research and documentation behind the claim had inconsistencies such that it could not be established that the output of the Prius was comparable to all 2.0 litre cars registered in 2005.[89] The advertisement could

---

85   David Hunter and James Salzman, "Negligence in the Air: The Duty of Care in Climate Change Litigation" 155 *University of Pennsylvania Law Review* (June 2007) at 102.

86   For example, in the United Kingdom, complaints are made to, and adjudicated by, the Advertising Standards Agency.

87   See, for example, the Australian Trade Practices Act 1974, Section 52, and the respective State Fair Trading Acts and the Trade Descriptions Act 1968 (England and Wales).

88   For further examples of ASA adjudications on green advertising, see www.asa.org.uk/asa/news/news/2007/ASA+Gets+Tough+On+Advertising+Green+Claims.htm as at January 28 2008.

89   For a full report on the adjudication see: www.asa.org.uk/asa/adjudications/Public/TF_ADJ_42615.htm.

not be cast again in the same form.

- A leaflet for Scottish and Southern Energy Group (SSE) encouraged consumers to join its "power2" scheme in order to reduce CO_2 emissions. The claim was headlined "*A good use of your energy*" and it stated that "*when you join power2, we supply cleaner, greener hydro-electricity to the National Grid, cutting CO_2 emissions. And we plant trees to balance out the CO_2 that your gas heating and household waste produces*". The complainant argued the claim as to tree planting could not be substantiated and that it was misleading. The response by SSE was that it would plant sufficient trees to absorb the amount of CO_2 produced by the average UK household. The ASA could find no evidence specifically to substantiate this claim, even though SSE had engaged the World Land Trust to plant 150,000 trees per annum, and the ASA held that SSE was in breach of code standards in substantiation and truthfulness, and that SSE could not use the advertisement again in its current form.

These, and other similar complaints[90] filed against automobile companies, highlight the significant trend towards the public monitoring of GHG-producing industries and products, and an increase in likelihood of knock-on costs to impacted industries.

(b)   *Directors' duties and environmental reporting*

Directors and officers of corporations have fiduciary obligations both to the company as a whole and its shareholders. This encompasses duties of due care and loyalty. As climate change continues to impact on the integrity of the environment, property and human health, so does it impact on company balance sheets as an economic issue. Shareholders now expect boards duly to inquire, be informed about, and apply adequate internal monitoring mechanisms to deal with the consequences of climate change.[91] It has been alleged[92] that companies in the United Kingdom, for example, are failing to factor climate-change risk into their investment decisions despite evidence that climate change will impact on asset values over the next 40 years.[93] This awareness, and the powers of corporate and financial regulators as well as shareholders (through derivative actions) to commence legal action, means the risk of this type of consequential litigation occurring is increasing.

With the availability of shareholder derivative actions in various jurisdictions[94] and climate change risks being associated with directors' duties, the scope for consequential litigation in this area is increasing as some argue that it is now

---

90   For example, in May 2007 a complaint was filed with the German Ministry of Finance against Volkswagen by the campaign group GermanWatch, which contended that Volkswagen had damaged the environment by expanding its range of luxury cars that pollute more heavily, and by conducting lobbying campaigns against legislation intended to protect the climate. This particular complaints procedure was sanctioned by the Organization for Economic Cooperation and Development (OECD) to monitor the activities of large corporations. See generally Kanter n 5 above.

91   J Smith and M Morreale, "Boardroom Climate Change", *New York Law Journal* July 24 2007.

92   Alex MacDonald, "UK Cos Not Factoring Climate Change Risk in Invest-Report", *Dow Jones International News*, October 23 2006.

93   Acclimatise, "The Adaptation Tipping Point: are UK Businesses Climate Proof?"

94   For example, in the United Kingdom, the Companies Act 2006 now allows for such claims for a "cause of action arising from an actual or proposed act or omission involving negligence, default, breach of duty or breach of trust by a director of the company" (Section 260(3)).

"reasonably foreseeable" that climate change risks should be taken into account in investment decisions. These risks are in addition to the potential consequential litigation arising out of financial services and corporate regulators and watchdogs enforcing listing rules, accountancy standards and corporations legislation.

In the United States, there has been a recent increase in shareholder resolutions under the Securities Act 1934 challenging management authority and behaviour in relation to climate change. Nearly 30 companies annually in the United States receive shareholder proxy resolutions calling for the basic disclosure of carbon and GHG information.[95] In the 2007 proxy season, a record 43 climate-related resolutions were filed by institutional investors with US companies[96] calling for proper disclosure of climate change risks, and specific responses to such risks, along with a call to set GHG reduction targets.

Corporate climate change disclosure attracted even more attention in September 2007 when two environmental groups and the financial officers of 10 states and New York City filed a petition with the US Securities and Exchange Commission (SEC) requiring the SEC to compel companies to disclose in their 10-K disclosures the risks that climate change can pose to profits.[97] The petition calls on the Commission to issue a rule clarifying that, under existing law, corporations should assess physical and financial climate risk and disclose it to the public. This process may also include formal adjudications in relation to existing disclosures from certain companies, in relation to which the Commission has the potential to take witness statements and conduct formal hearings. The petition is still under review by the SEC.

In addition, the Attorney-General of New York, Andrew M Cuomo, recently started an investigation into five energy companies to determine whether financial risk had been adequately disclosed in respect of their association with coal-fired power plants, by issue of subpoenas under state securities legislation.[98] Reportedly subpoenas were issued to the five energy companies in September 2007 and the investigation is ongoing. As of the date of writing, the subpoenas have not been made public.

Some companies respond to external pressures to report by engaging in voluntary reporting initiatives. Institutional investors such as pension funds have for years focused on climate-related risks and, through voluntary reporting initiatives such as the Carbon Disclosure Project (CDP), institutional investors seek detailed information on the largest global corporations' GHG footprints and management methodologies. Corporations which do disclose under the CDP and similar voluntary schemes[99] must be sure to disclose accurately in order to avoid any future disputes, notwithstanding the fact that such disclosure is voluntary.

---

95 Gary S Guzy, "A Change in the Weather – New Climate Change Challenges Increase the Potential for Litigation and Regulation", *MMC Viewpoint,* available on www.mmc.com/knowledgecenter/viewpoint/Guzy2007.php as at October 3 2007.

96 Carbon Finance, "Pressure Grows on US Companies to Act on Climate", *Carbon Finance,* Volume 4, Issue 8, August 2007 – see www.carbon-financeonline.com.

97 Ceres Petition Before the United States Securities and Exchange Commission; Petition for Interpretive Guidance on Climate Risk (September 18 2007); Petition Number: 4-547.

98 See Felicity Barringer and Danny Hakim, "New York Subpoenas Five Energy Companies", *New York Times,* September 16 2007.

99 Other examples include the Equator Principles for financial institutions, the UN Global Compact, and the Global Reporting Initiative.

4. Common legal themes

Whilst, as we have seen, the increasing public awareness of climate change and GHG emissions has recently led to the increased use of litigation as a means to combat or promote climate change issues, the legal questions and issues which arise in these proceedings are not necessarily new.

The legal issues which are particularly pertinent in climate change litigation can either act as shields for defendants (many times striking out or dismissing claims even before the court hears any substantive arguments) or swords for plaintiffs (depending on the type of climate change litigation being commenced, as discussed below). As more cases have come before the courts, precedents are being set by particular courts in different jurisdictions as to how these legal issues will be dealt with.

Key issues such as standing, forum and jurisdiction, justiciability and judicial competence, remedies, causation and scientific uncertainty pose a mixture of legal, political and scientific questions, some of which can be difficult to resolve by the judiciary alone, or otherwise inappropriate for the judiciary to address to the exclusion of governments and policymakers. These legal issues add to the complexity of conducting any climate-change-related litigation and of advising on prospects of success.

4.1 Standing

In US jurisprudence, standing analysis begins with Article III, § 2 of the Constitution, which limits federal judicial power to the adjudication of "cases" and "controversies". Accordingly, in order to support standing in Federal Court, a plaintiff must demonstrate that:

- a particularised injury has been suffered (inquiry);
- a causal connection exists between the injury and the conduct complained of, so that the injury is fairly traceable to the challenged action of the defendant (causation and immediacy); and
- it must be likely, as opposed to merely speculative, that a favourable court decision will relieve the injury complained of (redressibility).[100]

In *Massachusetts v EPA*, the Supreme Court held that the State of Massachusetts has standing to challenge the EPA's failure to regulate emissions of carbon dioxide and other greenhouse gases based on injuries sustained by Massachusetts resulting from climate change.[101] The EPA had argued that, inasmuch as climate change is a classic example of widespread harm, Massachusetts had not suffered a "particularized injury". The court initially noted, however, that a litigant to whom Congress has "accorded a procedural right to protect his concrete interests" – such as the right under 42 U.S.C. § 7607(b)(1) for Massachusetts to challenge EPA's rejection of a rulemaking petition as arbitrary and capricious – "can assert that right without

---

100   See *DaimlerChrysler Corp v Cuno*, 126 S.Ct.1854, 1861 (2006) ("A plaintiff must allege personal injury fairly traceable to the defendant's allegedly unlawful conduct and likely to be addressed by the requested relief").
101   127 S.Ct.at 1452 to 1458.

meeting all the normal" standing requirements of "redressability and immediacy".[102] Given this procedural right, and a state's special quasi-sovereign interest in protecting "all the earth and air within its domain", the court found that Massachusetts was "entitled to special solicitude" in the standing analysis.[103] Operating under this relaxed standing threshold, the court found that Massachusetts had "satisfied the most demanding standards of the adversarial process" because "EPA's steadfast refusal to regulate greenhouse gas emissions presents a risk of harm to Massachusetts that is both 'actual' and 'imminent'".[104] Moreover, the court found a "substantial likelihood that the judicial relief requested" by Massachusetts would "prompt EPA to take steps to reduce that risk".[105]

With respect to redressibility, the court noted that while "it may be true that regulating motor-vehicle emissions will not by itself *reverse* global warming, it by no means follows that we lack jurisdiction to decide whether EPA has a duty to take steps to slow or reduce it".[106]

Not all plaintiffs will be granted the "special solicitude" given to the State of Massachusetts in this case. Tests for standing of course vary across jurisdictions and also according to the cause of action pleaded. For example, private parties will not usually be afforded relaxed requirements in an administrative law litigation action. A plaintiff seeking judicial review of a governmental decision or power will need to demonstrate a "sufficient interest"[107] in that decision or power. Similarly, plaintiffs in a claim for private nuisance must generally demonstrate having some title to the affected land. In relation to liability litigation where claims are made on the basis of negligence or nuisance relating to the impacts of global warming, it is more difficult for plaintiffs to establish standing where (currently) scientists and academics cannot arrive at a

---

102   *Ibid* at 1453.
103   *Ibid* at 1454 to 1455. Writing for a four-justice dissenting minority, however, Chief Justice Roberts disagreed with the court's decision to grant "special solicitude" to Massachusetts with respect to standing. *Ibid* at 1464 to 1465. After first noting that § 7606(b)(1) afforded states no special standing rights different from those granted to private litigants, the dissent argued that the majority misconstrued the court's earlier holding in *Georgia v Tennessee Copper*, 206 US 230 (1907), 127 S. Ct. at 1465. The dissent maintained that *Tennessee Copper* did not grant states elevated standing privileges based on their quasi-sovereign status but, rather, only empowered a state to bring suite in a representative capacity as *parens patriae* where its citizens had already satisfied the ordinary standing requirements of injury, causation, and redressibility (*Ibid*). "Far from being a substitute for Article III injury, *parens patriae* actions raise an additional hurdle for a state litigant: the articulation of a 'quasi-sovereign interest' apart from the interests of particular private parties" (*Ibid* (emphasis original)). The dissent also disagreed with the application of the doctrine to an action against the United States – "while a State might assert a quasi-sovereign right as *parens patriae* for the protection of its citizens, it is no part of its duty or power to enforce their rights in respect of their relations with the Federal Government. In that field it is the United States, and the State, which represents them" (*Ibid* at 1466).
104   127 S. Ct. at 1455.
105   *Ibid*.
106   *Ibid* at 1458 (emphasis original) (citing *Larson v Valente*, 456 US 228,244 (1982) ("[A] plaintiff satisfies the redressibility requirement when he shows that a favorable decision will relieve his *every* injury")). Chief Justice Roberts's dissent found redressibility even more problematic than causation because "developing countries such as China and India are poised to increase greenhouse gas emissions substantially over the next century" – meaning that the domestic emissions at issue "may become an increasingly marginal portion of global emissions, and any decreases produced by petitioners' desired standards are likely to be overwhelmed many times over by emissions increases elsewhere in the world" (*Ibid* at 1469). As a result, the dissent found it unlikely that the particular injury in fact – the asserted loss of Massachusetts's coastal lands – would be redressed even if greenhouse gas emissions were reduced by EPA regulations (*Ibid* at 1470).
107   In a judicial review in England and Wales, pursuant to Section 31(3) of the Supreme Court Act 1981.

consensus regarding the actual consequences of global warming.[108] Therefore, courts find it difficult to determine whether any given plaintiff has suffered an injury in fact, or to ascertain whether a defendant's emissions contributed to any such injury.[109]

4.2   Forum and jurisdiction

As has already been discussed, climate change litigation (and in particular, liability litigation) will commonly involve cases where defendants based in one jurisdiction are sued for alleged damage caused to a plaintiff located in a different jurisdiction. This can bring with it various practical and procedural obstacles, such as validly serving originating process or complying with other procedural rules.[110] However, of greater importance to plaintiffs and defendants alike is one of the major defences to any climate-change litigation claim which spans multiple jurisdictions, being that of *forum non conveniens*. In general, in deciding whether it is appropriate and proper to adjudicate in any particular case, a common law court will consider such matters as whether the tort or other cause of action in question was committed within the jurisdiction concerned, whether any damage suffered occurred within the jurisdiction, whether a plaintiff would be effectively denied relief unless he or she were to be able to sue in the jurisdiction in question, and whether any other foreign court or tribunal is better placed to deal with the evidentiary or other matters raised by the claim, having regard to the interests of all the parties and the ends of justice.[111]

The judiciary in the United Kingdom has recently shown itself to be sympathetic to aggrieved plaintiffs who can demonstrate a real and remediable loss arising in a foreign jurisdiction. In *Lubbe v Cape*, five employees[112] suffering from asbestosis brought an action against the English parent company, Cape plc, of their employer, for its alleged failure to take proper steps to ensure that proper working practices were followed throughout its subsidiary company's asbestos mining operations in South Africa, in circumstances where Cape plc knew, or should have known, that exposure to asbestos was gravely injurious to health. The plaintiffs sought to make their claim in the English courts and the question of *forum non conveniens* was heard by various courts (at first instance and on appeal) as an interlocutory matter.[113] When more than 3,000 plaintiffs sought to be joined in a group action against the defendant after the first successful appeal by the five original plaintiffs, the matter again came before the courts, this time the House of Lords,[114] to consider the questions of *forum non conveniens* and abuse of process which were raised by the defendant.

The House of Lords held that the *forum* defence could not hold in circumstances

---

108   Blake R Bertagna, "'Standing' Up for the Environment: The Ability of Plaintiffs to Establish Legal Standing to Redress Injuries Caused by Global Warming", 2 *Brigham Young University Law Review* 415 (2006).

109   See for example *Korsinsky v EPA* (2005) No 05 (iv 859, 2005 US Dist. Lexis 21778 (SD. NY. September 29 2005) – also referred to in this chapter under section 4.3 "Justiciability" below.

110   However, most jurisdictions provide rules as to service of process on foreign defendants, see Kerr at n 17 above.

111   See *Spiliada Maritime Corporation v Cansulex Ltd* [1987] AC 460, [1986] 3 All ER 843.

112   Including, in some cases, personal representatives, of the employee's estate.

113   Initially by writ issued on February 14 1997 in the High Court of England and Wales, Queens Bench Division, then in the Court of Appeal on July 30 1998 ([1998] CLC 1559) and November 29 1999 ([2000] 1 Lloyd's Rep 139).

114   *Lubbe v Cape plc* [2000] 4 All ER 268.

where the plaintiffs would have been denied justice had they commenced proceedings in the South African courts. This was because: (i) it would have been improbable that the plaintiffs would have had access to professional representation and expert evidence in South Africa, and this would amount to a denial of justice; and (ii) the lack of established procedures in South Africa to handle group actions would have been an unreasonable obstacle for the plaintiffs, and it was clear that the most efficient, expeditious and cost-effective way of handling the plaintiff's claims was by way of group litigation.[115]

This decision of the House of Lords in *Lubbe v Cape*, whilst not a climate change suit, has significant implications for the future conduct of climate change litigation, and, in particular, liability litigation where the liability of multinational corporations present in different jurisdictions is in issue.

In the United States, whilst ultimately overturned by the US Supreme Court, in the Court of Appeals hearing of *Massachusetts v EPA*, again, in the context of standing, one of the court's considerations was that, given that global warming was harmful to humanity at large and not just to the petitioners, the correct forum to address the alleged harm was the executive arm of government and not the courts.[116]

Legal practitioners should also be aware of international agreements relating to jurisdiction. For example, in relation to suits within the European Union, Article 2 of the Brussels Convention on Jurisdiction and the Enforcement of Judgments in Civil and Criminal Matters 1968 ("Brussels Convention") provides that an individual can be sued in the place of his principal residence, including for matters relating to tort, delict or quasi-delict.[117] The Brussels Convention has been adopted by the European Union as a regulation in broadly similar terms to the original text and therefore applies within the European Union.[118] The defendant in *Lubbe v Cape* was sued separately on similar grounds in England by four other plaintiffs claiming exposure to asbestos and asbestos products in Italy (a party to the then Brussels Convention).[119] Unlike Cape plc's position on *forum* as against the South African plaintiffs, Cape plc had no jurisdictional objection to the prosecution of the action by the Italian plaintiffs in the English courts on the basis of Article 2 of the then Brussels Convention compelling the English courts not to decline jurisdiction in favour of the Italian legal system.

4.3   Justiciability

Under the US Constitution, justiciability turns on whether "the duty asserted can be judicially identified and its breach judicially determined, and whether protection for the right asserted can be judicially molded".[120] Among the factors in determining the existence of a non-justiciable political question is the impossibility of deciding an issue without "an initial policy determination" of a clearly non-judicial and discretionary character.

---

115   *Ibid per* Lord Bingham of Cornhill.
116   Judge David Sentelle in *Massachusetts v EPA*, 415 F.3d 50 (D.C. Cir. 2005).
117   Article 5(3).
118   Council Regulation (EC) No 44/2001 on jurisdiction and the recognition and enforcement of judgments in civil and commercial disputes, known as the Brussels Regulation.
119   [2000] 4 All ER 268.
120   *Baker v Carr*, 369 U.S. 186, 198 (1962).

In the public nuisance suit of *State of Connecticut, City of New York et al v American Electric Power Company Inc et al* (the *American Electric,* or *AEP,* case),[121] the defendant "top 5" producers of CO_2 in the United States were sued on the alleged basis that they did not make use of practical, feasible and economically viable options for reducing their respective CO_2 emissions and that this unmitigated contribution to global warming would, in turn, cause damage to the property of the plaintiffs, which included public land designated for recreational and educational uses which was prone to damage from increased sea levels. Ignoring for the moment the problems associated with seeking damages for "future" potential harm as opposed to identifiable actual harm suffered, the United States District Court for the Southern District of New York dismissed the case on justiciability grounds. It held that global warming was a legislative issue and that until an initial policy determination had been made on the matter, the court was not in a position to pass judgment:

"... because resolution of the issues presented here requires identification and balancing of economic, environmental, foreign policy and national and security interests, an initial policy determination of a kind clearly for non-judicial discretion is required ... Thus, these actions present non-justiciable political questions that are consigned to the political branches not the Judiciary."[122]

The various remedies sought by plaintiffs in the *AEP* case – an order capping carbon dioxide emissions and mandating annual percentage reductions – were held to be of a "transcendentally legislative nature".[123] Such relief would require the court to engage in a multifaceted and complex policymaking exercise, "all without an 'initial policy determination' having been made by the elected branches".[124] In this regard, it has been suggested that limiting the range of remedies sought so that they relate directly to the harm suffered will decrease the chances of courts holding climate change matters non-justiciable.[125] This case was on appeal at the time of writing.[126] Likewise, in *California v General Motors Corp,*[127] the court dismissed California's global warming-based public nuisance tort claim against several car manufacturers on justiciability grounds identical to those in the *AEP* case at first instance.[128]

---

121 406 F.Supp.2d 265 (S.D.N.Y. 2005). In this case, eight states, the City of New York and three private plaintiffs brought a public nuisance action against American Electric Power, The Southern Company, Tennessee Valley Authority, Xcel Energy Inc and Cinergy Corporation, allegedly the five largest emitters of CO2 in the United States.
122 Judge Loretta Preska, September 19 2005.
123 *Ibid.*
124 *Ibid* at 272 to 273.
125 *Ibid* at 86.
126 Oral arguments regarding the matter were heard on June 7 2006, and supplemental briefing was allowed by the court regarding the impact of *Massachusetts v EPA* on the issues presented by the appeal, particularly with regard to any effect on the analysis of the doctrine of pre-emption or whether the plaintiffs' claims are displaced by congressional legislation. To date the court has not issued a decision.
127 F.Supp.2d (N.D. Cal. Sept 17 2007).
128 The court was concerned that it was being asked "to make an initial decision as to what is unreasonable in the context of carbon dioxide emissions. Such an exercise would require the Court to create a quotient or standard in order to quantify potential damages that flow from Defendants' alleged act of contributing [to] California's carbon dioxide emissions. [The] adjudication of [California's] claims would require the Court to balance competing interests of reducing global warming emissions and the interests of advancing and preserving economic and industrial development. The balancing of those competing interests in the type of initial policy determination to be made by the political branches, and not this Court."

The question of justiciability also arose in *Korsinsky v EPA*,[129] where among other things the plaintiff New York resident claimed that, after learning the dangers of climate change, he had developed a mental illness. The court here considered that even if these allegations were true, their intervention in finding for the plaintiff would not redress the plaintiff's problems and so the matter was non-justiciable.

Justiciability is a significant hurdle for plaintiffs framing their pleadings in such a way that effectively requires a court to stand in the shoes of the government in order to provide the redress required. For this reason, pleadings need to be carefully considered by plaintiffs, and equally carefully scrutinised by defendants in climate change related suits, for relevant justiciability issues.

4.4   Judicial competence

Closely related to the issue of non-justiciability, is the question of whether the courts are well enough equipped to consider the complex scientific and economic questions raised in climate change litigation. This is the question of judicial competence. It is argued by some that judges lack the specialised skills required to analyse highly technical scientific information about global warming and climate change.[130] In administrative law litigation, for example, where plaintiffs challenge governmental authorities on the basis of a failure properly to consider environmental and climate change impacts in granting approval to the construction of major projects, there is an argument that the adjudicator must be able to interpret the scientific data:

"[Risk assessment] requires lawyers to understand biological and statistical sciences, critique their normative and political function and translate them into values of the law and political system .... [However], lawyers have not been educated to this task and it is not an easy transition to make."[131]

In any form of climate change litigation, defendants may attempt to strike out claims on the basis of the above. It may be argued that specialist governmental authorities or governmental working parties are better equipped to deal with claims arising out of climate change. However, in administrative challenges to governmental decision making by judicial review, as set out in section 3.2 above, it is less likely that this argument will succeed, given that governments are accountable to the public, and in the great majority of jurisdictions are subject to judicial review wherever there has been an administrative breach of the law. In any event, the usual modern approach is for the courts to inquire whether a reasonable person could have come to the decision in question without misdirecting himself on the law or the facts in a material aspect[132] and it is the decision-making process which is in issue not the decision itself. In contrast, in any merits review or liability litigation, where the

---

129   No 05 (iv 859, 2005 U.S. Dist. Lexis 21778) (S.D.NY. September 29 2005).
130   Pidot n 51 above at 5.
131   M Lyndon, "Risk Assessment, Risk Communication and Legitimacy: An Introduction to the Symposium" (1989) 14 *Columbia Journal of Environmental Law* 290.
132   *Halsburys Laws of England* Volume 1(1)(21) – Power to Determine Ambit of own Authority. In addition, in some countries, certain specialist environmental courts have been created where the judiciary and technical lay-persons alike gain an increasing understanding of the technical, scientific issues raised in the disputes which come before them. Moreover, courts and tribunals have always decided legal issues relating to torts, causation, damages, and negligence on the basis of the available expert evidence at the time and, as discussed, these issues – even in the context of climate change – are not new.

technical merits of a decision are reviewed, or the scientific aspects of causation are in issue respectively, a judicial competence argument may be more plausible to the extent that technical lay adjudicators are not already involved.[133]

4.5   Remedies

In the event that a court or tribunal were to order damages for, say, property damage caused by a defendant's contribution to climate change, such damages would need to be proportional to the defendant's contribution to the damage. This causes obvious technical and scientific challenges in determining the degree to which any particular defendant is held to be responsible for the damage, and in turn offers claimants little redress in circumstances where they might not be able to provide any conclusive scientific evidence. The ability to demonstrate redressability is also a factor in considering legal standing, as considered above.

Emissions limits, for example, are generally the realm of the legislature not the courts. The remedies sought by claimants in climate change litigation cases therefore need to be properly thought out by both lawyer and client.

Remedies sought by plaintiffs in climate change litigation may include injunctive relief, compensatory damages and declaratory relief. For example, the main remedy for nuisance is injunction such that the defendant is ordered to cease from continuing the nuisance. However, this will prove little comfort to plaintiffs suing for property damage which has already occurred as a result of a "freak" storm or flood and, in any event, an injunction will probably only be effective insofar as the defendant is exceeding emissions beyond the amount permitted by law (generally under a statutory licence). Legal commentators have argued that climate change creates a need for more creative remedies, particularly for climate change nuisance litigation, such as court orders requiring defendants to purchase emissions offsets credits from the carbon market as a means of abatement.[134] Whether these kinds of remedies are sought, and considered by the courts in the future, remains to be seen.

Another matter to consider is that an award of damages will not generally be made, even where causation and damage is proven, if the damage is too remote. Remoteness is the judicial control mechanism which regulates the extent of a defendant's liability.[135] In actions for negligence and nuisance, the test for remoteness is whether a reasonable man should have foreseen the damage occurring.[136] The requirement of reasonable foreseeability puts an important restriction on liability for emitters of CO_2 who find themselves defending such an action. Independent of the complexities of proving causation for global warming, courts will also be facing questions of whether a particular defendant should have foreseen his actions would not only (i) cause global warming, but also (ii) cause the damage complained of.

---

133   For example, a planning inspector in a planning inquiry in England and Wales, or a Commissioner in the New South Wales Land and Environment Court.

134   Kirsten H Engel, "Harmonizing Regulatory and Litigation Approaches to Climate Change Mitigation: Incorporating Tradeable Emissions Offsets into Common Law Remedies", The University of Arizona Legal Studies Discussion Paper No 07-10 (March 2007) at 14.

135   David Allen et al, *Damages in Tort* (2000) Sweet & Maxwell at 82.

136   *Overseas Tankship (UK) v Morts and Dock Engineering Co Ltd (The Wagon Mound)* [1961] AC 388.

4.6   Causation and scientific uncertainty

Causation is a key issue in climate change litigation and deserves special attention. Causation is a critical element in tort-based claims such as negligence and nuisance, and equally relevant in civil-law jurisdictions to the question of legal liability. It is therefore of prime importance to understand the science of climate change in order properly to prepare and understand evidence required in litigation. The not inconsiderable task of any plaintiff in common-law jurisdictions alleging damage to the environment, property or human health caused by climate change, which was in turn caused as a result of the actions or inaction of any defendant, is to prove on the balance of probabilities (sometimes referred to as a 50% plus 1 chance) and to the relevant codified standard in civil law countries, that such actions or inaction:

- caused or contributed to, global warming; and
- this global warming led to specific regional climate change which itself caused or contributed to the damaged alleged in the pleadings.

These are two related but distinct limbs of causation which have been described as "general" and "specific" causation respectively.[137] The challenge of demonstrating a causal link in relation to climate change is particularly onerous when attempting to establish a link between the general incidence of global warming (contributed to by any number of emitters located in different countries) and a specific climate change event allegedly causing a plaintiff's particular loss. However, as discussed in section 3.1(a) above, specific causation may not be a requirement in an action for public nuisance.

(a)   The science of climate change causation

There is a vast divergence of opinion as to when scientists began to agree that climate change was a real issue. As early as 1956, the *New York Times* published an article entitled "Warmer Climate on Earth May be Due to More Carbon Dioxide in the Air".[138] Documentaries such as Al Gore's *An Inconvenient Truth* are entering popular culture, and various other media spectacles challenge and question whether humans have contributed to climate change. As a result, it is certain that the debate will continue until scientists are able to prove to society whether the "greenhouse effect" is in fact causing global warming, which is in turn responsible for the colder winters, hotter summers, severe weather storms, flooding and rises in sea levels and which are themselves in turn impacting on the environment, property and human health.

Science has gone some way since 1956 in establishing this causal link. The link between science and potential causes of action cannot be overstated. For example, on the current scientific knowledge available, climate change[139] has been claimed to be linked to (among other things):

---

137   Engel n 135 above at 18 and see *Sterling v Velsicol Chem Corp*, 855 F. 2d. 1188, 1200 (6th Cir. 1988).
138   TA Howard and KE Ryan, *"'Hot Enough For You?' Global Warming, Prospective Corporate Liability Claims and General and Professional Liability Coverage Implications"* Wiley Rein & Fielding LLP 2006 at 3 citing Jurriaan Kamp, *"The Courthouse Effect"*, Ode, June 2006, at 29.
139   "Climate change" can be characterised as increases in temperatures, rises in sea level, and a greater incidence of droughts, floods and catastrophic weather events. See Figure 1.2 in Smith n 12 above at 10.

- denying certain people a place to live;
- endangering public health through increases in microbial infection;
- impacting on certain industries such as tourism and causing economic disruption generally;
- decreasing water quantity and quality; and
- causing damage to public infrastructure in coastal areas, as well as energy and utilities infrastructure located in coastal areas.

Importantly, perhaps the most definitive and authoritative position on the science of climate change has been promulgated by the Intergovernmental Panel on Climate Change (IPCC) which, in engaging scientists respected world-wide, have prepared a series of assessment reports[140] and concluded with "very high confidence"[141] that the net effect of human activities since 1750 has been one of warming. Depending on individual jurisdictions' rules of evidence and the admissibility of the IPCC reports as regards climate change generally, or otherwise the use of such reports by expert witnesses to prepare evidence on how specific climate change impacts the subject of a dispute, these studies may be highly relevant in a court room in arguing causation. This is discussed in more detail next.

(b)   The judicial approach to causation

In most common-law countries, the traditional test for causation is the "but for" test, which questions whether the injuries complained of would have occurred but for the acts or omissions of the defendant. This test has been criticised and considered inappropriate where it has been found that there is more than one cause, or more than one potentially liable defendant, to which damage can be attributed.[142] In the context of climate change and global warming, it would be impossible to attribute the knock-on climatic effects to one sole emitter of GHG. The standard of proof for causation is "on the balance of probabilities", which as discussed above is sometimes interpreted as a "50% plus 1" or more chance of an assertion being correct.[143] Importantly, the IPCC's fourth assessment report concluded among other things that:

> "Most of the observed increase in globally-averaged temperatures since the mid-20th century is very likely due to the observed increase in anthropogenic GHG concentrations. It is likely there has been significant anthropogenic warming over the past 50 years averaged over each continent (except Antarctica)."[144]

It is important to note that "very likely" is attributed a greater than 90% chance confidence level and "likely" is given a greater than 66% chance confidence level by the IPCC. As has been observed by other commentators,[145] if the courts were to hold

---

140   The IPCC prepares assessment reports on scientific, technical and socio-economic information relevant for the understanding of human induced climate change, potential impacts and options for mitigation and adaptation. The latest is the 4th Assessment Report entitled "Climate Change 2007". See www.ipcc.ch for further information.

141   The confidence level of statements made with "very high confidence" by the IPCC indicates a 9 out of 10 chance of the statement being correct. See Introduction to the 4th Assessment Report at page 2.

142   See the Australian High Court decision of March v Stramere (1991) 171 CLR 506 and in the United Kingdom, Fairchild v Glenhaven [2002] UKHL 22.

143   See Smith n 11 above at 118.

144   Fourth assessment report Summary for Policymakers at 6.

this evidence admissible and to accept it, this is enough to meet the common law standard of proof. However, it does not prove causation as regards any one particular defendant or any one incidence of climate-change-induced environmental damage.

It has been alleged that it may now be possible to measure the percentage contribution of any one company, or group of companies, to GHG emissions globally.[146] Also, in 1997, the US Natural Resources Defense Council commissioned a study that concluded that 20 petroleum and coal producers together accounted for almost half of the world's carbon emissions[147] and another study in 2004 tables the GHG emissions of the top 100 electric power producers in the United States using publicly available information.[148] Whether these studies are technically accurate is a question beyond the scope of this chapter. However, the point to be made is that science is now at least claiming to be able to measure and account for emissions with a certain degree of precision. To date, however, a great deal of scientific uncertainty exists as to any one person's contribution to climate change.

The current inability of science to be able to determine the proportional liability of industry sectors and individual actors is important when considering the potential for creative judicial approaches to the question of causation both in common law and civil law jurisdictions. For example, in the unanimous decision of the House of Lords in *Fairchild v Glenhaven Funeral Services Ltd* (2002),[149] it was held that where it was accepted that two employers owed a duty of care to the plaintiff, and the plaintiff contracted mesothelioma in the course of his employment (a disease contracted from exposure to asbestos), then in circumstances where current science could not prove on the balance of probabilities that either one employer or the other was responsible for the damage caused, both employers became jointly liable for the total amount of damages owed to the plaintiff. The implications of this decision to determining causation in climate change actions is that even where the science of causation may not be mature enough specifically to hold any individual defendants liable for damage to health, property or the environment due to global warming, it may be sufficient (although, to date, still difficult) to prove that a group or class of defendants caused global warming in concert in order to obtain judicial redress. This again, could have a direct impact on the way in which causation for global warming or climate-change-related damage is assessed by the judiciary. It should be noted, however, that the scientific, technical and legal hurdles of establishing both "general" and "specific" causation remain significant, especially in the case of actions in private nuisance where the courts will require proof of causation of damage linked to a specific example of regionalised climate change[150] such as for

---

145   Smith n 11 above at 118.
146   The lead lawyer in *Comer v Murphy Oil* has been quoted as stating "we can prove how much carbon these companies have pumped into the air with great precision" – Gerald Maples, lead lawyer for the plaintiffs. See Kanter n 5 above.
147   Natural Resources Defense Council, "Kingpins of Carbon: How Fossil Fuel Producers Contribute to Global Warming" (1997) – see Kerr, Michael., n 17 above at 8.
148   Natural Resources Defense Council, "Benchmarking Air Emissions of the 100 Largest Electric Power Producers in the United States" (2004), available at: www.nrdc.org/air/pollution/benchmarking/default.asp as at August 16 2007.
149   *Fairchild v Glenhaven Funeral Services Ltd* [2002] All ER (D) 139 (Jun)
150   For more discussion on linking causation to specific regional climate change, see Smith n 11 above at 139.

example, proof that the GHG emissions of defendants A and B specifically caused the hurricane which caused damage to the claimant(s). This is where scientific knowledge remains limited, though it is improving.

One of the most radical approaches to probability which has been mooted is that of liability by the tortious creation of risk,[151] which by definition, eliminates the need to prove actual harm suffered and instead assesses liability solely from the perspective of the unreasonableness of the degree of risk imposed on a plaintiff.[152] However, currently in the United Kingdom there is no liability in tort or delict merely for increasing risks. The courts have instead established that a causal connection is required before liability can be found, in addition to establishing the reasonable foreseeability of harm.[153] With the complexities of the science of climate change, and the over-arching duties of the judiciary to administer justice, climate change case law may well develop in time to allow for a more relaxed view of liability.

Importantly, the House of Lords in the United Kingdom has held that causation in negligence was established where the claimant could prove that a tort "*materially increased the risk*" of an injury occurring[154] on the basis that the defendant's breach of duty made the risk of injury more probable even though it was uncertain whether it was the actual cause of the damage (in this case, dermatitis contracted from brick dust).[155] The relevant principles applied by the courts will always depend on the facts of the particular case (eg whether there is one known cause for the claimant's damage, or multiple possible causes). However, where a defendant's actions in a climate change suit are shown to have been a material contribution to the alleged damage to property, health and the environment, then the point is that there is judicial precedent to allow a degree of flexibility as to how liability is defined and apportioned in circumstances where scientific evidence is uncertain, and where there are multiple parties considered responsible.

5.   Conclusions

This chapter has sought to set out the broad drivers for climate-change litigation suits by discussing current and potential causes of action and the common legal themes arising from these causes of action. There has been much writing on specific examples of climate change litigation and the specific claims and defences being heard in various courts internationally and the respective chances of success of such actions in those courts and tribunals. Whilst the discussion of specific cases in this chapter has served to provide some examples of such matters, the chapter has rather sought to focus on the way in which the law is developing in response to public opinion and the science of climate change. The key legal themes arising out of

---

151   Robinson, *Probabilistic Causation and Compensation for Tortious Risk* (1985) 14 J *Legal Stud.* 779 to 786.
152   Richard Goldberg, *Causation and Risk in the Law of Torts: Scientific Evidence and Medicinal Product Liability* (1999) Hart Publishing, Oxford at 30.
153   *Ibid* at 32 and *McKew v Holland and Hannen & Cubitts (Scotland) Ltd* [1969] 3 All ER 1621.
154   See *McGhee v National Coal Board* [1973] 1 WLR 1 and *Fairchild v Glenhaven Funeral Services Ltd* [2002] All ER (D) 139 (Jun).
155   The judgment in *McGhee* in this regard was followed in *Fairchild*. However, in this case the cause of the injury was known (brick dust) and there were no other possible causes for the injury to the plaintiff.

climate change litigation introduce hurdles for claimants and defendants alike and need to be properly understood early in any disputes process to ensure claims and defences are properly drafted. Based on the growing public perception of global warming and its implications, there is an increasing risk to companies and governments globally of legal challenges, and therefore an increasing need for an awareness of the areas and bases for potential litigation so that sound risk-management techniques can be employed in order to adapt and respond to climate change and mitigate the effects of any legal action arising as a result.

The authors would like to thank and acknowledge the contribution of N Jonathan Peress and Jeffrey Kuhn, who are associates in the Albany office of Dewey & LeBoeuf LLP.

Real estate: developing buildings in cities

Tim Baines
John Bowman
Dewey & LeBoeuf

1. Introduction

"It was a town of machines and tall chimneys, out of which interminable serpents of smoke trailed themselves for ever and ever and never got uncoiled."
[Charles Dickens, *Hard Times*, 1854]

The environmental impacts of our cities have been acknowledged and legislated against for hundreds of years. Though London's recent initiatives addressing the energy use of buildings and climate change have been grabbing the headlines, the burning of coal was temporarily outlawed in London as far back as 1306 because of the pollution it caused. In 1909, more than 1,000 people died in Glasgow because of smog. Fifty years later, the English eventually caught up with the Scots when, in 1952, 4,000 people were killed by a week of London's "killer fog".[1]

1.1 More than just air

Since the Industrial Revolution, air pollution has stood out among the environmental impacts traditionally associated with urban environments. More recently, legislators have implemented legislation in respect of contaminated land and water in order to combat some of the negative environmental impacts of our cities.

Many of these "traditional" environmental issues are still highly relevant to cities in both developed and developing nations. However, the ever increasing prominence of climate change has caused the discussion to evolve. The recognition of the need to mitigate and adapt to climate change has led to a focus on energy use by cities and, in particular, the buildings of which they are composed.

1.2 The environmental impacts of buildings and cities

Buildings generally (not just in cities) consume 40% of the world's energy and account for one-third of greenhouse gases.[2] Cities are estimated to account for 75% of the world's energy use and greenhouse gas emissions from buildings to account for around 50% of cities' carbon dioxide emissions. In New York and London, this figure is more likely to be 70%.[3]

Cities are a significant contributor to climate change. Redressing their impacts at

---

1   "Bad Air Days – air pollution in the United States", *The Environmental Magazine*, November 1999 by April Reese.

2   www.reuters.com/article/ousiv/idUSN1618928020070517.

3   www.ethicalcorp.com/content_print.asp?ContentID=5238.

a global, regional and local level has the potential significantly to reduce the man-made causes of climate change. The application in Europe of more stringent standards to new and existing buildings could by 2010 reduce energy consumption by more than one-fifth of present levels and carbon dioxide emissions by up to 45 million tonnes per year.[4]

According to the United Nations Environment Program (UNEP),[5] better architecture and energy savings in buildings could do more to fight global warming than all limits on greenhouse gases agreed upon under the UN's Kyoto Protocol. However, more surprising is that studies have shown that energy efficiency improvements in buildings can be achieved at no net cost, or even at net financial gain.[6]

At this point, any debate about whether to act to reduce the climatic impacts of the buildings that surround us should have ended. The objective must now be to review the measures that have already been successfully implemented and "cherry pick" the most effective among them in order to achieve results quickly.[7]

1.3   The approach of this chapter

This chapter begins by introducing the concept of energy efficiency in buildings in order to provide some context to the subsequent discussion. A number of international, national and local responses to the climatic impacts of buildings are then described. This is followed by a more detailed discussion of emissions trading for buildings, documenting the concept of "green" in commercial agreements and the implications of climate change for property leases. Finally, some of the wider policy issues about what kinds of "legal" mechanisms should be used to address the climatic impacts of buildings are discussed.

The focus of this chapter is primarily on those initiatives that relate to the urban environment, particularly in relation to the non-domestic sector. This is because the size and concentration of such buildings and the levels of energy that they consume means that improving their design and fit-out can produce the greatest improvements most readily. However, many of these initiatives are equally relevant to buildings generally, including rural and suburban development.

We have not addressed many other aspects of cities relevant to energy use and climate change, including transportation systems, population density, and land use. Nor have we addressed any of the social, economic and geographic considerations that are relevant to the sustainability of cities.

---

4   Pekka Huovila et al, *Buildings and Climate Change: Status, Opportunities and Challenges*, United Nations Environment Programme (UNEP), 2007.
5   UNEP, *ibid*.
6   AB Vattenfall, Global Mapping of Greenhouse Gas Abatement Opportunities up to 2030, January 2007 and McKinsey & Company, A Cost Curve for Greenhouse Gas Reduction, *The McKinsey Quarterly*, 2007, Number 1.
7   The UK government has put forward a Climate Change Bill which would put into statute the United Kingdom's targets to reduce carbon dioxide emissions, through domestic and international action, to 26% to 32% below 1990 levels by 2020 and to at least 60% by 2050. Reducing the climatic impact of buildings could contribute significantly to this.

2.   What makes a green building?

2.1   Energy phases

UNEP has identified the distribution of buildings' energy use over their lifecycles.[8] These phases are set out below:

- *Phase one:* manufacturing of building materials and components (embodied energy);
- *Phase two:* energy used to transport materials from production plants to the building site (grey energy);
- *Phase three:* energy used in the actual construction of the building (induced energy);
- *Phase four:* energy consumed at the operational phase, for running the building when it is occupied (operation energy); and
- *Phase five:* energy consumed in the demolition process of buildings as well as in the recycling of their parts (demolition recycling energy).

Tackling the climate change effects of buildings must therefore be considered in relation to more than just the construction and operational stages of a building's life.

2.2   Methods of increasing building efficiency

According to the US Green Buildings Council (US-GBC) (see further below),[9] developing green buildings is one of the best strategies for meeting the challenge of climate change because the technology to make substantial reductions in energy and CO_2 emissions already exists. On average, LEED-certified buildings (see subsection 3.2(b) below) use 32% less electricity and save 350 metric tonnes of CO_2 emissions annually. Examples of measures given by US-GBC that can be taken to improve building performance include:

- incorporating the most efficient heating, ventilation and air-conditioning systems, along with operations and maintenance of such systems to assure optimum performance;
- using state-of-the-art lighting and optimising daylighting;
- using recycled content building and interior materials;
- reducing potable water usage;
- using renewable energy;
- implementing proper construction waste management; and
- using locally produced building materials.

2.3   Energy-efficient building models

A number of approaches to characterising the energy efficiency of buildings have been identified.[10]

---

8   Based on David Jones, *Architecture and the Environment*, New York, 1998, The Overlook Press.
9   www.usgbc.org/.
10   UNEP, *ibid.*

(a)   ***Low- and zero-energy buildings***

A distinction can be drawn between green buildings seeking to reduce energy use by 50% of that of a standard building, and those that seek to be zero-energy or "passive" buildings. Low-energy, rather than zero-energy buildings typically rely on traditional building methods, but increased levels of insulation, advanced building material (such as high-performance glass) and ventilation heat recovery systems.

Zero-energy buildings seek to produce as much energy as they consume. This requires a much less traditional approach to building which relies on renewable energy sources, such as solar and wind power, and environmentally efficient design. Energy created by the building can be stored for when it is needed, for example in batteries. Where buildings over produce energy, for example by way of excess solar power generated during the summer, this energy can be sold to national electricity grids. Over producing buildings may be termed "energy-plus" buildings.

(b)   ***Refurbishing buildings***

The principles of construction of new green buildings (eg those outlined in respect of US-GBC above) can equally be applied to refurbishment of buildings. Some building refurbishment initiatives are described below. The approach to refurbishment may also remove or substantially delay the consumption of demolition recycling energy.

(c)   ***Lifecycle performance and assessment***

Particularly in relation to the construction of new buildings, the energy performance of buildings over their useful life can be enhanced by implementing a system that guarantees that buildings meet certain performance standards, including in relation to energy performance. This requires interaction of a number of entities, including developers and construction companies, as well as bodies responsible for monitoring and assessing energy use. We have addressed some of these issues below.

(d)   ***Ecocities***

Where developers have the luxury of developing buildings as part of an entirely new community, it is possible for the concepts underlying green buildings to be addressed on a city- or at least a community-wide basis, in which entire communities are organised on a low-energy use basis.

3.   Responses at international, national and local levels

3.1   International responses

(a)   ***Examples of early international environmental initiatives relating to cities***

Since the 1990s, a number of international initiatives have developed in the field of "sustainable" cities. A discussion of "sustainability" is far beyond the scope of this chapter. Sustainability in the context of urban development encompasses a much wider range of social and economic factors than buildings' energy use alone. Though it may not have been apparent even at the time that all of these initiatives were originally conceived, it is now recognised that energy efficiency of buildings and their climate change impacts goes to the heart of sustainability in the urban environment.

(i)   Sustainable Cities Programme

The Sustainable Cities Programme (SCP) is a joint UN-HABITAT/UNEP programme established in the early 1990s to build capacities in urban environmental planning and management. The programme targets urban local authorities and their partners, and it is founded on broad-based stakeholder participatory approaches. One of the many concerns of this initiative is energy use in buildings. Currently, the SCP and its sister programme Agenda 21 operate in more than 30 countries worldwide. SCP adopts an environmental planning and management approach and supports the efforts that cities make in improving their environments.[11]

(ii)   The European Sustainable Cities and Towns Campaign

The Charter of European Cities and Towns Towards Sustainability, approved by the participants at the European Conference on Sustainable Cities and Towns in Aalborg, Denmark, on May 27 1994 (the Alborg Charter) includes a goal to increase end-use efficiency of products, such as energy-efficient buildings. It is a key policy statement for local sustainable development worldwide and gave birth to the Sustainable Cities and Towns Campaign in 1994.[12]

More than 2,500 local and regional governments from 39 countries have committed themselves to the goals of the Aalborg Charter and any local or regional government from any part of Europe which signs up to the Aalborg Charter automatically become a participant of the Sustainable Cities and Towns Campaign. The project aims to promote urban sustainability in Europe, to encourage the exchange of experience, to disseminate best local practices and to influence sustainable development policy at the European Union, member state, regional and local levels. It also includes a number of "toolkits" to facilitate achieving the Aalborg commitments.

(b)   C40 Large Cities Climate Leadership Group

These early examples of international initiatives aimed at bringing about change in the wider social and environmental aspects of cities serve as an important backdrop to more recent developments that relate very specifically to buildings' effects on climate change.[13]

In May 2007, leaders of municipal governments and international businesses from more than 30 world cities convened in New York for the second C40 Large Cities Climate Summit. The starting point for C40 Large Cities Climate Leadership Group (C40) is that cities are responsible for three-quarters of the world's energy consumption and, as such, the world's largest cities have a critical role to play in the reduction of carbon emissions and the reversal of dangerous climate change.

---

11   www.unhabitat.org/categories.asp?catid=540.
12   www.sustainable-cities.eu/.
13   www.c40cities.org.

It is hoped that through effective partnership working with the Clinton Climate Initiative (CCI),[14] C40 will help deliver emissions reductions and better energy efficiency. Sir Nicholas Stern, former Chief Economist of the World Bank and author of the seminal "Stern Report",[15] has said, *"The C40 Cities Climate Leadership Group is a tremendous idea and a fine example of the different dimensions of international collaboration."* Stern's much-publicised review analyses the potential costs and benefits to humans as a result of climate change. It cites buildings' greenhouse gas contribution as 8% of total emissions in 2000, and touts the potential effectiveness of minimum efficiency standards in diminishing this contribution.

The CCI will provide a range of solutions to the C40 partner cities to help reduce energy use and cut greenhouse gas emissions. These include:

- *Pooling the buying power of cities.* This will help lower the prices of energy-saving products and hasten development and uptake of new energy-saving technologies. The consortium will partner with vendors, leading to lower production and delivery costs and therefore lower prices. Key product categories will include, among others, building materials, systems, and controls.
- *Mobilising expert assistance.* This is intended to help cities develop and implement programmes that will lead to reduced energy use and lower greenhouse gas emissions. Technical help will be provided in different areas, including building efficiency.
- *Create and deploy common measurement tools.* The goal is that cities can establish a baseline on their greenhouse gas emissions, track reductions and share best practice.

(i)   How buildings can help

C40 has identified a number of ways in which buildings can help to tackle energy consumption and to use cleaner energy. They include:

- the use of solar power for buildings;
- creating building regulations, codes and standards that set out effective and realistic changes that make buildings cleaner and more energy efficient;
- carrying out energy audits of buildings;
- retrofitting buildings so as to improve energy efficiency; and
- installing more energy-efficient lighting.

(ii)   Energy Efficiency Building Retrofit Program

During the May 2007 C40 Large Cities Climate Summit, former US President Bill Clinton announced the creation of a global Energy Efficiency Building Retrofit Program,[16] part of the CCI. This brings together some of the world's largest energy service companies, banks and cities and it aims to reduce energy consumption in existing buildings.

It is hoped that the Retrofit Program will provide cities and private building

---

14   www.clintonfoundation.org/cf-pgm-cci-home.htm.
15   *The Economics of Climate Change*, 2007.
16   www.clintonfoundation.org/pdf/051607-cci-fact-sheet-building-retrofit-program.pdf.

owners with access to the funds needed to retrofit existing buildings with more energy-efficient products. Energy savings could be in the region of 20% to 50%.

Honeywell, Johnson Controls, Inc, Siemens and Trane will conduct energy audits, perform building retrofits, and guarantee the energy savings of the retrofit projects. This will provide the information needed by banks so that they can organise financing for the retrofit projects. ABN AMRO, Citi, Deutsche Bank, JPMorgan Chase, and UBS have committed to arrange $1 billion each to finance cities and private building owners to undertake these retrofits. The energy savings achieved by the retrofits mean that this expenditure and the cost of financing will be at no net cost. This initiative is likely to double the global market for energy retrofit in buildings.

(c)   *Sustainable mortgage-backed securities*

In a recent exciting and potentially international development involving green buildings, a partnership of leaders in the capital markets ("the Capital Markets Partnership") is attempting to tackle the priorities needed to stimulate the global economy, stop irreversible dangerous climate change and promote global sustainability by introducing "sustainable mortgage-backed securities" (MBS) into the international mortgaged-backed securities market.

The partnership consists of investment banks, investors, national governments and NGOs. It has completed the due diligence needed to launch sustainable MBS within existing bank operations in the $4 trillion global MBS market. Sustainable MBS are essentially bonds backed by a "pool" of green building mortgages. Investment banks have submitted sustainable MBS due diligence to the rating agencies responsible for rating MBS. If sustainable MBS penetrates the global market for mortgage securitisations, it is hoped that the benefits will stimulate the global economy, improve energy security, and help to prevent climate change by encouraging properties' green credentials.

The success of this initiative may hinge on a recovery from the 2007/8 global "credit crunch" which has blighted the asset-backed securities market.

(d)   *World Green Building Council*

The World Green Building Council (WGBC) was founded in November 1999. As at early 2008 there are 11 country members[17] with 17 emerging Green Building Councils. The WGBC "supports national Green Building Councils whose common mission is to create a sustainable built environment through market transformation".[18]

The WGBC's role is to:
- establish common principles for Green Building Councils (GBCs);
- serve as a global voice on behalf of Green Building Councils;
- support and promote individual Green Building Councils;
- establish clearing for knowledge transfer between Green Building Councils;
- encourage development of market-based environmental rating systems; and

---

17   The current country members are the United States, Australia, Brazil, Canada, Japan, India, Mexico (all founding members), New Zealand, Taiwan, United Arab Emirates and the United Kingdom.
18   www.worldgbc.org/.

- recognise global green building leadership.

The longer-term objectives of the WGBC are to:
- create a global market for green building through the creation of successful national Green Building Councils;
- be the lead global voice for global green building issues;
- represent no less than 60% of the global property industry through countries with Green Building Councils;
- have a dynamic web presence that serves as the pre-eminent portal for global green building news; and
- have collaborative relationships with all other complementary global organisations.

The ability of the Green Building Council movement to influence law and policy as it affects all buildings, commercial and residential alike, should not be underestimated. The Green Building Councils for both the United Kingdom and the United States (UK-GBC and US-GBC respectively, discussed further below) form part of the WGBC network.

(e)   International emissions trading for buildings

One international initiative which, despite its enormous potential to reduce carbon emissions by buildings, has not yet made significant progress is the possible extension of a global emissions trading scheme to include buildings. "Cap and trade" emissions reduction schemes reduce emissions by imposing an artificial "cap" on the amount of emissions that can legally be produced by a particular sector, which is then divided up between individual installations. Usually, installations subject to a cap-and-trade scheme are allocated or have to purchase allowances or permits that entitle them to emit a certain quantity of CO_2 and other greenhouse gases. Where an installation emits less than its individual cap, it will have a surplus of allowances that it can sell to (or "trade" with) other installations that have not performed below their cap.

Until recently, applying this model to buildings has been seen as very problematic. However, a collaborative Position Paper by Lend Lease, Lincolne Scott and Advanced Environmental has attempted to set out a vision of how an emissions trading scheme might work[19] According to their Position Paper, applying emissions trading to buildings has been seen as difficult due to the "split incentives" nature of the industry, pursuant to which it is likely that the entity responsible for developing a building is not its eventual owner, let alone its tenant.

The Position Paper states that a reduction of up to 60% of emissions could be saved using today's technology if an emissions trading scheme for buildings was introduced. It is possible that a scheme, if properly designed, could form part of a post-Kyoto international climate change agreement. The detail of the Position Paper is discussed further below.

---

19   Lend Lease, Lincolne Scott and Advanced Environmental, *Emissions Trading & The Built Environment*, December 2007.

(f)   *EU Energy Performance of Buildings Directive*

The international initiatives described above are voluntary or speculative in nature. However, in 2000, the European Commission released an Action Plan on Energy Efficiency which identified the need for specific measures in relation to buildings. This resulted in the enactment of the European Directive on The Energy Performance of Buildings (EPBD) on January 5 2003.[20] The principal objectives of the EPBD, which applies throughout member states of the European Union, are (i) to promote the improvement of the energy performance of buildings through cost-effective measures and (ii) to promote the convergence of building standards towards those of member states with the highest existing standards.

The EPBD includes provisions setting out a methodology for calculating the energy performance of buildings, the application of performance standards for new and existing buildings, certification schemes for buildings, and requirements relating to inspection and assessment of boilers and heating and cooling installations. The United Kingdom's implementation of the EPBD is discussed further below. However, it has not been entirely successful. On February 28 2008 the European Commission launched court proceedings against Belgium and the United Kingdom for failing to notify adequate national implementing measures to it in respect of the EPBD.

3.2   National responses

(a)   *United Kingdom*

(i)   *General*

Up to 50% of the United Kingdom's overall current energy consumption is associated with buildings, including the energy used to heat buildings and to power the equipment inside them. The present regulation of the built environment is high on the political agenda of the UK government. The effects of various government initiatives have filtered through to the design and construction of environmentally sustainable buildings, including the regulation of energy suppliers in relation to the provision of more efficient technologies to households and business.

(ii)   *UK Green Building Council*

In 2007, the UK Green Building Council (UK-GBC) was launched with a stated mission to *"dramatically improve the sustainability of the built environment by radically transforming the way it is planned, designed, constructed, maintained and operated"*.[21] The impetus for the UK-GBC came about following the 2004 Sustainable Buildings Task Group Report calling for sustainable building advisory bodies to be simplified and consolidated to provide a clear direction for industry.

(iii)   *Better Regulation Commission*

In its report dated February 2007, the Better Regulation Commission (BRC) made a

---

20   www.defra.gov.uk/ENVIRONMENT/energy/internat/ecbuildings.htm.
21   www.ukgbc.org.

number of recommendations including that by the end of 2007 all UK government departments and other public-sector concerns should have developed and implemented a plan for investing in public-sector energy conservation.[22] The BRC also welcomed and noted the current initiatives being developed by the UK government, primarily under the direction of the Department for Communities and Local Government (DCLG), for the development of carbon-zero homes.

(iv)   *Energy Performance Certificates*
The EPBD has been partly transposed into English law by the Energy Performance of Buildings Regulations.[23] Different types of buildings should display one of two types of certificate.[24] Energy performance certificates (EPCs) must be made available whenever buildings of a certain size are constructed, sold or rented. The EPC requirement is being phased in from April 2008. The EPC indicates on a scale of "A" to "G" (with "A" being the most efficient and "G" the least), how energy efficient a property is. EPCs are valid for 10 years and must be accompanied by an advisory report.

Display Energy Certificates (DECs) will be only required for large, public buildings occupied by public authorities or institutions which provide public service to a large number of people. This will include courts, hospitals, stations and schools. DECs need to be displayed and are valid for 15 months. The requirement for DECs comes into effect from October 10 2008. The "public service" requirement of DECs will mean that DECs in particular are likely to have a significant impact on buildings in cities where many public buildings are located.

(v)   *UK planning and building policy*
On December 13 2006, the UK government launched a consultation on a draft supplement entitled "Planning and Climate Change"[25] ("the Climate Change PPS") to *Planning Policy Statement 1: Delivering Sustainable Development* (PPS1). The intention was not for planning authorities to devise their own standards for the environmental performance of individual buildings, since these are set out nationally through the building regulations.[26] Rather, planning authorities in England would consider the environmental performance of proposed developments, taking particular account of the climate the development is likely to experience in its expected lifetime.

The response to the consultation has been the publication of "Planning Policy Statement: Planning and Climate Change Supplement to Planning Policy Statement

---

22   Better Regulation Commission, "Regulating to mitigate climate change – a response to the Stern Review", February 2007. The BRC was formed in January 2006 as an independent body which monitors and challenges the UK government's regulatory activity and provides advice on how to regulate better.
23   Energy Performance of Buildings (Certificates and Inspections) (England and Wales) Regulations 2007.
24   www.communities.gov.uk/planningandbuilding/theenvironment/energyperformance/certificates/displayenergycertificates/.
25   Planning Consultation – Planning Policy Statement – Planning and Climate Change – Supplement to Planning Policy Statement 1, Communities and Local Government, December 2006.
26   PPSs set out the government's national policies on different aspects of land-use planning in England and Wales and explain the statutory provisions and provide guidance on spatial planning matters and urban design issues. The building regulations, on the other hand, set baseline mandatory national standards for the health, welfare, safety and convenience of people in and around buildings and for the reasonable conservation of fuel and power used by those buildings.

1" in December 2007. The Supplement states that planning authorities, developers and other partners in the provision of new development should engage constructively and imaginatively to encourage the delivery of sustainable buildings. Accompanying guidance is currently in the process of being developed.

(vi) *BREEAM*

BREEAM,[27] the world's most widely used environmental assessment method for buildings, helps construction professionals understand and mitigate the environmental impacts of their developments. Its methodology is used in various stages and scales of the construction process, such as during materials manufacture and design, as well as during and after construction. BREEAM products implement the most up-to-date research and technology to reflect changing priorities in regulations and to ensure that BREEAM continues to represent best practice.[28]

Specific BREEAM assessments come in various forms, and can be tailored for offices (both at the design stage and operational stage), industrial buildings and retail complexes, to name a few. The BREEAM assessment process is revised as UK building regulations are updated. It considers various environmental impacts including management, wellbeing, energy, transport, water, materials and waste, land use, ecology and pollution. Credits are awarded to these areas according to performance and buildings (whether new, or being refurbished) are then rated on a scale of "Pass", "Good", "Very Good" or "Excellent".

While still completely voluntary in the commercial building context, the benefits for developers are stated as enhanced marketability (due to, among other things, reduced ongoing operating costs appealing to occupiers), increased investment security and higher rates of return on investment. BREEAM is clearly geared to UK buildings and the UK regulatory environment and is developed as such, although bespoke BREEAM assessments are possible for buildings outside the United Kingdom.

(b) **The United States**

The situation in the United States is little different from that in the United Kingdom. In 2004, total emissions from residential and commercial buildings constituted 38% of total US carbon emissions – more than either the transportation or industrial sectors.[29] In the United States, the growth in green buildings has been largely commercially driven by property developers and construction companies seeking to gain competitive advantage and engage in best-practice sustainable building construction, design and maintenance.

(i) *LEED and US Green Building Council*

American commerce and industry have pragmatically attempted to differentiate themselves from their competitors by adhering to voluntary best practice standards such as the Leadership in Energy and Environmental Design (LEED) green building

27   BRE Environmental Assessment Method, created by Building Research Establishment Limited (BRE).
28   www.breeam.org/.
29   Transport accounts for 33% and industry 29%. Buildings and Climate Change – publication by the US Green Building Council available at www.usgbc.org/DisplayPage.aspx?aspxCMSPageID=1617.

rating system. The green building movement in the United States has largely been attributed to the US Green Building Council (US-GBC). The US-GBC was formed in 1995 and administers LEED. Since that time, the US-GBC has evolved into 75 regional chapters and has a membership of more than 7,500 organisations from a broad range of sectors within the building industry. These have a common purpose to "transform the building marketplace to sustainability".[30]

LEED can be described as the US counterpart of BREEAM. It is the nationally accepted benchmark in the United States for the design, construction, and operation of high-performance green buildings. Like BREEAM, LEED has a rating system of "Certified", "Silver", "Gold" or "Platinum". The key areas of assessment within LEED are human and environmental health, sustainable site development, water savings, energy efficiency, materials selection and indoor environmental quality. LEED is developed and continually refined via an open, consensus-based process which is claimed to have made LEED the green building standard of choice in the United States for federal agencies and state and local governments. In order to earn LEED certification, a building must first meet certain prerequisites and performance benchmarks.

(ii)   *Green Globes*

The "second" US green buildings rating system is Green Globes™. This was brought to the US in 2005 by the Green Building Initiative, a non-profit organisation created to promote green building approaches. Users can gain one to four "globes" for levels of certification with ratings in seven categories, based on a 1,000 point scale. Green Globes is growing in popularity.

3.3   Local state/city specific Initiatives

(a)   **London**

(i)   *London energy policy*

Ken Livingstone, Mayor of London until May 2008 and Chairman of C40, pledged to cut the UK capital's CO2 emissions to 50% of 1990 levels by 2025, 25 years sooner than the government's plan for the rest of the United Kingdom, and by 20% of 1990 levels by 2010. His recent efforts to mitigate the effects of greenhouse gas emissions include: a partnership with London's theatre industry to diminish its emissions;[31] a collaboration with solarcentury, a renewable energy company, to advise boroughs on meeting their targeted emissions reductions;[32] the London Wind and Biomass Study; "Capacity building for planners and others implementing energy-related planning policy in London"; Skills for a Low Carbon London: Summary Report and Recommendations; Investing in London's Low Carbon Future; and more. The Mayor's building, City Hall, is itself a green building.

---

30   www.usgbc.org 'Who we are'.
31   www.london.gov.uk/view_press_release.jsp?releaseid=14179.
32   www.london.gov.uk/view_press_release.jsp?releaseid=8746.

(ii)   *London Climate Change Partnership*

London has identified that climate change will mean that London will experience increasing risks of flooding, overheating and drought. The London Climate Change Partnership (LCCP) was created to help London prepare for these impacts by identifying who and what will be affected, and proposing how to manage these changes.[33] This is an example of local initiatives that have the potential to make an impact on a broader than local scale. It is hoped that where London has taken the lead, other cities in the United Kingdom (and the rest of the world) may adopt similar strategies. As indicated in relation to California below, municipalities, as large landlords and local legislators, have huge procurement and policy development power.

The LCCP's objectives are to:

- embed adaptation to climate change into London policy documents;
- raise awareness of climate risks and opportunities across all sectors;
- commission research and develop adaptation guidance;
- increase the level of adaptation in new developments and existing builds; and
- provide simple information that is accessible for all Londoners.

Whilst these are all examples of London's adaptation to climate change, the pledge to reduce CO_2 emissions is a clear example of a climate change mitigation strategy. Some of the LCCP's other initiatives include the publication of a *Checklist for Development*, providing guidance for local planners and developers, and a *Good Practice Guide for Sustainable Communities*, which provides guidance for local planners.

The LCCP's publications also include *Business as Usual?*, a review of climate risks and opportunities for London's financial services sectors which includes questions and recommendations for the insurance, banking, pension, fund manager, infrastructure and utilities sectors. This approach creates parallels with some of the international infinitives driven by relations between the industry and financial sectors that are discussed above. The LCCP documentation makes it clear that energy use by buildings and climate change issues interact with all levels of society and effect a broad range of stakeholders.

(iii)   *London Climate Change Agency*

The London Climate Change Agency (LCCA)[34] was launched in June 2005 with the remit to work closely with the private sector to tackle climate change. In March 2006, it was announced that EDF Energy had been chosen to work in partnership with the LCCA to promote initiatives that will provide decentralised, more efficient energy supplies for London.

Founding supporters of the LCCA were BP, HSBC, Lafarge, Legal & General, Sir Robert McAlpine, and Johnson Matthey and support has also been provided by

---

33   www.london.gov.uk/climatechangepartnership/.
34   www.lcca.co.uk/.

Corporation of London, Carbon Trust, Energy Saving Trust and the Rockefeller Brothers Fund. The LCCA is receiving substantial support from the Mayor's business arm, the London Development Agency, and UK and global companies.

The LCCA is intended to be a key driving force in accelerating reductions in emissions in London. It will enter into partnerships with private-sector firms to deliver low- and zero-carbon energy projects and services which will be a combination of combined cooling, heat and power, energy efficiency, renewables and other technology in new developments and retrofit projects.

(iv)   *City of London Corporation*

The City of London Corporation,[35] which provides local government services for the Square Mile, has been purchasing renewable energy since the mid-1990s. The City's switch to the green electrical powering of all public buildings and street lighting in the Square Mile has cut its greenhouse gas emissions by 35% since 1997. It has also established the "City Climate Pledge" which aims to encourage City firms to manage their carbon footprints.

The City of London has created its own policy to ensure that its services and infrastructure continue to function well in the face of climate change. On June 8 2007 the City signed the "Nottingham Declaration", a voluntary commitment for local authorities to address the issues of climate change. This act echoed the UK government's leadership of efforts to tackle climate change at the 2007 G8 Summit.

The City of London also takes a keen interest in the role of the City in emissions trading (discussed elsewhere in this book) and has published a report entitled *Emission Trading and the City of London* (September 2006), written by the Consilience Energy Advisory Group. The report looks at the business opportunities offered by emissions trading, ascertains how the market has developed and identifies the next generation of trading opportunities. Further, in partnership with BP, Reuters and Zyen Consulting, the City of London is leading the London Accord, which is an investigation into the economics of solutions to climate change.

(v)   *London Accord*

The London Accord[36] has brought together teams from leading investment banks and research houses to publish a wide-ranging series of papers relating to the evaluation of investment opportunities in potential solutions to the impact, and mitigation, of climate change. It is a collaborative initiative and shares insights into the approaches and methodologies of leading investment researchers, measuring links between investment, finance and "carbon" returns, and it illustrates how to understand interactions between public policy and investment decisions.

---

35   www.cityoflondon.gov.uk/Corporation.
36   www.london-accord.co.uk.

(b)   *State of California*

(i)   *Green buildings*
The State of California has taken a leading role in the implementation of local green buildings strategies, and it exemplifies the ways in which large public bodies with great purchasing power and policy implementation capacities are able to implement energy efficiency strategies in a progressive manner.

Governor Schwarzenegger launched a Green Building Initiative in late 2004 and has committed California to improving the energy and environmental performance of existing and new state-owned buildings. This relates to the facilities it owns, leases, retrofits or maintains. Executive Order S-20-04 ("the Green Building Order") called for reducing electricity consumption in state buildings 20% by 2015. Reaching that goal will include a combination of benchmarking the energy efficiency of state buildings, and retro-commissioning and retrofitting facilities to ensure that energy systems are operated as efficiently as possible.

The Green Building Order invokes the LEED standards described above. California is pursuing LEED New Construction certification for its major construction and renovation projects and is seeking LEED Existing Building certifications for existing facilities in order to ensure energy-efficient building operations and maintenance practices. California is also encouraging and enabling schools built with state funds to be resource and energy efficient.

(ii)   *Green procurement in buildings*
In recognition of the fact that buildings and energy use relate to more than just the physical infrastructure of buildings, California state law requires state government to practice environmentally preferable purchasing. State buyers have a responsibility to buy products that give California the best value and source "environmentally preferable" products which are long lasting, of high quality, less toxic, reusable and easy to recycle, and which use fewer materials, water and energy, minimising the impact on California's natural environment.

In the context of buildings, this strategy extends to a carpet policy. California purchases 12 million square feet of new carpet each year. A purchasing policy called the "California Gold Sustainable Carpet Standard", requires companies selling carpeting to the state to ensure it contains at least 10% recycled fibre. Suppliers must ensure that old carpet fibres get recycled at specialised facilities and be certified by a third party as a maker of environmentally friendly and sustainable carpets.

4.   Legal and regulatory policy aspects of developing green buildings

4.1   Emissions trading for buildings
Emissions trading, discussed elsewhere in this book, continues to be central to the global approach to combating climate change. It is a market-driven model which is thought to allow emissions of greenhouse gases to be reduced at the point of least cost by the entities that have most control over their emissions. Emissions trading is also seen as a less burdensome alternative to taxation. It has been proposed that

emissions from buildings, until now not included in any emissions trading regime, could also be reduced in this way.

Emissions trading in respect of buildings could be introduced at an international, national or local level, and could potentially be incorporated into existing emissions trading schemes such as the EU Emissions Trading Scheme (though there are no current plans to do so). Though a number of voluntary emissions trading schemes have been successful, if emissions trading is to be implemented in an effective manner on a large scale, it is likely to require a formal legislative framework of some kind.

The model emissions trading scheme in respect of buildings suggested by Lend Lease, Lincolne Scott and Advanced Environmental (referred to above in subsection 3.1(e)), if implemented, could represent a milestone in the ability of developers and occupiers of buildings to contribute to combating climate change. This would have a particularly significant effect in cities, where the majority of large commercial buildings are located.

(a)   *How the scheme would work*

The scheme would work by differentiating between "permits" for design savings and "offsets" for operation emission savings. Green buildings councils would be used to monitor and verify emissions. According to the published Position Paper, design savings of buildings and systems such as lighting, heating and cooling can be assessed independently of climate, tenant and maintenance issues and do not vary year on year for a given building. Operational emissions relate to the energy sources that are selected and do vary year on year.

(b)   *Permits for design savings*

The details of the proposed scheme are thin. However, it is suggested that permits would be generated and allocated in respect of the construction of buildings. These permits would be allocated by independent verification organisations. Penalties would be set to encourage compliance and emitters would offset emissions in order not to pay a penalty.

It is not clear from the Position Paper how the level of a building's allocation of permits would be calculated. It is certainly envisaged that the permits would be traded in a market. However, it is unclear which entity would be responsible for compliance with this obligation. This could, for example, be the developer, the construction company or even the architect. It appears that this scheme would only work on a one-off basis – for instance in the year of construction of the building.

(c)   *Offsets for operational use*

The Position Paper then suggests that at an operational level each building would be allocated with a "business as usual" baseline by way of energy modelling. Each building would need to demonstrate an improvement on the baseline. Improvements in efficiency of a building's energy use appear then to be intended to result in the generation of offset credits. It is also acknowledged that adjustments would need to be made to take account of weather and tenant variances. Nationally consistent baselines and methodologies would need to be set for the regime to be implemented globally. Again, it is not clear which entity would be responsible for compliance with the scheme, but this could be the tenant or some other entity with operational control of a building.

Though many details of the proposed schemes remain to be elaborated on, they do provide a starting point for a policy discussion going forward.

4.2 So what does "green" mean?

Peter Britell and Smita Korrapati[37] have addressed many of the issues raised elsewhere in this chapter in relation to the difficulties of developing green buildings. They describe the importance of "green" issues for developers, architects, construction companies, lenders and tenants who are engaging in real-estate development projects. Some key areas of concern when dealing with these problems in the context of legal documentation are set out below.

(a) Identifying the relevant green standard

As discussed above, there are already a number of different "green" standards that are applied to buildings. Further, these codes are in a state of constant evolution. It is therefore important to refer to a reference date or version that defines exactly what standard is being applied to any development. Different entities involved in a development project may rely on different standards. Attempts should therefore be made at the initiation of a project to minimise the number of different standards that will be applied by different project-affected parties – even, or especially, where they are located in different jurisdictions. This will minimise the difficulties in dealing with inconsistencies in requirements, reduce the potential for disputes, minimise design costs and reduce legal fees.

(b) Consequences of defaults

Once counsel for all parties to a development have ensured that they have articulated the correct green rating standard in agreements affecting their clients, they must define their client's obligations with respect to that standard and consider what the consequences would be for their client if such standard was not met. For example, the consequences of failing to meet the condition of obtaining a green standard could be catastrophic for a developer. The development may lose funding, financing or tax credits. It may also fail to secure a certificate of occupancy, a document issued by a local government which states that the building is legally ready to be occupied. The development may lose a major tenant if a condition to lease commencement is not achieved. Where green standards are imposed in the contractual relationships between parties, a failure to comply with such consent may result in the termination of a lease, acceleration of a loan, and/or the foreclosure of a mortgage or damages.

---

37   "What does 'Green' mean?", *New York Law Journal, Trends in Real Estate and Title Insurance*, Monday June 11 2007.

(c)   *Monitoring implementation*
Britell and Korrapati rightly identify the need for constant monitoring of green standards during the implementation of a development, in part due to the relative novelty of green standards. This also needs to be implemented in legal documentation.

4.3   **The effects of climate change impacts and energy efficiency on parties to leases**
Property owners and investors, and others involved in the management or occupation of property, must also consider the impact of climate change and energy use on the leasing arrangements for buildings which are already let, or which they intend to let, and which may be occupied for a number of years to come.

Not only does the property industry need to reduce the effects of its buildings on the environment; it must also consider how to deal with the converse issue: what happens when the environment begins to have an adverse impact on buildings? What issues should owners and occupiers be considering?

(a)   *Existing leases*
Some of the primary issues relating to leases of existing buildings are:
- Who is, or should be, liable to carry out any necessary works in respect of adaptation to and mitigation of climate change, and who is, or should be, liable to pay for them?
- Can and should a landlord be entitled to either require tenants to repair, pursuant to their lease covenants, or charge the tenants via service charge for the cost to the landlord doing so?
- Do existing leases permit recovery of costs from tenants? Has one or more of the tenants negotiated exceptions or carve-outs? Has a tenant excluded, for example, capital expenditure or expenditure relating to work which is not in the nature of "repair" (eg where the item in question is not in disrepair (as legally defined) but its operational effectiveness is reduced or even prevented by the effects of climate change)?
- If there is no "disrepair", and no other relevant provision can be found within the leases' service-charge regime, do the insurance provisions provide any assistance? It is unlikely that most of the effects of climate change – other than those causing dramatic and immediate harm by a conventional insured risk such as flood – would be governed by a traditional lease provision relating to insured risks.
- If the situation becomes serious, could the landlord be liable for breach of the covenant for quiet enjoyment, nuisance or "derogation from grant", if the tenant's ability to occupy the property is significantly affected and the landlord fails to take reasonable steps to try and minimise the impact?

(b)   *New leases*
There are also a number of concerns which parties looking to lease or occupy property should seek to address in any new lease:
- Should buildings be required to meet certain green standards?

- Should landlords have the ability (at their discretion or with the agreement of the tenant (not to be unreasonably withheld?)) to "upgrade" buildings or plant and machinery to certain green standards?
- Could or should it be assumed that certain standards have been met at the point when rents are being reviewed?
- What will happen at rent review for leases in older buildings over the course of the next two or three review phases? If the market becomes sufficiently segregated, older buildings may start to be let at a discount.
- Should the landlord have the right to carry out significant works (notwithstanding who pays for them), which might be disruptive over a long period of time? What about quiet enjoyment – should there be an exception for work required to meet green standards, especially if this is to ensure the comfort or safety of occupiers or to meet other "worthy" objectives?
- What controls will tenants have? They will be concerned that their employees and visitors could be affected by a (sick and) tired building. These concerns (and others) will be weighed up against the cost implications of any course of action.
- With increasing numbers of tenants expressing a desire, or even a requirement, that the buildings they occupy should meet certain green standards (eg by reference to energy efficiency or one of the other standards such as BREEAM), are we heading towards a two-tier market where modern, environmentally-friendly and efficient buildings attract higher rents than buildings of traditional construction and operation?

It is not yet clear how the above questions will be dealt with, and it will take time for market practice to develop in these areas.

4.4   Wider legal policy issues

The area of green buildings remains relatively new and undiscovered from a legal perspective. New because, as we have seen, the energy use of buildings in cities has only recently become a mainstream issue of concern; undiscovered because the complicated web of law, guidelines and regulations relevant to this area has only recently been developed. Further, much of the progress that has been made in "regulation" of this area has been driven by non-legal codes, guidance and practice, many of which remain in their infancy.

It is clear that that there is now a plethora of initiatives at international, national and local levels relating to energy use by buildings. It is likely that this trend will continue to shape the development of cities and the buildings that they comprise over the coming years and that the existing range of initiatives will increase rather than reduce. However, is this constant promulgation and evolution of initiatives helpful? And what are the drawbacks of relying on largely voluntary initiatives?

(a)   New challenges created by relying on voluntary action

With a few exceptions, including the EPBD, regulation of climate-change-related "regulation" of buildings in cities has been driven by the voluntary sector. Where legislative bodies, such as the State of California and the Greater London Authority, have addressed this issue, they have often turned to voluntary codes such as LEED and BREEAM, in order to facilitate their implementation.

This voluntary approach is a clear break from traditional forms of law-making. The voluntary approach brings with it both advantages and disadvantages. These generic issues are shared with a number of other global initiatives which are not directly related to climate change.[38]

Advantages of relying on voluntary initiatives include increased speed of take-up, the ability for membership criteria to be inclusive and non-prescriptive, as well as flexibility and pragmatism of approach which is unconstrained by the fear of formal legal sanctions. This often leads to the rapid development of a "critical mass" which allows voluntary initiatives to become market standard.

The challenges posed by voluntary initiatives include the dangers of people not adopting the "spirit" of the initiative and instead engaging in "greenwash" (discussed further below at subsection 4.4(h)), the abuse or flagrant violation of standards that do not provide recourse to formal legal sanctions, and the presence of entities that deliberately do not adhere to voluntary standards in order to gain a competitive advantage over their peers.

(b)   *Lack of scrutiny of green building standards*
Green building councils and the standards that they promulgate are increasingly being turned to by traditional legislators. Where a regulation is passed by a local government that requires, for example, all public buildings to meet a specified green building rating, this effectively incorporates the relevant green building standard into local law. Whilst the legal act that imposes the requirement will be subject to scrutiny, the underlying green building standards are not promulgated by organisations that are subject to the same standards of transparency and accountability as traditional legislatures. Instead, they are usually implemented by representatives from industry and experts in the field. Further, there is a risk that modifications to underlying green building standards are subject to less scrutiny than changes to "traditional" laws.

(c)   *Scrutiny of green building compliance officers*
A separate but related issue is that, in professionals being accredited as qualified to monitor and review green building standards by Green Building Councils, those councils are increasingly playing a role traditionally reserved, in the United Kingdom at least, for branches of local government. Such professionals are likely to be subject to scrutiny and sanction of the relevant GBC, but may not be scrutinised by the authority that has imposed a particular standard.

As the importance and role of GBCs increase, these are issues that are likely to become increasingly important. The situation that has effectively been created can

---

38   Parallels can be drawn between some of the problems relating to the implementation of the Equator Principles in project finance transactions. These were discussed in detail in Banking on Responsibility, Part 1 of the Freshfields Bruckhaus Deringer *Equator Principles Survey 2005: The Banks*.

be characterised as self-regulation by the construction industry. This is an example of how the development of voluntary standards has led to a blurring of the traditional distinctions between private and public legal systems. The acceptability of this approach may be called into question with time, especially as green building criteria move from optional to mandatory.

(d)   *Need for qualified and expert personnel*
Related to this issue is the need for properly qualified and trained personnel to implement green building criteria. Whilst it may be a worthy ambition to implement green building requirements throughout a state, region, or even an entire country, this will rely on being able properly to fund and implement qualification and training procedures. This will in turn lead to a debate about which entity is best placed to pay for such measures. Environmental regulation and enforcement has traditionally been a cost born by local and national government, but it may be that in the future these costs are pushed through to the private sector.

(e)   *Green buildings are only part of the equation*
Much of the approach to tackling the issue of the effects of buildings on climate change has been focused on the development of green buildings themselves. As already noted, the role of buildings, though highly significant, is only part of the wider issue of the sustainability of cities. There is a danger that in focusing on energy use by buildings, some of the broader and equally significant issues may be overlooked. A green building may in itself be "green", but if it is located away from public transport, far from the residences of the people that will be occupying it, or managed and used in an unsustainable manner, its "green" credentials will be compromised.

A number of other issues are potentially highly relevant to the carbon footprint and wider sustainability of a green building. For example, does the furniture that will be used adhere to recognised environmental criteria? Is all wood used from sustainable sources? Is the off-site energy that will be consumed from renewable sources? What standards or codes should be adhered to in respect of these issues? How sustainable will recycling and energy consumption practices be? Who will monitor their implementation?

(f)   *Confusion*
The issues identified above are a potential source of great confusion for owners and occupiers of green buildings. As yet there is unfortunately no universally recognised approach to analysing and responding to all of these concerns in a coherent manner. It still remains extremely difficult and expensive to review the entire supply chain of the many separate elements that constitute a working building. Little progress has been made in finding a solution to this issue.

(g)   *Risk of being undermined by less scrupulous developers*
The risk of new and potentially complex initiatives being undermined by unscrupulous participants in a market is present in any regulated environment. However, it is particularly important that, where standards are being implemented in

a manner that relies extensively on voluntary initiatives, less scrupulous developers are not able to thrive by promoting cheap, inefficient buildings which offer all of the physical comfort and amenities of green buildings. This could potentially undermine some or all of the progress made by more progressive developers. However, it is difficult to legislate against this phenomenon where the state is relying on voluntary actions as the dominant legal framework.

(h)   *Greenwash*
A further difficulty linked to the implementation of voluntary initiatives is the accusation of "greenwash". Companies should be aware that in attempting to set themselves apart from peers by participating in carbon reduction initiatives, they are likely to attract increased scrutiny by environmental and civil society organisations whose attention they may have previously escaped. Organisations should be wary of making unintentionally misleading statements about the "green" credentials of their buildings, especially where, for example, they also operate other buildings that are far from green. As with all sustainable development reporting, enthusiasm must be tempered by the ability to rely on properly verified facts about the whole of an organisation's activities.

5.   Conclusion
Over the coming decades, buildings, particularly those in the urban environment, are well placed to play a significant role in combating climate change. Their current contribution to global greenhouse gas emissions is staggering. The scope for efficiency gains is such that many improvements can be made at no net cost, even when using existing technology. Further, tenants of buildings are increasingly prepared to pay a premium for "green" buildings which offer a reduced carbon footprint.[39]

It therefore seems incredible that, far from taking a constructive lead, traditional legislators, with a few exceptions, appear to have been entirely overtaken in the development of approaches to tackling buildings' climatic impacts by a plethora of non-governmental, non-binding initiatives driven by the private sector. Further, those legislators that have chosen to address this area have relied on green building standards and practices developed, for better or for worse, by commercial entities that remain outside of governmental scrutiny.

The use of voluntary mechanisms appears to have many advantages. Initiatives such as C40 and the Clinton Climate Initiative have developed innovative solutions that traditional law-makers are unlikely ever to have conceived. Further, their ability to circumvent the slow pace and bureaucracy of traditional legislatures has allowed for faster responses to be implemented.

These advantages have, until now, outweighed some of the disadvantages of "legislating" in a way that risks being subject to reduced scrutiny and which relies on self-governance by the commercial sector. Traditional law-makers have, until now, been incapable of devising a regime which, as is necessary, intervenes at local,

---

39   *CBI/GVA Grimley Corporate Real Estate Survey Winter 2007/2008.*

regional, national and international levels and which calls on the vast array of professional resources that are needed to tackle the climatic impact of buildings in cities.

However, now that the commercial sector has developed a seemingly workable approach to tackling the issue of buildings' energy use, traditional legislators may be required to intervene. One reason is that only traditional legislators have the power to impose a regime with real consequences for entities that choose to breach their obligations. This will be necessary if energy efficiency standards are to reach full implementation, particularly when the point is reached at which efficiency improvements will represent a net cost to building development. A second reason is that it will be impossible in any event for some "traditional" areas of the law, such as leases and construction and development contracts, not to confront some of the new issues posed by green buildings.

It must be hoped that governments will act quickly to capitalise on the apparently "easy win" of addressing the climatic impact of buildings in cities. The front door is wide open.

The authors would like to thank Nathan Rees, Edan Rotenberg and Joshua Cohen for their much valued help and contributions to this chapter.

Carbon sequestration

Juliette Addison
John Bowman
Paul Q Watchman
Dewey & LeBoeuf

"We have no choice but to succeed in developing [carbon capture and storage] CCS ... no matter how much effort we put into the development of renewables, oil and gas will continue to be our most important source of energy for years to come. That is why CCS is so important. We quite simply have to make it more environmentally friendly to use oil, gas and coal. Nothing less is sustainable."

Mrs Aslaug Haga, Norwegian Minister of Petroleum and Energy, March 5 2008[1]

1. Introduction

Sequestration is the term used to describe the removal of carbon dioxide (CO_2) from the atmosphere by carbon sinks such as the forests,[2] oceans[3] and soil.[4] This process has regulated the planet's climate since its beginnings. The more recent concept of carbon capture and storage (CCS), which refers to the artificial extraction of CO_2 from industrial processes and its permanent storage underground or under or into the seabed, has, however, provoked strong opinions on both sides of the climate change debate. On the one hand, CCS has been heralded as one of the most significant weapons available to combat climate change without having to change behaviour drastically in the short term. On the other, it has invited scorn from those who consider it to be a (currently) prohibitively costly, unproven and potentially unsafe distraction from other, more established greenhouse gas (GHG) mitigation

---

1   From an open hearing in The European Parliament, Brussels, March 5 2008 (see www.regjeringen.no/en/dep/oed/The-Ministey/Aslaug-Marie-Haga/Speeches-and-articles/2008/ccs-projects-in-norway.html?id=502599).

2   As trees photosynthesise and grow, CO_2 is removed from the atmosphere. However, as a forest becomes more mature, comprising a mix of old and young trees, it may still absorb more CO_2 than it emits above ground, but the organic matter it has deposited on the forest floor (humus) will slowly release CO_2 to the atmosphere or, indeed, it may be transferred to the soil by organisms which encourage decomposition. Forest fires and deforestation release CO_2 back into the atmosphere; the former, immediately, the latter depending upon the purpose of the deforestation (eg if for combustion for energy, then that release will be shortly after the trees have been cut down but if for timber to construct homes, it may be decades or centuries before the timber decays and releases CO_2 to the atmosphere).

3   It has been said that if all the CO_2 in the atmosphere were sequestered to the ocean, it would only raise the average concentration of CO_2 in the ocean by about 1.2% (see M Markels and T Barber (2001), "Sequestration of CO_2 by Ocean Fertilization", Poster Presentation for NETL Conference on Carbon Sequestration, p 6). Approximately one-third of anthropogenic emissions is estimated to be entering the ocean (see further, T Takahashi, SC Sutherland, C Sweeney, A Posson, N Metzl, B Tilbrook, N Bates, R Wanninkhof, RA Feely, C Savine, J Olafsson and YC Nojiri (2002) "Global sea-air CO_2 flux based on climatological surface ocean pCO_2, and seasonal biological and temperature effects", *Deep Sea Research* II, p 49: 1601 to 1622).

4   Soils contain more carbon than in global vegetation and the atmosphere combined. CO_2 is sequestered in soils as humus (see n 3 above). Several variables affect carbon stocks in soil and the potential for soil to sequester carbon including temperature, precipitation and the soil's chemical and physical properties.

measures. Further, critics have noted that CCS technology faces legal obstacles, economic constraints and, perhaps most worrying of all, the risk that leakage of CO_2 could, in a worst-case scenario, unravel previous CO_2 reductions and cause damage to ecosystems and organisms, including human beings.

2. Approach in this chapter

In this chapter, we will identify the different types of CO_2 sequestration and will briefly discuss the technologies available. Secondly, we will consider the current status of CCS projects around the world, the role of CCS as one of a portfolio of climate change mitigation options and the issue of leakage of CO_2, the likelihood of such leakage and its potential impacts. Thirdly, we will identify the key commercial/financial and legal challenges that need to be addressed at national, regional and international level to enable CCS to contribute effectively to GHG abatement in the near term. Finally, we consider the future of CCS.

3. What is sequestration and what is CCS?

As discussed above, sequestration may take place naturally by the uptake of CO_2 by "carbon sinks" or, secondly, by artificial means. CCS falls within the category of artificial sequestration, as does deep ocean injection.[5] There is a third category of sequestration in which artificial techniques are used to enhance natural sequestration: these include ocean fertilisation[6] and mineral sequestration.[7] Both techniques require considerably more research and development to ensure their economic and environmental viability as CO_2 mitigation strategies and so are beyond the scope of this chapter.

---

5   Deep ocean injection refers to the injection of fluid CO_2 to ocean depths greater than 1,000 metres via tailpipes from ships or the deposit of solid blocks of CO_2 into the ocean. Recent developments in international law which prohibit the injection of CO_2 into the water column combined with the inclusion of CCS in such international instruments suggest that CCS technology (rather than some of the other artificial or enhancement-of-natural-sequestration techniques set out in this chapter for example) is the preferred capture technique in future (for further, see sections 9.1(b) and 9.1(c) below).

6   Ocean fertilisation refers to the addition of iron (although other nutrients such as nitrates, phosphates and silica may also be added) to low-cholorophyll ocean waters which are deficient in such nutrients to stimulate the growth of "blooms" of phytoplankton. This leads to a consequent increase in the quantities of CO_2 sequestered from the atmosphere by such phytoplankton via photosynthesis. When the plankton die, they sink to deeper waters where they are either eaten by animals and bacteria or settle on the ocean floor. It is reported that such sequestered CO_2 on the ocean floor will remain for around 1,600 years (for further, PM Williams, and ERM Druffel (1987) "Radiocarbon in dissolved organic carbon in the central North Pacific Ocean", *Nature*, pp 246 to 248, p 330, cited at p 3 of M. Markels and T Barber T (2001)).

7   Mineral sequestration is the reaction of CO_2 with various minerals to form solid, geologically stable carbonates which permanently isolate CO_2 – this process occurs naturally over hundreds of years. Recent technology aims to expedite this by adding crushed olivine or serpentine to CO_2 from one or more power plants in a carbonation reactor until the desired level of carbonation is achieved. A further advantage of the technology is that the raw materials necessary (eg magnesium-based minerals) are readily available. However, whilst the process gives off heat and produces carbonated minerals and residue, both of which add value and could offset the costs of sequestration, the heat produced is low grade and difficult to recover. Also, to quicken the rate of reaction, high pressures and temperatures are required (which are costly). For further, see P Goldberg, C Zhong-Ying, W O'Connor, R Walters and H Ziock, "CO$_2$ Mineral Sequestration Studies in US", undated, see www.netl.doe.gov/publications/proceedings/01/carbon_seq/6c1.pdf.

CCS refers to the capture and separation (whether before or after combustion)[8] of CO_2, its compression and transport to a storage location and then its injection for the purposes of permanent disposal into suitable geological formations. Such formations may be onshore (as in the United States and Canada in the context of acid gas injection) or offshore (more likely to be the case in Europe) and may include depleted oil and gas reservoirs, deep saline formations and unmineable coal seams.[9] Such formations may also partly extend beneath both the onshore and offshore territory of a state (a hybrid formation) as in Australia.

CO_2 is injected at sufficiently high pressures and depths (more than 800 metres) to ensure that it becomes (and remains) a supercritical fluid. Supercritical fluids diffuse better than ordinary gases or liquids and occupy considerably less space than gases or liquids. Once injected, there are various trapping mechanisms which operate to prevent the CO_2 from escaping.[10]

The injection of CO_2 has been carried out, principally in the oil and gas industry, on a small scale for longer than 30 years in order to augment the amount of these fuels that can be recovered from reservoirs (known as enhanced oil/gas recovery (or EOR or EGR respectively)).[11] For example, in the United States, the Permian Basin, West Texas, contains the greatest concentration of EOR projects worldwide and Petrochina Company Limited (a subsidiary of China National Petroleum Company (CNPC)[12]) has implemented several EOR research projects since the 1960s.It is understood that 30% to 60% or more of a reservoir's original oil can be extracted using EOR.[13]

---

8   Pre-combustion CCS technology is commonly used in the production of fertilisers and hydrogen; separation is easier due to the higher concentrations of CO_2 in the gas stream and the high pressure applied. Post-combustion CCS refers to the capture of CO_2 after combustion of the fossil fuel, usually using a liquid solvent. This is the technique which would be applied to existing power plants (ie where CO_2 would be removed from the flue gases). Post-combustion CCS technology is largely understood and established. Another technique is called oxyfuel combustion, where nearly pure oxygen is used for combustion instead of air, resulting in a flue gas which is almost pure CO_2. Other technologies (such as capturing CO_2 directly from the atmosphere) are still in the early stages of development.

9   CO_2 storage in basalt and oil shale formations is also possible but more research and development is required in this area before this becomes a viable alternative. For example, India's National Geophysical Research Institute is currently testing its feasibility.

10 These operate simultaneously and also on different timescales to keep CO_2 trapped underground. They include: physical trapping of CO_2 below an impermeable layer of rock (caprock); hydrodynamic trapping (in saline formations, CO_2 dissolves in brine and then migrates from the storage site); mineral trapping (CO_2 reacts with the minerals in the storage formation and caprock to produce stable carbonates (for artificial enhancement of mineral sequestration, see above n 8)); and adsorption of CO_2 onto organic matter in coal and shale. Interactions between these various mechanisms are complex, evolve with time and are highly dependent upon local conditions. For further, see Intergovernmental Panel on Climate Change, IPCC *Special Report Carbon Dioxide Capture and Storage; A Special Report of Working Group III of the Intergovernmental Panel on Climate Change*, Sections 1,6.3, 5.2.2, 5.7.3.4, Table 5.5 (see http://arch.rivm.nl/env/int/ipcc/pages_media/SRCCS-final/IPCCSpecialReportonCarbondioxide CaptureandStorage.htm).

11 Enhanced coal bed methane (ECBM) refers to the use of CO_2 to enhance the recovery of the methane present in unmineable coal beds through the preferential adsorption of CO_2 on coal. In this chapter, EOR, EGR and ECBM will be referred to in aggregate as EOR.

12 CNPC netted $27 billion in 2007: see Reuters, "China's Largest Oil Producer nets $27 Bln profit", April 7 2008, see www.ibtimes.com/articles/20080407/cnpc.htm.

13 See US Department of Energy, www.fossil.energy.gov/programs/oilgas/eor/index.html.

3.1 Who is taking the lead?

CCS has some influential advocates, internationally[14] (especially in Canada,[15] Australia,[16] the United States[17]and China[18]). There has recently been increased media scrutiny on climate change, and CCS has drawn the attention of a wide variety of stakeholders, ranging from those in the commercial research and development spheres through to prominent political supporters of CCS, such as the EU Commission, the Council of the European Union,[19] the Norway and United Kingdom (UK) governments and, more recently, countries as diverse as Poland,[20] the Netherlands[21] and Algeria.[22]

---

14   2007 marked the tenth anniversary of the Carbon Sequestration Program, in the United States, a collaboration between the US Department of Energy, Office of Fuel Energy and National Energy Technology Laboratory, which focuses on developing both core and supporting technologies. It aims to develop by 2012 techniques which capture 90% of CO_2 achieving 99% permanence at a less than 10% increase in the cost of energy services (for further, see US Department of Energy, Office of Fuel Energy and National Energy Technology Laboratory, *Carbon Sequestration Technology Roadmap and Program Plan 2007*, at p 5). Also, the Carbon Sequestration Leadership Forum, established in 2003, is a voluntary climate initiative of developed and developing nations that accounts for around 75% of all manmade emissions.

15   For example, the Canadian Prime Minister recently announced a collaboration between the federal government and the state of Saskatchewan to combine state-of-the-art carbon capture technology with EOR and carbon sequestration to reduce Canada's GHG emissions annually by a million tonnes whilst generating up to 100 megawatts of clean power (see SK Estevan, "Canadian PM announcement on CCS", March 25 2008, see www.pm.gc.ca/eng/media.asp?category=1&id=2036).

16   The first geosequestration project in the southern hemisphere was launched in the state of Victoria, Australia, in March 2008 (see P Mercer, "Australia to begin carbon capture", April 2 2008, see news.bbc.co.UK/1/hi/world/asia-pacific/7325782.stm). Also, early indications suggest that Australia's equivalent of the Stern Review will recommend the making of "substantial commitments to support private research, development and commercialisation activities related to carbon capture and storage by established coal-based electricity producers ..." (Garnaut Climate Change Review Interim Report to the Commonwealth, State and Territory Governments of Australia, p 51, see www.garnautreview.org.au/CA25734E0016A131/WebObj/GarnautClimateChangeReviewInterimReport-Feb08/$File/Garnaut%20Climate%20Change%20Review%20Interim%20Report%20-%20Feb%2008.pdf). This report is expected to be released in September 2008.

17   Various states in the United States are in the process of enacting/amending existing laws in order to govern CCS. For example, the first laws establishing a regulatory framework for CCS were signed by the Governor of Wyoming (March 3 2008). House Bill 89/HEA 18 recognises that surface owners control the underground pore spaces where CO_2 could be stored or sequestered and House Bill 90/HEA 25 conferred upon the Wyoming Department of Environmental Quality the authority to regulate the long-term storage of CO_2.

18   China has prioritised CCS as a key research area in important, national research and development plans as follows: (i) China's Scientific & Technological Actions on Climate Change; (ii) Medium & Long-Term Science and Technology Plan of China; (iii) State High-Tech Program (863) R&D Project; and (iv) China's National Climate Change Programme.

19   At the Council's Spring meeting on March 14 2008, the Council put forward guidelines for future workstreams with particular emphasis upon the importance of the legal framework for carbon capture and storage.

20   Poland, a country with large coal reserves, recently announced its ambition to develop CCS technologies (see UCL, Faculty of Laws, "Poland and the Netherlands signals on CCS", March 19 2008, see www.ucl.ac.UK/cclp/ccsnews.php).

21   A pilot post-combustion capture plant was launched in April 2008 in Rotterdam by CATO, a national €25 million public/private research partnership into clean fossil fuels. The plant is fitted adjacent to a 1040MW coal-fired plant run by E.ON and will sequester around six tonnes of CO_2 daily (see R Van Noorden, "Dutch power ahead with carbon capture", April 4 2008, see www.rsc.org/chemistryworld/News/2008/April/04040802.asp).

22   For example, see the In Salah storage CCS project in Algeria, which is attached to the production of natural gas (the carbon content of natural gas from In Salah is around 4% to 9%, but needs to be less than 0.3% to enter the European market). There is a joint venture between Statoil, Sonatrach (the Algerian National Oil & Gas company) and BP. For further information, see www.opec.org/home/Press%20Room/EU-OPEC%20presentations/HaddadjiSonatrach%20Algeria.pdf.

Commercially, CCS is being explored as a necessary option both by companies individually[23] and acting in partnership (eg the CO_2 Capture Project in the United States,[24] the Integrated CO(2) Network in Canada[25] and the Cooperative Research Centre for Greenhouse Gas Technologies in Australia[26]). Current operation of commercial-scale[27] CCS projects is limited, the most prominent being CCS storage projects at: (i) Sleipner West, off the coast of Norway (which has operated since 1996 and is the oldest carbon storage project in the world);[28] (ii) Weyburn, Saskatchewan, Canada (operating since 2000); and (iii) the In Salah storage project in Algeria (2005). More recently, commercial-scale CO_2 storage projects have been planned for Gorgon, Australia (to commence operations from 2008 to 2010); Carson, Southern California (2009); Draugen, off the coast of Norway (2010); and Mongstad, Norway (a test centre is scheduled to be in place in 2011 with a full-scale CCS project operational in 2014). Smaller demonstration projects have been undertaken at Nagaoka, Japan,[29] Frio, Texas,[30] the K12-B gas field offshore from the Netherlands[31] and, most recently, a former gas field near Warrnambool, west of Melbourne, Australia.[32]

Politically, many governments appreciate the potential of this new technology, not just as a climate change mitigation option (see below), but also as a major industry which has the potential to create high-skilled employment and generate wealth. Some commentators have cited CCS as a parallel industry to the whole fossil fuel industry with an estimated world market of £150 billion per year.[33] Similarly, another commentator recently predicted that construction of CCS plants alone could become a $1.5 to $2 trillion per year business, as important globally as the construction of oil platforms.[34]

---

23   Energy and utility companies Statoil and Chevron Texaco as well as Shell, Schlumberger, Anglo Coal, Rio Tinto and Petróleos Mexicanos (the state-owned Mexican petroleum company) have all been linked to CCS research and development. The Swedish utility Vattenfall, Europe's fifth largest generator of electricity is an investor in the prestigious Norwegian Mongstad project (see above) and recently confirmed that it "cannot meet our target of cutting emissions by 50% by 2030 without [CCS]" (Staffan Gortz, head of communications for CCS projects, March 12 2008, "Vattenfall says it needs carbon capture to hit CO_2 cut goals", see Dow Jones & Company, Inc. *Dow Jones International News*.)

24   This is a joint project comprising eight of the world's leading energy companies, including Chevron Texaco, ENI, Norsk Hydro ASA and Shell. It aims to develop new technologies to reduce the cost of capture from combustion sources and safely sequester it underground by means of research, developing guidelines for maximising safe geological storage and actively transferring and making available new technologies. The US Department of Energy and the European Commission also are involved. For further, see www.co2captureproject.org/contacts/contactsP2.htm.

25   Known as ICO(2)N, this is a proposed system for large-scale CCS in Canada and it has a wide range of participating companies including Opti Canada Inc, Suncor Energy Inc, Syncrude Canada Ltd, Imperial Oil Ltd, Conoco Phillips and Canadian Natural Resources Ltd. For further, see www.ico2n.com/

26   Known as CO2CRC, this is an unincorporated joint venture of Australian and global industry, plus Australian academics undertaking leading research into CCS technologies amongst other things. Participants include CSIRO, Xstrata, Stanwell Corporation Limited, New South Wales Department of Primary Industries and the Australian Government. For further, see www.co2crc.com.au/about/

27   Meaning projects which each capture and store approximately 1 million tonnes of CO_2 per year.

28   Some 7.5 million tonnes has been stored to date.

29   See uregina.ca/ghgt7/PDF/papers/nonpeer/273.pdf.

30   See uregina.ca/ghgt7/PDF/papers/nonpeer/574.pdf.

31   See uregina.ca/ghgt7/PDF/papers/peer/534.pdf.

32   See "Australia to begin carbon capture", April 2, 2008 at n 18 above.

33   N MacErlean "How Europe can Seize the Market in Carbon Capture", *The Observer*, May 6 2007.

34   J Acher, "Saudi, Norway back carbon capture for CDM", February 18 2008, see www.reuters.com/article/ELECTU/idUSL1831690120080218?sp=true.

There also appears to be a "race to CCS" in terms of demonstrating a full-scale project and, as a global leader, exporting such technology to other countries (particularly the developing world). The United Kingdom launched its long-awaited competition to develop the country's first commercial-scale demonstration of CCS using post-combustion capture on a coal-fired power station providing at least 300MW of energy in November 2007[35] and aims for operations to commence between 2011 and 2014. In the European Union, the Commission committed to substantially increasing the funding for demonstration of CCS, making it a major priority for 2007 to 2013.[36] The Commission proposed that all new coal-fired power plants built in the European Union after 2020 should include CCS or be "capture ready" for the later addition of CCS[37] and, to this end, supported the bold industry initiative established in 2006 by several major coal-using energy companies which aims to have 10 to 12 demonstration CCS projects in place by 2015.[38] The United Kingdom has sponsored various projects overseas (including the near Zero Emissions Coal initiative (nzec)[39] with China) and has formed alliances with other countries with interest in CCS (eg Norway). Equally, the European Union has set up the CCS Cooperation Action initiative within China–EU–UK (the COACH project).[40] In light of the above, it is easy to see why the Norwegian Prime Minister has spoken of his country's efforts related to CCS as Norway's "moon-landing project".[41]

4. How can CCS contribute to climate change mitigation?

4.1 Current position

"What does it mean to be rich? It means you can travel, have heating or cooling systems and motive power, and all in great luxury. All depends on purchasing cheap energy. All depends on having access to cheap energy ... Now think about what it would mean to be rich without access to energy. Let me spell it out: no access to transport, to driving fine cars or

---

35   The competition is coordinated by the Department for Business Enterprise and Regulatory Reform (BERR), the UK Government department responsible for business relations and energy issues. BERR has indicated that the demonstration project will need to run for at least 15 years in order reliably to demonstrate the full chain of CCS technologies (although this is subject to discussion with bidders). Applications for the pre-qualification stage of the UK demonstration project closed on March 31 2008. RWE npower confirmed that it would enter the competition as leader of a consortium of companies (BOC, Cansolv Technologies Inc., IM Skauge, The Shaw Group Inc. and Tullow Oil plc) and E.ON, Scottish Power and Scottish and Southern Energy have all expressed interest. Reportedly, at least one major petroleum company abandoned a CCS project into which it had invested considerable funds, due to the delays in the launch of this competition. For further information, see www.berr.gov.UK/energy/sources/sustainable/carbon-abatement-tech/ccs-demo/page40961.html.

36   Communication from the Commission to the Council and the European Parliament, Sustainable power generation from fossil fuels: aiming for near-zero emissions from coal after 2020, January 10 2007 (COM (2006) 843 final), paragraph 3.1 at p 6.

37   See Communication from the Commission, January 10 2007, n 39, paragraph 3.2.

38   The Zero Emission Fossil Fuel Power Plant Technology Platform (see www.zero-emissionplatform.eu/website/).

39   Intended to address the challenge of tackling increasing GHG emissions from the use of coal in China (see www.nzec.info/).

40   COACH aims to develop and demonstrate near-zero coal emissions technology in China and the European Union via CCS technology. The last two phases of the programme are to design a demonstration plant during 2008 to 2010 and to construct and operate the demonstration plant during 2010 to 2014.

41   See Norwegian Minister of Petroleum and Energy, n 2.

indeed to any flying, to cooking – no air conditioning in Southern Europe in summer or heating in winter in Northern Europe."
Dr Eddie O'Connor, CEO of Airtricity[42]

The above illustrates the inextricable link between energy and wealth. Developed countries, and now, increasingly, developing countries and emerging markets, have taken or are taking for granted the standard of living guaranteed by a continuous and cheap energy supply. This is one of the reasons why CO_2 emissions have increased by more than 20% since 1997[43] and are forecast to reach nearly two-and-a-half times the current levels by 2050.

This is unlikely to change in the short to medium term. However, two factors have recently forced developed countries to reconsider the above position. First, the need (accepted as necessary by most governments, civil society and the scientific and industrial communities) to tackle climate change rapidly by reducing GHGs, especially CO_2 emissions, domestically and internationally. Second, the need to ensure a secure, reliable and diversified energy supply, a goal highlighted with increasing regularity by politicians, industry associations and non-governmental organisations (NGOs) alike, is a pressing concern of developed as well as emerging markets and developing countries. Rising energy prices and demand – oil prices having recently reached the previously unimaginable price of $120 per barrel[44] (and may well still continue to rise) – coupled with the "politicisation of energy supply"[45] has forced energy-dependent nations to reconsider their energy policy, and there are increasingly instances of energy-producing countries appearing to use this as a means of exercising influence over their consumer countries.[46] This is especially the case for the United Kingdom, which is increasingly reliant upon oil and gas imports having ceased to be energy self-sufficient some time ago.[47]

4.2 International, regional and national responses
National and regional responses to the first challenge include the European Union's unilateral targets first to reduce EU GHG emissions by at least 20% by 2020[48] and, second, to ensure that 20% of the European Union's energy comes from renewable

---

42 Address by Dr Eddie O'Connor, CEO of Airtricity at the European Energy Forum Dinner/Debate in the European Parliament, September 12 2006.
43 International Energy Agency (IEA), "Legal Aspects of Storing CO2", 2007, p 12.
44 AFX News Limited, Rigzone News, "Oil Hits New Records As Supply Fears, Weaker Dollar Fuel Buying," April 15 2008 see www.rigzone.com/news/article.asp?a_id=60237.
45 Referring to the greater reliance by high-energy-using countries upon supplies of oil and gas from politically less stable parts of the world.
46 For example, Russia is a major supplier of oil and gas to many EU countries including several "energy islands" (ie countries such as Estonia, Latvia and Lithuania, which are entirely dependent upon energy from Russia). In the 1990s, Russia provided most other ex-Soviet states with subsidised energy. However, Russia's recent attempts to charge market value for its natural resources have led to disputes with several states, culminating in January 2006 with it cutting off of gas supplies to Ukraine. For further, see news.bbc.co.UK/1/hi/world/europe/5167062.stm
47 Historically, the United Kingdom met its energy demands using coal, oil and gas obtained from the rich reserves of the North Sea.
48 Endorsed by the European Council in March 2007. The Council also endorsed an EU objective of a 30% reduction in GHG emission by 2020 provided that other developed countries would commit themselves to comparable emission reductions and economically more advanced developing countries would contribute adequately according to their responsibilities and respective capabilities.

sources (currently only 8.5%)[49] by 2020 and, third, to increase energy efficiency by 20% by 2020. The European Council reaffirmed that developed countries should collectively reduce their emissions by 60% to 80% by 2050 compared to 1990. Similarly, the United Kingdom has set its own ambitious domestic goals, including targets to reduce CO_2 emissions by 26% to 32% by 2020[50] and by at least 60% by 2050.[51]

Notwithstanding the fact that "climate change and energy security [are]... the two greatest energy challenges we face",[52] it is evident that the world's voracious appetite for fossil fuels for energy and industry is not one which can be curbed overnight. Policymakers recognise that the transition to a low- (or no-) carbon economy, based on energy obtained from renewable, non-fossil sources will be a slow and gradual one. This is evinced by the fact that coal demand is actually expected to increase its share of the global primary energy market from 41% to 43% by 2030. Even the United Kingdom, which is attempting to position itself as a "green leader", as demonstrated by its pioneering UK emissions trading scheme, its landmark Climate Change Bill[53] and its commitment to renewables and energy efficiency, still uses coal, oil and gas to satisfy around 90% of its current energy demands.[54] Further, it is estimated that by 2020 the majority of the United Kingdom's energy will still be supplied by fossil fuels.

4.3   CCS as one of a portfolio of GHG mitigation options

It is recognised that no single technology option will provide all the emission reductions necessary to achieve stabilisation of GHG concentrations and, equally, no single source of energy will provide security of supply while ensuring a reduction in GHG emissions. There is broad consensus that a portfolio of (existing and emerging) climate change mitigation options is the most effective and least expensive way to reduce CO_2 levels. Such options would include greater energy efficiency in industry, buildings and transport together with increased use of renewable energy (eg wind, hydro, biomass, solar, wave and tidal), nuclear power[55] and fuel switching to low or zero carbon technologies (eg from coal to gas).

---

49   See EU Commission, Press Release: "Boosting Growth and Jobs by Meeting Our Climate Change Commitments", January 23 2008.

50   See Climate Change Bill [HL] 2007/8, Bill 97, 54/3, Part 1, Clause 6 (1)(a).

51   See Climate Change Bill, *ibid*, Part 1, Clause 2(1).

52   Department for Business Enterprise & Regulatory Reform, *Meeting the Energy Challenge: A White Paper for Nuclear Power*, January 2008, paragraph 20, p 16.

53   The Bill aims to enshrine into statute long-term CO_2 targets which should be achieved over shorter periods of time (five years, beginning with 2008 to 2012). The Bill proposes to create a new independent body to manage the United Kingdom's carbon budget targets (the Committee on Climate Change), which will, amongst other things, have a specific role in reporting on progress. Finally, the Bill will be used to support emissions reductions through specific policy measures – for example, implementation of the carbon reduction commitment and a mandatory cap-and-trade scheme covering energy use emissions from large, non-energy-intensive organisations.

54   See *Meeting the Energy Challenge*, n 58, paragraph 4.02 at p 105.

55   The UK government recently agreed with the recently published fourth report of the Intergovernmental Panel on Climate Change (IPCC) that "nuclear power could have a role to play alongside other low carbon energy sources in reducing carbon emissions" (see *Meeting the Energy Challenge*, n 58, paragraph 54 at p 187). It also estimates that existing nuclear power stations save between 5% and 12% of the United Kingdom's total CO_2 emissions (compared with fossil-fuelled power stations) and that ruling out nuclear power would increase the risk of failing to meet the United Kingdom's long-term carbon reduction goal (see *Meeting the Energy Challenge*, n 58, p 18).

CCS has been identified as one of the portfolio of climate change mitigation options and a key weapon in the battle against climate change. CCS would contribute to security of energy supply since it would allow fossil fuels, especially coal, to remain a key part of the energy mix in a carbon-constrained world. In addition to reducing CO_2 emissions and leading to improved local environmental quality, it is argued that CCS would also result in greater economic efficiency and competitiveness.

CCS, once deployed on a commercial scale, represents a way to reduce GHG concentrations rapidly and (crucially for some nations) without necessarily having to change behaviour in the short term. Some estimate that CCS could be responsible for a global reduction in GHG emissions of up to 27% by 2050 and of 25% to 30% in the 27 EU member states by 2030 (as against 2000). Equally, in the United Kingdom, it is estimated that CCS might reduce emissions from fossil fuel power plants by as much as 90%. Most importantly, the Intergovernmental Panel on Climate Change (IPCC) report has confirmed that 50% to 90% of the global CO_2 emissions reductions needed until 2100 to stabilise concentrations of CO_2 at 450 ppm will come from CCS.

As to where the CO_2 will be stored, various stakeholders appear confident that not only do suitable rock formations for CCS storage exist throughout the world, but that they also offer a large capacity compared with current need.[56] The EU Commission concluded in January 2008 that, broadly speaking, there is enough storage capacity for each EU member state to store its own emissions, provided that the optimistic estimates made regarding aquifer storage potential were borne out.[57] Although it is difficult to state with certainty, it is thought that capacity exists to store several decades' worth of current global CO_2 emissions (approximately 30 Gt CO_2/year). The IPCC gives an estimated range of the economic potential for the cumulative global reduction of emissions from CCS in this century of 220 to 2200 Gt CO_2.[58] By comparison, current EU ETS emissions are of the order of 2 Gt CO_2/year.[59]

Of course, such predictions may well be adjusted in future years, due to the fact that geologists have only recently started estimating the storage capacity of geological formations and that their techniques are still relatively new. Second, and more important, the above predictions are based on the assumption that the CO_2 will be permanently isolated from the atmosphere (ie that there will be no short- or long-term leakage of the stored gas), which we shall discuss in greater detail below.

---

56   For example, see International Energy Agency, *Geologic Storage of Carbon Dioxide – Staying Safely Underground*, January 2008, p 11.

57   Commission of the European Communities, Commission Staff Working Document – Accompanying document to the Proposal for a Directive of the European Parliament and of the Council on the geological storage of carbon dioxide, Impact Assessment, COM (2008) X final, January 23 2008 (the draft CCS Directive Impact Assessment) see p 5.

58   See IPCC, *Special Report Carbon Dioxide Capture and Storage: Summary for Policymakers: A Special Report of Working Group III of the Intergovernmental Panel on Climate Change*, n 11 above, paragraph 19, p 12.

59   Commission of the European Communities, Commission staff working document accompanying document to the Proposal for a Directive of the European Parliament and of the Council amending Directive 2003/87/EC so as to improve and extend the EU greenhouse gas emission allowance trading system, Impact Assessment, SEC (2008) 52, January 23 2008, paragraph 3.5, p 49 (the draft EU ETS Directive Impact Assessment).

5. Leakage

Leakage of CO_2, at whichever stage of the CO_2 chain, and whether gradual or sudden, refers to the release of CO_2 back into the atmosphere, thus undermining the effectiveness of CCS as a global climate-change mitigation measure. Consequently, it is important that any regulatory framework ensures that zero (or, more realistically, minimal) leakage is permitted to occur via stringent site selection, characterisation, monitoring, reporting and verification procedures (see section 9.7 below).

CO_2 leakage from a storage site may result in two types of damage. Environmental, health and safety damages refers to the *local* damage which CO_2 leakage may have upon the environment, ecosystems and human beings it may come into contact with. A sudden and large leak of CO_2 could damage marine and terrestrial ecosystems (leading to acidification of groundwater and/or the ocean, as applicable) and, if its concentration were to exceed 7% to 10% in the air,[60] would pose immediate danger to ecosystems and organism life and health (as evidenced by the 1,700 human fatalities at Lake Nyos, Cameroon in 1986).[61]

The second type of damage has a more *global* effect and refers to the reversal of local and/or global efforts to reduce atmospheric CO_2 levels (we shall refer to this as climate change damage). This form of damage is particularly serious, as it may lead to GHG stabilisation targets being jeopardised without any warning. Further, as CO_2 does not respect national boundaries, poor management and/or monitoring of storage sites in one country could negate in whole or in part previous GHG mitigation measures taken diligently in another country. Such climate change damage would require regulators to trace and (depending upon how CO_2 credits are dealt with under emissions trading schemes (see section 8 below), reclaim any credits generated for stored CO_2 or require surrender of credits in respect of leaked emissions perhaps decades or centuries after their original grant. Such an exercise could potentially be administratively difficult or even impossible if, for example, the original beneficiary of the credits had ceased to exist at the date of the leak.

Supporters of CCS including the IPCC argue that, based on current experience, properly selected and managed storage sites are "very likely"[62] to retain more than 99% of stored CO_2 for longer than 100 years and are "likely"[63] to exceed 99% over 1,000 years. Such proponents of CCS cite examples such as the CCS project at Weyburn where, since 2001, about 2 million tonnes of CO_2 have been injected in combination with EOR and where, so far, no leakage has been detected.[64] Also, it is argued that, by analogy with oil

---

60   CO_2 normally comprises only around 0.04% of the air in the atmosphere.

61   On August 12 1986, a large cloud of CO_2 emitted from Lake Nyos in Cameroon (which is located in the crater of a volcano) swept through a local village killing 1,700 people and thousands of cattle by asphyxiation.

62   "Very likely" means a probability of between 90% and 99% (see IPCC, *Special Report Carbon Dioxide Capture and Storage: Summary for Policymakers: A Special Report of Working Group III of the Intergovernmental Panel on Climate Change*, n 11 above, paragraph 25 at p 14.

63   "Likely" means a probability of between 66% and 90% (see IPCC, *Special Report Carbon Dioxide Capture and Storage: Summary for Policymakers: A Special Report of Working Group III of the Intergovernmental Panel on Climate Change*, n 11 above, paragraph 18 at p 12).

64   See International Energy Agency, "Legal Aspects of Storing CO_2" n 48 above, 2007, p 17. Equally, various commentators have, over the years, looked to the largest demonstration of sub-seabed CO_2 storage (Sleipner) and noted that there has not been any leakage of injected CO_2 (see Rob Arts et al, "Recent Time-Lapse Seismic Data Show No Indication of Leakage at the Sleipner CO_2 Injection Site", *Proc. Seventh Int'l Conf. Greenhouse Gas Control Techns* (WW Rubin et al, eds, 2004)).

and gas storage operations, the risk of CO_2 migration is low. This is countered by the view that there is insufficient data from CCS projects to support or deny these assertions.[65]

Local and climate change damages could have a number of causes, including mechanical failure (eg a pipe weakened by corrosion) or seismic activity (eg an earthquake or volcanic eruption). What is certain is that, according to several studies, leakage rates must be less than 0.01% per year to be acceptable to all IPCC emissions scenarios[66] and that leakage rates of more than 1% per year will be costly for future generations.[67]

6. The challenges to CCS

As stated above, CCS has the potential, combined with other climate change mitigation measures, to facilitate a gradual shift towards a future fossil-free society. Further, the commitment of global governments, multilateral organisations, some sectors of industry and other stakeholders to CCS is evident and growing. However, before it can be deployed on a wide scale, there are several commercial or financial, legal and technical barriers which need to be addressed. We shall consider the most significant of these below.

7. Financial incentivisation of CCS

CCS is a technology which has been, and still is, almost exclusively driven by political concerns over climate change and diversification of energy supply (save in the very limited case of EOR, where sequestration has been driven by commercial factors as discussed above). This is a view that is even recognised by the European Commission.[68] Consequently, as there is currently no strong, independent commercial rationale for CCS, some forms of incentivisation are critical to encourage current and prospective operators in CO_2-intensive industries (such as power generation) to install CCS technology into existing plant ("retrofitting") and/or constructing new plant with such technology.

This lack of investor and operator appetite for CCS is compounded by several factors. First, whilst elements of the technology (eg capture and transportation) are well established in small-scale operations (eg EOR), there is no experience on a large scale[69] of the entire process (from capture and compression, through to the transport, injection and geological storage) from start to finish. Considerable investment in research and development (estimated at around €1 billion between now and 2020 by the European Commission, based on industry estimates) will need to be spent to "up-scale" CCS technology to cope with the large volumes of CO_2 which would be required for its commercial application.[70]

---

65   For example, see Matt Elkington, "Taking the Long View", July to August 2007, *Environmental Finance*.
66   For example, see RP Hepple, SM Benson (2002): "Implications of surface seepage on the effectiveness of geologic storage of carbon dioxide as a climate change mitigation strategy", *Proceedings of the Sixth International Conference on Greenhouse Gas Control Technologies* GHGT-6, September 30 – October 4 2002, Kyoto Japan, Vol 1, pp 261 to 266, J Gale and Y Kaya (eds).
67   For example, see Greenpeace, Submission to HM Treasury Consultation on Barriers to Deployment of Carbon Capture and Storage, undated (see http://www.hm-treasury.gov.UK/media/2/A/carbon_16_greenpeace.pdf).
68   See draft CCS Directive Impact Assessment, n 64 at paragraph 2.3(61), p 21.
69   See n 29 above for "large scale" definition.
70   See Communication from the Commission to the European Parliament, the Council, the European Economic and Social Committee and the Committee of the Regions – *Supporting early demonstration of sustainable power generation from fossil fuels*, COM(2008)) 30 final, SEC(2008) 47, SEC(2008) 48, COM/2008/0013 final, paragraph 2, p 4.

Second, the high initial capital costs (CAPEX) of retrofitting CCS technology into existing power plants (or constructing new power plants with such technology) means that is it proving to be economically unviable and prohibitively expensive. Such CAPEX costs are likely to add €70 per tonne of CO_2 to the cost of power generation. Third, the higher operating costs (OPEX) of such CCS technology are also a powerful deterrent. The principal such cost is the additional energy that is required to capture and compress the CO_2 (known as the "energy penalty"). This is illustrated by the fact that a power plant with CCS uses between 10% and 40% more energy than a plant of equivalent output without CCS. A connected concern is that the cost of oil and gas prices has recently spiralled (with a commensurate effect upon the cost of the electricity which is needed for CCS processes). Thus, the energy penalty is two-fold.[71] The counterargument offered by proponents of CCS is that, with a concerted research and development and demonstration effort, the costs of CCS may be reduced by 50% between now and 2020, which will necessarily encourage commercial deployment.[72] Further, such CAPEX and OPEX costs are expected to decrease further thereafter, as know-how and economies of scale take effect.

Finally, the lack of financial incentives is perhaps the most commonly cited reason for poor CCS uptake. Several countries (eg Australia) have provided state funding for CCS demonstration projects. Whilst the UK government has made it clear that its single demonstration project will receive some funding[73] (as has the European Commission for its 12 to 15 demonstration projects), the Commission has also stated conclusively that no subsidy for the technology in the post-demonstration phase will be forthcoming in the European Union.[74]

Therefore, the most powerful incentive for power generators and energy-intensive industries is likely to be the recognition of CCS under the EU Emissions Trading Scheme which, at the time of writing, has been proposed and appears to be imminent. This is discussed further below.

8. EU Emissions Trading Scheme (EU ETS)

The EU ETS has been described as the spearhead and "one of the most important instruments" of EU climate policy due to its ability to achieve absolute emission reductions in an economically efficient manner.[75] Unlike "command and control" type, state-imposed mechanisms, the EU ETS is a market-based mechanism which aims to secure emission reductions at the lowest possible cost wherever and however it is cheapest to do so. This is exemplified by the fact that EU installations may

---

71 It is reported that several stakeholders, including those in energy-intensive industries and those who gave contributions via an internet consultation on the EU ETS review website, expressed concern over the possible impact on the price of electricity of the inclusion of CCS into the EU ETS (see draft EU ETS Directive Impact Assessment, n 67 above, at p 226, see http://ec.europa.eu/environment/climat/emission/pdf/com _2008 _16_ia_en.pdf)).

72 See Communication from the Commission, to the European Parliament et al. – *Supporting early demonstration of sustainable power generation from fossil fuels*, n 79, p 4.

73 See BERR, *Project Information Memorandum – Competition for a Carbon Dioxide Capture and Storage Demonstration Project*, November 19 2007, paragraph 2.7, see www.berr.gov.uk/files/file42478.pdf

74 See draft CCS Directive Impact Assessment, n 64 above, January 23 2008, p 5.

75 European Commission, *Proposal for a Directive of the European Parliament and of the Council amending Directive 2003/87/EC so as to improve and extend the greenhouse gas emission allowance trading system of the Community*, COM(2008) 30 final, January 23 2008 (draft EU ETS Directive).

acquire credits generated outside the European Union under the Clean Development Mechanism (CDM) and Joint Implementation (JI) to meet their allowance caps. By constraining a previously free activity (emitting CO_2), the EU ETS has, since January 1 2005, "put a price on carbon".

8.1   Current position

The EU ETS is regulated by Directive 2003/87/EC of the European Parliament and of the Council of October 13 2003 establishing a scheme for greenhouse gas emission allowance trading within the Community and amending Council Directive 96/61/EC (the EU ETS Directive).[76]

The EU ETS Directive is currently subject to a review pursuant to Article 30. This process resulted in the publication of a draft legislative proposal by the Commission for a directive amending the EU ETS Directive (the Draft EU ETS Directive),[77] which is now being debated by the Council and European Parliament. One of the issues being considered is how to recognise CCS activities in the EU ETS. Various options have been proposed including: first, annual crediting of the installation which stores the CO_2 less the "energy penalty"[78] (the crediting option). Some commentators suggested the creation of a new CCS credit which would be distinct from existing EU ETS credits, but would be fungible for trading on the EU ETS. This option has three principal disadvantages: first, the administrative and practical difficulty of recovering credits in the event of seepage of some of the stored CO_2, especially if such seepage took place years or decades after the original CCS credits were granted. Second, this option would create a value for captured CO_2 and so could actually encourage greater production of CO_2 from activities currently outside the EU ETS – something of a perverse incentive. Finally, the creation of a new type of credit (a CCS credit) would add considerable delay and complexity to this area.

A second option was considered which comprised treating stored CO_2 as not having been emitted at all, therefore obviating the need for the surrender of (and also, the crediting of) any allowances in this respect (the neutral option). Of course, in the event of leakage (as above), the operator would be required to submit a suitable number of allowances as at the date of the leak (with the same difficulties as set out above).

A further factor which needs to be considered, regardless of whether the crediting or neutral option is adopted, is the treatment of installations which use CO_2 for EOR. It could be argued that by recovering more oil or gas (or coal-bed methane as applicable), ultimately more CO_2 directly[79] and indirectly[80] will be emitted to the atmosphere. Consequently, there is an argument to suggest that, under the crediting option, the number of credits earned for the stored CO_2 should be reduced by the energy penalty for EOR. Equally, under the neutral option, there is a strong argument that CO_2 credits in respect of direct and indirect emissions from EOR will need to be

---

76   OJ L 275, 25.10.2003 pp 32-46.
77   See draft EU ETS Directive, n 84.
78   See section 7 above.
79   For instance, the process of EOR requires considerably more energy to be expended than oil, gas or coal-bed methane recovery without EOR.
80   Via the eventual combustion (whether for energy or industry) of the additional recovered oil, gas or coal-bed methane as a result of the EOR process.

surrendered (an exception from the general principle that stored CO_2 will not be treated as emitted).

Currently, all elements of the CO_2 chain (capture, transport and storage) can be "opted in" under Article 24 of the EU ETS Directive. This approach confers all the risk and liability for emissions upon one installation rather than separating such liability to installations throughout the chain. At the time of writing, only the United Kingdom has decided to opt-in for CCS during Phase II (2008 to 2012).

Therefore, the current and default position is that emissions which are captured and safely isolated from the atmosphere are neither recognised as credited nor as not emitted under the EU ETS. We shall consider below recent proposed changes which will significantly impact upon the attraction to operators, investors and incumbents of the EU ETS.

8.2   First line of incentivisation?

The EU ETS internalises the true environmental cost of burning fossil fuels and, as mentioned above, puts a price on carbon. As a corollary, therefore, the recognition of CCS under the EU ETS would, if adopted, also create a value upon the permanent isolation of CO_2 from the atmosphere via CCS.

Recently, a first step towards internalising the principal externality of CCS deployment (ie its reduction of CO_2 emissions) has been taken. The Commission's draft proposal for a directive amending the EU ETS Directive,[81] published on January 23 2008, made two important amendments affecting CCS for the (proposed) Phase III period of the EU ETS (from 2013 to 2020).[82] It fell short, however, of making CCS mandatory by 2020 (discussed further at section 9.13 below).

First, if the proposal is accepted as drafted, installations carrying out the capture, transport and geological storage of GHGs shall be expressly included in Annex I to the draft EU ETS Directive (which lists the installations which are subject to the EU ETS). If passed, this will replace the unsatisfactory and ad hoc "opt-in" status quo under Article 24. Second, in order to provide the necessary incentives for geological storage of emissions, installations using CCS technology will not be required to buy and surrender allowances in respect of emissions stored in geological formations.[83] Instead, emissions which are stored using CCS will be treated under the EU ETS as not having been emitted (ie the adoption of the neutral option). Of course, in the event that any CO_2 were to escape from a storage site, the operator would have to purchase allowances under the EU ETS to cover the leakages. It should be noted, however, that the European Union is not adopting the same approach for CCS[84] as it has for low-carbon technologies, which it wishes to encourage by granting free allowances (eg as proposed from 2013 under the EU ETS for Combined Heat and Power).

Although in the period 2013 to 2020 very few CCS projects will be operational,[85]

---

81   See draft EU ETS Directive, n 84.
82   The draft EU ETS Directive has not yet been formally accepted and therefore the length of Phase III may change.
83   See draft EU ETS Directive, n 84 above, January 23 2008, Recital 16.
84   See draft EU ETS Directive, n 84 above, January 23 2008, Article 10(a)(2).
85   See draft EU ETS Directive Impact Assessment, n 67 above, paragraph 3.5.4, p 50.

the above two amendments will encourage greater investor confidence in CCS technology as they provide greater certainty and a clearer signal to the market as to the future of CCS in the EU ETS.

Other proposed material changes to the EU ETS under the draft EU ETS Directive are also likely to increase demand for CCS. These include the end of national allocation plans in favour of an EU-wide cap which will impose much tighter limits upon permitted emissions, an end to free allocation (which will only be permitted in limited circumstances of "carbon leakage" (ie energy-intensive industries relocating to areas which are subject neither to mandatory caps on emissions, nor mandatory CCS)) and restricted recourse to non-EU-generated credits. These, if successfully passed, will impose greater upward price pressure on carbon allowances in Phase III. It is highly likely that the power sector will be forced by the above amendments to consider CCS deployment more seriously, as it is proposed that installations in this sector will be required to purchase by way of auctioning 100% of their allowances from 2013 onwards (there will be no free allocation).[86] For this reason, it is not surprising that other energy-intensive industries (such as the steel and cement sectors) have already expressed interest in exploiting the abatement potential of the CCS.[87]

Finally, as at the time of writing, there are strong indications that the EU ETS will be extended to other sectors[88] and other gases (such as perfluorocarbons emissions from the aluminium sector and nitrous oxide from the production of nitric, adipic and glycoxalic acids). Currently, we are not aware of any other GHG (save for certain exceptions)[89] being sequestered under geologic formations and understand that such practices are in their infancy. However, it does suggest that, in time, all six GHGs will be permitted to be permanently stored in geological sites. This will necessitate detailed consideration, beyond the scope of this chapter, as to whether such injection of other GHGs, whether alone or mixed with CO_2, will breach waste regulations. Further assessment will be needed to consider how these GHGs behave under high pressure within geological formations; the effect they will have upon geology around the storage site; how they will react with *in situ* minerals; their solution velocity; and the effects of exposure to elevated concentrations of these GHGs in the biosphere.

8.3 Clean Development Mechanism and Joint Implementation

There is a substantial body of opinion including support from DEFRA, BERR, 50 large UK industries and several NGOs[90] and the Norwegian Government,[91] that the Kyoto

---

86   The reason given for this is because the power sector is largely insulated from external competition (and therefore will be immune from "carbon leakage") and will be able to pass on the full opportunity costs of having to acquire such credits to its consumers.

87   See draft EU ETS Directive Impact Assessment, n 67 above, Annex I, Agenda Item 7, p 181.

88   For instance, CO_2 emissions from petrochemicals, ammonia and aluminium industries.

89   Natural gas, which contains methane (which is a GHG), has been sequestered under geologic formations in jurisdictions including the United States and the United Kingdom. Acid gas (which may contain methane) has also been sequestered, particularly in the United States.

90   For example, on March 6 2007 these disparate parties issued a Manifesto for the EU-ETS, including a call for CDM and JI projects to be eligible for EU ETS credits.

91   The Norwegian Government has agreed to lobby with Saudi Arabia for CCS to be included in the CDM (see J Acher, n 37).

flexible mechanisms (Joint Implementation (JI) and the Clean Development Mechanism (CDM)), or, at the very least, the CDM alone, should include CCS activities.[92] It is most likely that, out of JI and CDM, CCS will be added (subject to the issues discussed below) to the CDM based on current[93] and prospective investment activity and areas of potential CCS deployment. This accords with the underlying purpose of the EU ETS, that is, that it is a market-based mechanism the aim of which is to achieve global GHG emission reductions regardless of location and at the lowest cost. Equally, the addition of CCS as a qualifying project to the CDM would satisfy the CDM's stated purpose (ie to assist "non-Annex I" countries to the UN Framework Convention on Climate Change (UNFCCC) to achieve sustainable development and to contribute towards the ultimate objective of the UNFCCC[94] by assisting Annex I parties to achieve compliance with their quantified emissions limitations). This is also sensible given that, as discussed below, the participation of developing countries and emerging markets in CCS is critical if ambitious global and regional emission reduction targets (such as the European target to reduce GHGs by 60% to 80% below 1990 levels by 2050) are to be achieved.

CDM projects must meet certain legal requirements. One of these is that the project must provide real, measurable and long-term benefits related to the mitigation of climate change and must deliver reductions in emissions that are additional to any which would occur in the absence of the certified project activity.[95] The project must also contribute to the sustainable development of the developing country and a complex baseline study (carried out in-house or by an external consultant), and a validation (completed by an independent certification company) will be required.[96] The associated transaction costs of such a baseline study have been considered a barrier for JI and CDM, especially given the fact that the market prices of the credits generated are fairly low.[97] There has been uncertainty for years as to whether CCS projects may qualify under the CDM for several reasons, the most significant of which has been the fact that it cannot be guaranteed that CO_2 stored in geological formations would be permanently stored. However, similar permanence concerns affect forestry projects under JI and CDM and have been addressed by the issuance of temporary credits. Secondly, an accounting and baseline methodology for CCS will need to be carried out and it will be necessary for emissions arising from capture, transport and injection (amongst other things) to be taken into account in the

---

92   For example, see draft EU ETS Directive Impact Assessment, n 67 above, Annex II, at p 227.
93   For example, the In Salah project in Algeria.
94   This is as follows: "... to achieve, in accordance with the relevant provisions of Convention, stabilization of greenhouse gas concentrations in the atmosphere at a level that would prevent dangerous anthropogenic interference with the climate system. Such a level should be achieved within a time frame sufficient to allow ecosystems to adapt naturally to climate change, to ensure that food production is not threatened and to enable economic development to proceed in a sustainable manner" Article 2 of the UNFCCC (see unfccc.int/resource/docs/convkp/conveng.pdf).
95   See UNFCCC, Decision 3/CMP.1 *Modalities and procedures for a clean development mechanism* as defined in Article 12 of the Kyoto Protocol, FCCC/KP/CMP/2005/8/Add.1, March 30 2006, Section F, Article 43.
96   *Ibid*, UNFCCC, Decision 3/CMP., Articles 44 to 48.
97   During 2007, the price for Certified Emission Reductions (credits generated under the CDM) for delivery in December 2008 fluctuated between approximately €13.50 to €18 compared with €17 to €25 in the same period for EU allowances (EUAs) (see www.pointcarbon.com/getfile.php/fileelement_137496/CJM20080416.pdf).

baseline. Third, regarding storage permanence, a definition for storage effectiveness and an acceptable way for dealing with leakage will need to be found. In light of the above, whereas it is likely that additionality and baseline development could be satisfied by CCS, there may be more difficultly regarding the storage permanence and sustainable development criteria.[98] However, it appears that, in light of the proposed inclusion of CCS in the EU ETS, this may now change. It is understood that a final decision on whether to include CCS in the CDM will be taken at the next Conference of the Parties/Meeting of the Parties to the UNFCCC in December 2008.

In summary, environmental integrity is crucial to the success of the EU ETS. Therefore, at the same time as efforts are made to include CCS in the EU ETS (by way of the neutral option as described above), it is also important that a clear, effective, regulatory framework is established which deals with practical, legal and commercial issues in a way which provides the certainty that operators, their lenders and other stakeholders consider to be a prerequisite of their substantial investment in such CCS technology. We will consider these issues below.

9.   Enabling a regulatory framework for carbon storage

Although national and international laws already exist which regulate particular aspects of CCS and its risks (eg water contamination, liability for local environmental damage, necessary licences, decommissioning), these are highly unlikely to have been enacted with CCS in contemplation. Therefore, some of the risks of CCS are not adequately regulated and require, first, removal of unnecessary barriers to CCS activities in current legislation and, second, either amendment of existing legislation or the enactment of stand-alone specific legislation to cover those risks. We shall consider below, briefly, international and regional efforts to remove legal barriers to the geological storage of CO_2, with particular emphasis upon the European Union, before considering the key elements necessary for a regulatory framework for carbon storage.

9.1   International law

Offshore CCS will necessarily trigger the application of public international marine environmental protection law due to the risks to marine ecosystems of leakage of CO_2. This is of relevance because a high proportion of CO_2 storage sites are likely to be offshore.

(a)   United Nations Convention on the Law of the Sea (UNCLOS) 1982

UNCLOS, described as "a constitution for the oceans",[99] regulates a wide range of uses of the world's oceans and seas including shipping, marine research and the exploitation of natural resources. States are subject to a general obligation to protect and preserve the marine environment[100] and specifically to take all measures

---

98   See HC de Coninck, *Project Based Kyoto Mechanisms and CO2 Capture and Storage*, undated, p 3 (see www.ecn.nl/fileadmin/ecn/units/bs/CCS/vancouver-hdc.pdf).

99   Taken from the title of an article of the same name entitled "A Constitution for the Oceans", Remarks by Tommy TB Koh, of Singapore, President of the Third United Nations Conference on the Law of the Sea, undated, see www.un.org/Depts/los/convention_agreements/texts/koh_english.pdf.

100   UNCLOS, Article 192.

necessary to prevent, reduce and control pollution of the marine environment from any source using best practicable means and in accordance with their capabilities.[101] The wide definition of "pollution" could possibly include CO_2. There is, however, no clarity on this point. Currently, it appears that the transportation of CO_2 by vessel (eg ship or pipeline) to an injection platform constitutes "dumping"[102] and therefore is subject to UNCLOS.

Certain factors suggest that formal clarity of UNCLOS regarding CCS is unlikely to be achieved. The first is the need for considerable negotiation and cooperation between states, with a core minimum of support required; and the second is the "framework nature" of UNCLOS. The latter means that greater clarity is intended to be supplied by more specific, subsequent instruments such as the London Convention and Protocol and the OSPAR Convention (considered below).

(b)   *Convention on the Prevention of Marine Pollution by Dumping of Wastes and other Matter (the London Convention) 1972*[103]

The London Convention, concluded in 1972 and which entered into force on August 30 1975, prohibits the dumping at sea of "industrial wastes" specified in its Annex I and requires certain other wastes to be dumped only upon obtaining a prior (special[104] or general[105]) permit. As originally drafted, it was unclear whether the London Convention prohibited CCS due to the wide definition of "waste" (remedied in part by the introduction of the "industrial waste" category in 1996), the fact that CO_2 was not originally specified in either Annex I or II, the fact that it did not deal with sub-seabed storage and also the nature of some of the exemptions to the prohibition on dumping (eg if the CO_2 were to be reinjected into the seabed following the normal operation of an installation for EOR, this would be permitted).

This was clarified in part by the 1996 Protocol to the Convention on the Prevention of Marine Pollution of Wastes and Other Matter 1972 (the London Protocol) which entered into force on March 24 2006. It will apply in parallel with the Convention until such time as sufficient parties have ratified the Protocol. The London Protocol went considerably further than the London Convention, prohibiting the dumping of all wastes save for those contained in a "reverse" list in Annex 1 (which originally contained only seven categories).[106] Secondly, it requires contracting parties to apply the precautionary principle rather than just be guided by it (as in the London Convention).

However, most significant of all was the amendment to exclude sub-seabed storage of CO_2 from the scope of the London Protocol. Australia, sponsored by France, Norway and the United Kingdom, successfully submitted a proposal (adopted

---

101   UNCLOS, Article 194(2).
102   "Dumping" means "any deliberate disposal of wastes or other matter from vessels, aircraft, platforms or other man-made structures at sea .... for the purposes of mere disposal thereof (unless such placement is not contrary to the aims of this Convention)" (Article 1 (5)(b), UNCLOS)).
103   See http://nosinternational.noaa.gov/conv/lonprot.html#ARTICLE%201.
104   Those wastes listed in Annex II of the London Convention require a special permit.
105   Those wastes listed in Annex III of the London Convention require a general permit.
106   Article 4, the London Protocol. The reverse list includes dredged material, sewage sludge, fish waste and inert or inorganic material.

unanimously by all contracting parties in November 2006) to add an eighth category of permitted dumping activity (ie "carbon dioxide streams from carbon dioxide capture processes for sequestration") provided:

- disposal is into sub-seabed geological formations;
- these streams consist "overwhelmingly" of CO_2 (although they may contain incidental associated substances derived from the source material and the capture and sequestration processes used);
- no wastes of other matter are added for the purposes of disposal; and
- such sequestration may only occur upon the grant of a permit by the contracting party's government which complies with certain conditions specified in Annex 2 to the Protocol.[107]

This marks a considerable step forward not only because of its broad scope – the Protocol applies to all marine waters (including the seabed and subsoil thereof) other than the internal waters of contracting states[108] – but also because it has set a precedent for other regulations to follow in order to specifically permit CCS.[109]

However, the London Protocol is subject to certain limitations. First, the above amendment to permit sub-seabed sequestration of CO_2 will only bind parties to the London Convention who have also ratified the London Protocol. For example, the United States, Brazil, Finland, the Netherlands, Morocco and Argentina have signed but not yet ratified the Protocol. Consequently, until such time as these countries do so, they would appear to be bound only by the less stringent London Convention (which does not expressly permit CCS activities).

Second, several clarifications and issues need to be addressed. As these are similar to those for the OSPAR Convention,[110] these are referred to below. One such amendment refers to Article 6 of the Protocol which was considered by a Legal and Technical Group on Transboundary Carbon Sequestration Issues on February 25 to 27 2008. Article 6 prohibits contracting parties from allowing the export of wastes to other countries for dumping or incineration at sea. The group concluded that Article 6 as drafted would exclude transboundary transport of CO_2 and proposed two significant amendments in response. First, an amendment which would permit cross-border transport for storage in another state and, second, an amendment sought by Germany, Italy and Greenpeace that such transboundary transport should only take place "if disposal of CO_2 from a particular source is not feasible". It remains to be seen whether either of the above amendments will be adopted.

(c) *Convention for the Protection of the Marine Environment of the North East Atlantic (the OSPAR Convention) 1992*

The London Convention encourages contracting parties with common interests in

---

107 Annex 1(4), the London Protocol.
108 However the London Protocol does not include sub-seabed repositories accessed only from land (see Article 1(7)).
109 For example, see OSPAR Convention and draft CCS Directive below.
110 1992 OSPAR Convention, Convention for the Protection of the Marine Environment of the North-East Atlantic, see www.ospar.org/eng/html/convention/ospar_conv1.htm. Described further in subsection 9.1(c).

the same geographical area to enter into regional agreements for the prevention of pollution.[111]

One such treaty is the OSPAR Convention which governs protection of the marine environment in the North-East Atlantic and the North Sea – an area which, due to the number and size of depleted oil and gas fields, is likely to be one of the first areas of significant development of CCS projects and therefore is of particular interest. Members include the European Union (represented by the Commission) and many of its member states.[112]

The OSPAR Convention entered into force in March 1998 and is considered to be the strictest legal framework governing the marine environment. The Convention prohibits the dumping of all wastes, unless specifically listed in Annex II (none of which, as originally drafted, could be construed as including CO_2). However, the OSPAR Convention's scope was wider than that of the London Convention in that it specifically included polluting activities in the sub-seabed and subsoil. Further, it contained restrictions concerning pollution from land-based sources depending upon the sources and nature of the CO_2 placement.

There have been several significant recent amendments to the OSPAR Convention which facilitate CCS in the North-East Atlantic region. First, on June 28 2007, the OSPAR Commission[113] agreed to adopt a decision which will amend the OSPAR Convention. These amendments will bring the Convention into line with the 1996 London Protocol by permitting the storage of CO_2 in geological formations under the seabed subject to the same conditions as stated in the first three sub-paragraphs under section 9.1(b) above, plus an additional fourth condition, to the effect that the CO_2 streams are intended to be retained in these formations permanently and will not lead to significant adverse consequences for the marine environment, human health and other legitimate uses of the maritime area.[114] As under the London Protocol, such storage must be permitted by the Contracting States' relevant national authorities and any such authorisation shall be carried out in accordance with their OSPAR Guidelines for Risk Assessment and Management of Storage of CO_2 streams in Geological Formations, as updated from time to time.[115] Finally, the parties must notify OSPAR's executive secretary if they decide to issue a permit for CCS activities.

Second, the Commission decided expressly to exclude placement (which includes disposal) of CO_2 into the water column of the sea[116] or on the seabed for CCS

---

111 Article VIII, London Convention.
112 At the time of writing, there are 15 Contracting Parties to the OSPAR Convention comprising Belgium, Denmark, Finland, France, Germany, Iceland, Ireland, Luxembourg, the Netherlands, Norway, Portugal, Spain, Sweden, Switzerland and the United Kingdom. For further, see www.ospar.org/eng/html/welcome.html.
113 The OSPAR Commission is made up of representatives of the governments of the Convention's Contracting Parties (see n 127).
114 OSPAR Convention, Annex II, Article 3, new sub-paragraph (f)(iv)) as amended by OSPAR Decision 2007/2 on the Storage of Carbon Dioxide Streams in Geological Formations, Annex 6 (Ref §2.10c), paragraph 2.1 (for OSPAR Decision 2007/2, see www.ospar.org/asp/ospar/download.asp?ftp=%5C%5Cserver%5Corg%5Cdbase%5Cdecrecs%5Cdecisions%5C07%2D02e%7E1%2Edoc&function=4).
115 See OSPAR Decision 2007/2, n 129, at paragraph 3.1.
116 The same approach is adopted in Article 2(4) of the draft CCS Directive, n 153 at p 16.

purposes,[117] due to the "potential negative effects". This was because the Commission was "convinced that such storage is not a sustainable storage option, is likely to result in harm to living resources and marine ecosystems and is thus neither a viable solution with regard to mitigating climate change nor compatible with the aims of the Convention".[118] This amendment was motivated by OSPAR's findings on ocean acidification, documented in 2006, which confirmed that high levels of atmospheric CO_2 are changing ocean carbon chemistry at least 100 times faster than at any time in the last 100,000 years.[119] The parties' competent authorities' must ensure that the correct regulations and authorisations are in place for CCS activities and that these, in turn, comply with the OSPAR Guidelines for Risk Assessment and Management of CO_2 Streams in Geological Formations. The above amendments represent the result of five years of work led by Norway, the Netherlands, France and the United Kingdom, parties with considerable political, economic and environmental interest in expediting offshore CCS deployment as soon as possible.

As discussed above, the London Protocol amendments to include CCS were adopted without any opposition. Consequently, it is possibly that the OSPAR amendments could also be adopted in short order, provided that the ratification process under the Convention is complied with (Article 15). This stipulates that for those Contracting Parties which have ratified, accepted or approved amendments, the amendments will only come into force on the thirtieth day after receipt by the depositary government (currently France) of such notification of such ratification, acceptance or approval by at least seven Contracting Parties.[120] At the time of writing the above amendments are not yet in force.[121]

In summary, the amendments to the London Protocol (which came into force in February 2007) and the OSPAR Convention (which have yet to be adopted) mark an important first step towards the widespread deployment of CCS. However, clarity in both instruments is needed in several areas, including the definition of "overwhelmingly" in the context of CO_2 purity issue (see section 9.9 below), the extent to which discharges from land-based sources need to be authorised and regulated, and how transboundary transport of CO_2 will be treated under the London

---

117   It should be noted that such storage is permitted if it results from normal operations as described in Article 1(g)(i) of the OSPAR Convention, or is for the purpose other than the mere disposal thereof as described in Article 1(g)(ii) of the OSPAR Convention and is in accordance with its provisions. See OSPAR Decision 2007/1 to Prohibit the Storage of Carbon Dioxide Streams in the Water Column or on the Sea-bed, Annex 5 (Ref §2.9b) (see www.ospar.org/asp/ospar/ download.asp?ftp=%5C%5Cserver%5Corg%5Cdbase%5Cdecrecs%5Cdecisions%5C07%2D01e%7E1%2Edoc&function=4).

118   Ibid, OSPAR Decision 2007/1 at Recital 7.

119   See OSPAR Commission, "Effects on the marine environment of ocean acidification resulting from elevated levels of CO_2 in the atmosphere", 2006, at www.ospar.org/documents/dbase/publications/p00285_Ocean%20acidification.pdf. Effects included reduced pH and lower concentrations of carbonate ions, which makes it more difficult for marine animals to build carbonate shells. Surface waters of the world oceans have already experienced a pH reduction of about 0 to 1 pH units and further reductions of the order of 0.2 to 0.3 (or greater) may be seen by 2100.

120   Thereafter, the amendment shall enter into force for any other Contracting Party 30 days after that Contracting Party has deposited its instrument of ratification, acceptance or approval of the amendment (OSPAR Convention, Article 15).

121   In respect of this legislation, France is the depositary government and it was expected that France would begin the ratification process by corresponding with the Contracting Parties in late 2007 (see Personal Communication; Corinne Michel, OSPAR Commission, August 20 2007, cited in Ian Havercroft and Ray Purdy, Carbon Capture and Storage – A Legal Perspective, see, n 227 at note 17).

Protocol (Article 6 as discussed above) and the OSPAR Convention.

9.2 The European Union

Within the European Union, efforts have begun to create a comprehensive regulatory and legal framework to govern the three stages of the CCS process (capture, transport and storage). Generally, a conservative approach has been taken so that the default option for regulating a CCS element is the existing legal framework if it regulates activities of a similar risk.

(a) Capture

Broadly, the key stages of the carbon capture process (eg solvent stripping of CO_2 for post-combustion capture, air separation for oxyfuel combustion and gasification for pre-combustion capture) are already conducted in industrial processes performed by power or chemical plants. Consequently, the risks posed by these activities at the capture phase of the CCS chain are similar to those in the chemical/power generation sectors.

Commentators, including the EU Commission, have therefore concluded that legislative instruments such as Council Directive 96/61/EC of September 24 1996 concerning integrated pollution prevention and control (the IPPC Directive)[122] adequately regulate the risks of carbon capture. One potential outstanding activity, however, is whether CO_2 compression and the presence of compressed CO_2 in large quantities may constitute a dangerous substance warranting application of the Seveso II Directive.[123] The Directive affects around 8,000 establishments which store quantities of dangerous substances above a certain threshold (as defined by reference to its Annex I). Incumbents mainly comprise chemical, petrochemical and energy installations – and it is no coincidence that these are the very sectors which may need to consider CCS in the near future in order to achieve compliance with their more restricted allocations under the EU ETS. Certain parties (such as the Health and Safety Executive (HSE) in the United Kingdom) consider that CO_2 should be governed by this Directive and requested that this be considered by the Committee of Competent Authorities (CCA)[124] as part of the Commission's review of the Seveso II Directive (launched on February 26 2008). At the time of writing, the Seveso II Directive is under examination by the CCA (scheduled for April 2008 in Slovenia and October 2008 in France). If successful, CCS installations will be subject to the Directive's notification, accident reporting and inspection requirements and those with dangerous chemicals above the "upper tier" will also have to provide a safety

---

122   OJ L257, 10.10.1996, p 26 Directive as last amended by Regulation (EC) No 166/2006 of the European Parliament and of the Council (OJ L 33, 04.02.2006, p 1).

123   The Seveso II Directive refers to Council Directive 96/82/EC of December 9 1996 on the control of major-accident hazards involving dangerous substances OJ L 10, 14.01.1997 pp 13 to 33 as amended by Directive 2003/105/EC of the European Parliament and of the Council of December 16 2003 amending Council Directive 96/82/EC on the control of major-accident hazards involving dangerous substances OJ L 345, 31.12.2003 pp 97 to 105. It is considered to be the legal and technical instrument to fulfil the obligations of the European Community arising out of UN Economic Commission for Europe Convention on the Transboundary Effects of Industrial Accidents, 1992.

124   The CCA's role is to ensure the coherent implementation and consistent application of the Seveso II Directive and to give guidance on its general application.

report (including a major accident prevention policy and a safety management system), emergency plans and information to the public.

(b)   *Transport*

In the event that the CO_2 injection site is located some distance away from the CO_2 source, the CO_2 will need to be transported in fluid form, most commonly by pipeline or by ship.

Pipeline transportation of CO_2 is a mature and well-regulated practice, particularly in the United States.[125] In the European Union, the risks posed by CO_2 transport by pipeline are broadly covered by Council Directive 85/337/EEC of June 27 1985 on the assessment of the effects of certain public and private projects on the environment[126] (the EIA Directive) for pipelines longer than 40km and with a diameter of more than 800mm. It should be noted that the EIA Directive can also regulate assessment of the environmental impact of the capture and storage elements of the CCS chain. At UK level, the Health and Safety Laboratories (an agency of the UK HSE) has stated that CO_2 which is transported by pipeline at pressures and temperatures below those that categorise CO_2 as dense-phase or supercritical exhibits major accident potential.[127] Pending further research, the UK HSE may propose amendments to the Pipelines Safety Regulations[128] to include CO_2 as a dangerous fluid.

Equally, the other principal method of transporting CO_2 (by ship) could be more than adequately deemed to be controlled by existing legislation in respect of liquefied natural gas (LNG) and liquefied petroleum gas (LPG). Similarly, the risks of local environmental damage caused by a leakage of CO_2 were deemed to be suitably covered by the Environmental Liability Directive[129] and the risks of liability for climate change damage were assessed to be adequately dealt with under the existing EU ETS Directive.[130]

(c)   *Storage*

We will consider in more detail the legal and practical issues relating to the storage element of the CCS chain, as this is a "significant novel element of CCS".[131] Whilst there are some existing legislative instruments regulating similar activities (eg natural gas storage, EOR and also landfill), in contrast to capture and transport there is currently no single regulatory system which is readily adaptable to the risks arising

---

125   For instance, around 4,800km of CO_2 pipelines exist in the United States alone (see International Energy Agency, *Geologic Storage of Carbon Dioxide – Staying Safely Underground*, n 63 above, January 2008, p 12).

126   OJ L 175, 05.07.1985, p 40. Directive as last amended by Directive 2003/35/EC of the European Parliament and of the Council (OJ L156, 25.06.2003, p 17).

127   House of Commons, Select Committee on Science and Technology, Memorandum from the Department of Business, Enterprise and Regulatory Reform, "Update on Carbon Capture and Storage (CCS) Developments since the Government's Response of April 24 2006 to the Committee's Report: Meeting UK Energy and Climate Needs: The role of Carbon Capture and Storage (First Report of Session 2005-06 HC 578), October 2007 see Recommendation 31 (see www.publications.parliament.UK/pa/cm200607/cmselect/cmsctech/1108/1108we11.htm).

128   See Pipelines Safety Regulations 1996 (SI 1996/825) which came into force on April 11 1996.

129   Directive 2004/35/EC.

130   Directive 2003/87 EC as amended at n 85 above.

131   See draft CCS Directive Impact Assessment, n 64 at paragraph 5.3(107) at p 29.

as a result of geological storage of CO_2. Existing laws would require extensive and complex amendment before they could be applied to CO_2 storage risks due to the fragmented nature of the regime and the number of legal gaps.[132] For example, adopting the conservative approach described above, the Commission recently considered whether CO_2 storage risks could be adequately regulated under the EU ETS Directive (which would be the simplest option for legislators, regulators and operators as it would require no legislative change either at EU or national level). However, this advantage was dismissed due to its lack of effectiveness and the fact that it failed to deal with significant other issues (eg regulation of impurities in the CO_2 stream; permitting requirements; liability for local environmental damage; private/public transfer of liability; and financial provision to cover future liabilities).[133] Equally, applying existing environmental legislation in a "patchwork" manner would not only add a layer of complexity but also fail to address all of the necessary CO_2 storage risks. For instance, applying the IPPC Directive would also trigger the need for an EIA (requiring a prior impact assessment, with public consultation), but the IPPC Directive lacks provisions requiring operators to take out financial securities for operations to cover closure, decommissioning (ie post-closure) and stewardship costs in the event of operator insolvency.[134]

Overall, therefore, recent developments have suggested that a stand-alone framework, tailored to the specific risks of CO_2 storage is the preferred option in the European Union. This, combined with the EIA Directive, would, in the opinion of the Commission, provide "complete regulatory coverage tailored to the needs of CCS".[135] We consider the key elements of such a regulatory scheme below.

9.3   Key elements of a CCS regulatory scheme

Several international jurisdictions have taken significant steps forward towards the development of a legal and regulatory scheme to govern CCS projects. Most recently, as touched upon above, in the European Union, the Commission has prepared a draft directive to govern a regulatory scheme. It is understood that the regulatory scheme is likely to become binding in 2008.

We consider below the key areas of a potential regulatory framework for CO_2 storage projects which will impact significantly upon the success or otherwise of CCS projects towards effectively reducing climate change and achieving GHG reductions. Fundamentally, a successful regulatory and policy framework for CCS:

- must be based upon an integrated risk assessment for CO_2 leakage;
- requires a consistent, flexible and transparent basis for regulation of CCS projects to ensure the environmentally sound, safe and reliable operation of CCS activities;
- should remove unnecessary barriers to CCS activities in current legislation (considered at section 9.1(a) to (c) above and section 9.14 below);

---

132   For further, see Norton Rose, ERM, ECN, *Identification of Gaps and Obstacles for CCS in Existing Legislation*, 2007.
133   For further, see draft CCS Directive Impact Assessment, n 64 at paragraph 5.4(12) at p 30.
134   See draft CCS Directive Impact Assessment, n 64 at paragraph 5.4.2 (117).
135   See draft CCS Directive Impact Assessment, n 64 at paragraph 5.5 (128).

- should provide appropriate incentives proportionate to the CO_2 reduction benefits (considered above at section 7);
- must deliver investment certainty for CCS project operators, funders and regulators;
- should inspire public confidence that CO_2 will be safely and effectively stored and that natural resource management, environmental impacts and health and safety issues will be addressed; and
- should encourage increased research and development and tran~~~ technology.

(a) *Site selection and site characterisation*

The first step in the regulatory framework will be to ensure that storage sites are carefully selected to ensure a high degree of safety and security of CO_2 storage. Improper site selection and characterisation increase the probability of leakage due to CO_2 migration which, in turn, will undermine public, operator and regulator confidence in the project. Policymakers in many jurisdictions agree with the IPCC's pronouncement that the selection of an appropriate site is the best way of reducing as far as possible any risks posed by leakage of CO_2 over the long term.[136]

The commitment to ensuring the complete containment of the stored CO_2 for the indefinite future is a common theme in several jurisdictions. In Europe, the EU Commission has proposed that this may be achieved by stipulating that a site should only be selected if there is "no significant risk of leakage, and if in any case no significant environmental or health impacts are likely to occur".[137] Equally, the "no significant impact test" in Australia will be a pre-condition for approval to undertake CCS activities proposed under the Ministerial Council on Mineral and Petroleum Resources (MCMPR) Regulatory Guiding Principles and determined on a case-by-case basis.

Site characterisation will be the means to determine that there is no significant risk of leakage. Good site characterisation involves the study of the underlying geology of the prospective storage site and surrounding area (the storage complex).[138] The principal objective of site characterisation is to consider how the injected CO_2 will behave generally (eg how it reacts with *in situ* minerals; its possible interactions with other activities such as the exploration of hydrocarbons;[139] its rate of migration; its potential to induce seismicity and any potential leakage pathways (eg abandoned

---

136   See Ministerial Council on Mineral and Petroleum Resources (MCMPR), *Carbon Capture and Geological Storage, Australian Regulatory Guiding Principles 2005*, November 2005, p 19.

137   Commission of the European Communities, Proposal for a Directive of the European Parliament and of the Council on the geological storage of carbon dioxide and amending Council Directives 85/337EEC, 96/61/EC, Directives 2000/60/EC, 2001/80/EC, 2004/35/EC, 200612/EC and Regulation (EC) No 1013/2006, January 23 2008, COM (2008) XXX (the draft CCS Directive), Recital 15 and Article 4(2).

138   This is the term used in the draft CCS Directive and means the storage site and surrounding geological domains which can have an effect on overall storage integrity and security (see draft CCS Directive, *ibid*, n 153, Article 3 (6)).

139   The need to manage interaction with the petroleum industry in Australia was identified as a major challenge in developing the regulatory framework due to the fact that many prospective CCS locations are located within the "footprint" of oil and gas production (see Dr John Bradshaw, Chief Scientist CCS, Geoscience Australia on behalf of Margaret Sewell General Manager, Resources Division, Department of Industry, Tourism and Resources, Development of Australia's Legislation and Regulatory Guidelines for CCS, June 20 2007).

or adequately sealed wells and caprock)).[140] General siting guidelines are being drafted in Australia, the United States, Canada and throughout the European Union.

Notwithstanding the above generic guidelines, because each CCS project site will be unique, the characterisation and management of geological and technical uncertainty will require methodologies and the technologies tailored to the particular site.[141]

The site's specific characteristics will also need to be weighed up against the following practical factors which may influence a site selector's decision as to the proposed storage site, particularly in the near term:

- proximity to a source of (plentiful) high-purity streams of CO_2 (such as natural gas processing, hydrogen and ammonia manufacturing, or processes using oxyfuel pre-combustion);
- sites already served by existing infrastructure (eg former sites previously used for oil/gas extraction) would prove attractive, thus minimising the cost of transporting the CO_2 (as is the case in Australia); and
- proximity of the source to the proposed storage site.

These practical considerations will be in the regulator's thoughts due to the need, in the near-term at least, to achieve the economies of scale necessary in order to make CO_2 an effective and attractive GHG mitigation option. Such considerations will also necessarily give some countries an advantage over others regarding early deployment and demonstration of CCS projects. For example, the 500 largest CO_2 point sources in the United States are predominantly coal-fired plants, and 95% of these are located within approximately 80km of at least one proposed geologic storage formation.[142] Equally, preliminary research suggests that few large-point sources are located close to potential ocean storage locations, with most located near large urban and major industrial areas[143] with a few subject to the occasional notable exceptions (eg a significant proportion of Australia's storage capacity is far from population centres, with a considerable number of potential offshore sites).

9.4   Permitting/licensing

(a)   General themes

There is broad consensus, whether in international (eg the London Protocol),[144] regional (eg the OSPAR Convention),[145] or national proposals/legislation,[146] and whether affecting onshore or offshore geological formations that the storage of CO_2 in geological formations must be permitted by the relevant authorities.[147] The

---

140   Site characterisation will often be by way of computer simulation and/or 3D modelling.
141   International Risk Governance Council, Regulation of Carbon Capture and Storage, undated p.6 (see www.irgc.org/IMG/pdf/Policy_Brief_CCS.pdf).
142   International Energy Agency, Near-Term Opportunities for Carbon Dioxide and Storage, 2007, paragraph 4.1 at p 16.
143   IPCC, *Special Report Carbon Dioxide Capture and Storage; A Special Report of Working Group III of the Intergovernmental Panel on Climate Change*, n 11 above, pp 8 to 9.
144   See Article 4, London Protocol, which states that Contracting Parties shall adopt administrative or legislative measures to ensure the issuance of permits and permit conditions to comply with Annex 2.

exploratory permit, drawing on experience from the oil and gas industries must be limited in time and volume area.[148]

The reason for this is, to borrow the phrasing of the European Commission, because the storage permit is recognised as the core instrument to ensure that the requirements/obligations of the relevant instrument are met and that such storage occurs in an environmentally sound manner.[149] Clearly, the permits and their conditions will provide the mechanisms for enforcement by the relevant authority to ensure that their environmental integrity is not undermined by breach.

Secondly, a further common element, whether relating to offshore or onshore geological formations, is that an environmental impact assessment or equivalent is required prior to such permit being granted. In the international arena, in relation to offshore formations in all marine areas governed by the London Protocol, this is described as an "impact evaluation".[150] More specifically, in the North-East Atlantic region under the OSPAR Convention, it is described as a "full risk assessment and management process ... to the satisfaction of the competent authority".[151]

9.5 EU projects

Additional permits may be required under existing and proposed legislation if the proposed CCS project (whether relating to the capture, transport or storage phase) is located in the European Union. First, there are strong indications from the EU Commission[152] that capture installations, storage sites and pipelines for the transport of CO_2 streams with a diameter of more than 800mm and length of more than 40km for the purposes of geological storage will soon constitute "projects"[153] and require mandatory impact assessments under the EIA Directive.

Article 7 of the EIA Directive is also of particular relevance to CCS projects located in the European Union, as it is foreseeable that a storage site or pipeline, for example, will straddle the jurisdiction of another country. Article 7 stipulates that if a member state is aware that a project is likely to have significant effects on the environment in another member state, or where a member state is likely to be significantly affected and so requests, the member state shall send a description of the project and information on the nature of the decision which may be taken. Finally, such member states would

---

145   See OSPAR, *Decision 2007/2 on the Storage of Carbon Dioxide streams in Geological Formations*, 25-29 June 2007, OSPAR 07/24/1-E, Annex 6 (Ref. §2.10c). This prohibits Contracting Parties from permitting storage of CO_2 streams in geological formations without authorisation or regulation by the competent authorities and in accordance with the OSPAR Guidelines for Risk Assessment and Management of Storage (as updated from time to time). A permit shall only be granted if a full risk-assessment and management process has been completed to the satisfaction of the competent authority and that the storage will not lead to significant adverse consequences for the marine environment, human health and other legitimate uses of the maritime area (see paragraph 3.1).
146   See Energy Bill, n 174 below, Part 1, Chapter 3, Clause 16(2) (a).
147   See draft CCS Directive, n 153, Chapter 3, Article 6, p 18.
148   Draft CCS Directive, n 153, Recital 16, p 11 and Article 5, p 18. See also Energy Bill, n 174, Part 1, Clause 16(2)(c).
149   Draft CCS Directive, n 153, Recital 17, p 12.
150   See London Protocol, 1996, Annex 2, paragraph 17.
151   See OSPAR, Decision 2007/2, n 162, Article 3.1 at p 2.
152   *Ibid*, draft CCS Directive, n 153, Chapter 7, Article 29, Amendment of Directive 85/337/EEC.
153   "Project" means the execution of construction works or of other installations or schemes, or other interventions in the natural surroundings and landscape including those involving the extraction of mineral resources (see Article 1(2) EIA Directive)).

be required to take the results of the consultation and information gathered under the EIA process into consideration in the development consent procedure.[154]

9.6   United Kingdom

In addition to the relevant EU law (see above), various consents may need to be sought regarding CCS activities in the United Kingdom. The consents, legislation and regulators involved will depend largely upon whether the proposed storage site is onshore or offshore.

The Energy Bill[155] (at the time of writing, this Bill is currently being considered by Parliament) proposes, among other things, the creation of a licensing regime for the offshore storage of CO_2 in, under or over the territorial sea other than the territorial sea adjacent to Scotland or waters in a zone designated for gas importation and storage.[156]

The onshore injection of CO_2 might trigger the application of the Landfill Directive,[157] the directive known as the Water Framework Directive[158] and the hazardous substances regime, as well as the domestic planning system as regulated under the Town and Country Planning Act 1990.

The Planning (Hazardous Substances) Act 1990 requires hazardous substances consent to be obtained if hazardous substances are present on, over or under land in an amount at, or above, a controlled quantity.[159]

9.7   Monitoring, reporting and verification (MRV)

As under the EU ETS, a robust MRV framework is fundamental to ensuring that the CCS project maintains its integrity during its operational life and does not undermine local or global climate change mitigation measures. This will also encourage greater operator and public confidence in CCS.

Several CCS regimes[160] require submission of a monitoring plan by an operator at the stage that a permit application is made. This ensures that operators have considered and evaluated how best to manage the risks of leakage upfront, and at a time when the competent authority has most bargaining power. The plan should cover monitoring of fugitive emissions at injection facilities, the volumetric flow at injection wellheads, the storage site and storage complex as well as, preferably, the CO_2 plume[161] and the surrounding environment[162] during the operational phase. Such monitoring will have several objectives: first, to compare the modelled and the actual behaviour of the injected CO_2 – it is critical to see whether it is behaving as expected, or whether there

154   *Ibid*, EIA Directive, Article 8.
155   Energy Bill, Bill 79 2007 to 2008, Part 1, Chapter 3 (see www.publications.parliament.UK/pa/cm200708/cmbills/079/08079.i-vi.html)
156   *Ibid*, Energy Bill, Part 1, Chapter 3, Clause 16(3).
157   OJ L 182, 16.07.1999 pp 1 to 19, Council Directive 1999/31 EC of April 26 1999 on the landfill of waste.
158   Directive 2000/60/EC of the European Parliament and of the Council of 23rd October 2000 establishing a framework for Community action in the field of water policy (O.J L327, 22.12.2000, p 1).
159   Planning (Hazardous Substances) Act 1990, Clause 4(1). The "controlled quantity" is specified by the Secretary of State (Clause 5(1)(a)(ii)).
160   For example, see Energy Bill, n 174, Part 1, Chapter 3, Clause 16(3).
161   For example, chemical analysis of the injected material (see draft CCS Directive, n 153, Annex II, paragraph 1.1(h)).
162   For example, ascertaining the reservoir temperature and pressure may help determine CO_2 phase behaviour and state (see draft CCS Directive, n 153, Annex II, paragraph 1.1(i)).

is any migration or leakage. Secondly, if there is any such leakage, it is necessary to identify whether it is a threat to and/or damaging the environment or human health. Thirdly, such schemes need to detect any significant adverse effects resulting from leakage and also to assess the long-term isolation prospects for the injected CO_2.

Best-practice monitoring technology should also be used and legislation should require that such plans should be updated regularly (eg at least every five years) to take account of new technical developments. Updated plans should be resubmitted to the competent authority within a certain timeframe.

Typically, an operator will be required to report regularly (at a frequency to be determined by the regulator) on specific aspects of the monitoring for that period. Independent verification of the operator's report is also necessary and a "mitigation framework" should be in place to ensure that, in the event of leakage, the operator takes the necessary corrective measures.[163] Further, an element of regulator enforcement (on a routine and non-routine basis) should also be an integral part of the scheme.[164]

Most importantly, given the long-term nature of carbon storage, effective MRV is necessary to ensure that certain health and safety and environment standards are met before the transfer of the project back from the private sector to government.

9.8   Liability

(a)   Operational liability

Liability risk at the start of the CCS project is likely to be fairly low but will increase during its operational life as more CO_2 is injected into the site due to the increase in its fluid pressure. Liability for local damage caused by CO_2 leakage will generally be assumed by the operator. It is likely that, as for oil and gas, operators will be able to obtain insurance for damage-related costs in the event that they occur during the operational period. Insurers themselves may wish to include a form of catastrophe insurance in case liability costs end up being higher than expected. In the European Union, local damage to health or property will generally be covered by existing local law, and local environmental damage will be covered under the Environmental Liability Directive. Liability for climate change damage will also be covered, if (as expected) CCS is included within the EU ETS Directive (see above).

The situation becomes more complicated in the event that the operator is dissolved or goes into insolvency, or where the regulator withdraws the storage permit (as a result, for instance, of breach of condition). Currently, neither EU nor UK law has been crystallised on this issue. Parallels with the contaminated land regime might, however, be drawn in that the "polluter pays" principle[165] could apply

---

163   For example, the draft CCS Directive proposes that operators will be required to submit with their application for a storage permit a proposed monitoring plan, a proposed corrective measures plan and a provisional post-closure plan (see n 153 at Article 16(2)).

164   See draft CCS Directive, n 153, Article 15.

165   This is the principle according to which the polluter should bear the cost of measures to reduce pollution according to the extent of either the damage done to society or the exceeding of an acceptable level (standard) of pollution (Glossary of Environment Statistics, Studies in Methods, Series F, No 67, United Nations, New York, 1997 as cited on the OECD website (see http://stats.oecd.org/glossary/detail.asp?ID=2074)).

in the first instance, but in the event that the original polluter cannot be found, then the next appropriate person can be held liable.

(b) Closure and post-closure liability

The matter of closure and post-closure liability is perhaps the most contentious aspect of a regulatory framework relating to CCS activities. This is due to the inherent uncertainty as to how injected CO_2 will behave over the timescales involved and therefore the considerable potential that exists for the unravelling of any previously achieved climate change mitigation. Most commercial stakeholders consider that a private-to-public transfer of responsibility for closed storage sites is an essential precondition to encouraging the requisite investor confidence to encourage CCS commercialisation.[166] It is also recognised, given the long-term nature of CO_2 storage and its potential risks to the environment and human health, that such a transfer of responsibility is necessary for public safety, too.

Policymakers are faced with a difficult balance as to exactly when such liability should transfer: too early and operators may appear to have received a "windfall" or state aid (in that they will have profited from the upside of the transaction without having to bear any risk and this in turn would risk competitive distortion).[167] However, if the trigger for such transfer is set too late, private-sector investors will be reluctant to assume responsibility for storage sites in such an "open-ended" way.

Of all potential approaches, the preferred method, at least for the European Union, appears to confer some certainty to operators at the outset that their liability will end at an ascertainable point in the future (rather than at the member states' discretion, or at a fixed time after closure, both of which would risk competitive distortion).[168] This stipulates that an operator will remain responsible for post-closure maintenance, MRV, and corrective measures pursuant to a post-closure plan submitted at the time of the operator's application which, among other things, would require the site to be safely closed and sealed. The legal requirement to submit a post-closure plan is an established one in UK[169] and EU[170] law and, more recently, in voluntary codes such as the Equator Principles.[171] Responsibility, including full legal liability, will only transfer to the member state once evidence has been provided (and approved by both its competent authority and the EU Commission) that CO_2 will be wholly isolated for the indefinite future or that the risk of future leakage is low.[172] Therefore, whilst the site represents a significant risk, it

---

166   For example, see World Resources Institute, Carbon Capture and Storage Background Document Illinois Climate Change Advisory Group, May 2 2007, pp 2 and 3.
167   See draft CCS Directive Impact Assessment, n 64, paragraph 6.2.2 (152), p 39.
168   See draft CCS Directive Impact Assessment, n 64, paragraph 6.2.2, pp 38 to 39.
169   Section 29 of the Petroleum Act 1998 requires oil and gas licensees to submit a detailed decommissioning programme for each installation or pipeline, showing how the installation will be removed, re-used or recycled. Failure to comply is a criminal offence.
170   Under the IPPC regime, certain operators when they decommission a permitted site are obliged to restore it to its condition at the time of the grant of the original permit.
171   For new project financings with a total projected capital cost of $10 million or more funded by an institution which has adopted the Equator Principles (an EPFI), the Equator Principles require a borrower obtaining funding from the EPFI (for instance, to construct a CCS plant) to covenant to decommission that plant in accordance with a decommissioning plan (Principle 8(d)). In practice, however, anecdotal evidence suggests that very few such plans are being submitted to EPFI, notwithstanding this requirement in the Equator Principles. For further, see www.equator-principles.com/
172   For example, see draft CCS Directive, n 153 at Article 18(1).

will remain the operator's liability. The advantages of this option are that it complies with the polluter-pays principle whilst ensuring fairness for operators in that they will accept liability on the same objective performance basis. Further, the proposed review of draft approvals by the Commission (and its issue of an opinion) will help achieve consistency of implementation of the Directive and greater public confidence as a result.

(c)   ***Financial provision from operators regarding closure and post-liabilities***

There is now greater certainty that, in the European Union at least,[173] financial provision or any other equivalent will need to be established by operators to cover closure and post-closure liabilities in the event of operator insolvency. Similar financial provision is required under the Landfill Directive[174] and the directive governing the management of waste from extractive industries.[175] The draft CCS Directive suggests that Member States shall ensure that such provision (or equivalent) is submitted at the time of the application for a storage permit. Indications are that such provision will be kept after closure of a storage site until responsibility for the storage site is transferred to the competent authority. Such liabilities will need to include climate change damage, that is, liabilities under the EU ETS Directive to surrender allowances (which would, presumably, need to be purchased at the date that the leak was noticed) in respect of any leaked emissions. Such liabilities in the European Union would probably exclude liability for local damage to health and property (as these would already be governed at state level) and for local environmental damage (already governed by the Environmental Liability Directive).

(d)   ***Mechanisms for funding post-transfer leakage costs by the state***

A critical issue which has provoked considerable discussion is how to fund post-transfer leakage costs once responsibility has passed back to the state. These range from cash accounts and bonds, through to insurance and mutual funds. Existing insurance policies are available to address blow-outs of wells for oil and gas operations which, by analogy, could be applied to CCS. Equally, general insurance requirements may cover CCS storage activities (eg the Sleipner project was included within Statoil's general insurance cover).[176] Market trends from analogous cases suggest that the prospects for being able to insure against CO_2 leakage are now reasonable,[177] although other commentators consider that it is possible that insurers would be reluctant to write such policies for 20 to 30 years, particularly with the inherent uncertainties currently surrounding the industry. Consequently, this scarcity of policies could impact significantly upon the premium payable.[178]

Another option would be the creation of a special contingency fund into which operators would contribute. This is a model which has been used in other regimes

---

173   See draft CCS Directive, n 153 at Recital 28 and Article 19.
174   See Landfill Directive, n 176, Article 8(a) (iv).
175   OJ L 102, 11.04.2006, pp 15 to 34, Article 14, Directive 2006/21/EC of the European Parliament and of the Council of March 15 2006 on the management of waste from extractive industries and amending Directive 2004/35/EC – Statement by the European Parliament, the Council and the Commission.
176   See draft CCS Directive Impact Assessment, n 64, paragraph 6.2.7.2 (172) at p 43.
177   See draft CCS Directive Impact Assessment, n 64, paragraph 6.2.7.2 (173) at p 44.
178   See Matt Elkington, n 73 at p 40.

facing potential long-term liabilities coupled with limited longevity of commercial operations and an element of protection of the public interest.[179,180] The advantage of this option would be that funds should be available to remedy leakages regardless of the fate of the site operator. Clearly, a certain amount of infrastructure would be needed to administer such a fund (which could prove costly to establish and maintain). More fundamentally, it would not be certain that the amount in any fund would actually be enough to meet the costs of remedying any leakages that arose.

9.9 CO_2 classification

The issue of whether stored CO_2 is classified as waste[181] or as a commodity (under existing regulations or under a future regulatory framework) is important to the CCS project's commercial viability and is not a purely academic concern. This is because, typically, there are greater and more onerous restrictions when dealing with waste (and in particular, hazardous waste)[182] than if the substance is considered to be an industrial product/resource.[183] Examples of such regulatory burdens which apply to "waste" in the European Union include: the need for waste licensing; restrictions on the transfer and closing of storage facilities; the need for financial guarantees or other equivalent insurance; and restrictions upon transboundary shipments of waste.[184] Secondly, as a connected point, classification as a waste tends to have a significant impact on the public's perception of the substance in question.

It is preferable to achieve CO_2 purity (or as close as possible to this), first because impurities may corrode pipes through which the CO_2 is being transported, and secondly to establish public confidence that CCS is not being used to dispose of other

---

179   In the United Kingdom, the Nuclear Liabilities Fund (NLF) was established in November 2004 to meet the decommissioning costs of nuclear power plants in the United Kingdom. The NLF is partly funded by the UK government and partly by British Energy plc (it is the only privately owned nuclear generator in the United Kingdom, operating eight nuclear power stations in the United Kingdom). The government sold 450 million shares of its stake in the company on June 1 2007, raising £2.34 billion, net proceeds of which have gone to the NLF.

180   In Canada, since 1989, acid gas has been injected into geologic formations to comply with sulphur emissions regulations. All parties holding a permit to inject acid gas (which contains hydrogen sulphide, a poisonous and flammable chemical) must contribute to an "orphan fund" used to meet costs of suspension, abandonment and reclamation of orphaned wells.

181   In the European Union, waste is defined as "any substance or object ... the holder discards, intends to discard or is required to discard" (see Article 1(a) of Council Directive 75/442/EEC as amended by Directive 91/156/EEC of July 15 1975 on Waste (the Waste Framework Directive), OJ L 194, 25.7.1975, p 47 as amended by Directive 91/156/EEC (OJ L 78, 26.03.1991, p 32)). There is a similar emphasis on discarded material in the United States, too. The European Court of Justice (ECJ) has for the past 30 years consistently applied a broad, purposive interpretation to the EU definition. The ECJ has established a three-stage test for determining whether production residues with economic value are considered to be waste (for further, see Paul Q Watchman, John Bowman, Simon Read and Juliette Addison, Carbon Capture and Storage: Burying the Problem of Climate Change, June 11 2007, see www.deweyleboeuf.com/files/News/2c4d6f0e-e563-48ee-b37a-474c5a08acd6/Presentation/NewsAttachment/5868f860-fadc-4e49-b758-4d09e2b55225/5589.pdf).

182   Pursuant to European Community Council Directive 91/689/EEC on hazardous waste OJ L 377, 31.12.1991, p 20 (the Hazardous Waste Directive). "Hazardous wastes" are wastes with one or more of the characteristics set out in Annex III to the Hazardous Waste Directive which are dangerous to health or the environment. The list of hazardous wastes is consolidated in the European Waste Catalogue.

183   For example, most states in the United States have classified CO_2 as an industrial commodity for the purpose of EOR projects.

184   For example, see Regulation (EC) No 1013/2006 of the European Parliament and of the Council of June 14 2006 on shipments of waste (12.07.2006). Producers of CO_2 are under a "duty of care" to ensure that they transfer waste to a licensed waste-management handler.

waste. However, notwithstanding the above ideal, there is consensus (in international and regional instruments and among commentators) that, in practice, it is "almost inevitable"[185] that a certain level of contamination will be contained within the resultant stream. The draft CCS Directive adopts the same language as the London Protocol and OSPAR Convention in that CO_2 streams for sub-sea bed CO_2 storage will need to "consist overwhelmingly" of CO_2, although such streams may contain "incidental associated substances" derived from the source material and the capture and sequestration processes used. Clarity as to the exact quantities of CO_2 permitted in such streams is required, but clearly certain operators will be able to comply with these obligations more easily than others. For example, the stream resulting from oxyfuel is almost pure CO_2, in contrast to post-combustion CO_2 streams which will contain traces of the capture solvents.

However, the difficulty with the current waste regime in the United Kingdom and the European Union is that, if these impurities are categorised as hazardous wastes under Annex III of the Hazardous Waste Directive,[186] then they will need to be separated out from the non-hazardous waste for disposal where technically and economically feasible. Whilst it is improbable that such separation as part of a CCS project will be technically and economically feasible, the mere fact that such a possibility exists in theory (eg using scrubbing technology), coupled with the complicated waste framework which exists in the European Union and other jurisdictions, might be enough to deter potential CCS investment.

Consequently, if in a particular jurisdiction a prospective operator were subject to laws which classified CO_2 as waste (in particular, hazardous waste), this could disincentivise such a prospective operator from setting up a CCS project in that jurisdiction (depending upon how onerous, complicated and expensive the waste regime in that location might be). Such dissuasion could possibly result in an overall increase, not a decrease, in GHG emissions due to "red tape". The same may be true where a CO_2 storage project crosses territorial borders of states but the classification of the CO_2 of the national authorities on either side of the border is different.

In future, states will need to prescribe appropriate quantitative (rather than qualitative) impurity levels to confer greater certainty upon stakeholders. This has not yet been possible due to the evolving nature of CCS technology.

9.10 Property rights

CCS investors/operators (together with any funders with security) will require certainty that, as owners, they may manage or restrict the access of others, appropriate the benefits of the property and enforce their property rights (eg in the case of geophysical trespassing). However, these rights will need to be balanced with the (sometimes) competing rights of oil, gas and other mineral title holders (eg over reservoirs and injection sites). Transboundary CCS projects will face differing legal regimes regarding title, access, liability and other critical issues.

One possible contractual solution may be to use unitisation agreements (as in the

---

185   See draft CCS Directive Impact Assessment, n 64, paragraph 6.3 (175) at p 44.
186   See Hazardous Waste Directive, n 202.

oil and gas fields in the United States and Canada). This would clarify the identity of the stakeholders and the nature of their roles. However, this would require consensus from all parties together with standardisation of such contracts.

Currently, there is no global uniformity on the issue of whether ownership of the sub-surface passes with ownership of the surface. Equally, the ownership and protection of other resources (such as minerals, water and pore space) may differ from jurisdiction to jurisdiction. It would be sensible for such a framework to apply uniform rules to this issue, particularly given that many CCS projects will inevitably cross national boundaries.[187]

9.11   Equal access to transport networks and storage sites

As commercial deployment of CCS progresses, and more operators come to the market, it will be necessary to enshrine in the enabling legal framework a principle of equal and non-discriminatory access to CO_2 transport and storage. This will be necessary to provide comfort to operators that CO_2 captured can actually be transported and stored at a cost which is reasonable and is not prohibitively expensive. This will be particularly important if CCS is made mandatory (see section 9.13 below). In the European Union, where offshore CO_2 storage is the likely option for CCS (as opposed to onshore storage), landlocked countries and/or those with very limited access to the coast will, without regulatory intervention, be at a considerable disadvantage as compared to islands and coastal states. For instance, Switzerland as an OSPAR contracting party will be permitted to carry out sub-seabed CO_2 storage but, unless it is granted rights to access CO_2 transport and storage, its participation in the OSPAR Convention will be rendered nugatory. This is particularly the case given the stricter allocation to which the EU member states will be subject under the EU ETS.[188]

The above objective may be achieved by way of two different approaches at EU level. First, there could be a general right of access to networks of pipelines (some of which may already be in existence from EOR, oil and gas and other activities) and storage sites, granted on a non-discriminatory, transparent and fairly priced basis and subject to limitations on access on grounds of public interest only. Alternatively, a more targeted approach could be adopted by way of specific rules aimed at ensuring effective market access for all market players, including new entrants, in a similar way to that used to expedite the liberalisation of the electricity[189] and gas[190] sectors in the European Union, as well as setting non-discriminatory rules for access conditions

---

187   For instance, in Canada, the government owns the subsurface.
188   For example, the cap for Phase II (2008 to 2012) of the EU ETS represents a reduction of almost 140 million allowances compared with verified emissions in 2005 from installations covered by the EU ETS (ie a cut of 6.8%) (see EU Commission Press Release, "Emissions trading: Commission adopts amendment decision on the Slovak National Allocation Plan for 2008 to 2012", December 7 2007 at http://europa.eu/rapid/pressReleasesAction.do?reference=IP/07/1869&format=HTML&aged=0&languag e=EN&guiLanguage=en).
189   OJ L 176, 15.07.2003 pp 7 to 56, Directive 2003/54/EC of the European Parliament and of the Council of June 26 2003 concerning common rules for the internal market in electricity and repealing Directive 96/92/EC.
190   OJ L 176, 15.07.2003, p 57, Directive 2003/55/EC of the European Parliament and of the Council of June 26 2003 concerning common rules for the internal market in natural gas and repealing Directive 98/30/EC.

to natural gas transmission systems.[191]

Currently in the European Union there are indications that the second approach specified above may be adopted. The draft CCS Directive states that member states shall take necessary measures to ensure that potential users are able to obtain access to CO_2 transport networks and to storage sites for the purposes of storage of the produced and captured CO_2, provided the access shall be in manner prescribed by the member state taking into account several, sometimes conflicting, factors.[192] It is possible that, as for the liberalisation of the electricity and gas markets, such an approach may enable new entrants to CCS to complete on a level playing field as existing incumbents (particularly those in the oil and gas industry, who may already have know-how and experience of EOR).

9.12   Intellectual property issues

Intellectual property (IP) refers to rights granted to creators and owners of works resulting from human intellectual creativity. IP rights are customarily protected via patents or trademarks (which both require registration) or copyright and trade secrets (which both are unregistered).

It is important for CCS operators/investors to understand (and protect) the differing nature of IP rights at each stage of the CCS chain. As the technology required to transport and to inject CO_2 is similar to other fluids (such as petroleum), it is likely that this technology will be widely available from different suppliers in the relevant jurisdiction. However, the largest area of IP is likely to be in the earlier stages, namely site selection and capture. Knowledge as to the location of a good storage site is likely to be very valuable and hence should be protected (by trade secret rather than patent). The capture technologies will also involve more IP, which should be protected by patent, ranging from materials such as CO_2-resistant injection cement for injection wells, catalysts and solvents, through to the processes of capture and process integration). The IP rights in these capture technologies are held by relatively few individuals and tend also to be protected by patent.

Operators/investors and their lawyers should also be aware of the applicable IP laws, methods of protection and the likelihood of enforcement of such laws in the jurisdiction of the CCS project. This is particularly the case in developing countries and emerging markets, where regimes for protection and enforcement of such rights may not be as robust as in developed countries. For example, until relatively recently[193] CCS proponents from Europe and the United States were reluctant to invest in CCS projects in China and India, fearing economic loss due to IP right infringement. Whilst China's IP framework (a system which developed rapidly in the

---

191   OJ L 289, 03.11.2005 pp 1 to 13, Regulation (EC) No 1775/2005 of the European Parliament and of the Council of September 28 2005 on conditions for access to the natural gas transmission networks.

192   Storage and transport capacity; the need to refuse access where the technology of the new entrant is incompatible with the existing technology and cannot be reasonably overcome; and the fact that CO_2 transport network operators and operators of storage sites may refuse access on the basis of lack of capacity (provided that substantiated reasons are given for any refusal). See draft CCS Directive, n 153, Chapter 5, Article 20.

193   StatoilHydro and India's Oil and Natural Gas Corporation (ONGC) announced in February 2008 their joint venture to explore potential for CCS (and CDM) opportunities in India (Reuters, "StatoilHydro, India's ONGC to explore CCS projects", February 6 2008, see http://UK.reuters.).

1980s) is compatible with international standards, investors have been deterred by the fact that IP rights are enforced by administrative agencies which can only impose fines and not award damages (which are a considerably more effective deterrent to a potential infringer). However, joint ventures and non-disclosure agreements are just two of the methods that Western CCS proponents are using to protect their IP rights.

As for other new sectors (eg renewables) which depend upon new technology, the successful deployment of CCS is linked to the satisfactory protection of the IP used in CCS. If the owner of the IP is not confident that its rights will be properly protected and that others will be made to pay to use that IP, it will be less likely to agree to transfer it. Of course, this may conflict with the policy imposed by the regulatory authority in the jurisdiction (eg new entrants to certain regulated industries (such as telecommunications) are entitled to rights to "interconnect" into existing infrastructure).

9.13   Mandatory CCS

Clearly, the financial incentivisation described above (see section 7) will not be required if the installation of CCS plant in new plant and/or retrofitting of existing plant is made compulsory. This is a discussion which has been considered in detail in the European Union. There are several options in the European Union for making CCS mandatory in:

- new coal-fired power from 2020 onwards;
- new coal- and gas-fired power from 2020 onwards;
- new coal-fired power only from 2020 and a retrofit of existing plant (constructed between 2015 and 2020) from 2020; or
- new coal- and gas-fired power from 2020 and a retrofit of existing plant (constructed between 2015 and 2020) from 2020.[194]

Whilst mandatory CCS has been considered extensively, it has not, so far, been implemented in the European Union. This is not to say that it has been ruled out altogether. One of the reasons for preferring an "enabling" rather than a "mandatory" framework is that, as touched upon above, market-based mechanisms are usually more effective than traditional "control and command" policies. Second, it was found that mandatory CCS would be felt disproportionately by a small number of EU member states. For example, in relation to the most onerous scenario (fourth sub-paragraph above), 75% of CCS would, based on current distributions of coal- and gas-fired power plants, occur in four member states (Germany (with 35% of such efforts), followed by Poland, the United Kingdom and Belgium). Such compulsion might also encourage "carbon leakage" (as discussed at section 8.2 above). This could act as a perverse incentive, actually resulting in greater global output of GHGs than before.

At the time of writing, it appears that there is little will in the European Union (with the exception of some NGOs) for mandatory CCS because the additional know-how gained would not compensate for the initial costs incurred by industry.[195] It is

---

194   See draft CCS Directive Impact Assessment, n 64, pp 3, 4, 5, 49 to 75 and 85 to 87.
195   For more, see draft CCS Directive Impact Assessment, n 64, paragraph 17 at p 5.

also thought that combined policies of investment in research and development and demonstration, plus the proposed inclusion of CCS in the EU ETS, would ensure a robust carbon price which would incentivise the market to introduce the technology voluntarily without having to resort to compulsion. However, it has been made very clear by the Commission that mandatory CCS is the next step if the power sector and energy-intensive industries do not voluntarily move early into CCS deployment, as evidenced by the Commission's own statement that "the policy-makers will be obliged to look at the option of compulsory application of CCS technology as the future only way forward".[196] Clearly, if CCS becomes mandatory, this will impact upon the profit margins and projections of operators. This has led to a climate of uncertainty in the market as power companies and others are already considering now how future CCS regulation will impact their current and proposed projects.[197]

The only element of compulsion in respect of CCS under the proposed EU regime is a provision in the draft CCS Directive which would require amendment of the Large Combustion Plants Directive.[198] This would require all combustion plants for which the original construction or operating licence is granted after the entry into force of the draft CCS Directive to have suitable space on the installation site for the equipment necessary to capture and compress CO_2. Further, it would also require an assessment to have taken place as to the availability of suitable storage sites and transport networks, as well as the technical feasibility of retrofitting for CO_2 captured.[199]

The Large Combustion Plants Directive applies to combustion plants with a rated thermal output of 50MW or more, irrespective of the type of fuel used (solid, liquid, or gaseous) – a typical "large-point source" of CO_2. A similar amendment has recently been tabled in the US Congress. This would prohibit the grant of a licence to new coal-fired power stations under the Clean Air Act unless that permit required the power station to use "state-of-the-art control technology to capture and permanently sequester carbon dioxide emissions from such unit".[200] If successful, this amendment will immediately require new prospective operators to factor this requirement into their plans when looking for new premises – in essence, they will need to find larger plots of land to accommodate the CCS technology than would previously have been the case. This may have effects on land prices and may drive up the sale value of large pieces of land, particularly those near potential storage sites.

---

196   See Communication from the Commission, to the European Parliament et al – Supporting early demonstration of sustainable power generation from fossil fuels, n 79, paragraphs 5.1 and 7 at pp 9 and 11 (see http://eur-lex.europa.eu/LExUriServ/LexUriServ.do?uri=CELEX:52008DC0013:ENNOT).

197   For example, in April 2008, E.ON asked the UK government to delay the grant of planning permission for its £1.5 billion Kingsnorth power plant (which would be the United Kingdom's first coal-fired power station for 20 years) until the government had finished its consultation on CCS. E.ON appears to be reluctant to construct a new power station if future legislation means that the newly constructed station is not capable of being fitted with CCS technology. For further, see Mark Milner, The Guardian, "E.ON Delays Coal-fired Power Plant to Await Carbon Capture Ruling", April 2 2008, see www.guardian.co.uk/environment/2008/apr/01/carbonemissions.biofuels.

198   Directive (2001/80EC) of the European Parliament and of the Council of October 23 2001 on the limitation of emissions of certain pollutants into the aim from large combustion plants OJ L309, 27.11.2001, p 1.

199   As proposed by the draft CCS Directive, n 153, Recital 37.

200   HR5575, 110th Congress, 2D Session, March 11 2008, see http://oversight.house.gov/documents/20080311112442.pdf SEC. 2. MORATORIUM.

9.14 Adaptation of existing legislation

As discussed above, several significant steps in international law have been recently taken in order to remove obstacles to CCS. Efforts are being made within the European Union as a whole and in the United Kingdom in particular to excise and/or amend provisions in existing laws to ensure that the outcome is a clear, effective, regulatory system without overlap and confusion.

At EU level, several key directives will be affected. Suggested necessary amendments are referred to below.

(a)   EIA Directive[201]

The EIA Directive stipulates which categories of project will be made subject to an environmental impact assessment, what procedure is to be followed and the content of the assessment.

It has been suggested that, due to the significant potential environmental impacts of CCS projects, installations for the capture of CO_2, pipelines for the transport of gas, oil, chemicals and pipes for the transport of CO_2 streams for the purposes of geological storage (with a diameter of more than 800mm and a length of more than 40km, including associated booster stations) and storage sites too will be expressly referred to as projects in Annex I for which an EIA[202] is required under Article 4(1)[203] This is especially the case as the EIA Directive (Article 7(4)) already states that the member states involved must consult on the potential transboundary effects of projects and the measures envisaged to reduce or eliminate such effects and must agree on reasonable time frames for the duration of any consultation period.

(b)   Landfill Directive[204]

Currently, the injection and storage of CO_2 may constitute "landfill" within the definition set out in the Landfill Directive. Equally, as the directive prohibits landfilling using all liquid wastes and, as discussed above, CO_2 is injected as a "supercritical fluid", suitable amendment will be required.

(c)   Water Framework Directive[205]

This directive is an ambitious attempt to bring fundamental change to the European Union's fragmented and outdated water policy in favour of a more holistic approach. The directive is being phased in over several years and by 2013 will have replaced certain existing instruments entirely.

The directive covers surface waters, coastal waters, estuaries and groundwater and its main purpose is to achieve good surface-water status and good groundwater status in all waters by the end of 2015. Article 11(j) currently prohibits the direct discharge of pollutants (as which CO_2 could feasibly be described) into groundwater subject to

---

201   See n 141 above.
202   An EIA shall consider the direct and indirect effects of a project on: (a) human beings, fauna and flora; (b) soil, water, air, climate and the landscape; (c) material assets and the cultural heritage; and (d) the interaction between the factors mentioned at (a), (b) and (c) above (Article 3, EIA Directive) .
203   See Article 29 of the draft CCS Draft Directive, n 153 at p 28.
204   See n 176 above.
205   See n 177 above.

certain exemptions (eg the injection of natural gas or LPG for storage purposes into geological formations which, for natural reasons, are permanently unsuitable for other purposes).[206] Various commentators[207] and the European Commission consider it would be sensible to amend this section to include an exemption for CCS activities too.

10.   The future for CCS?

We have identified above several commercial and legal obstacles which, unless addressed, will significantly affect the potential for CCS to operate as an effective GHG mitigation strategy. We shall now consider below two further challenges which are more global in their scope. It is also, broadly speaking, more difficult to predict the outcome of these two issues as they entirely depend upon the act of third parties and, at the date of writing, little significant progress in either area has been made.

10.1   The participation challenge

Several studies conclude that on a global level, to be most effective, CCS will need to be deployed first in developed countries and then, from 2020 onwards (when emissions from developing countries will exceed those of developed countries), in developing countries which have plentiful domestic coal resources[208] (eg China, India and the countries in South East Asia) and which will profit from strong security of supply to meet their growing energy demands.

It could be argued that this is a further facet of the "participation challenge" (ie encouraging developing countries and emerging economies to submit willingly to mandatory international climate change caps and participate in trading of allowances).[209] It is to be hoped that, subject to the same strict caps on emissions as Annex I countries under the Kyoto Protocol for example, such countries would necessarily and voluntarily view CCS as a significant way to achieve such emission reductions in the short term. However, it is possible that, for many of the same reasons cited by developing countries and emerging markets for resisting mandatory caps on GHGs, in the short term, pleas for investment by such countries in CCS technology may fall upon deaf ears. This is first because there may well be no legal regime in place to regulate such risks, nor sufficient incentives; and, second, due to the difficulty that power and other potentially affected operators would have in obtaining the necessary funds to pay for the CAPEX, OPEX and other costs required to establish (or retrofit) CCS plant. Finally, some of these countries may be lacking the (general) corporate culture of regulatory compliance which is (usually) in evidence in the United Kingdom, for example.

---

206   Water Framework Directive, n 177, Article 11(j).

207   See Ian Havercroft and Ray Purdy, *Carbon Capture and Storage – A Legal Perspective*, at paragraph 4(iii), see www.un.org/esa/sustdev/sdissues/energy/op/ccs_egm/presentations_papers/havercroft_paper_legal.pdf.

208   In terms of known reserves, coal is the most abundant fossil – around 150 to 250 years' worth of coal remain at current production rates (see draft CCS Directive Impact Assessment, n 64, paragraph 2.2 at p 16).

209   George W Bush also used the "participation challenge" as a reason to explain the US rejection of Kyoto, that is, that Kyoto would exempt from compliance "80% of the world, including ... China and India [which] would cause serious harm to the US economy".

The above discussion demonstrates the need for a globally committed and implemented approach to the problem of climate change mitigation. Regardless of whether legal obligations exist or not, most citizens would agree that there is a collective responsibility and duty upon all states to participate in achieving global GHG emission reductions. However, the difficulty of engagement is an obstacle which will need to be surmounted before such participation can take effect.

10.2 Public confidence

Finally, policymakers are acutely aware of the need to build confidence in the public, NGOs and other parts of civil society. This should be achieved by demonstrating that CO_2 will be safely and effectively transported and, most importantly, stored underground or under the sea and that it will not leak out of the storage formation into the atmosphere (or, that if it does leak, corrective measures will be taken to stop the leak if there is a significant risk of harm to human or other health or life).

Gaining the public's confidence is a challenge that faces all countries wishing to use CCS, including developing countries. In countries where there is no established precedent for fluid storage activity at all (eg India), the vast majority of the public are unaware of the concept of CCS, let alone its risks and advantages. In such countries, no analogy with natural gas/acid gas storage for example can be drawn. In these cases, the public will need to be engaged and persuaded as to the merits of CCS, and this will be a long and gradual process.

However, there is no guarantee that the public in countries which are familiar with long-term fluid storage (eg the United Kingdom) will accept CCS willingly. In the United States and Canada in particular, where onshore storage will be the preferred storage choice for CCS, it is likely that individuals and communities will require comfort as to the safety of onshore CO_2 transport networks and, equally, onshore storage.

Proponents of CCS including operators and their funders should be aware that, whilst some NGOs are in favour of CCS, others are pragmatic but many are strongly opposed. Furthermore, the effect of negative publicity engendered by a zealous NGO upon the operators and their funders' business should not be underestimated. Consequently, it seems sensible that, especially for the early few projects, CCS development standards (as established by the regulatory framework discussed above) should be realistically high. This should reduce the chances of accidents or leakage to a minimum, which in turn, over time, will earn gradual confidence in civil society.

11. Conclusion

As seen above, there has recently been a noticeable shift in the way that CCS is viewed. After 30 years of being thought of as nothing more than a method of enhanced resource recovery, its potential as a climate change abatement option has brought CCS into the commercial, political and legal limelight. There are considerable – some would say unrealistic – expectations as to how successful such technology will be in acting as a short-term "bridge", whilst developed and developing countries and emerging economies chart the path towards a fossil-free future. Equally ambitious are the hopes that the widespread deployment of CCS will create high-skilled employment, wealth and knowledge transfer which will benefit developed, developing and emerging markets alike.

Clearly, there are still numerous challenges to be overcome, including the need for a harmonised, consistent, transparent and flexible regulatory framework, for financial incentivisation and for answers to difficult questions such as how best to deal with long-term post-closure liability, IP rights and equal access to transport and storage sites. A further hurdle to overcome will be the need to win the confidence of an increasingly "climate-change aware" public – one that is conscious of the "energy penalty" incurred by carbon capture techniques, critical of the possible diversion of resources away from renewables and energy efficiency towards CCS projects, and suspicious that power companies and heavy fossil-fuel users' support for this "fossil fuel enabling technology" may be a tactic to delay policy changes rather than a serious response to climate change.[210]

---

210   D Hawkins, *Stick it Where?? – Public Attitudes toward Carbon Storage* (undated), p 1, see www.netl.doe.gov/publications/proceedings/01/carbon_seq/1c2.pdf.

About the authors

Juliette Addison

Associate, Dewey & LeBoeuf

jaddison@dl.com

Juliette Addison is an associate in the environment, health and safety group of Dewey & LeBoeuf and is a member of the firm's global climate change group. Miss Addison has considerable experience in environmental and climate-change-related work, particularly for clients in the oil, gas and mining sectors. She has significant experience of the regulatory issues surrounding the European Union Emissions Trading Scheme (EU ETS). She has also assisted clients with issues relating to contaminated land (drawing on her former practice as a Real Estate lawyer at Freshfields Bruckhaus Deringer) and sustainable finance, including the Equator Principles and corporate social responsibility. Her articles on climate change range from consideration of the EU ETS to carbon capture and storage.

Tim Baines

Associate, Dewey & LeBoeuf

tim.baines@dl.com

Tim Baines is an associate in the environment, health and safety department of Dewey & LeBoeuf and a member of its climate change group. Mr Baines specialises in environmental and climate change issues.

He has particular experience of regulatory and compliance issues under the EU Emissions Trading Scheme and emissions trading documentation. Mr Baines also has experience of planning (zoning) and legal and quasi-legal sustainable development issues (including corporate social responsibilty (CSR) generally, the Equator Principles, the Principles for Responsible Investment and directors' duties in the United Kingdom). His work has been published in a number of journals and he has lectured, advised on and been consulted in relation to CSR-related issues in the United Kingdom and the United States.

John Bowman

Partner, Dewey & LeBoeuf

john.bowman@dl.com

John Bowman provides advice in relation to non-contentious environmental law, planning (zoning) law, and regulatory matters (including regulation of the electricity sector, carbon emissions and trading). He advises across a range of climate-change-related matters, including the EU Emissions Trading Scheme (advising on challenges to individual company allocations, compliance generally, and new sector entrants), the Kyoto flexible mechanisms (CDM and JI) and alternative ways of addressing carbon dioxide emissions such as carbon capture and storage.

Mr Bowman also advises on the consents process for major infrastructure projects, including power stations (nuclear, coal, gas, CHP, biofuel), gas storage facilities, roads, airports, mineral developments, railways, mixed-use developments, development on government land, and large-scale residential projects. In addition, he assists clients in the assessment and management of planning and environmental risk in the context of mergers and acquisitions and complex financing transactions.

Iain Calton
Senior Manager, Deloitte
icalton@deloitte.co.uk

Iain Calton is a senior manager in Deloitte's energy, infrastructure and utilities group delivering accounting advice to both audit and non-audit clients. He has experience of dealing with clients both on the trading and compliance side of emissions accounting. He is a member of the Institute of Chartered Accountants in Scotland.

Mr Calton also has experience in derivative accounting and is part of a specialist group focusing on valuation and accounting for energy contracts. He is one of the derivatives specialists within Deloitte UK, which exposes him to a wide variety of derivative instruments and accounting.

Mr Calton's previous roles include secondment as a technical accounting manager to an energy company, accounting for acquisition and disposal of oil and gas assets, as well as contract and derivative accounting.

Peter D Cameron
Director of Research and Professor of International Energy Law & Policy, CEPMLP, University of Dundee
peterdcameron@btinternet.com

Dr Peter D Cameron is Professor of International Energy Law and Policy at the Centre for Energy, Petroleum and Mineral Law and Policy (CEPMLP) at the University of Dundee (UK) and former Director of the International Institute of Energy Law at the University of Leiden (The Netherlands) and Professor at the European University Institute at Florence, Italy. On an independent basis, he has also been a legal advisor and expert witness on petroleum, energy legislation and transactions, gas and electricity regulatory issues, and energy

and environmental taxation for international organisations, corporate clients and governments, with more than 25 years' experience. He is a Fellow of the Chartered Institute of Arbitrators (FCIArb), and a Special Member of the AIPN.

Christopher Carr
Counsel, Vinson & Elkins LLP
ccarr@velaw.com

Christopher Carr is co-chair of the climate change practice group at the international law firm of Vinson & Elkins. He advises on a variety of environmental matters including those involving climate change, transactional and regulatory matters, and environmental enforcement and litigation. Mr Carr recently served two years as senior counsel at the World Bank, where he was a legal advisor to the Bank's Carbon Finance Unit. He advised on matters related to the Clean Development Mechanism (CDM) and Joint Implementation (JI) provisions of the Kyoto Protocol. He also advises on US greenhouse gas issues, including both transactional and legislative matters. Mr Carr has provided counsel on a range of issues associated with structuring and negotiating carbon transactions. He is a graduate of the Columbia University School of Law and Brown University.

Jose A Cofre
Associate, Dewey & LeBoeuf
jose.cofre@deweyleboeuf.com

Jose A Cofre is an associate in the environment, health and safety group based in the London office of Dewey & LeBoeuf and is a member of the firm's global climate change practice. Mr Cofre has significant experience advising clients on both contentious and non-contentious planning, environmental and climate change regulatory matters, particularly in the mining, oil and gas, and energy sectors. He holds a B.Business (Finance major) and an LLB (with first-class honours) from the University of Technology, Sydney and completed graduate studies in environmental law at the Sydney University Law School. Prior to joining Dewey & LeBoeuf, Mr Cofre worked in the Sydney office of Clayton Utz specialising in planning and environmental law where, in addition to his corporate/regulatory environmental work, he was responsible for running various civil and administrative litigious matters on behalf of electricity companies and road and rail regulators engaged in property, planning and environmental disputes.

Peter Crowther

Partner, Dewey & LeBoeuf
peter.crowther@dl.com

Dr Crowther heads the EU and competition practice at Dewey & LeBoeuf, working out of the London and Brussels offices. His practice embraces contentious and non-contentious competition law, EU and national merger control, state aid, public procurement, trade and general EU law advice. Dr Crowther also provides ongoing commercial and corporate advice to an international client base.

Angela Delfino

Associate, Dewey & LeBoeuf
adelfino@deweyleboeuf.com

Angela Delfino is an associate in the environmental and climate change group at the London offices of Dewey & LeBoeuf. Her academic career includes time spent at the University of Lisbon, LMU in Munich, UCL in London, and the New York University School of Law. She has also worked for PLMJ law firm in Lisbon, the Directorate-General Environment of the European Commission in Brussels, and the Center for International Environmental Law in Washington, DC. She has published several articles on climate change and corporate social responsibilty issues.

Helen Devenney

Director, Deloitte
hdevenney@deloitte.co.uk

Helen Devenney is a director in Deloitte UK's indirect tax practice, where she is a member of the energy, infrastructure and utilities team. She is a qualified chartered accountant and also chairs the Chartered Institute of Taxation's Environmental Taxes Working Group.

Ms Devenney specialises in advising businesses in the energy sector, and her clients range from upstream oil and gas companies to players in the UK nuclear industry. She has in-depth knowledge of the indirect tax implications of commodity trading around Europe.

Ms Devenney has extensive experience in advising businesses on managing their environmental tax obligations and on the indirect tax consequences of the greenhouse gas and renewable obligation trading schemes. She negotiated with HM Revenue & Customs & Excise on the VAT treatment of the voluntary emissions trading scheme introduced in the United Kingdom and has since been advising businesses and funds on European and global emissions trading issues.

Steven Ferrey

Professor of Law, Suffolk University Law School
sferrey@suffolk.edu

Steven Ferrey is Professor of Law at Suffolk University Law School and has been Visiting Professor at Boston University School of Law and Harvard Law School. He is the author of six books and more than 75 articles on the energy-environmental legal and policy interface. These books include *The Law of Independent Power* (25th ed 2007), a three-volume treatise, as well as *Renewable Power in Developing Countries: Winning the War on Global Warming* (2006). His articles on energy policy during the past five years have appeared in law reviews at Harvard, Duke, William & Mary, University of Virginia, Boston College,

NYU and Stanford University. Mr Ferrey advises the United Nations and World Bank on carbon and energy regulation in developing countries in Asia, Africa, and Latin America.

Lucie Fish

Associate, Dewey & LeBoeuf
lfish@deweyleboeuf.com

Lucie Fish is an associate at Dewey & LeBoeuf, advising on aspects of EU competition law, including control of mergers and joint ventures, cartels and abuse of market power, state aid and anticompetitive agreements. Miss Fish also advises on corporate law aspects of mergers and acquisitions.

Anthony Hobley

Partner, Norton Rose LLP
anthony.hobley@nortonrose.com

Anthony Hobley is a partner at Norton Rose and heads the firm's global climate change and carbon finance team. He was previously General Counsel to the Carbon Funds and Director of Legal Policy at Climate Change Capital, where he advised on CDM and JI projects including the biggest private syndication of a carbon transaction. Anthony is chairman of the Carbon Markets Association and a board member of the Voluntary Carbon Standards Association.

Anthony has a first-class honours degree in Chemistry with Physics and a Masters Degree in Environmental Law. He specialises in climate change, carbon finance and clean energy law. He advised the EU Commission on the preparation of the EU Registries Regulation for an EU-wide system of greenhouse gas registries. He currently advises investment banks, carbon funds, project developers and corporates in the carbon market. He lives in Kent and is married with two daughters.

John McMorris

Vice President, Forest Systems LLC
jmcmorris@forestsystems.com

John McMorris is a founder and vice president at Forest Systems, handling business development, regulatory affairs and government relations. Forest Systems develops large-scale forestry projects which balance portfolio value between conventional timber products, carbon offsets and renewable energy fuel stock. Previously, Mr McMorris was a founder and Senior Vice President at both AES AgriVerde – a joint venture between the AES Corporation and AgCert International plc, established to develop greenhouse gas mitigation projects in Asia, eastern Europe and Africa – and AgCert International plc, one of the first large-scale CDM project developers (serving in various roles including intellectual property development and chief operating officer). During his time with these firms, Mr McMorris helped to develop both CDM/JI methodologies and projects representing approximately 10% of the CDM project sites worldwide. He has been developing technology start-up companies for approximately 15 years, building on a systems engineering and business background.

Sarah Nolleth

Senior Manager, Deloitte
snolleth@deloitte.co.uk

Sarah Nolleth is a senior manager in Deloitte's energy, infrastructure and utilities practice, specialising in corporate tax. She is a qualified chartered accountant.

Ms Nolleth advises businesses in the renewable energy and carbon trading sectors and has significant international tax experience. Her clients range from independent renewable energy companies to government bodies involved in reducing carbon emissions.

Ms Nolleth has extensive experience of the renewable energy and carbon trading sectors, and has advised on a number of transactions within these areas. She has also advised on a number of AIM listings and the establishment and structuring of renewable energy and carbon funds.

Christopher Norton
Partner, Lovells LLP
Christopher.Norton@lovells.com

Christopher Norton is a partner in the corporate department at Lovells LLP, a leading international law firm with 26 offices in the main financial centres of Europe, Asia and the United States. Christopher joined Lovells in October 2007 from Baker & McKenzie LLP.

Christopher specialises in environment and international climate change law. His practice includes advising clients on the international legal regime relating to climate change, the UK and EU emissions trading schemes, renewable energy projects and acting on the sale and purchase of carbon credits.

Courtney A Queen
Associate, Dewey & LeBoeuf LLP
cqueen@dl.com

Courtney A Queen is an associate in the Boston office of Dewey & LeBoeuf LLP. She is a member of the environmental, health and safety group at the firm and she also practices within the firm's climate change group. Courtney is a 2006 graduate of Vermont Law School and is admitted to practice in the Commonwealth of Massachusetts.

Simon Read
Solicitor, Pinsent Masons LLP
Simon.read@pinsentmasons.com

Simon Read is a solicitor in Pinsent Masons' planning and environment team. Mr Read specialises in clean energy and climate change issues, and has advised on a wide range of matters including the EU Emissions Trading Scheme, CDM projects, investment in carbon funds, acquisitions

of carbon project developers, emission reductions purchase agreements, carbon trading documentation, power purchase agreements and energy from waste projects. Aside from his clean energy and climate change practice, Mr Read advises on a broad range of environmental matters including IPPC, wastes management and outsourcing, contaminated land, environmental disputes, general regulatory advice, and environmental due diligence and the drafting of complex warranties and indemnities in property and corporate transactions. Mr Read is a regular contributor to numerous publications on climate change and environmental issues and holds an LLM in Environmental Law.

Nicholas Rock
Partner, Dewey & LeBoeuf
nicholas.rock@dl.com

Nicholas Rock is a partner in the environmental, health and safety and litigation groups of Dewey & LeBoeuf. Dewey & LeBoeuf is a globally recognised law firm with 27 offices around the world. Mr Rock is based in the firm's London office and specialises in contentious and non-contentious environmental law. He handles the environmental aspects of complex commercial transactions and projects, major environmental pollution incidents, the remediation and redevelopment of large property portfolios, and environmental permitting and licensing issues; but he has particular expertise in climate change law and practice. He regularly advises companies on their participation in the regulated and voluntary carbon markets, in particular the European Emissions Trading Scheme and CDM and JI overseas emissions reduction projects.

Flavia Rosembuj
Senior Legal Counsel, World Bank
frosembuj@worldbank.org

Flavia Rosembuj is a senior legal counsel in the co-financing and project finance unit of the legal vice presidency of the World Bank, where she works on carbon finance legal issues.

Ms Rosembuj received her JD degree from the University of Barcelona in 1991 and her Doctorate in 2004. She obtained a Masters in Law from the University of Paris at Sorbonne in 1992 and continued her postgraduate studies at the University of Brussels.

Ms Rosembuj has been a professor at the University of Barcelona and a visiting scholar at Columbia University. Prior to that, she has worked at Spain's largest law firm, and at the international law firm, Freshfields.

She is a member of the Barcelona and Paris Bar Associations. She is the author of a book on the European Union emissions trading scheme and numerous papers on the legal framework for using market mechanisms for environmental protection.

Anju Sanehi

Counsel, Hunton & Williams
asanehi@hunton.com

Anju Sanehi is Counsel at Hunton & Williams. She specialises in environmental and energy regulation, with a focus on climate change law and emissions trading. Ms Sanehi was previously Regulatory Counsel at American Electric Power where she led the UK regulatory team in respect of the company's renewable fuel interests and on negotiating emission allocations in respect of the company's generation assets. Ms Sanehi sat on the influential JEP which represented the United Kingdom's major coal-fired generators and negotiated with government on implementation of the EU Emission Trading Scheme and proposed trading arrangements under the Large Combustion Plant Directive. She has also been involved in lobbying on issues affecting the energy, power and infrastructure sectors.

Seb Walhain

Director Environmental Markets, Fortis
seb.walhain@nl.fortis.com

Seb Walhain has an MSc in Environmental Sciences, policy specialisation. From 1996 until 1999, Mr Walhain taught strategic energy management and environmental accounting at the University of Amsterdam's faculty of Economics. From 1999 until 2003 he was manager of environmental products at Nuon Energy Trade & Wholesale. Following a period of work in business development in Nuon Renewables, he set up a leading environmental products trading desk. In 2003, Mr Walhain established Europe's first financial institution carbon desk at Fortis. The desk aims to reduce greenhouse emissions efficiently through portfolios of reduction projects, and to use those reductions to optimise and ensure compliance for a pan-European corporate client portfolio. The activities of this desk range from valuing environmental benefits in long-term discounted cash-flow models for project finance, to short-term pure trading and long-term hedging.

Mike Wallace

President, Wallace Partners
mike@wallacepartners.net

Mike Wallace, President of Wallace Partners, has more than 15 years of international environmental consulting experience. He is a specialist in the field of environmental governance, where corporate environmental performance intersects with traditional corporate governance. Mr Wallace's international experience in the area of environmental assessment, measurement and quantification enables him to provide specialised guidance to corporations, NGOs and government agencies. He has worked with numerous Fortune 500 companies on the development and implementation of sustainability initiatives. Mr. Wallace has authored numerous articles on corporate environmental performance, has participated in international working groups on the subject and speaks regularly on the topic of environmental measurement, reporting and management. He also serves as the North American representative for Trucost plc, a research firm specialising in environmental performance measurement of publicly traded companies. Trucost holds environmental data on more than 4,200 companies and has the world's largest collection of quantified and comparable CO_2 emissions data.

Paul Q Watchman
Partner, Climate Change Practice Group,
Dewey & LeBoeuf
paul.watchman@dl.com

Paul Q Watchman is co-chair of Dewey & LeBoeuf's global environmental, health and safety practice group and the leader of its climate change group. Having practised law for more than 30 years, Paul's climate change practice now includes advising on the development of carbon projects under the Kyoto Protocol, carbon capture and storage projects, renewable energy projects and green buildings, as well as emissions trading. He has advised major energy and oil and gas clients, insurance companies and financial institutions on climate change litigation.

In addition, Paul has a wide-ranging practice in environmental, planning and regulatory issues. Paul has represented a large number of industrial conglomerates buying and selling businesses around the globe. This has involved multijurisdictional due diligence and the negotiation of complex forms of environmental protection for clients.

Paul also has a particularly keen interest in corporate social responsibility, human rights and business practices. He has been involved in ground-breaking work for the United Nations on the fiduciary duties of pensions funds, unit trusts and insurance companies. In 2006, Paul was named as one of the six key international figures in the development of sustainable finance.

Martijn Wilder
Partner, Baker & McKenzie
martijn.wilder@bakernet.com

Martijn Wilder is the lead partner of Baker & McKenzie's global climate change and emissions trading practice. Mr Wilder is regarded as one of the leading legal experts in the area, having worked in it for more than 10 years. Representing an international client base, he has advised multinational clients such as the World Bank, the Asian Development Bank and a number of governments on the development of climate change and emissions trading laws and he advises clients on international carbon transactions on a daily basis. Martijn is also chairman of the New South Wales Premier's Greenhouse Advisory Panel; he is on the governing board of the renewable Energy and Energy Efficiency Partnership (REEEP); he is vice-president of the International Law Association (Australian branch); he is a governor of World Wildlife Fund; and president of TRAFFIC (Oceania). Martijn has published widely in the climate change and international law area.

Index